Woman Triumphant

WOMAN TRIUMPHANT

Feminism in French Literature
1610–1652

IAN MACLEAN

Fellow of the Queen's College, Oxford

Oxford
At the Clarendon Press
1977

Oxford University Press, Walton Street, Oxford OX2 6DP

OXFORD LONDON GLASGOW NEW YORK
TORONTO MELBOURNE WELLINGTON CAPE TOWN
IBADAN NAIROBI DAR ES SALAAM LUSAKA ADDIS ABABA
KUALA LUMPUR SINGAPORE JAKARTA HONG KONG TOKYO
DELHI BOMBAY CALCUTTA MADRAS KARACHI

© *Oxford University Press 1977*

British Library Cataloguing in Publication Data
Maclean, Ian, b. 1945
    Woman triumphant: feminism in French literature,
    1610–1652
Bibl.—Index
ISBN 0–19–815741–x
1. Title
301.41′2′0944   HQ 1613
Women—France—Social conditions
Arts, French

*Printed in Great Britain
at the University Press, Oxford
by Vivian Ridler
Printer to the University*

for
Pauline

Preface

THE heroic age of Marie de Médicis, Louis XIII, and Anne of Austria is well known for the prominence enjoyed by women. Their influence in religious activities such as public charity and mysticism, in literary circles both as critics and authors, in politics and statecraft, and even in the military arts has been fully chronicled by historians of the period.[1] The privileged position occupied by women in French literature of the first half of the seventeenth century has also been long recognized. Charles Sorel comments on it in *De la connoissance des bons livres* of 1671;[2] Antoine-Léonard Thomas accords it exhaustive treatment in his *Essai sur le caractère, les mœurs et l'esprit des femmes dans les différens siècles* published in 1772; since that time, many writers have treated the topic, sometimes as an introduction to discussions of feminism in their own age,[3] sometimes with a more scholarly concern for historical perspective. Outstanding among the latter group are Georges Ascoli, whose illuminating article on 'Les idées féministes en France' appeared in 1906,[4] and Gustave Reynier, who published *La femme au XVIIe siècle: ses ennemis et ses défenseurs* in 1929. In recent years, a steady stream of articles and chapters in books on genres or individual authors has furthered the study of what we may call 'feminism' in this period.[5]

---

[1] See G. Fagniez, *La femme et la société française dans la première moitié du XVIIe siècle*, Paris, 1929; H. Bremond, *Histoire littéraire du sentiment religieux en France*, Paris, 1930, ii. 2; E. Magne, *Voiture et l'Hôtel de Rambouillet. Les années de gloire, 1635-48*, Paris, 1930; V. Du Bled, *La société française du XVIe siècle au XXe siècle*, Paris, 1902-4, iii. 213-58, iv. 203-45; A. de Payer, *Le féminisme au temps de la Fronde*, Paris, 1922; C. Romain, *Les guerrières*, Paris, 1931. One might add to this list the biographies of prominent women of this period by Victor Cousin and Emile Magne.

[2] See below, pp. 201-2.

[3] A notorious example is Théodore Joran (*Les féministes avant le féminisme*, 1ère série, Paris, 1911; 2e série, Paris, 1935).

[4] *Revue de synthèse historique*, xii. 25-57, 99-106, 161-84.

[5] The most important of these are the studies of M. Magendie (*La politesse mondaine et les théories de l'honnêteté en France au XVIIe siècle, de 1600 à 1660*, Paris, 1925, i. 88-105, 120-48, 188-237); R. A. Sayce (*The French biblical epic in the seventeenth century*, Oxford, 1955, pp. 78-9, 245); B. Treloar ('Some feminist views in France in the seventeenth century', *AUMLA*, x (1959), 152-9); and A. Stegmann (*L'héroïsme cornélien, genèse et signification*, Paris, 1968, ii. 268-73).

The use of this word in the context of the seventeenth century may, however, give rise to certain misapprehensions which should be dispelled. Ascoli defines feminism as 'l'attitude d'esprit de ceux qui répugnant aux délimitations infranchissables et aux exclusions arbitraires, se refusent à admettre une inégalité naturelle et nécessaire entre les facultés des hommes et des femmes, par suite entre leurs droits'.[6] Here we may perceive two interrelated elements: the assertion of the moral and intellectual equality of the sexes, and the demand that this be recognized in a new social dispensation. Although it is true that in nearly all feminist works of this period some relaxation of the marital and social oppression of women is advocated, no far-reaching reforms are suggested.[7] What is more, the rhetorical nature of much writing in favour of women casts doubt on the sincerity of motive of the writer and the seriousness of his arguments. Feminism may better be described as a reassessment in woman's favour of the relative capacities of the sexes. This definition allows not only for texts which propose the equality of the sexes, but also those which attempt to establish the superiority of woman over man; it presupposes, however, an account of the contemporary conception of the female sex, against which background any reassessment must be measured. For this reason, this study of feminism opens with a brief account of the Renaissance notion of woman.

According to Rosalie Colie, woman's nature is 'one of the great subjects of Renaissance paradoxy'.[8] Feminist and anti-feminist writing is a genre with a rhetoric of its own, which is described in the second chapter of this book. The fortunes of the traditional *Querelle des femmes* in the seventeenth century are short-lived, for around 1630 there emerges out of moralistic literature a new mode of feminist writing. Not only does this mode overturn traditional attitudes and aspire to artistic features of presentation, including copious book illustrations, but it also explores more fully the questions of marriage and the social rôle of women; these topics are discussed in succeeding chapters.

[6] *Revue de synthèse historique*, xiii. 25.
[7] Cf. Fagniez, *La femme et la société française*, p. 102: 'ce féminisme-là [that of the seventeenth century] n'a consisté que dans la revendication de la parité intellectuelle et morale des deux sexes: il n'y a rien de commun avec ce qu'on peut appeler le féminisme économique, avec celui qui cherche à ouvrir le plus de débouchés possible à l'activité féminine.'
[8] *Paradoxia epidemica: the Renaissance tradition of paradox*, Princeton, 1966, p. 53.

After this examination of feminist writings as such, imaginative literature comes under scrutiny, and with it the aesthetic dimensions of feminism. These are examined first in the context of the visual arts where they pertain to literature, and then in elements of the style of feminist writings which reflect the taste and sensibility of the period and the connection between feminism and baroque.

It is hoped that this study will contribute to the understanding of literary texts by identifying an influence, feminism, which is born of intellectual and social debates, and which affects the sensibility of the age. Such an inquiry courts many dangers: the temptation to trade in generalities, the falsification of ideas when taken out of context, and the exclusion of large areas of evidence are some of them. In my attempts to come to terms with these problems, I have received assistance from many scholars who have helped me to venture into areas of study new to me, and to eradicate countless errors. It is a great pleasure to be able to record some of these obligations: the first is that which I owe to Richard Sayce of Worcester College, Oxford, who suggested this topic to me as a doctoral thesis for the University of Oxford, and who in supervising the thesis gave me the benefit of his great erudition and incisive criticisms as well as providing a constant source of encouragement and enthusiasm. I was given valuable guidance by my examiners, Dr. M. Gerard Davis of St. Hilda's College, Oxford, and Professor M. A. Screech of University College, London, who also lent me unpublished notes on sixteenth-century feminism in France. Charles Schmitt of the Warburg Institute read parts of the manuscript with characteristic thoroughness and acumen, and gave me the benefit of his knowledge and time; among my former colleagues at the University of Leeds, Dr. George Hainsworth and Professor T. E. Hope gave me much useful advice. The late Professor Edgar Wind opened my eyes to the problems inherent in the visual arts and iconology; I am indebted also to Mr. K. V. Thomas of St. John's College, Oxford, for information about the sociological and historical aspects of feminism, and to my former tutors, the late Iain Macdonald of the Queen's College, and Duncan Stewart of Wadham College, Oxford, for much patient help and encouragement.

I should like to express my deep gratitude for the generous assistance which I have received from librarians everywhere, but especially from those of the Taylor Institution, the Bodleian Library, the British Museum, the Fawcett Library of Feminism, the Bibliothèque Nationale, the Bibliothèque de l'Arsenal, the Bibliothèque Mazarine, the Bibliothèque Historique de la Ville de Paris, the Bibliothèque Sainte-Geneviève, the Bibliothèque de la Sorbonne, the Bibliothèque de la Faculté de Médecine, the Bibliothèque Marguerite Durand, and the Bibliothèque Municipale de Versailles. I have also received much practical help: the Department of Education and Science, the Board of the Faculty of Medieval and Modern Languages at Oxford, the Sir Ernest Cassel Educational Trust, the University of Leeds, and the Queen's College, Oxford, have all been generous in financial assistance for travel abroad and for typing. My greatest debt is to my wife Pauline, who has suffered with the patience of Griselda the many absences and inconveniences caused by this undertaking, and who has spent many hours improving the quality of the English and the coherence of the arguments.

Oxford
April 1975

Contents

List of Plates

(between pages 208 and 209)

For permission to reproduce photographs, the author makes grateful acknowledgement to the Library of the Taylor Institution (Plates 1, 8, 14, 20, 21, 23), the Bibliothèque Nationale, Paris (Plates 2, 4, 5, 11, 12, 13, 16, 18, 19, 22, 26), W. B. Henderson, Esq. (Plate 3), the British Library (Plates 6, 7, 9, 10, 24, 25), the Bodleian Library (Plate 15), and the Bibliothèque de l'Arsenal, Paris, and Mme Colomb-Gérard (Plate 17).

Note on References

In transcribing titles of books and proper names, I have followed the convention of modernizing *u* and *v*, *i* and *j*, of resolving ampersands and printers' abbreviations (˜ and ;), and of retaining the minimum of capitals.

In transcribing from sixteenth- and seventeenth-century texts, I have resolved only ampersands and printers' abbreviations, retaining the original punctuation, the distinction between *u* and *v*, *i* and *j* as in the text, and all capitals. In transcribing from modern editions, I have followed the conventions of the editor.

The few abbreviations used in the notes and bibliography are recorded here:

All Souls	The Codrington Library, All Souls College, Oxford
Ars	Bibliothèque de l'Arsenal, Paris
AUMLA	*Journal of the Australasian Universities Modern Language Association*
BHR	*Bibliothèque d'Humanisme et Renaissance*
BHVP	Bibliothèque Historique de la Ville de Paris
BM	The British Library, British Museum
BN	Bibliothèque Nationale, Paris
BSHAF	*Bulletin de la Société de l'Histoire de l'Art français*
FMLS	*Forum for Modern Language Studies*
Lyons	Bibliothèque Municipale, Lyons
Madrid	Biblioteca Nacional, Madrid
Maz	Bibliothèque Mazarine, Paris
MLN	*Modern Language Notes*
PG	*Patrologiae cursus completus, series graeca*, ed. J.-P. Migne (Paris, 1857–1904)
PL	*Patrologiae cursus completus, series latina*, ed. J.-P. Migne (Paris, 1844–1904)
Queen's	Library of the Queen's College, Oxford
RSH	*Revue de Synthèse Historique*
Ste Geneviève	Bibliothèque Sainte-Geneviève, Université de Paris
Taylor	Library of the Taylor Institution, Oxford

I

The Renaissance Notion of Woman

IN order to understand the scope of feminist literature at some
point in the past, it is first necessary to have some idea of the
popular conception of woman at that time; for feminist literature
encourages a reassessment of the capacities and status of woman,
and in so doing rejects or modifies notions generally held about
her. There are many problems encountered in attempting this.
Is it legitimate to take information from texts of different dates?
How is it possible to establish what is authoritative in intellectual
debates at any one time? Is there a uniquely French notion of
woman, or is the notion common to all Western Europe? What
sort of evidence reflects best the popular conception which one is
trying to describe? It would be possible to discuss such problems
at great length; in this chapter, I shall try to show that commentaries and debates on ancient and Christian authoritative texts,
written in Europe between 1500 and 1630 and widely circulated,
provide a coherent picture of the female sex which satisfies the
needs of this study. This picture may be summarized in the
form of a set of commonplaces which constitute the background
of feminist literature in the seventeenth century. The central
interest of this chapter lies in the field of the history of ideas; for
this reason, no attempt has been made systematically to compare
theory with practice, intellectual with social history, although
comparisons are included where they seem useful. As will be
seen, the notion of woman is, as it were, molecular in structure,
consisting of an interdependent network of assumptions taken
from different intellectual spheres; for the sake of clarity, woman's
status in theology, in anatomy and medicine, in law, and finally
in moral philosophy and politics will be considered in turn.

There had been debates both in the early Church and during the
Middle Ages about the differences between the sexes;[1] these are

[1] See Jerome, *Epistolae*, lxxxiv, *PL* xxii. 743–52; Pierre-Daniel Huet, *Origeniana*
(first published 1668), ed. Migne, *PG* xvii. 991.

recorded by Renaissance commentators, but in most cases not revived. For Catholic theologians of this period, it is not surprising that Aquinas is an important source for the formulation and resolution of questions about the theological status of women; it seems that he is also used by some Reformers, whose discussion of this topic does not differ markedly from that of Catholic writers.[2] As the *Summa theologica* is influential, it is to be expected that Aristotle's views on the physical world and on ethics will appear in conjunction with patristic writing; these views will be considered in their own right in another section of this chapter. It is convenient here to follow the sequence of related questions asked by theologians: first, is a woman a human being (that is, having a mortal body and an immortal soul)? Is she made in the image of God? Is she an imperfect version of man, and if so, in what form will she appear after resurrection? Finally, is she the equal of man in theological terms?

Is woman a human being? An anonymous satirist of the bibliolatry of anabaptists revived the question in a *Disputatio nova contra mulieres qua probatur eas homines non esse*, published in Germany in 1595.[3] This work enjoys a certain notoriety in the following century, and is a useful compendium of commonplaces about the inferiority of woman to man, both biblical and pagan, but it does not provoke anything but refutation. Conclusions drawn from glossing Genesis and St. Paul, as well as a wealth of *argumenta e nihilo*, are intended by the writer not to prove his case, but rather to expose the dangers of the anabaptists' literal

---

[2] See, for example, Johann Gerhard, *Loci theologici*, Jena, 1610–22. Gerhard was a prominent Lutheran theologian. The edition quoted below is that published in Geneva in 1639.

[3] Usually attributed to Valens Acidalius, although he strenuously denies authorship (*Epistolae*, ed. Christianus Acidalius, Hanau, 1606, p. 339). The work was refuted by Simon Gediccus (Leipzig, 1595), and attacked by both physicians (e.g. J. P. Lotz, *Gynaicologia*, Rintheln, 1630) and jurists (e.g. J. U. Wolff, *Discursus: de foeminarum in jure civili et canonico privilegiis, immunitatibus et praeeminentia*, Rostock, 1615). Marie de Gournay alludes to it in her *Égalité des hommes et des femmes* (ed. M. Schiff, Paris, 1910, p. 70). An extended version of it appears in German in 1615 (republished in 1642) as a debate between a Jesuit and a Benedictine monk. The text appears with Gediccus's refutation as a *Disputatio perjucunda* at The Hague in 1638, 1641, 1644, at Paris in 1683, 1690, 1693; an Italian translation is printed at Leone in 1647. On this and other attempts to show that women are not human beings see Pierre Bayle, *Dictionnaire historique et critique*, Rotterdam, 1697, i. 86, ii. 1228; Gerard Vossius, *De origine idololatriae*, iii. 48, in *Opera omnia*, Amsterdam, 1700, v. 361–2; *Histoire des conciles*, ed. H. Leclercq, Paris, 1909, iii. 1, 211–12.

approach to the understanding of the Scriptures, and cannot be considered as serious.[4]

Is woman made in the image of God? There is no doubt that man is made in His image (Gen. 1 : 26–7); if St. Paul's commentary on the relevant verses in Genesis seems to suggest women may not be,[5] Augustine's long commentary on the meaning of image, to which Aquinas refers, settles the issue in the Western Church, and all Renaissance theologians seem to follow his line, except where the doubt provides a moral stick with which to beat the vanity of women.[6] At the same time, however, as asserting that woman as well as man is made in the image of God, they reflect St. Paul's conviction that greater dignity and pre-eminence reside in the male sex.[7]

Is woman a perfect creation of God, or is she an imperfect version of a male? The anatomical implications of this much-debated question are examined below; in theological discussion, Aquinas's question on the *productio mulieris* provides an answer often repeated by later commentators:

It seems that woman ought not to have been produced in the original production of things. For the Philosopher says that the female is a male *manqué*. But nothing *manqué* or defective should have been produced in the first establishment of things; so woman ought not to have been produced then . . .

Only as regards nature in the individual is the female something defective and *manqué*. For the active power of the seed of the male tends to produce something like itself, perfect in masculinity; but the procreation of a female is the result either of the debility of the active

---

[4] The texts most helpful to the writer are Gen. 1 : 26–7 (no explicit statement that woman is made in the image of God); Gen. 2 : 21–3 (the creation of woman); Gen. 3 : 16 (subordination of Eve to Adam); Eph. 4 : 12 (use of *vir* and not *homo* to designate the saved); 1 Tim. 2 : 15 (women's salvation is in the procreation of males). The *argumenta e nihilo* include the absence of mentions of women in biblical genealogies, the fact that no woman is described as *homo* in Holy Writ, the fact that there is no mention of the resurrection or damnation of a woman. This last assertion is false (see Acts 5 : 10), and illustrates the humour underlying many of the theses of the disputation.

[5] See Augustine, *De Genesi ad litteram*, xii. 42, PL xxxiv. 452. The Pauline text is 1 Cor. 11 : 7. Gerhard refers to 'disputationes quaedam veterum' on this question (*Loci theologici*, ii. 202–3). See also Aquinas, 1a 93. 4; and Pierre Grégoire, *De republica*, Frankfurt, 1597, vii. 11, p. 444.

[6] See below, p. 41.

[7] Aquinas, 1a 92. 1; Luther links this Pauline belief with 1 Pet. 3 : 7 (woman the *vasculus infirmior*) (*Commentarii in Genesim*, in *Opera omnia*, Wittenberg, 1580, vi. 15ᵛ). See also N. Selneccerus, *In Genesim commentaria*, Leipzig, 1569, p. 115.

power, of some unsuitability of the material, or of some change effected by external influences, like the south wind, for example, which is damp, as we are told by Aristotle.

But with reference to nature in the species as a whole, the female is not something *manqué*, but is according to the tendency of nature, and is directed to the work of procreation. Now the tendency of the nature of a species as a whole derives from God, who is the general author of nature. And therefore when he established a nature, he brought into being not only the male but the female too.[8]

The need for this apology of Aristotle's views is, however, obviated if those views are no longer held to be authoritative; some theologians use anatomical arguments to show the equality of the sexes rather than those proposed by Aquinas.[9]

If woman is considered as imperfect, even if only as regards her individual nature, will she participate in the resurrection in the form of a woman, or as a man, or as some sort of sexless being? This question caused debate in the early Church, and some contention in the Middle Ages.[10] The Lutheran theologian Gerhard seems to consider this point as seriously as the other problems

---

[8] 1a 92. 1. For the use of this argument see Gerhard, *Loci theologici*, vii. 853–5; Cornelius A Lapide, *In omnes divi Pauli epistolas commentaria*, Paris, 1638, pp. 509–11. See also M. A. Screech, *The Rabelaisian marriage*, London, 1958, p. 94; Rabelais, *Tiers livre*, 32. Another account of woman's inferiority is given in Thomas de Vio's (Cajetanus's) *Commentarii in quinque Mosaicos libros*, Paris, 1539, p. 25: Eve is created from Adam as he sleeps; 'homo enim dormiens semihomo est. Et similiter principium generans mulierem semivirile est. Et propterea a philosophis mulier dicitur vir laesus.'

[9] See André Valladier, *La saincte philosophie de l'ame*, Paris, 1614, pp. 818–19, quoted below, pp. 41–2; François Dinet, *Le theatre françois, des seigneurs et dames illustres*, Paris, 1642, ii. 2.

[10] Biblical *loci* are Matt. 22: 29–30 (marriage in heaven); Gal. 3: 28 (sex in heaven); Eph. 4: 12 (resurrection as perfect 'males'); 1 Cor. 15: 24 (no subjection in heaven: therefore women must be changed into men in order to be equal to men). Huet, *Origeniana*, gives a summary bibliography of patristic texts on this topic. After Augustine's comments in *De civitate Dei* (xxii. 17, *PL* xli. 778), there seems to be a lull in the debate. Medieval texts include Peter Lombard, *Sententiae*, ii. 20, iv. 44; Aquinas, *Suppl.* 81. 3; and Duns Scotus, who according to A Lapide (*In omnes Pauli epistolas*, pp. 509–10) and Gerhard (*Loci theologici*, viii. 853) argues that all women except the Virgin Mary will become males in heaven. Renaissance editors of Scotus insist, however, that these words are an interpolation (see Duns Scotus, *In quatuor libros Sententiarum quaestiones*, ed. Hugo Cavellus, Antwerp, 1620, p. 228; *Opera omnia*, ed. Franciscus Lychetus, Lyons, 1639, vi. 2, 824–5). For Calvin's rather different approach see his *Commentarii in epistolas ad Ephesios*, in *Opera omnia*, Amsterdam, 1667, vii. 341 ('Quisquis ergo vir est in Christo, ille demum omni ex parte est absolutus'), and Conrad Pellikan, *In omnes apostolicas epistolas commentarii*, Zürich, 1539, p. 383.

raised by woman's theological status, and uses Aquinas's arguments to show that women are resurrected in the form of women;[11] while all Renaissance theologians would agree with his conclusion, not all are as tolerant of discussion of such speculative points of dogma.[12]

Are men and women equal before God? Gregory I's assertion of the equality of all men, referred to by Aquinas on several occasions, would seem to suggest that they are;[13] Basil's argument that equal reward for good and equal punishment for evil in the next life proves the equality of the sexes is a supporting text popular with feminist writers.[14] There remain, however, two difficulties: the subordination of wife to husband (Gen. 3: 16), and the question whether men and women are equally prone to sin. The first difficulty is much debated in the Renaissance, which saw a profound reassessment of Christian marriage.[15] Even enlightened writers concede woman's subordinate position to her husband, which they attribute to the different capacities of the sexes;[16] in this they follow Aquinas, whose distinction between various forms of subordination answers the problem caused to commentators by Gregory's argument of the equality of all men.[17] Although in marriage authority is vested in the husband, both he and his wife should be equally committed to the institution of marriage and the family; in their insistence on this, Renaissance moralists reflect the new understanding of St. Paul's teachings on matrimony.[18]

The relative propensity of the sexes to good or evil is connected with the ability to resist temptation and to perform acts of virtue.

---

[11] *Loci theologici*, viii. 853–5; see also A Lapide, *In omnes Pauli epistolas*, pp. 509–11; Wolfgang Musculus, *In Epistolas Pauli ad Galatas et Ephesios commentarii*, Basle, 1569, ii. 108.   [12] See below, p. 41.

[13] *Moralia in Job*, 31: 15, PL lxxxvi. 203; *De regula pastorali*, ii. 6, PL lxxvii. 34; Aquinas 1a 92. 1; *Suppl.* 52. 1.

[14] *De hominis structura*, i. 22, PG xxx. 34–5; for the use of this argument see Simon Majolus, *Colloquia physica*, Mainz, 1615, i. 3, p. 47; Nicolas L'Archevesque, *Les grandeurs sur-eminentes de la tres-saincte Vierge Marie*, Paris, 1638, pp. 485–6; Jacques Du Bosc, *La femme heroïque*, Paris, 1645, i. 29. See also Clement of Alexandria, *Paedagogus*, i. 4, PG viii. 259–62.

[15] See below, p. 21.   [16] See below, pp. 105–6.

[17] 1a 92. 1; *Suppl.* 52. 1. Aquinas argues that subordination must be distinguished from subjection; the former is authority exercised over a person for his own good; the latter, for the good of the person exercising the authority.

[18] The relevant passages in St. Paul are 1 Cor. 7; Eph. 5: 22–33; 1 Tim. 2: 9–15. See Screech, *The Rabelaisian marriage*, pp. 66–83, 104–25.

It seems that woman's greater mental frailty is generally conceded; Tertullian's accusation that woman in the form of Eve was the *janua diaboli*[19] leads to a discussion in the Middle Ages about the gravity of the sin of Eve compared to that of Adam, in which no consensus is reached, except that less is expected of Eve than of Adam.[20] From this, and from the apostolic description of woman as the weaker vessel,[21] the appellation *fragilior sexus* is derived; this in turn is reflected in the interpretation of verses in the Old Testament about woman, such as Ecclus. 42: 14, 'melior est iniquitas viri quam mulier bene faciens et confundens in opprobrium.'[22] The assumption of woman's smaller capacity for virtue and greater tendency to sin is of considerable importance to this study, as it can give rise to the paradox of strength in weakness, when a woman, endued with less potential moral strength than man, performs acts of virtue greater than those achieved by man; this paradox underlies the depiction of the *femme forte*.[23] The agency of grace in heroic actions by women is not denied, but is argued to be an indication of God's special dispensation for woman.[24]

Most Renaissance theologians seem therefore to accept that woman is not quite the equal of man in the manner of her creation, nor is she as well endowed as he is with moral apparatus; but this inequality is attached to her existence in this life only, as is her subordination to her husband in marriage, and it is agreed that she will share equally in the joys of paradise. The disparity in capacity for virtue is reflected in the religious proscriptions suffered by the female sex: women are not allowed to speak in church, to teach doctrine, to administer the sacraments. Even those theologians who argue the equality of the sexes in all things do not inveigh against these unequal religious practices.

At the base of Aristotle's writings about natural philosophy there seems to be a division between 'male' and 'female' principles

---

[19] *De cultu feminarum*, i. 1, *PL* i. 1419.
[20] Peter Lombard, *Sententiae*, ii. 22; Aquinas, 2a 2ae 163. 4, 165. 2.
[21] 1 Pet. 3: 7.
[22] See below, pp. 42–4. Other prominent texts from the Old Testament are Ecclus. 25: 23 (woman's anger) and Eccles. 7: 28 (absence of goodness in all women). For discussion of Prov. 31: 10–29 (the Alphabet of the Good Woman) see below, p. 21 and pp. 81–2. A compendious list of Old Testament *loci* is found in Antoine de Balinghem, *Scriptura sacra in locos communes digesta*, Cologne, 1659, i. 599–606.
[23] See below, pp. 67 ff.   [24] See below, pp. 73, 188–9.

in nature, the former being active and formative, the latter passive, material, and 'deprived' or incomplete without the male principle.[25] It is this division which is reflected in the most famous and most debated commonplace about woman in Aristotle, to be found in the *De generatione animalium*, where she is described as a 'πεπηρωμένον': the Latin formulations most commonly encountered are *mas mutilatus, aberratio naturae, defectus naturalis, animal occasionatum*.[26] Renaissance commentators examine a sequence of related problems deriving from this commonplace: first, is woman a monster (that is, in Ambroise Paré's formulation, 'chose outre le cours de Nature'[27])? Is she an animal, where man is an *animal rationale*? Is she less perfect than man, and if so, in what respects? Finally, does this imperfection, if it is accepted to be such, affect the working of her mind?

Before considering these questions, a brief word must be said about the vexed position of the authority of various ancient writings. It has been shown that Plato and Galen are set against each other by Renaissance anatomists,[28] as are Galen and Paracelsus;[29] it seems that by the end of the sixteenth century the supporters of Galen gain the upper hand, although by this time most doctors are eclectic in their choice of authority.[30] In the case of medical writings about women, there is a collection of Arabic, Greek, Medieval, and Renaissance treatises entitled *Gynaecea*, which appears first in 1566, and contains most of the

---

[25] *Physics*, i. 9 (in which Aristotle refers to a similar Platonic concept, expressed in *Timaeus*, 50c); also *Metaphysics*, i. 8; *De generatione animalium*, i. 20; *De historia animalium*, ix. 1. For references to this division see Aquinas, 1a 92. 1; Gabriele Falloppio, *Tractatus de metallis seu fossilibus*, xi, i *Opera omnia*, Frankfurt, 1600, i. 300: 'Ea proportio, quae est inter materiam et formam, est etiam inter foeminam et marem. Nam foemina sustentatur mari, et appetit marem, tanquam suam perfectionem, quemadmodum et materia appetit formam, tanquam optatum et amatum ex Aristotele in I Physic.'; see also Du Bosc, *L'honneste femme*, Paris, 1633–6, i. 224: François de Grenaille, *L'honneste mariage*, Paris, 1640, pp. 206–7.

[26] *De generatione animalium*, ii. 3; iv. 6.

[27] *Des monstres et prodiges*, ed. J. Céard, Geneva, 1971, p. 3.

[28] See Screech, *The Rabelaisian marriage*, pp. 84–103.

[29] For a discussion of Paracelsus's attitudes towards woman and sex (which do not appear to be very influential) see W. Pagel, *Paracelsus: introduction to philosophical medicine in the era of the Renaissance*, Basle and New York, 1958, p. 238 ff.; id., *Das medizinische Weltbild des Paracelsus*, Wiesbaden, 1962, pp. 62–70; P. Diepgen, 'Paracelsus und das Problem der Frau', *Nova acta Paracelsiana*, viii (1957), 49–54.

[30] For examples, see *Gynaecea*, ed. Israel Spachius, Strasbourg, 1597, pp. 1002–3; Rodericus A. Castro, *De natura mulierum* (first published 1603), Hamburg, 1662, passim.

important material before Rodericus A Castro's *De natura mulierum* of 1603.[31] In both these works, the presence of debates about ancient texts suggests the continuing tradition of Renaissance medicine in spite of new experimental approaches; the survival of these debates may be seen in the context of the survival of Aristotelianism as a whole.[32]

Whether woman is a monstrous creature or not is debated in the context of the commonplace from the *De generatione animalium* referred to above, and Aristotle's assertion in the *Metaphysics* that man and woman belong to the same species.[33] Besides satirical or virulently anti-feminist works—the *Disputatio nova contra mulieres*, Giuseppe Passi's *I donneschi diffetti*, and Trousset's *Alphabet de l'imperfection et malice des femmes*[34]—there are no defences of the proposition that women are monstrous; vigorous refutation may be found in several medical texts.[35] In some texts the idea of physical monstrosity is linked with the suggestion in Plato's *Timaeus* (91A) that women incarnate the souls of men who in a previous life had been debauched: 'animas eorum, qui in vita existentes male, et praeter iustitiam vixissent, in foeminea corpora, quasi imperfecta et montruosa recipi'.[36]

The animality of woman is linked with a commonplace taken from Plato (*Timaeus*, 91A–D) usually quoted in the form in which Erasmus rendered it in the *Praise of Folly*: 'Plato dubitare videtur, utro in genere ponat mulierem, rationalium animantium an brutorum.'[37] Plato's text merely suggests that the womb itself may be considered as an independent being in woman, an *animal avidum generandi*, endowed with senses and being able to move of its own accord. The debate falls into two sections: first is woman an animal (that is, possessed of mortal life but not of reason)?

---

[31] *Gynaecea* was republished in 1577, 1586–7, and 1597; A Castro's work appeared at least four times between 1603 and 1662.

[32] See C. B. Schmitt, 'Towards a reassessment of Renaissance Aristotelianism', *History of science*, xi (1973), 159–93.

[33] *Metaphysics*, x. 9.

[34] *Disputatio nova*, thesis xliii; *I donneschi diffetti*, Venice, 1599, p. 8; *Alphabet de l'imperfection et malice des femmes*, Rouen, 1631, p. 418.

[35] e.g. Martinus Weinrichius, *De ortu monstruorum commentarius*, Breslau, 1595, ii. 65ᵛ–69ᵛ; Bartholomaeus Keckermann, *Systema physicum*, Hanau, 1617, pp. 593–601.

[36] Paolo Zacchia, *Quaestiones medicolegales*, 3rd edn., Amsterdam, 1651, p. 470; Grégoire, *De republica*, p. 446; see also Montaigne, *Essais*, ed. Thibaudet and Rat, Paris, 1967, iii. 5, p. 834.

[37] *Opera omnia*, Leyden, 1703–6, iv. 418.

second, is the womb an animal in its own right? The first of these questions is linked to the theological issue, already mentioned, of whether women have souls; only the facetious *Disputatio nova contra mulieres* seems to make much of this.[38] On the second question, most doctors conclude against Plato at the end of the century that the womb is an organ like any other,[39] although it seems that some earlier Platonists try to uphold his view.[40] The associated belief that woman is prey to almost boundless lust because of her need to satisfy the cravings of her womb survives, however, in medical and popular literature.[41]

On the more general question of imperfection, a wider and less unified debate may be discerned, which may indicate that commentators took this problem more seriously. Of all commonplaces, the ones associated with woman as an imperfect male persist longest: Bartolomeo Castelli's *Lexicon medicum* gives as a first definition for woman 'imperfectior mare' as late as in 1713.[42] It would seem, however, that there is only one defence of the proposition by an anatomist after 1600, that by Caspar Hofmann, in a commentary on Galen's *De usu partium corporis*: Chapter 14 of this work is an extended gloss on Aristotle's assertions in the *De generatione animalium*.[43] Following Galen closely, Hofmann produces two reasons why woman may be described as an imperfect male: the first that she is colder in humours and temperature, the most perfect beings being the hottest; the second, that the female genitalia are imperfect versions of the male, and have remained internal 'ob caloris debilitatem'. Hofmann also implies that since woman's function is to bear children, and since she cannot do this without the co-operation of the male, she is in herself incomplete; there may be in this a reminiscence of Aristotle's concept of deprivation.[44]

[38] See also Jacques Yver, *Le printemps d'Yver*, Paris, 1572, ff. 102–3. There seems to be no mention of the Muslim belief that women do not have souls until Montesquieu (*Lettres persanes*, cxli), where the belief is attributed by a Muslim to the Jews. [39] See A Castro, *De natura mulierum*, i. 6, pp. 17–19.
[40] See Screech, *The Rabelaisian marriage*, pp. 84–103.
[41] See Jean Aubery, *L'antidote d'amour*, Paris, 1599; Jacques Ferrand, *De la maladie d'amour*, Paris, 1623; Trousset, *Alphabet*, pp. 43–9.
[42] *Lexicon medicum graecolatinum*, Leipzig, 1713, s.v. *femina*.
[43] *Commentarii in Galeni de usu partium corporis*, Frankfurt, 1625, pp. 307–10; there is also one theological commentary by Sebastian Meyer (*Augustae laudes Divinae Majestatis e divinis Galeni de usu partium libris xvii selectae*, Freiburg, 1627, pp. 197–8) which accepts Galen's text as authoritative.
[44] See Aristotle, *Physics*, i. 9.

These reasons for considering woman an imperfect version of man, accepted by Aquinas, are gradually undermined in the course of the sixteenth century. Evidence from ancient texts is shown to be equivocal: it is not clear that all ancient authorities agree whether man or woman is the hotter.[45] Several reactions may be discerned among commentators to the doubts raised by this diversity of opinions: apart from the conservative anatomists who try to reconcile all ancient authorities, and are faithful to Aristotle's concept of female imperfection,[46] there are two groups of doctors who turn this confusion to the advantage of woman's anatomical status: the first, inspired by the writings of Julius Caesar Scaliger, argues that men and women are of the same bodily temperature, and that no ancient authority is correct on this point;[47] the second contends that bodily temperature is not a sign of perfection or imperfection, but rather of function: women must retain food and fat in order to be able to feed the foetus.[48]

Similar reasoning disposes of Galen's proof of female imperfection from physical formation. The Parisian doctor André Du Laurens refutes Caspar Bauhin's argument that there is any direct comparison to be made between the genitalia of man and woman; such differences as exist are accounted for by the different rôles played by the two sexes in procreation, not by the conditions prevalent at the moment of conception, which

---

[45] Galen, *De usu partium corporis*, xiv, argues that women are colder; Hippocrates, *De morbis mulierum*, i, argues that 'calidiorem sanguinem mulier habet, ideoque viro calidior est'. The *De morbis mulierum* is no longer considered to be the work of Hippocrates (see E. Littré, *Hippocrate, œuvres complètes*, Paris, 1839, i. 373), but is found in all Renaissance editions of the *Opera omnia*. See also Hieronymus Cardanus, *Contradicentia medica*, ii. 6, in *Opera omnia*, Lyons, 1663, vi. 645-54.

[46] e.g. Mauricius Cordaeus, *In librum priorem Hippocratis de morbis mulierum commentarius*, in *Gynaecea*, pp. 502-7; Johannes Zecchius, *Tractatus de pulsibus*, Frankfurt, 1650, pp. 933-5.

[47] Scaliger, *Exercitationes*, cclxxiv (first published 1576), Frankfurt, 1592, pp. 832-8; Martinus Akakia, *De morbis muliebribus*, prolegomena, in *Gynaecea*, p. 745; A Castro, *De natura mulierum*, ii. 13, pp. 94-5; iii. 8, pp. 126-35.

[48] This also explains why women alone menstruate (unlike men, they cannot use up excesses of matter in producing bodily hair), why they are generally fatter, sleepier, of paler skin and softer flesh, why they do not go bald, and why they burn better than men on funeral pyres (see Nicolaus Rocheus, *De morbis mulierum curandis*, iii, in *Gynaecea*, p. 65; Hieronymus Mercurialis, *De morbis mulierum*, vi. 1, in *Gynaecea*, p. 257; Akakia, *De morbis muliebribus*, i, in *Gynaecea*, p. 746; Albertus Bottoni, *De morbis mulierum*, xiv, in *Gynaecea*, p. 348; A Castro, *De natura mulierum*, ii. 13, p. 97). The Aristotelian *locus* is in *De historia animalium*, iv. 11.

Aquinas mentions as an Aristotelian theory.[49] Galen's two arguments are thus discredited in nearly all circles by the end of the sixteenth century, but his views survive in the associated question of the action of bodily temperature on the workings of the mind. In spite of Scaliger's exposure of the possible absurdities to be derived from an inflexible application of Galen's theory of the humours,[50] there is much contemporary speculation about the effect of the dominant cold and moist humours in woman, more in feminist and anti-feminist literature than in medical works themselves. Beliefs about woman's greater inconstancy, greater powers of memory and imagination, greater compassion for others, greater propensity to fear and despair, more violent passions, smaller capacity for active virtue, in many ways derived from passages of Aristotle's *De historia animalium*,[51] persist well into the seventeenth century.[52]

Thus in medical debates one may discern a conservative desire to maintain the general context of medical science while having the freedom to tamper with details within that structure; there is an awareness of the contradictions implied in accepting all ancient authority, coupled with the practice of taking or rejecting whichever tenets are suitable or unsuitable to an argument. This reactionary audacity of anatomists does not disturb the tranquil existence of commonplaces in the popular mind which are repeated outside the context of scholarly debate with conviction

[49] Bauhin, *Theatrum anatomicum*, i. 32–3, Frankfurt, 1605, pp. 210–12; Du Laurens, *Historia anatomica humani corporis*, viii. 1–2, Frankfurt [1600], pp. 280–4. For a more detailed comparison of male and female genitalia, see Aemylius Parisanus, *De microcosmica subtilitate pars altera*, Venice, 1635, pp. 107–10, who asserts that 'recentiores quidam et doctissimi dicunt partes genitales omnino similes cum marium genitalibus' but does not mean by this that the female are an inferior version of the male. The argument about sex determination at conception is connected with the question whether woman as well as man has semen or a *vis formatrix*; Aristotle (*De generatione animalium*, i. 20, ii. 4) and Galen (*De semine*, ii) do not agree on this point. The former argues that the male alone is endowed with a *vis formatrix*, which, in perfect conditions, would naturally reproduce its producer; hence woman is the result of imperfect conception. For Renaissance discussion of this topic, see Ludovicus Mercatus, *De mulierum affectionibus*, i. 2, in *Gynaecea*, p. 807; A Castro, *De natura mulierum*, ii. 3, pp. 43–9; Ambroise Paré, *De hominis generatione*, 1–2, in *Gynaecea*, pp. 404–5; Cardanus, *Contradicentia medica*, iv. 11, in *Opera omnia*, vi. 768–9.

[50] *Exercitationes*, cclxxiv, pp. 832–8; see also Mercurialis, *De morbis muliebribus*, i. 1, in *Gynaecea*, p. 209.

[51] *De historia animalium*, iv. 11, ix. 1. See also other peripatetic philosophers, Avicenna, *De animalibus*, viii. 3; Albertus Magnus, *De animalibus*, i. 2, 11.

[52] See below, pp. 46–50.

and trust: woman, the imperfect male endowed with dubious rationality and a weaker physical constitution. While one may detect a movement towards a more sympathetic appraisal of women, it cannot be said that any of these anatomical works establish their equality with men in so striking a way as to impress itself on an audience wider than a few like-minded scholars.[53]

In the sphere of legal studies, one may trace a similar debate to that already examined in the sphere of medical writings, which seems to follow a similar chronology and a similar progression from what might loosely be called an anti-feminist to a feminist position. This debate is pursued in philologically inspired glosses on the *Digest*, the *Codex*, and the *Institutes*, and is connected with the purging of all interpolation and error from those documents. Fifteenth-century commentators had tried to deal with the problem of interpreting the words and formulas *homo, mulier, masculus, si quis, quicunque*. Their glosses seem to arouse little ire in their time, whereas their greatest successor, Jacques Cujas, unleashed a storm of protest over a chapter in his *Observationes et emendationes* relating to the Roman law of homicide (*lex Cornelia de sicariis*):

The Roman emperors considered infanticide to be punishable by death; the murderer of a man was punished in the same way. The law therefore pursued homicide with an avenging sword. It was possible to doubt whether the law covered the murder of infants, as the *lex Cornelia* says 'who kills a human being [*homo*]', hence the name of the crime [homicide] . . . in the same way it was possible to doubt whether the murder of a woman is covered by the law. Now an infant is not a human being; nor, properly speaking, is a woman (see the passage 'quis aliquid'§ abortionis in the section *De poenis* of the *Digest*). But in the *lex Julia et Papia* the meaning of 'human being' [*homo*] is extended by the jurists, as in the *lex Cornelia*, to include 'woman' too.[54]

---

[53] Ancient ideas generally rejected about women have not been discussed here, e.g. the belief that females are conceived on the left side of the womb and males on the right (see Hippocrates, *Aphorisms*, v. 48; Mercatus, *De mulierum affectionibus*, iii. 4, in *Gynaecea*, p. 103; Cardanus, *Contradicentia medica*, iv. 11, in *Opera omnia*, vi. 768–9).

[54] *Observationes*, vi. 21, in *Opera omnia*, Lyons, 1606, iv. 1484. Gerard Vossius says that Cujas intended this chapter to be a joke (*De origine idololatriae*, iii. 48, in *Opera omnia*, v. 361–2). For a similar facetious reading of the same text see Scipio Gentilis *Parergorum libri II*, Frankfurt, 1588, i. 3, pp. 9–11.

The offending words would seem to have been 'woman, properly speaking, is not a human being' ('foemina item proprie non est homo').[55] Of all the refutations, the most cogent and most quoted is that of Johannes Goddaeus in his commentary on *Digest* 50. 16 *De verborum significatione*.[56] Goddaeus's intention is to establish as an axiom that 'masculino sexus foemininus non modo extensivae significationis beneficio sed maxime sermonis proprietate comprehenditur'. He begins by asserting that women as well as men are made in the image of God, referring to Gen. 1 : 26–7, that pagan philosophers stress the community of species between men and women, and that in origin, matter, and form no distinction is to be made between the sexes. Goddaeus next turns to the question of woman's inferiority to man, quoting the commonplaces discussed above from the *Timaeus* and the *De generatione animalium*, but denies strenuously that such inferiority (which he appears to accept) implies distinction of species. After a technical refutation of Cujas's legal arguments, he continues with an eloquent passage in which, in the same way as Basil had done in another context, he shows that equality of punishment implies equality of humanity. He goes on to show how *si quis*, *quicunque*, and other such formulas apply in most cases to both sexes, using both legal and biblical illustrations, and concludes that the only limitations are those imposed by law or custom.[57] Later commentators all praise Goddaeus's elegance and precision, and extend his gloss to other texts.[58]

It has been seen that Goddaeus appears to accept women's natural inferiority to man, and reproduces theological and anatomical arguments to establish it. This inferiority is enshrined in one of the most aggressively anti-feminist passages of the *Digest*, which appears in the *De regulis juris antiqui* (50. 16. 2):

Women are excluded from all civil and public offices; and thus they

[55] See also Franciscus Hoeltich and Johannes Waltz, *Quaestio foemina non est homo*, Wittenberg, 1672, for another treatment of this topic.

[56] *Commentarius repetitae praelectionis in tit. xvi libri l pandectarum*, Nassau, 1614 (5th edn.), pp. 32–46.

[57] Where *si quis* refers to a function which a woman may not fulfil, such as magistrature; also where the meaning of the text excludes women, as in references to crimes such as rape.

[58] See Johannes Harpprecht, *Tractatus criminalis*, Frankfurt, 1603, p. 381; Hieronymus Treutler, *Selectae disputationes ad jus civile*, Marburg, 1603, i. 18–19; Wolff, *Discursus*, H2ᵛ; Joachimus Eberartus, *Bonus mulier*, n.p., 1616, E3ᵛ–4ᵛ.

may not be *judices*, nor magistrates, nor advocates; nor may they intervene on another's behalf in law, nor act as agents.[59]

This *regula* is well known in the Renaissance as a commonplace, and finds its way into many feminist and anti-feminist tracts, as well as into Classical digests such as Rhodiginus's *Lectiones antiquae*.[60] The fragment draws extensive comment from Renaissance jurists;[61] representative of their interpretations is a volume which collects together the commentaries of five eminent scholars on the *De regulis juris antiqui*, published in Lyons in 1593.[62] Twenty-nine folio pages explore these lines, outlining the position of women in Roman, Holy Roman, and Canon law, and examining this in connection with their anatomical and theological status. The commentators are concerned with both the prohibitions in law relating to women and the prerogatives in their favour, and all refer to exceptions which break the rule.[63] For the purpose of this study, it is most interesting to establish what reasons are adduced to justify these prohibitions and prerogatives.

One jurist (Francus) refers to the historical event which is said to have caused the prohibition (Calpurnia's notorious behaviour);[64] others content themselves with the more general reasons. Cagnolus argues that women are inferior to men in the imperfection of their anatomy, in their lack of active virtue,[65] in their dependence on men, symbolized in the manner of their

---

[59] 'judices': those who decided on the facts of a civil or criminal case; people on the *album judicum* (see W. W. Buckland, *A textbook of Roman Law*, 2nd edn., Cambridge, 1950, pp. 635 ff.); 'postulare' is here translated as 'to be an advocate' (see ibid., p. 91).

[60] See Cornelius Agrippa's rhetorical version of it in his *De nobilitate et praecellentia foeminei sexus*, Antwerp, 1529, C7^{r-v}, quoted below, p. 16; *Disputatio nova contra mulieres*, thesis xlix; Nicolas Angenoust, *Le paranymphe des dames*, Troyes, 1629, p. 6; Lotz, *Gynaicologia*, pp. 164–5; Caelius Rhodiginus, *Lectiones antiquae*, xiii. 33, Geneva, 1620, col. 720.

[61] See Martinus Lipenius, *Bibliotheca realis juridica*, Frankfurt, 1679, s.v. *femina*, *mulier*, for a bibliography of commentaries on this text; also the collection in the Bodleian Library, Oxford, pressmarks Diss. E 139–140 Jur.

[62] The five jurists, and the dates of first publication of their commentaries, are Philippus Francus (1499), Philippus Decius (1525), Jacobus Ferrarius (1546), Hieronymus Cagnolus (1576), Jacobus Raevardus (1584).

[63] There is no agreement as to the number of prohibitions and prerogatives: Decius, for example, finds 39 of the former and 14 of the latter; Francus, 32 and 26.

[64] *Commentarii ad titulum Digestorum de regulis juris antiqui*, Lyons, 1593, p. 53.

[65] Cf. Aquinas, 1a 92. 1, quoting Augustine: 'semper honorabilius agens patiente', and below, p. 18.

first creation, and in the specific religious injunction: 'vir est caput mulieris' (Eph. 5: 23). Women are excluded from public life because they must uphold the modesty of their sex, because they are inconsistent, of poor judgement, prone to emotionalism, and unable to keep secrets.[66] Ferrarius also refers to their imperfect faculties; he then describes woman's desire to govern and dominate in order to compensate for her weakness, and points to the disastrous consequences of letting her do so;[67] he concludes with a quotation from the *Digest* (*De senatoribus*, 1. 9. 1): 'maior dignitas est in sexu virili.' References to the *fragilitas*, *imbecillitas*, *inconstantia* of women are everywhere apparent in these commentaries; almost as common are references to custom (which one commentator generously allows to be the major factor in women's exclusion from public office)[68] and to modesty, the prime virtue of the female sex, which public appearances would endanger:[69] 'in muliere maior honestas requiritur.'[70]

In these and other commentaries, prerogatives are listed as well as prohibitions; these were brought together by Joannes Bassianus in the fifteenth century,[71] and by two jurists who write against the *Disputatio nova* in the early years of the seventeenth century, Johannes Ulricus Wolff (*Discursus : de foeminarum in jure civili et canonico privilegiis, immunitatibus et praeeminentia*) and Joachimus Eberartus (*Bonus mulier*). Wolff shows all the signs of a genuine enthusiasm for a feminist movement, and concludes his work with a ringing peroration, calling Plato a fool for doubting whether women were men or beasts, and demanding that Tertullian and St. Augustine be punished for calling woman the gate of the devil.[72] Eberartus's work is more difficult to assess, as it seems to be compounded of truth and error, seriousness and humour, insults to Catholicism, and ribaldry; but its conclusion is an accurate refutation of Cujas and a humane rejection of the tenets of the *Disputatio nova contra mulieres*. Both Wolff and Eberartus argue that women are unfairly treated by the law, and that their *deterior conditio* is the result of custom, not of difference in capacity to men; in the commentaries on the *De regulis juris*, however,

---

[66] *Commentarii de regulis juris*, pp. 50–1.
[67] Ibid., pp. 47–8; Eve, Helen, Deianira, and Cleopatra are cited in this context.
[68] Ibid., p. 48, with special reference to acting as judges.
[69] Ferrarius here quotes the opening paragraph of Plutarch's *Mulierum virtutes* (see below, pp. 20 and 74).   [70] Ibid., p. 31.
[71] See Francus, *Commentarii de regulis juris*, p. 57.   [72] *Discursus*, H2^{r-v}.

even the prerogatives which women enjoy under the law are ascribed to unflattering causes: presumed ignorance of the law and of social custom, lack of common sense, muddle-headedness, rashness, and a tendency to emotionalism.[73]

In spite of the writings of feminist jurists, the theoretical justification of the *deterior conditio* of women in law is reproduced in commentaries of the seventeenth century;[74] in practice, it is therefore not surprising to find that the legal position of women is far inferior to that of men. Cornelius Agrippa's declamation *De nobilitate et praecellentia foeminei sexus* of 1529 gives a graphic description of woman's legal deprivation and social enslavement:

By the excessive power of male tyranny, which prevails against divine justice and the laws of nature, women's liberty is denied to them by law, suppressed by custom and usage, and eradicated by upbringing. For as soon as a woman is born, she is imprisoned in the home in a state of idleness from her earliest years on, and is not allowed to wield anything other than needle and thread, as though she were incapable of more lofty activities. Once she has reached the age of puberty, she is given over into the jealous control of a husband, or shut up for ever in the vestals' prison . . . she is excluded from public and civil offices by law: furthermore she is debarred from jurisdiction, judgement, adoption, from giving surety, from acting on another's behalf, from tutelage, from guardianship, from criminal cases and cases concerning wills . . .[75]

Agrippa does not mention laws relating to succession and inheritance, which provoke some discussion during the early years of the seventeenth century;[76] these are marked by a strong masculine bias especially in France, where Salic law prevents a woman succeeding to the throne, and where special legislation has to be enacted to allow a woman to be regent.[77]

Most of the legislation relating to women is concerned with

[73] *Commentarii de regulis juris*, pp. 37–8.

[74] e.g. Johannes Jacobus Draco, *De foeminis ad officia publica non recipiendis*, Altdorf, 1620; Everardus Bronchorst, *In titulum Digestorum de diversis regulis juris antiqui enarrationes* (first published 1624), Leyden, 1648, pp. 6–7.

[75] Antwerp, 1529, C7r–v.

[76] Notably Gregorius Rolbag, *Certamen masculofoemineum super aequitate utilitate et necessitate differentiarum sexus in successionibus, quibus exstantibus masculis excluduntur foeminae in Italia, Gallia, Hispania et Germania*, Speyer, 1602; also discussion of the von Rechenberger v. Sprinzenstein case (for a bibliography of this see Lipenius, *Bibliotheca realis juridica*, p. 196).

[77] See J. Portemer, *La femme dans la législation royale des deux derniers siècles de l'Ancien Régime*, Paris, 1959, p. 9.

women as married persons,[78] for unmarried women are considered to be minors, at least until the age of twenty-five, when they may claim limited rights of inheritance, while remaining under the guardianship of their parents or nearest male relative. The law allows the husband to administer his wife's property, and this right may only be wrested from him if he shows himself to be notoriously extravagant; in such cases, a separation of goods may be obtained. Only in commerce are women allowed to keep for themselves the profits of their own dealings. Civil divorce is, of course, out of the question, and annulment favours the wife no more than it does the husband, except in cases of impotence and non-consummation, which are much discussed at the end of the century.[79] A *séparation de corps* is possible, however, if the husband is in prison, or if the wife commits adultery, or in cases of mal-treatment of the wife. This last condition is not as straightfor-ward as it may sound, for although it is the most common cause of separation in France at this time, marital cruelty entails more than wife-beating, which is sanctioned by law to a 'reasonable' degree.[80] Adultery is theoretically punishable by death in the case of the husband, and by claustration or forfeiture in the case of the wife, but in practice the wife's misdemeanours are punished more severely than those of the husband, for which he is rarely indicted. Of all conditions of women, only the widow enjoys any real privileges, for she has the wardship of her children and the dis-pensation of her husband's goods and property. In all other respects, women are legally bound to their husband's or guar-dian's dictates and cannot go to law without his permission except in cases of marital cruelty.[81]

The only important legal change in this period in France con-cerns the conditions for marriage. In the early part of the sixteenth century, if the marriage vows were pronounced, regardless

[78] For discussion of marriage law by jurists see André Tiraqueau, *De legibus connubialibus* (5th edn., Paris, 1554) and Joannes Nevizzianus, *Sylvae nuptialis libri sex*, Paris, 1521.

[79] See Antoine Hotman, *Traité de la dissolution du mariage par l'impuissance et froideur de l'homme ou de la femme*, Paris, 1581 (*Second traité*, Paris, 1610); Vincent Tagereau, *Discours de l'impuissance de l'homme ou de la femme*, Paris, 1611.

[80] See O. de la Brosse, *Saint François de Sales: les femmes mariées*, Paris, 1967, Introduction, p. 20.

[81] For a more detailed treatment of the legal status of women at this time see E.–V. Telle, *L'œuvre de Marguerite de Navarre et la querelle des femmes*, Toulouse, 1937, pp. 69–85.

of the presence of witnesses or of the consent of parents, then annulment became also impossible, especially if consummation ensued. Such a state of affairs could easily lead to bigamy and misalliance. Writers of this period are very doubtful whether children are the best judges of whom they should marry; Rabelais, Marguerite de Navarre, and Jean de Coras are all eloquent advocates of the *mariage de raison* and the consent of parents.[82] The twenty-fourth session of the Council of Trent in 1563 made the reading of banns, the presence of witnesses, and the consent of parents obligatory under canon law, and those conditions became necessary under civil law in France ten years later. The new legal position led, however, to the opposite abuse of parents marrying their children off for financial or social motives, without paying due consideration to the wishes of the parties involved in the marriage.[83]

One does not encounter the same wealth of commentary on the status of women in the sphere of moral philosophy as in theology, medicine, and law; since most discussions of virtue presuppose active virtue, and since women are characterized by passive virtue, they are tacitly excluded from a wide section of such writings.[84] The most quoted passages on this topic in ancient texts are taken from Plato's *Republic*, where one interlocutor seems to suggest that men and women are equally suited to all forms of political activity;[85] from Aristotle's *Politics* and the *Economics* (attributed to Aristotle by Renaissance commentators), where the virtues of men and women are said to be complementary and not identical;[86] and from Plutarch, whose moral treatise entitled *Mulierum virtutes*

---

[82] See Screech, *The Rabelaisian marriage*, pp. 69–85.

[83] See La Brosse, *Saint François de Sales*, Introduction, p. 17; J. Gaudemet, 'Législation canonique et attitudes séculières à l'égard du lien matrimonial au xviie siècle', *XVIIe siècle*, cii–ciii (1974), 15–30.

[84] The association of passive virtue with women is found in anatomical writing (Aristotle, *Physics*, i. 9; *De historia animalium*, iv. 11, ix. 1; Cardanus, *Contradicentia medica*, ii. 6, in *Opera omnia*, vi. 645–54); legal commentaries (Cagnolus, in *Commentarii de regulis juris*, p. 51 'viri [virtus] enim est agere, et mulieris pati'); theological tracts (see above, p. 14 n.), as well as in moral philosophy (Aristotle, *Economics*, i. 3; Seneca, *Epistulae morales*, xcv; Montaigne, *Essais*, ed. Thibaudet and Rat, iii. 5, p. 863).

[85] *Republic*, v and vii; also *Laws*, vii and *Meno*, 72A–73C. See also Diogenes Laertius, *Antisthenes*, in *Lives*, vi. 12. The *Republic* can also be adduced to support the opposite argument (see Francus, in *Commentarii de regulis juris*, p. 51).

[86] *Politics*, i. 1, 9; *Economics*, i. 3.

argues the case for equal virtue of the sexes.[87] There is little consistent reference to other ancient texts.

There are two related questions to be considered here: does an identical set of virtues and vices apply to men and women? do women and men have the same rôle to play in the running of the state? One coherent Renaissance text on these topics which attracts attention in Italy and France is Torquato Tasso's *Discorso della virtù feminile e donnesca*, which first appears in 1582.[88] Tasso revives the difference of opinion in ancient texts, and simplifies it into a debate between Plato and Aristotle. He makes an initial distinction between two sorts of virtue: intellectual virtue (relating to speculative reason) and affective virtue (from the concupiscible and irascible appetites), which is Thomist or Aristotelian in origin.[89] Women, he argues, do not need to practise intellectual virtue;[90] their rôle is entirely defined within the context of affective virtue. Tasso then introduces the idea that each sex has a dominant virtue, one which both sexes need to practise, but which is more important to one than to the other; the dominant virtue is chastity in the case of women, and courage in the case of men. The dominant vice for each sex becomes the antithesis of the dominant virtue (lack of chastity, cowardice), and the most excusable vice the antithesis of the dominant virtue of the other sex. Thus for men it is most unforgivable to be cowardly, and most forgivable to be unchaste; for women, the vice of *impudicitia* is most to be abhorred, and cowardice the least reprehensible vice. Chastity and courage are seen, therefore, in some sense as opposite virtues when placed on a sexual spectrum. Tasso goes further, and attributes some virtues to men and some to women, producing thereby a kind of sexual ethics; men may be virtuous in practising eloquence, liberality, courage, magnificence; women

---

[87] The opening paragraph is often quoted by feminist writers: see Tasso, *Discorso della virtù feminile e donnesca*, in *Le prose diverse*, ed. C. Guasti, Florence, 1875, ii. 204–5; Du Bosc, *La femme heroïque*, i. 37; Hilarion de Coste, *Les eloges et vies des reynes . . .*, Paris, 1630, ā1ʳ⁻ᵛ; Angenoust, *Paranymphe des dames*, p. 39.

[88] Translated into French in 1632 by Jean Baudoin; refuted by Lucrezia Marinella (*La nobiltà et l'eccellenza delle donne* (first published 1600), Venice, 1621, pp. 171–4) and Pierre Le Moyne (see below, pp. 83–4).

[89] See 1a 2ae 58 (distinction between moral and intellectual virtue); 1a 2ae 22–3 (distinction between irascible and concupiscible appetites); Aristotle, *Nicomachean Ethics*, i. 13; *De anima*, ii. 3. Tasso seems to have mixed the terminology of passions and virtues. See also A. H. T. Levi, *French moralists*, Oxford, 1964, pp. 19–20.

[90] *Della virtù feminile e donnesca*, ed. Guasti, ii. 209.

by being silent (one remembers 1 Tim. 2: 11–12), economical, chaste, modest. The implication is that it is inappropriate for a woman to be eloquent and liberal, or for a man to be economical and silent, although not, of course, unvirtuous. Public honour is also more suitable to a man than a woman.[91]

Tasso then encounters a problem in his discussion: what if moral duties clash with political duties? What if, as a royal person, one is encouraged to be eloquent, liberal, magnificent, and as a woman economical, silent, and modest? This problem leads to a discussion of the relationship between moral and political virtues; the practice of the former, argues Tasso, leads to personal happiness, and the practice of the latter, to the proper functioning of the state. The moral virtues assigned to woman are suitable to a member of the bourgeoisie or lesser nobility; they do not appear to be so to a princess, who is enjoined by her royal status to practise the heroic virtues. Tasso argues that the first duty of a princess is to her royal status; it is therefore forgivable, though regrettable, if she neglects her moral virtues such as chastity in the pursuit of her royal virtues, as was the case with historical figures such as Semiramis and Cleopatra. The princess is, as it were, a man by virtue of her birth, and hence the masculine standard of morality applies to her. It is clear that such an argument was bound to attract refutation.[92]

Tasso's problem concerns only women of high birth; for other classes, there is a natural continuity from moral to political virtue. Moralists divide such women into three groups—the unmarried, wives, and widows—and make separate moral provision for each group. Unmarried women are kept in tutelage and trained for marriage or the veil; wives are subordinate by theological and legal decree to their husbands. Their rôle is to preserve, where that of the husband is to acquire;[93] to remain at home, while the

---

[91] See Plutarch, *Mulierum virtutes*, which begins with the question whether women should enjoy public acclaim for virtuous acts. Plutarch's essay establishes the fame of a number of women of antiquity; early Renaissance feminist writing often takes the form of a compilation of biographies of women (e.g. Boccaccio, *De claris mulieribus*). See below, p. 26.

[92] See below, pp. 83–4.

[93] *Conservare* and *acquirere* are concepts taken from Aristotle, *Economics*, i. 3; see also *Politics*, i. 8 and *Nicomachean Ethics*, viii. 12. For Renaissance commentaries on these passages see John Case, *Thesaurus œconomiae, seu commentarius in Œconomica Aristotelis*, Oxford, 1597, pp. 145–204; Keckermann, *Synopsis disciplinae œconomicae*, Hanau, 1607, pp. 8–30, 105–6; Hennigus Arnisaeus, *Doctrina politica in genuinam*

husband has a wider ambit; to avoid the public eye while the
husband seeks to attract it; to keep the family unit together by
practising the moral virtues of obedience, chastity, fidelity,
loyalty, and forbearance. The biblical portrait of the good woman
(Prov. 31 : 10–29) includes among her virtues a fine business
sense and an aptitude for home management. There is little in this
description of the duties of husband and wife in marriage to cause
a clash between pagan and Christian writers; St. Paul's teachings
coincide happily with those of Plutarch and Aristotle.[94] Only
widows of this class of women acquire any independence; the
virtues most highly recommended for them are continence and
piety.[95]

Tasso states that intellectual virtue is not within woman's
compass. It would seem that he means speculative mental activity,
for it is generally accepted that moral reading can do women no
harm; Vives allows them some of the Church Fathers, the lives
of the saints, and some ancient moralists, and Erasmus even
advocates the Bible.[96] This exclusion from a wide area of learning
is bitterly contested by women who are made to while away the
time with traditional female activities such as spinning, sewing,
embroidery, and home management. It is a common feature of
feminist writing to demand the right of education. Whereas,
however, most feminist writers are willing to concede that learning is appropriate to and useful for woman's private morality,
even the most enlightened deny that the fruits of such learning
should be carried over into her marriage or social existence.[97]

A last aspect of political morality concerns woman's involvement in public life. The commonplace taken from the *De regulis
juris antiqui* which deals with women's exclusion from civil offices
has already been discussed: two other ancient commonplaces

methodum quae est Aristotelis, reducta, Frankfurt, 1606, pp. 47–101; Johannes Magirus,
Corona virtutum moralium (commentarii in libros Ethicorum Aristotelis ad Nicomachum),
Frankfurt, 1601, p. 795.

[94] See 1 Cor. 7; Eph. 5: 22–33; 1 Tim. 2: 9–15; Plutarch, *Conjugalia praecepta*;
Aristotle, *Economics,* i. 1–3.

[95] The most influential Renaissance work on the behaviour of women of this
class is that of Juan Luis Vives, *De institutione foeminae Christianae* (first published
1523). See also Ruth Kelso, *Doctrine for the lady of the Renaissance,* Illinois, 1956.

[96] Vives, *De institutione foeminae Christianae,* Antwerp, 1524, i. 3, C3ʳ–C4ᵛ. The
chapter begins by listing the books girls should not read, prominent among which
are novels; Erasmus, *Paraclesis,* in *Opera omnia,* v. 140.

[97] See below, pp. 53–7.

might be mentioned here which describe the practical effects of woman's involvement in politics. In the first, Aristotle criticizes the Spartans for allowing women any part in public life because of their lascivious natures.[98] Most Renaissance commentators agree that Mars and Venus do not mix, although their famous encounter, as well as that of Hercules and Omphale, provides material for emblematists who argue that they do.[99] A second commonplace is taken from Plutarch's *Life of Cato* (viii), in which Cato comments on the insidious power exerted by women over their husbands; this power is ascribed by some moralists to the awareness of their weakness and their desire to compensate for it.[100] This imperiousness, as well as their lustful nature, throws into doubt women's ability to sustain the rigours of public office. While it is not uncommon to find references in feminist works to Plato's supposed view that women are suitable for all offices of the state, it is very rare to find a work which wholeheartedly supports their involvement in public life.[101]

Nowhere is a discrepancy between theory and practice more apparent than in the case of politics in this period: for all the opinions recorded above, women's involvement in the public life of the Renaissance as members of guilds, prominent figures in religious administration, patrons of learning and polite society, queen regents, and even sovereigns is well known to both contemporaries and posterity. Such a discrepancy leads contemporaries to ask whether these famous women are exceptional in their own sex, or whether they are an indication that all their sex possesses such virtue which is repressed by law and custom.[102] A discrepancy of similar scale is to be detected in the notion of woman itself, derivative, in part at least, from humanism; the

---

[98] *Politics*, ii. 7; see also Justus Lipsius, *Politica*, ii. 3, in *Opera omnia*, Lyons, 1613, ii. 52.

[99] See below, pp. 215-18.

[100] See below, pp. 75 n.; Ferrarius, in *Commentarii de regulis juris*, p. 47.

[101] For discussion of rule by women in tracts of political theory see Jean Bodin, *Les six livres de la republique*, Paris, 1580, vi. 5, pp. 1001-13; John Case, *Sphæra civitatis*, Oxford, 1588, i. 3, pp. 32-4, 40-1; Pierre Grégoire, *De republica*, vii. 11, pp. 443-79; Keckermann, *Systema disciplinae politicae*, Hanover, 1607, i. 2, pp. 40-3; Joannes Stephanus Menochius, *Institutiones politicae e sacris scripturis depromptae*, Lyons, 1625, i. 5, pp. 63-73. All these writers except Case conclude against female rule, except in emergency. See also below, pp. 58-62.

[102] See below, pp. 79 ff.

enhancement of the dignity of mankind, which is at the centre of humanism, does not seem to affect in any way the low status of women. Both discrepancies indicate the deep-rooted nature of the ancient and Judaeo-Christian commonplaces examined in this chapter. These commonplaces emerge from a study of scholarly texts, often written by enlightened men, who are prepared to question the validity of ancient opinions. In spite of their doubts and questionings, the commonplaces filter through their works, and reappear in more popular literature. Purely literary evidence for a popular conception of woman is in itself unsatisfactory; but the presence of a recurring set of commonplaces in scholarly works of various disciplines, and in feminist and anti-feminist writings, may be taken as an indication of the generally held notion which we are trying to describe. It would seem unlikely that writers on women could have been unaware of the majority of these commonplaces; and their audience too must have been familiar with them.[103]

The interrelationship of these commonplaces has emerged to some degree from this study of them. Theologians refer to anatomy, anatomists to theology, jurists to theology and anatomy, moralists to all three. The interrelationship of specific commonplaces about woman is established in interdisciplinary studies such as Franciscus Vallesius's *De iis quae scripta sunt physicè in libris sacris* of 1588, in which Aristotle's 'imperfect male' theory is reinforced and justified by an exegesis of Genesis,[104] by Simon Majolus's *Colloquia physica* of 1615, where a theologian, a doctor, a philosopher, and a soldier all discuss the nature of women,[105] and Sebastian Meyer's *Augustae laudes Divinae Majestatis e Galeni de usu partium libris xvii selectae*, printed in 1627.[106] Parallels between Judaeo-Christian and Classical commonplaces are indeed striking: the manner of Eve's creation suggests the commonplace *imperfectior viro*;[107] the first sin recalls the jurist's belief in woman's *imbecillitas animi*; the curse of subordination to husband equates with woman's *deterior conditio* in law; the pains of childbirth suggest Seneca's *pati natae*; the Alphabet of the Good

---

[103] An example of the use and currency of these commonplaces is to be found in book iii of Castiglione's *Il Cortegiano*.

[104] *De iis quae scripta sunt physicè in sacris libris*, Lyons, 1588, pp. 50–8.

[105] *Colloquia physica*, pp. 47–59.

[106] See above, p. 9 n.

[107] See above, p. 4 n.

Woman in Proverbs is consistent with Aristotle's division between conservative and acquisitive rôles for woman and man.
Supported by such a powerful concordance of authorities, it is
not surprising that the notion of woman in the Renaissance was
so impervious to change.

II

The Traditional *Querelle des Femmes* in the Seventeenth Century

FEMINIST and anti-feminist writing belongs to a tradition which, in one sense, is timeless, for the relative merits of men and women and the different psychologies of the sexes are naturally among the most prominent literary preoccupations of any age. This is reflected in imaginative literature in France throughout the later Middle Ages and the Renaissance; at these times the idealistic cult of woman founded in courtly love or in neo-Platonism has as its counterpart a satirical and realistic investigation of the vices and failings of the female sex, often in the context of marriage. A tradition which is more specifically feminist also has its roots in the Middle Ages, although it flourishes most vigorously between the fifteenth and seventeenth centuries. In this, the prominent topics are the right of woman to man's homage, respect, and gratitude for her services to him, the demand that fidelity in marriage should be considered as important for husband as for wife, and the plea that woman should be allowed to educate herself and perhaps thereby play a more active rôle in society. These two traditions intermingle, and constitute together the *Querelle des femmes*, which is characterized by indiscriminate plagiarism and the repetition of stock arguments by both feminist and anti-feminist writers.

Although the positions taken up by writers in the debate reflect to some extent their sympathies for one side or the other (this is certainly the case with Christine de Pisan, the author of a *Livre de la cité des dames* at the turn of the fifteenth century, as well as with most women who write subsequently in favour of their sex), this genre is written to amuse its readers rather than persuade them. This is most obvious in the case of anti-feminist works, but it can be true also of those written in defence of women, even by such renowned feminists as Cornelius Agrippa, whose *Declamatio de nobilitate et praecellentia foeminei sexus* (1529) is a seminal work, containing many of the arguments encountered in later French feminist treatises.[1] These arguments include the series of theological proofs of female excellence *e nomine* (Eve means life, whereas Adam means earth in Hebrew), *ex ordine* (Eve was the last created thing, and therefore the most perfect being in creation), *e materia* (Eve was made of living flesh, whereas Adam was made of earth), *e loco* (Eve was created in paradise, Adam outside), and *e conceptione* (woman bore God, which man could not do).[2]

It is difficult to isolate formal characteristics of the genre, as from its inception works appear in verse and in prose, in dialogue form and as discursive arguments. Some elements are, however, worthy of mention. Compilations of biographies of famous women are frequently encountered, often derived from Boccaccio's *De claris mulieribus*;[3] these are intended in some cases to illustrate the female capacity for all manner of virtue, but may also be moralistic works, in which the outstanding qualities of women of the past highlight the frailty and deficiencies of those of the present. In the sixteenth century, the dialogue form emerges as a popular medium for writers in the debate. Although it would be possible thereby to present a balanced case, this is rarely done, and it is more common to find that the dialogue is slanted in one or the other direction. Jacques Tahureau, Madeleine and Catherine des Roches, and Cholières are among those who use this form to discuss feminist topics. Finally, it is a feature of the debate that adversaries of a tract or poem will borrow or parody the form chosen by their opponent; this occurs in the *Querelle des amyes* of the 1540s[4] and in the less well-known *Querelle du mariage* of the end of the century.[5] It remains true to say, however, in spite of these formal links, that the genre in general is characterized much

[1] See Telle, *Marguerite de Navarre*, pp. 43–68; M. A. Screech, 'Rabelais, de Billon and Erasmus', *BHR* xiii (1951), 241–65.

[2] For medieval antecedents of these arguments see P. Meyer, 'Mélanges de poésie française', *Romania*, vi (1877), 501.

[3] e.g. Ravisius Textor (ed.), *De memorabilibus et claris mulieribus* (1521); Alexandre Vandenbusche, *Recueil des dames illustres en vertu* (1574–5); le sieur du Souhait, *Pourtraicts des chastes dames* (1600).

[4] See M. A. Screech, 'La querelle des amyes', *BHR* xxi (1959), 103–30.

[5] See *Le mariage honni par Desportes, louangé par Blanchon, Le Gaynard, Rouspeau*, ed. H. Vaganay, Mâcon, 1908; Mme Liébaut, *Les misères de la femme mariée* (n.d., *c.* 1597); Courval-Sonnet, *Satyre menippee sur les poingnantes traverses et incommoditez du mariage* (1609).

more by the evidence it adduces than by the way in which this is set out.

Between the Middle Ages and the sixteenth century a change in attitudes towards women seems to have taken place;[6] writings in their favour come to the fore under the influence of neo-Platonism and the revival of courtly love traditions, and the anti-feminist stance becomes less fashionable. Influential female patrons of the arts and the rise of salons and court life also help bring about this change. None the less, a taste for both feminist and anti-feminist writing continues throughout the century, as is attested not only by new works, but also by the republication of medieval texts.

It has long been established that there were literary debates about women in the first half of the seventeenth century in France. Ascoli lists twenty-one feminist and anti-feminist works between 1595 and 1655,[7] and Reynier mentions many other texts which are more peripheral.[8] Both of these scholars confine their researches for the most part to France, although it is clear from contemporary bibliographies that Italian, German, Spanish, and neo-Latin works were known to French writers.

Two such bibliographies, both in manuscript, are particularly rich in references. Among the Dubuisson-Aubenay manuscripts in the Bibliothèque Mazarine there is a volume entitled *Mulieres virtutibus et scientia praeditae cum praefixis authoribus qui earum laudes scripserunt*. This also contains a *Traité de la perfection des femmes comparée à celle des hommes*, dated variously 1617 and 1618, probably written by Dubuisson-Aubenay himself.[9] Appended to the *Traité* are notes intended either for inclusion or as corrections, collected together during two significant periods, 1617–18 and 1645–51. These notes, which are in the main extracted from

---

[6] For fuller accounts of medieval and sixteenth-century feminism see A. Campaux, *La question des femmes au XVe siècle*, Paris, 1865; A. Lefranc, *Œuvres de François Rabelais, le tiers livre*, Paris, 1931, Introduction, pp. xxx–lxix; Telle, *Marguerite de Navarre*, pp. 43–68; Kelso, *Doctrine for the lady of the Renaissance*. There is also the less trustworthy study by L. M. Richardson, *The forerunners of feminism in the French literature of the Renaissance*, Baltimore, London, and Paris, 1929.

[7] 'Essai sur l'histoire des idées féministes en France du xvie siècle à la révolution', *RSH* xiii (1906), 99–100.

[8] *La femme au XVIIe siècle*, Paris, 1929, *passim*.

[9] For fuller details and attribution see bibliography. The *Traité* was written in reply to Ferville's *Cacogynie, ou méchanceté des femmes*, Caen, 1617.

printed sources (hence the bibliographical interest of the manuscript), are brought together haphazardly under such headings as
'qui laudes mulierum scripserunt', 'mulieres uarijs ornatae virtutibus', 'prudentes', 'politicae et bellatrices', 'hospitales', 'miseri-
cordes', 'liberales et beneficae', 'religiosae', 'pudicae', 'in coniugio
fideles'. The *Traité* is similarly ordered, containing an exhaustive
list of moral virtues with copious examples of women endowed
with them. Many of the works to which the author refers (classical authors, Church Fathers, contemporary or near-contemporary
historians, and feminist writers such as Boccaccio and Agrippa)
were not written specifically in honour of women; nor should
those written by women, of which he includes a great number, be
considered necessarily as feminist writings. None the less, even
after a careful elimination of much of his material, there remains
a formidable body of contemporary or near-contemporary writing
which is directly relevant to this investigation.

A second manuscript bibliography of similar scope may be
found in Louis Jacob's *Bibliothèque des femmes illustres par leurs
écrits*, which was finished in 1646.[10] It is by virtue of this work
that Louis Jacob earned a place among the feminist writers listed
by Antoine-Léonard Thomas in 1772.[11] It was also known to
contemporaries.[12]

While it seems that Dubuisson-Aubenay uses all manner of
sources with equal readiness, other authors make sharp distinctions between the different categories of feminist writing; Du
Bosc, in *La femme heroïque* of 1645, criticizes harshly works on
this subject which he considers to be frivolous or irresponsible:

C'est vne merueille de remarquer les extrauagances, où se sont em-
portez ceux qui ont voulu preferer excessiuement vn sexe à l'autre.

[10] For fuller details see bibliography.
[11] See *Essai sur le caractère, les mœurs et l'esprit des femmes dans les différens siècles*,
Paris, 1772, p. 93.
[12] e.g. Hilarion de Coste, *Eloges et vies des reynes* . . . , ii. 170. Some printed works
also contain suggestions for further reading, e.g. Laurens Le Peletier, *De la chasteté,
et combien l'incontinence est dommageable*, Angers, 1635, p. 351; 'qui voudra voir d'auantage [des Tiltres, Excellences, et Dignitez du deuot Sexe Feminin], qu'il lise le
Traicté de Plutarque qu'il a fait de leurs loüanges [i.e. the *Mulierum virtutes*], S.
Hierosme sur l'explication du Psalme 18, *Coeli enarrant gloriam Dei* &c, S. Iean
Chrisostome sur l'Homelie de la decolation de S. Iean Baptiste [respectively *PL*
xxvi. 924–7 and *PG* lix. 485–90], Bocace [*De claris mulieribus*], le liure des Loix
Connubiales de Monsieur de Tiraqueau, Conseiller en la Cour de Parlement, et
plusieurs autres Autheurs et Historiens . . .'

Que de paradoxes ridicules sur cette matiere! que de fatras de Volumes! que de faux raisonnemens! iamais on ne vit tant de problémes, et de controuerses que sur ce sujet: et il semble que ce soit la matiere du monde, dont la plus part ayent traitté auec moins de iugement. Il y en a peu qui ayent touché auec sobrieté les auantages particuliers de l'vn et de l'autre sexe: fort peu de personnes ont loüé ou blasmé les femmes auec temperament: il y en a qui ont tellement éleué l'homme, et qui luy ont attribué tant de priuileges, qu'il semble que les femmes ne soient pas capables d'aucune belle action, et qu'elles soient d'vne espece inferieure à la sienne. Ils ont fait de gros Volumes remplis d'iniures et d'inuectiues contre les Dames; et ont traitté vn sexe innocent auec tant d'indignité et de mespris, que je ne puis comprendre comment on a permis l'impression d'ouurages semblables: il y en a d'autres aussi qui ont trop affecté le parti contraire, et qui ont traitté les Dames de diuinitez et de Deesses; comme si les hommes n'estoient nez que leurs valets; comme si la femme estoit toute la fleur de l'espece, et que l'homme n'en fut que l'excrement et la crasse; c'est ainsi qu'ils ont discouru sur ce sujet, sans iugement et sans equité; aigrissant les deux sexes l'vn contre l'autre, et prenant plaisir d'entretenir vn diuorce si dangereux, et si plain d'inhumanité.[13]

Although it is clear from this that in seventeenth-century eyes there are various categories of feminist writing, it should be stressed, however, that certain features of argumentation and a large body of evidence are common to most feminist and anti-feminist works.

It is possible that Du Bosc had in mind the one noteworthy debate about women in the traditional manner at this time; this is provoked by Trousset's *Alphabet de l'imperfection et malice des femmes*. Sporadic outbursts of polemic also occur, and these are often accompanied by reprints of sixteenth-century or even earlier *facetiae* and popular works,[14] in many cases printed on the Pont

---

[13] *La femme heroïque*, i. 39–41.

[14] e.g. *Recueil des exemples de la malice des femmes, et des malheurs venus à leur occasion* (1596), which is answered by a *Deffence en faveur des dames de Lyon, avec un discours de l'excellence et beauté de la femme* (1596); Alexandre Vandenbusche, *Sommaire des dames illustres et vertueuses* (1603, first printed 1574–5); *La rejouissance des femmes sur la deffence des tavernes et cabarets* (1613); Cholières, *La guerre des masles contre les femelles* (1614, first printed 1588); *Advis salutaire et tres-necessaire aux gens de bien, qui se laissent battre par leurs femmes* (1615, first printed 1610); *Le purgatoire des hommes mariez, avec les peines et les tourmentz qu'ils endurent incessamment au subject de la malice et mechanceté des femmes* (1619, probably written in reply to the republication of Mme Liébaut's *Misères de la femme mariée* in the same year); *Les quinze joyes de mariage* (reprinted 1606 and 1620); *Les singeries des femmes de ce temps découvertes* (1623); *Le fantastique repentir des mal mariez* (1623); *La constance des femmes nouvellement descouverte* (1627);

Neuf, where the presses were very active, thanks to a relaxation of restrictive legislation against them at this time.[15] In the provinces also such republication is not uncommon.[16] Together with such works, there appear more compendious writings, such as the *Discours en la faveur des dames contre les mesdisans* (1600), Jacqueline de Miremont's *Apologie pour les dames* (1602), which is in verse, and Marguerite de Valois's letter in answer to François Loryot's essay 'Pourquoy le sexe feminin est fort honoré de l'homme' in his *Secrets moraux* of 1614.[17]

These works form a prelude to Alexis Trousset's *Alphabet de l'imperfection et malice des femmes*, which was first published in 1617. In that year also appeared Jean Besly's *Plaidoyer . . . sur les mondanités des femmes et pucelles* and Ferville's *Cacogynie, ou méchanceté des femmes*, which Trousset owns to be his inspiration, and from which he quotes.[18] It is not clear why 1616–17 should be a time of such anti-feminist activity not only in France but elsewhere: Lotz mentions a 'dialogus vernaculus . . . interlocutoribus Fr. Andrea, mulierum osore, Ord. Bened. et Patr. Eugenio, Soc. Jesu. defensore; in quo multa in insontem sexum è sacris literis detorquentur';[19] Giambattista Barbo wrote a work entitled *L'oracolo overo invettiva contra le donne* and in England John Swetnam published an *Arraignment of lewd idle froward and inconstant women*, which provoked a minor literary debate of its

and the copyists and plagiarists of Desportes's 'Stances du mariage': Courval-Sonnet, *Satyre menippee sur les poingnantes traverses et incommoditez du mariage* (1608), which is attacked in the *Contre-satyre pour la deffence des dames* (1609), answered in turn by Courval-Sonnet; and the author of the *Brief discours pour la reformation des mariages*.

[15] See Mongrédien, *La vie littéraire au XVIIe siècle*, Paris, 1947, pp. 35–59.
[16] Loys Costé printed at Rouen in 1602 the following collection of sixteenth-century *facetiae*: *Les tenebres de mariage*; *Discours joyeux de la patience des femmes obstinees contre leurs maris*; *Le plaisant quaquet et resjuyssance des femmes pource que leurs maris n'yvrongnent plus en la taverne*; Pierre Rigaud reprinted Jean de Marconville's *De l'heur et malheur de mariage* and *De la bonté et mauvaistié des femmes* (both of which first appeared in 1564) at Lyons in 1602; Abraham Cousturier published Guillaume Coquillart's *Les presomptions des femmes* at Rouen c. 1600.
[17] *Les secrets moraux*, Paris, 1614, pp. 63–90. Marguerite's letter was printed in Loryot's *Fleurs des secrets moraux* of the same year, in an unpaginated gathering with duplicated signatures at the beginning of the volume, indicating that it had been included between printing and binding.
[18] *Alphabet*, pp. 209–10.
[19] *Gynaicologia*, p. 31. The German title is *Grund- und probierliche Beschreibung / Argument und Schlußarticul . . . belangend die Frag / Ob die Weiber Menschen sein / oder nicht?* Reprinted 1643.

own.[20] It has been suggested that Marguerite de Valois might be the target of the *Alphabet*,[21] which is dedicated 'à la plus mauuaise du monde', but as she died in 1615 it would seem somewhat unlikely, whereas Leonora Galigai, who was burned as a witch in July 1617, and who appears to have aroused considerable passion, to judge from the copious literature of invective published in pamphlet form,[22] is a more immediate source of anti-feminist feeling.

Ferville's *Cacogynie* enjoyed some success, being reprinted at least four times in full between 1617 and 1650,[23] but this is eclipsed by that of the *Alphabet*, republished at least eighteen times between these dates.[24] All editions except the first bear the name Jacques Olivier 'licencier aux Loix, et en Droict Canon' on the title-page; this is almost certainly a pseudonym for Alexis Trousset, a Franciscan who published other works at this time.[25] His *Alphabet* of female vices is not original; it is an amplification of that written by St. Antoninus Forciglioni,[26] Archbishop of

---

[20] First printed 1615; it was answered by Esther Sowernam, *Ester hath hang'd Haman; or an answere to a lewd pamphlet, entitled the arraignment of women* (1617); *A mouzell for Melastomus. Or an answere to that pamphlet made by Jo. Sw* . . . (1617); Rachel Speght, *Vindication of women . . . against J. Swetnam* (1619).

[21] By Paul Lacroix, in the *Catalogue Pixérécourt*, Paris, 1838.

[22] See the pamphlets in the Bibliothèque Nationale with the pressmarks Lb36 1074–91, and A. Ungherini, *Manuel de bibliographie biographique et d'iconographie des femmes célèbres*, Turin and Paris, 1892–1905, s.v. Galigai.

[23] Viz. Caen, 1617, Paris, 1618, 1619, and Lyons, 1650.

[24] Viz. Paris, 1619, 1623, 1626, 1630, 1631, 1634, 1636, 1638, 1643; Rouen, 1630, 1631, 1634, 1638, 1640, 1646; Lyons, 1628, 1646, 1648.

[25] See Alexandre Cioranescu, *Bibliographie de la littérature française du XVIIᵉ siècle*, Paris, 1966–7, s.v. Trousset. The attribution is founded on the decipherment of a *sonnet acrostiche* (*Alphabet*, p. 351), which L'Escale indicates in his *Alphabet de l'eccellence et perfection des femmes*, Paris, 1631, p. 31. At least two other sources describe the author of the *Alphabet* as a 'cordelier' (Dubuisson-Aubenay and the anonymous *L'excellence des femmes avec leur response à l'autheur de l'Alphabet*, Paris, 1618). There are several comments in the *Alphabet* and the *Response aux impertinences de l'aposté capitaine Vigoureux* which suggest that the writer is not a cleric (e.g. 'Ie suis marié, i'ay femme et enfans', *Response aux impertinences*, Paris, 1617, p. 78), but in spite of these, the attribution seems very probable.

[26] See Antoninus, *Tertia pars totius summe*, Venice, 1503, i. 25, ff. 48–9; there is another edition in 1542 at Lyons, followed by a translation into Spanish four years later (*Tractado en que se da a conoscer las condiciones, y propiedades de las mugeres, va por su Abecedario agora nuevamente traducido de latin en romance por un doctissimo varon*). See also J. Mauritius, *Zeege-pralende loftooneel der vrouwelyke sexe, tegen dat vuyl en leelyk A.B.C. vol hatelyke namen der vrouwen, uytgebraakt van de papen, en voornamelyk van . . . Antoninus*, Amsterdam, 1704. See also E. Hobert, *Die französische Frauensatire unter Berücksichtigung der antiken Tradition*, Marburg, 1967, pp. 29–33.

Florence at the end of the fourteenth century, which was in turn
inspired by the Alphabet of the Good Woman in the Old Testament.[27] Stripped of its excessive bias against women, Trousset's
work is little more than a moralistic text condemning a list of
vices arranged in alphabetical order;[28] there is therefore some
truth in the author's assertion:

> Mon dessein n'a esté, que pour blasmer en l'vn et l'autre sexe, et
> particulierement au feminin, les diffamations qui les rendent con-
> temptibles et mesprisables aux yeux de Dieu.[29]

At one point he even promises to compose a work in honour of
'les vertus heroïques et les perfections singulieres des femmes
sages et discrettes'.[30] His adversaries, however, take no account of
these qualifications in their attacks on his work, and nearly all
the apologies in favour of women published in answer to the
Alphabet are in the form of lists of moral virtues opposed to the
vices of Trousset's work.

Trousset's *Alphabet* has a *Privilège du roi* dated 30 August 1617;
the first refutation, entitled *La defense des femmes, contre l'alphabet
de leur pretendue malice et imperfection*, has a *Privilège* dated 3 October.
Its author describes himself as 'le sieur Vigoureux, capitaine du
chasteau de Brye-Comte-Robert'; both Trousset and La Bruyère
refer to him as 'Barbier, aduocat en conseil'.[31] His tract, which
rests on the tenet 'les femmes sont telles que les hommes les
rendent', provokes two replies, one from Trousset (*Response aux
impertinences de l'aposté capitaine Vigoureux, sur la defense des femmes*)
and le sieur de La Bruyère's *Replique à l'antimalice ou defense des
femmes du sieur Vigoureux*, both from the same printer (Jean

---

[27] Prov. 31: 10–29; the Venerable Bede wrote a commentary on this Hebrew
alphabet, entitled *Libellus de muliere forti*, printed in 1612, and known to Dubuisson-
Aubenay (PL xci. 1039–52).

[28] Viz. avidissimum animal; bestiale barathrum; concupiscentia carnis; duellum
damnosum; estuans aestas; falsa fides; garrulum guttur; herinnis armata; invidio-
sum ignis; kaos calumniarum; lepida lues; mendacium monstrosum; naufragium
vitae; odii opifex; peccati auctrix; quietis quassatio; regnorum ruina; sylva super-
biae; truculenta tyrannis; vanitas vanitatum; xanxia Xerxis; yurongnesse eshontée;
zelus zelotypus. Some letters in Antoninus's alphabet are different, viz. avidum
animal; dolorosum duellum; naufragii nutrix; prima peccatrix; ymago idolorum.

[29] *Alphabet*, p. 338.

[30] *Alphabet*, p. 22. He may even have done this, if he is the author of the *Traicté
de l'excellence du sexe fœminin, et des prerogatives de la mere de Dieu* (1635), which was
published by a person describing himself as 'Guerry' (? cured of misogyny).

[31] *Alphabet*, p. 366; *Replique à l'antimalice*, Paris, 1617, p. 101.

Petit-Pas),[32] and both bearing the same date of *Privilège*, 27 October 1617.

These works are followed by a cascade of denunciation: in 1618 there appeared *L'excellence des femmes, avec leur response à l'autheur de l'alphabet*, in which was reprinted the letter sent by Marguerite de Valois to Loryot; le chevalier de L'Escale's *Champion des femmes, qui soustient qu'elles sont plus nobles, plus parfaites et en tout plus vertueuses que les hommes*, which contains a counter-alphabet of female perfections; Bernier's *Apologie contre le livre intitulé Alphabeth de la meschanceté des femmes*; and two reprintings of Ferville's *Cacogynie*. The following year saw the republication of four earlier works, Etienne Pasquier's *Monophile* (which first appeared in 1554), Mme Liébaut's *Misères de la femme mariée* of more recent date, Marie de Romieu's *Discours admirable de l'excellence des femmes*, and possibly Martin Le Franc's *Champion des dames*, originally written in the fifteenth century.[33] Also in 1619 Trousset added a 'friant dessert . . . de plusieurs histoires pour les courtisans et partisans de la femme mondaine', based on traditional material, as was the *Alphabet*.[34]

Nor did the pace slacken; in the following three years appeared Louis Le Bermen's *Bouclier des dames* (1621), Gaillar's *Bouclier des femmes* (1620), Marie de Gournay's *Egalité des hommes et des femmes* (1622), and finally an Italian work, Cristoforo Bronzini's *Advocat des femmes ou de leur fidelité et constance . . . traduit d'italien en françois par S.D.L.* (probably L'Escale),[35] which appeared in 1622. Yet when Honorat de Ménier published in 1623 *La*

[32] This printer also produced the first edition of Trousset's *Alphabet*. To some degree, it would seem that the debate is stimulated by printers; Petit-Pas republished Pasquier's *Monophile*, a very pertinent work to the debate, in 1619, and on the feminist side, Thomas Arnaud d'Armosin printed several works by sixteenth-century authors (Marie de Romieu's *Brief discours que l'excellence de la femme surpasse celle de l'homme*, which first appeared in 1581, republished with a new title in 1619; Mme Liébaut's *Misères de la femme mariée*, first published *c*. 1597, reappears also with a new title in 1619) as well as original works (Dydimus des Armosins, *Les trophees celestes, ou se peuvent voir les genereux et immortels faicts des femmes illustres*, 1620).

[33] Dubuisson-Aubenay writes of an edition of this work at this date.

[34] It is an amplification of the adage 'mulier est deus in ecclesia, angelus in via, daemon in domo, bubo in fenestra, pica in porta, capra in horto, faetor in lecto' attributed by Giuseppe Passi to Alexander Aphrodiseus (*I donneschi diffetti*, p. 5); see also Gabriel Meurier, *Thresor de sentences dorees, proverbes et dicts communs*, Rouen, 1579, p. 87.

[35] Dubuisson-Aubenay talks of 'le chevalier de L'Escale abbreviateur de Christophe Bronzini'.

perfection des femmes. Avec l'imperfection des hommes qui les méprisent,
he writes:

> L'on a bien iuste subiect de s'estonner, voyant que ceux qui ont faict
> veu de chasteté et de continence (comme l'autheur du liure qui court
> de la malice des femmes) se meslent de detracter de tout le sexe feminin,
> et font des liures plains de calomnie contre l'honneur des femmes, sans
> qu'il se trouue personne qui les en reprenne ouuertement . . .[36]

A similar indication of the enduring popularity of Trousset's
Alphabet may be found in the new version of L'Escale's *Champion
des femmes*, printed in 1631, in which the author laments that 'on
imprime son meschant liure tous les iours de nouueau'.[37]

On the anti-feminist side in the early 1620s there appeared two
works, one a parody of Marie de Gournay's *Egalité des hommes et
des femmes*, entitled *La response des dames et bourgeoises de Paris au
caquet de l'accouchée* (1622), the other by Rolet, with the title
Tableau historique des ruses et subtilitez des femmes (1623). Apart from
reprints, the last work written in answer to Trousset's *Alphabet*
to appear is Angenoust's *Paranymphe des dames*, published in
1629. During the following decade, several moralistic works
condemning the behaviour of leisured women appeared, and a
new approach to feminist questions may be traced in the writings
of Faret, Du Bosc, and Grenaille; but these are more relevant to
the reassessment of the social rôle of women than to the traditional genre.

Several neo-Latin works of the 1630s and 1640s, published in
Holland and probably known in France,[38] fall within the scope of
this inquiry. In 1638 the *Disputatio perjucunda qua anonymus probare
nititur mulieres homines non esse* was reprinted, and in 1644 two more
anonymous works appeared, *Hippolytus redivivus id est remedium
[amoris sive ars] contemnendi sexum muliebrem*[39] and *Cupido triom-
phans, vel ratio cur sexus muliebris omni amore et honore sit dignissimus.*[40]
While most writing in French at this time does not fall into the
category under consideration here, there are a few texts which
should be mentioned; in the *Nouveau recueil des pieces les plus*

[36] *La perfection des femmes*, Paris, 1625 (1st edn. 1623), ã3ʳ.

[37] *Alphabet de l'eccellence et perfection des femmes*, pp. 10–11.

[38] See Samuel de Sorbière, *Lettres et discours sur diverses matières curieuses*, Paris,
1660, lxiii, p. 437.

[39] 'Autore S.I.E.D.V.M.W.A.S.'. The missing words, essential for the sense,
are supplied from G. F. de Bure's transcription in his *Bibliographie instructive* of
1765.   [40] 'Autore H.H.V.O.G.'.

agreables de ce temps, there is a *Discours de l'ennemi d'amour et des femmes,* which is followed by a *Response à l'ennemi d'amour et des femmes,* both probably printed for the first time in this volume which appeared in 1644. The debate on the subject 'Quel est le plus noble de l'homme ou de la femme?' in the *Conferences du Bureau d'Adresse* of 1634[41] also belongs to the traditional genre. From the sporadic appearance of works in the genre after 1630, it may be safely concluded that the traditional *Querelle des femmes* is a feature only of the first three decades of the seventeenth century, and that had it not been for Trousset's *Alphabet,* it would scarcely have figured in the seventeenth century at all.

It cannot be said that these texts merit serious consideration for their literary qualities. A certain number of their authors are lawyers or clerics, and it is possible to detect echoes of forensic rhetoric and sacred eloquence; yet it is often difficult to decide whether striking qualities of style are due to ineptitude or design.[42] If *elocutio* is unremarkable, *dispositio* is scarcely more noteworthy; most writers are content to follow the construction of previous texts, or, in composing refutations, to use the same form as their adversary. *Inventio* is also conventional; little new evidence or argumentation is introduced into the genre. Yet it is this last element which merits most attention here, for it is the most characteristic facet of the genre, and is even reflected in the writings of Du Bosc and Le Moyne, who profess to reject traditional approaches to the praise of women.

Most writers set out to prove the superiority of one sex or the other (Marie de Gournay, who points this out, claims originality in that she asserts the sexes to be equal), and base their case on a combination of authority, example, and ratiocination. The relative merits of these three methods of argumentation are debated in the more serious writings: Marie de Gournay prefers the 'auctorité de Dieu mesme, des arcsboutans de son Eglise et de ces grands hommes qui ont servy de lumiere à l'Univers' to examples (which are 'trop communs') and 'raisons' ('puisque les opiniastres les pourroient debattre').[43] Ménier claims, however, that

---

[41] Printed in the *Premiere centurie des questions traitees ez conferences du Bureau d'Adresse,* Paris, 1634, pp. 204–8.

[42] This does not apply to later feminist writing; see below, pp. 239 ff.

[43] *Egalité des hommes et des femmes,* ed. Schiff, p. 63.

'L'Escriture saincte ne se doit alleguer, que pour preuue de choses sainctes',[44] and prefers examples. If the competence of the authority in question is challenged, then the weakness of this form of argumentation becomes apparent: where Trousset relies on Tertullian, Le Moyne denounces the misogyny of this doctor of the Church;[45] Du Bosc describes the author of Ecclesiastes as a 'Philosophe réueur',[46] where Trousset emblazons his title-page with a quotation from this book;[47] Dinet even attacks several 'Philosophes du Christianisme' for their 'propositions ridicules' on the subject of women.[48] Authority in the form of quotation from Holy Writ remains, however, one of the most powerful weapons in the hands of anti-feminists, and ʲfeminists counter this by enthusiastic, but sometimes wayward, glosses on the damning verses in Genesis, Proverbs, Ecclesiastes, Ecclesiasticus, and St. Paul. Second to the authority of the Scriptures is that of the Church Fathers, who are pillaged for apposite quotations, often taken out of context.[49]

Ratiocination is not considered by either feminists or anti-feminists to be a convincing method of argument.[50] Imprecise generalizations about society, anatomy, and psychology, often facetious speculation on the relative importance of men and women, facile comparisons with nature may all come under the description of 'raisonnements', and it is not surprising that the more serious writers take little account of them. As for Cartesian

---

[44] *Perfection des femmes*, p. 21.

[45] *Alphabet*, pp. 245–6. 405; Le Moyne, *Les peintures morales*, Paris, 1640, i. 202.

[46] *L'honneste femme*, i. 224: 'et n'estoit-ce pas vn Philosophe réueur qui soustenoit publiquement que de mille Hommes à peine on en trouuoit vn constant, mais de toutes les femmes pas vne seule.' Cf. Eccles. 7: 29, quoted hereafter.

[47] 'Virum de mille unum reperi; mulierem ex omnibus non inveni'. It is possible that Du Bosc is referring to Trousset in the quotation given above, or to both Trousset and the author of Ecclesiastes.

[48] *Le theatre françois, des seigneurs et dames illustres*, ii. 3; those he mentions by name are Almaric, a heretic who had a following in Paris in the mid-sixteenth century (see M. de la Bigne, *Sacrae bibliothecae sanctorum patrum*, Paris, 1589, iii. 1338), and Lefèvre d'Etaples.

[49] Such quotation is often taken from commonplace books rather than the original works: for examples of these see Luis de Granada, *Sylva locorum communium*, Lyons, 1586; Filippo Diez, *Summa praedicantium*, Lyons, 1592; Jean Dadré, *Loci communes similium et dissimilium*, Cologne, 1603. The first of these is anti-feminist in its selection of quotations about women; the latter two, predominantly feminist.

[50] See *La femme genereuse*, Paris, 1643, p. 42: 'les exemples [meuuent] bien plus que les raisonnemens, puisqu'ils sont des raisonnemens effectuez et reduits en pratique'; and François de Grenaille, *L'honneste mariage*, p. 275.

logic and method, this is first employed in a consistent manner by Poullain de la Barre in his *De l'égalité des deux sexes. Discours physique et moral où l'on voit l'importance de se défaire des préjugés* of 1673, and is rarely encountered in these texts.

Example is the most popular method of argument, fulfilling a dual function, as it provides both a proof and a model of behaviour. For this reason, moralists use it with great frequency, since it is a simple and direct method of teaching, accessible to the understanding of everyone, whereas the 'meilleures preuues' drawn from moral philosophy 'ne sont connues qu'à ceux qui la sçauent parfaitement'.[51] Writers are, however, aware that even this method has its drawbacks; not only can one prove anything by examples,[52] but also they are relative to 'temps, lieux, religions, mœurs, aages, sexe et esprit',[53] and are applicable to a limited number of cases. For all this, the attractions of enumeration (which in the eyes of these writers is a persuasive, and hence desirable, feature of style) make the use of example as proof universal.

In some cases, where example is used in a statistical way, the effect is quite powerful, as in the following passage from d'Audiguier du Mazet's *Censeur censuré* of 1652:

Ie maintiens qu'à proportion du nombre des Femmes qui ont iamais commandé, il s'en trouuer[r]a plus de bonnes et moins de mau[u]aises, et qu'entre les Roys et les Souuerains qui ont Regné dans le monde, il s'en trouuera plus de ceux qui se sont laissez emporter a leurs passions que de ceux qui ont aymé leurs Peuples, et agy auec vn amour paternel.[54]

If, on the other hand, the writer is attempting to be impartial, the flaws in this method of argumentation are clearly exposed.[55] Du Bosc claims that the most effective method is comparison, in which he sees a combination of authority, example, and reasoning:

Il n'est pas malaisé de juger, qu'on ne peut establir plus fortement la gloire des Dames, qu'en comparant leur Vertu à celle des hommes: parce que ces raports ou ces comparaisons que ie fais, sont fondez sur

[51] d'Ablancourt, in the preface to Du Bosc's *Honneste femme*, i. ī4ᵛ–ōlʳ.
[52] Ibid. ããlᵛ.
[53] Ibid. ãã2ʳ.
[54] *Le censeur censuré*, Paris, 1652, p. 14.
[55] See Claude Maillard, *Le bon mariage*, Douai, 1643, p. 270, for an excellent example of this.

l'experience, et sur les effets; et cette façon d'argumenter est la plus
forte, aussi bien que la plus sensible tout ensemble, parce qu'elle joint
le raisonnement à l'exemple: les autres façons de raisonner sont trop
generales, trop maigres, et trop decharnées; et par consequent moins
sensibles et moins palpables . . .[56]

and elsewhere he declares 'ce ne sont icy ny visions, ny paradoxes,
ny vaines subtilitez; ce sont de puissantes preuues, et d'autant
plus autentiques, qu'elles ioignent la force du raisonnement auec
l'authorité des exemples; mais des exemples illustres, solides et
tirez le plus souuent des sainctes Lettres.'[57]

In the main, however, writers in the traditional genre are
content just to convince, or even just to amuse; since Charles
Estienne's translation of Ortensio Landi's *Paradossi*, entitled
*Paradoxes, ce sont propos contre la commune opinion, debattus en forme
de declamations foreuses, pour exerciter les jeunes advocats en causes
difficiles* of 1553,[58] which contains a 'Declamation que l'excellence
de la femme est plus grande que celle de l'homme', there were
several paradoxes of this nature published in France, among them
Alexandre de Pontayméri's *Paradoxe apologique, où il est fidellement
demonstré que la femme est beaucoup plus parfaite que l'homme en
toute action de vertu* (1594). Even Agrippa, writing of the declamation, points out the essentially specious nature of his own feminist composition,[59] and the author of *La Femme genereuse* of 1643
writes as a conclusion to this work:

Ie suppose que comme nonobstant l'opinion de Copernice qui tient
que la terre se meut, et que le ciel est immobile, l'ancienne opinion qui
establit le contraire existe. Que tout de mesme nonobstant toutes mes
raisons et mes preuues, qui buttent à faire passer les femmes en tout et
par tout au dessus des hommes, que tout ce que i'ay allegué soit tenu
pour paradoxe, et que le sentiment contraire le doiue emporter . . .[60]

The relative merits of *paradoxe* and *commune opinion* are much

[56] *La femme heroïque*, i. 79.   [57] Ibid. i. 274.
[58] Reprinted in 1554, 1558, 1561, 1583, 1603, and 1638.
[59] *Apologia adversus calumnias, propter declamationem de vanitate scientiarum* . . .
intentatas, xlii, in *Opera*, Lyons, n.d., ii. 326-7: 'proinde declamatio non judicat, non
dogmatizat, sed quae declamationis conditiones sunt, alia joco, alia serio, alia
falsè, alia severè dicit: aliquando mea, aliquando aliorum sententia loquitur, quaedam vera, quaedam falsa, quaedam dubia pronunciat . . . multa invalida argumenta
adducit . . .', quoted by Screech, 'Rabelais, de Billon and Erasmus', 246.
[60] *La femme genereuse*, pp. 168-9.

debated at this time,[61] and such discussion may be linked with the baroque aesthetic.[62]

Many feminists write in dialogue form, and here also most are concerned to amuse rather than to convince, although, after the practice of Erasmus, one interlocutor is usually far more unreasonable than the other. Some writers go further, and end their dialogue with the conversion of the anti-feminist to the feminist point of view, as does Jean Juliard,[63] or even have both interlocutors speaking in favour of women, as is the case in Cristoforo Bronzini's dialogue.[64] Non-sequiturs are very common, and it is not unusual to find no train of argument whatsoever. This applies also to the relationship between the anti-feminist works and their refutations; Trousset stresses again and again that he is only attacking the 'femmes mondaines', the 'courtisanes', and the 'debauchees'. 'Ie prie les vertueuses de m'excuser', he writes at one point, 'et leur demande bien humblement pardon, ie n'attaque que les meschantes',[65] and elsewhere he declares:

I'espère pourtant et croy fermement, que les sages et discrettes ne me sçauront malgré, par ce que comme les contraires mis aupres l'vn de l'autre paroissent dauantage, aussi ces satyres et anatomies de vices feront esclatter de plus en plus le lustre, la noblesse, la prestance, et les vertus des bonnes femmes, que ie soustiens estre en assez grand nombre . . .[66]

His adversaries, however, take no note of such riders, and base their refutations on the assumption that he is attacking woman-kind as a whole. Trousset and La Bruyère in turn accuse these writers of defending 'les femmes mondaines',[67] even though feminist writers make it clear that they are only writing in defence of the virtuous. Such wilful disregard of the stated intentions of both sides of the debate transforms the *Querelle* into a 'dialogue de sourds'.

---

[61] See the *Cinquième et dernier tome du recueil general des questions traittees és conferences du Bureau d'Addresse*, Paris, 1655, pp. 49–52, 'S'il vaut mieux suiure les opinions communes que les paradoxes'.

[62] See below, pp. 239 ff.

[63] See *Les amours de l'amant converty*, Lyons, 1604.

[64] See *L'advocat des femmes*, Paris, 1622.   [65] *Alphabet*, p. 205.

[66] Ibid., p. 332; see also pp. 16 and 23. Such qualifications are common in anti-feminist works; see Ferville, *La méchanceté des femmes*, p. 3 (second edition of the *Cacogynie*) and *Estranges propheties sur les mondanitez des femmes et des filles de ce temps*, n.p., 1632, p. 2.

[67] *Response aux impertinences*, p. 23; *Replique à l'antimalice*, p. 12.

This brief account of the methods of argumentation employed by writers in the traditional genre should be completed by an analysis of the evidence used in feminist and anti-feminist texts. Here one curious omission may be noted. Although in Germany and England at this time there are works dealing with the legal status and prerogatives of women (J. U. Wolff's *Discursus: de foeminarum in jure civili et canonico privilegiis, immunitatibus et prae-eminentia* of 1615 and the anonymous *Lawes resolutions of women's rights: or the Lawes provision for women* of 1632), in France no such tract appears, in spite of the fact that many of the feminist writers of this period are connected with the law;[68] in fact, very little reference to legal prerogatives of any kind is made. Another aspect of feminist writing abroad is also rare in France; that is, the vilification of the male sex as a means of promoting feminist claims.[69]

Theological evidence

(i) *Genesis*

The principal arguments drawn from Genesis to prove the superiority of women over men are found in most seventeenth-century works of the genre. The glosses on *locus, ordo, nomen,* and *materia* are repeated or modified according to the attitude of the writer: Trousset adroitly turns the argument from *materia* against women;[70] Caillet reverses the significance given by feminist writers to *ordo*;[71] moralists such as Du Bosc and Grenaille strip the creation of woman of both its feminist and anti-feminist overtones, and interpret the event as an indication of the need for

[68] e.g. Le Bermen, Angenoust, Barbier-Vigoureux, Saint-Gabriel (*Le merite des dames*, Paris, 1655), to name but a few.

[69] See Giuseppe Passi, *La monstruosa fucina delle sordidezze de gl'huomini* (1603); Lucrezia Marinella, *La nobiltà et l'eccellenza delle donne, co' difetti e mancamenti de gli huomini* (1600); Lucrezio Bursati, *La vittoria delle donne, nella quale si scuopre la grandezza donnesca e la bassezza virile* (1621). For Spanish examples of man-hating females, see B. Matulka, 'The feminist theme in the drama of the Siglo del Oro', *Romanic Review*, xxvi (1935), 191–237; M. McKendrick, 'The *bandolera* in Golden Age Drama', *Bulletin of Hispanic Studies*, xlvi (1969), 1–20.

[70] *Alphabet*, p. 93: 'Dieu formant le corps de la femme d'vne coste dure et craquetarde, et celuy de l'homme de terre sourde et muette, c'estoit vn prejugé que l'homme seroit de sa nature, taciturne et silencieux, et la femme cacquetarde et babillarde.'

[71] *Le tableau du mariage*, Orange, 1635, p. 138: '[La femme] a eu l'honneur d'auoir esté formee dans le Paradis terrestre, hors duquel l'homme auoit esté crée: Si est-ce toutesfois qu'elle doit reconoistre qu'elle a esté formée de la coste de l'homme. et apres l'homme, et pour l'amour de l'homme.'

mutual respect and fidelity in marriage.[72] In a similar way, the sin of Eve can either be seen as a proof of woman's evil nature and susceptibility to temptation, or as an indication that she was superior to man before the Fall (since it was she who took the decision to eat the apple), or merely as demonstration of the frailty of mankind.[73]

The question whether woman is made in the image of God is another problem set by Genesis. Augustine's interpretation of the Pauline understanding of the relevant verses[74] is often cited by anti-feminists who claim that she is not; but there is little development of this except as an excuse for preaching against cosmetics and jewellery. Valladier writes in the following terms on this subject:

Peut-estre ont pensé ces Docteurs que les femmes mondaines, portans le plus souuent l'image du Diable, ne pouuoyent porter l'image de Dieu? Et qu'eussent-ils dit s'ils eussent veu les vanitez de nostre siecle? Ne vous semble-t-il pas que la pluspart ressemblent plustost à des Diables, qu'à Dieu?[75]

Marie de Gournay has less patience with these authorities, which she describes as 'certains ergotistes anciens'.[76] There is occasional reference also to the theological problem of resurrection and sex, as in La Mothe Le Vayer's *Dialogue du mariage* of 1631:

Beaucoup ont creu auec S. Augustin et le subtil docteur Lescot, que les femmes ne participeront à la resurrection generale, qu'en changeant de sexe, et perdant le feminin pour le viril.[77]

Valladier sees it necessary to refute this also:

Ceux qui demandent si les femmes ressusciteront en ce sexe de femme, sont et tres-oiseux et fort vains, et trop ignorans, abusans des aureilles de l'auditoire . . . Ioinct que la femme est autant ou plus parfaicte, voire

---

[72] *L'honneste femme*, ii. 322–3 : '[la femme] ne fut pas tiree des pieds ny de la teste, mais du costé, pour monstrer qu'elle ne doit pas estre ny Esclaue, ny Maistresse, mais Compagne'; see also Grenaille, *L'honneste mariage*, pp. 110–11 and 216 ff.
[73] The denunciation of the sin of Eve in anti-feminist works is universal. For examples of the feminist argument, see Gaillar, *Le bouclier des femmes*, Paris, 1621, pp. 8–9, and Marguerite de Valois, *Lettre*, in Loryot, *Fleurs des secrets moraux*, d3r–v.
[74] PL xxxiv. 452–3.
[75] *La saincte philosophie de l'ame*, pp. 813–14; see also the anonymous *Tableau des piperies des femmes mondaines*, Paris, 1632, ff. 26v–30r.
[76] *Egalité des hommes et des femmes*, ed. Schiff, p. 70.
[77] Oratius Tubero, *Quatre autres dialogues* [Paris, 1631], p. 408. Lescot is of course Duns Scotus (see above, p. 4 n.). A playfully dishonest reference to sources. See also Montaigne, *Essais*, ed. Thibaudet and Rat, iii. 5, p. 835.

sans comparaison plus merueilleuse en la difference de son sexe, que nous au nostre : n'y ayant rien de la nature corporelle, de plus miraculeux, que de conceuoir, et former, et organizer l'enfant.[78]

Not all Church Fathers produce anti-feminist glosses on these verses, and it is worth mentioning that one of the most striking arguments in favour of the equality of women and men is drawn from Basil's commentary on Genesis.[79]

An analytical account of this evidence does not do justice to its cumulative effect, which can be discerned in the following passage from Marguerite de Valois's letter to Loryot:

Partant puis que [la femme] sur-passe l'homme en toute sorte d'excellence, de perfection, et de dignité, et que toutes choses se rapportent au plus excellent, plus parfait et plus digne, comme sa derniere fin : il faut dire la femme auoir est[é] faicte, comme chef de toute la creation du monde, et son dernier œuure, qui possede le Transcendant de toutes choses créees en plus pur et parfaict degré. Et par consequent, elle est vne digne offrande pour estre presentee à Dieu, et pour estre plus capable de luy rendre graces de toutes celles, qu'il a espanduës en la Nature, et sur toute sa creation.

Et tout ainsi qu'il n'y a rien en la Nature, si digne d'estre dict estre fait pour Dieu, que la femme : aussi toutes choses en la Nature estans soubs elle, et l'homme mesme, elles ne peuuent estre dictes faictes que pour la femme, ne pouuant sans se rabaisser et faire tort à sa dignité, se dire faicte pour autre que pour Dieu.

Que si on la dict estre descheuë de l'excellence de sa creation, par la menace que Dieu luy fist pour le peché de la pomme, disant en courroux, et par punition qu'elle seroit assuiettie à son mary : cela monstre qu'auparavant elle luy estoit superieure : et pour ce iuste courroux, il ne la priua de l'excellence de son Estre, l'ayant choisie pour mere de Dieu, honneur auquel le sexe de l'homme n'est point paruenu. Parquoy encores il doibt honneur et submission à la femme, comme à la mere de son Dieu.[80]

(ii) *Ecclus. 42: 14: 'melior est iniquitas viri quam mulier bene faciens et confundens in opprobrium'*

This text poses no problem for anti-feminist writers, who do little more than repeat it: 'si la compagnie et la frequentation des femmes, mesmes vertueuses et bien faisantes, est vne cuitable contagion', writes Trousset, 'que doit-on penser de celles qui

---

[78] *Saincte philosophie de l'ame*, pp. 818–19.   [79] See above, p. 5.
[80] *Lettre*, in *Fleur des secrets moraux*, d3^r–v.

prodiguent miserablement le bien et l'honneur?'[81] It presents, however, a considerable trial of ingenuity for those who attempt to gloss it in a way which is not to the dishonour of women. Nicolas L'Archevesque offers the following feminist interpretation in his *Grandeurs sur-eminentes de la Vierge Marie* of 1638:

Vn peu auant ce verset, l'Ecclesiastique auoit dit: Ne veuillez demeurer parmy les femmes; en suitte de quoy il adiouste: Mieux vaut l'iniquité de l'homme que la femme bien faisant, et confondant en opprobre. Son intention donc est d'aduertir, qu'il y a plus de danger, et de tentation au peché sale, en conuersant auec vne femme qui a quelques traits de beauté, quand bien elle seroit en oraison, et donneroit l'aumosne aux pauures, que d'estre en la compagnie d'vn meurtrier ou d'vn yurongne. Non que la vertu d'vne femme soit moindre que le vice d'vn scelerat: mais parce que l'homme est si fragile, que quand il verroit vne femme bien faire, il ne laisseroit de la conuoiter bien qu'il luy en deust arriuer du mal. Ce n'est pas la beauté de la femme, et encore moins ses bonnes œuures, qui sont la cause efficiente et formelle qui confond l'homme, et qui le font tirer à mespris: mais c'est sa propre concupiscence . . .[82]

Bernier, in his *Apologie contre l'Alphabeth* of 1618, produces a similar gloss.[83] This verse is also mentioned in various other works at about this time.[84]

In 1641 Louis Machon published a work entitled *Discours ou sermon apologetique, en faveur des femmes,*[85] devoted entirely to an interpretation of this verse; he gave it the sub-title *Question nouvelle, curieuse et non jamais soutenue,* which as a description hardly does justice to his immediate predecessors, not to speak of earlier commentators such as Agrippa and Erasmus.[86] His own gloss seems to be original:

Quand l'Autheur de l'Ecclesiastique a mis en auant cét enigme, ou plutost ce Paradoxe, il semble que par vne addresse toute Diuine et merueilleuse, il ait voulu apporter vn contrepoid égal à l'orgueil et

---

[81] *Alphabet*, p. 145.

[82] *Grandeurs sur-eminentes de la Vierge*, Paris, 1638, p. 568.

[83] *Apologie contre l'Alphabeth*, Paris, 1618, p. 39.

[84] See Grenaille, *L'honneste mariage*, p. 319; *Cinquiesme et dernier tome des questions traittees és conferences du Bureau d'Addresse*, p. 47.

[85] It would appear that this sermon was in fact preached; such a medium for feminist discussion is, however, not unusual, as Valladier, Pierre Du Moulin, Sufrin, and others all treat feminist topics from the pulpit.

[86] See Erasmus, *Enchiridion militis Christiani*, in *Opera*, Leyden, 1703–6, v. 17, quoted by Telle, *Marguerite de Navarre*, pp. 53–4; Agrippa, *De nobilitate foeminei sexus*, in *Opera*, ii. 529–31, quoted by Telle, p. 54.

presomption des femmes, qui de leur naturel estant toutes paistries
dedans la vanité, et l'amour d'elles-mesmes; par vne saincte apparence,
et vn remede plus salutaire qu'agreable, a feint de mespriser iusqu'à
leur propre vertu, preuoyant bien qu'elles trouueroient assez de
moyens et d'artifices, pour s'esleuer plus qu'elles ne doiuent, et
s'en faire accroitre beaucoup dauantage qu'il n'en est pas.[87]

The conclusions which he draws from this (that the concupiscence
and vice resultant from the beauty of women 'sont plustost des
marques et des assurances veritables de leur pouuoir dessus les
hommes, que non pas preuues de leur malice ny de leur foiblesse'[88])
are strikingly feminist. The discussion of this verse may also be
associated with moralistic literature condemning the company of
women, such as Matthieu Lambert's *Discours du danger et peril
qu'il y a de converser et hanter trop familiarement avec femmes, tant
seculieres que religieuses* (1596) and Théophile Raynaud's *Dissertatio
de sobria alterius sexus frequentatione per sacros et religiosos homines*
(1653).

(iii) *The New Testament*

The figures of Our Lord and the Virgin Mary appear prominently in these works, and a full treatment of this aspect of
feminist writing will be undertaken in a later section.[89] The argument that it is to the great honour of the female sex that a woman
gave birth to God ('quod homo non potuit') has already been
quoted;[90] Marie de Gournay retails this with similar material in
her *Egalité des hommes et des femmes*:

Si les hommes se vantent, que Jesus-Christ soit nay de leur sexe, on
respond, qu'il le falloit par necessaire bien seance, ne se pouvant pas
sans scandale, mesler jeune et à toutes les heures du jour et de la nuict
parmy les presses, aux fins de convertir, secourir et sauver le genre
humain, s'il eust esté du sexe des femmes: notamment en face de la
malignité des Juifs . . . D'ailleurs, l'advantage qu'ont les hommes par
son incarnation en leur sexe; (s'ils en peuvent tirer un advantage, veu
cette necessité remarquée) est compensé par sa conception tres precieuse au corps d'une femme, par l'entiere perfection de cette femme,
unique à porter nom de parfaicte entre toutes les creatures purement

[87] *Discours ou sermon apologetique*, Paris, 1641, pp. 34–5.   [88] Ibid., pp. 60–1.
[89] pp. 71–4.   [90] See above, p. 42.

humaines, depuis la cheute de nos premiers parens, et par son assumption unique en sujet humain aussi.[91]

Ferville's unusual gloss on Pilate's wife's dream (Matt. 27: 19) also merits inclusion here:

Le diable ennemy juré du genre humain et partisan du monde et de la chair, à bien sçeu choisir la femme pour l'euersion de nostre gloire: quel autre esprit que luy a solicité la femme de Pilate, afin qu'elle persuadast son mary de casser la sentence, où gisoit nostre redemption?[92]

Many other examples of ingenious and often heterodox interpretation of Holy Writ could be adduced but these would not elucidate any further the use made of this sort of evidence in the traditional genre. A last commonplace, patristic in origin, should, however, be mentioned. The description of women as the *sexe dévot*,[93] which they earned because of the charitable actions of those of their sex who served Christ during his ministry, is given prominence in most feminist works. Bernier merely uses the commonplace as an argument in favour of his thesis that women are more devout than men;[94] Nicolas Caussin is less specific:

La deuotion est vne vertu hereditaire à nostre sexe [le sexe des femmes], c'est le premier partage que Dieu nous a fait, c'est le tiltre que l'Eglise nous donne, c'est la plus illustre marque de nostre noblesse.[95]

Suzanne de Nervèze, addressing the Almighty, is more eloquent and periphrastic:

[La femme] est aussi l'abregé de vos grandeurs, l'éclat magnifique de votre gloire et le plus cher attrait de vos adorables dilections: les sacrez cahiers sont remplis de leurs vertus, le Paradis de leur pieté et toute la terre de leurs aymables merueilles. . . . C'est le deuot sexe cheri de Dieu, et idolastré mesme de ses aduersaires . . .[96]

[91] *Egalité des hommes et des femmes*, ed. Schiff, pp. 75–6; see also Suzanne de Nervèze, *Apologie en faveur des femmes*, in *Œuvres spirituelles et morales*, Paris, 1642, pp. 91–2.

[92] *La méchanceté des femmes*, p. 118. For glossing on the Alphabet of the Good Woman (Prov. 31: 10–29) see below, pp. 81–2; interpretations of St. Paul's dicta about marriage will be discussed below (pp. 82 ff.).

[93] A Marian prayer in the Breviary (one of the 'commemorationes communes de S. Maria quando non dicitur ejus officium parvum') reads: 'Sancta Maria, succurre miseris, juva pusillanimis, refove flebiles, ora pro populo, interveni pro clero, intercede pro devoto foemineo sexu . . .'

[94] *Apologie contre l'Alphabet*, p. 8.

[95] *La cour sainte*, Paris, 1640, ii. 270.

[96] *Œuvres spirituelles et morales*, pp. 85–6.

Aquinas's comment on devotion and the female sex, to which some writers refer, is, however, scarcely feminist in implication:

If contemplation were the proper cause of devotion, then those who are best disposed for contemplation would be the most devout. But this is not the case, because devotion is frequently present in simple men and in women in whom is found a lack of capacity for contemplation.[97]

Medical evidence

The Aristotelian 'imperfect male' theory is much discussed in the early seventeenth century, and seems still to be at issue as late as 1656.[98] Anti-feminists merely record Aristotle's view as this is expressed in the *De generatione animalium*; some feminist writers try to reinterpret this in a way less offensive to women, as does the author of *L'innocence de Chymène* of 1638:

Si Aristote a dit que la femme étoit faite dauanture et sans intention de la nature on s'est trompé de croire que ce fut pour quelque imperfection, la femme étant parfaite en son étre et rendant la nature humaine accomplie en sa perfection: mais ç'a été pour faire voir que la femme n'a point tant d'obligation à la nature qu'à l'amour, lequel donne la vie par sa disposition auec l'Auteur de la nature.[99]

François Dinet, however, merely scorns the idea as absurd:

Ie ne sçay quelle raison auoit Aristote, et quelques Medecins qui l'ont suiuy en son opinion, de dire que la femme estoit engendrée par accident, et contre le dessein de ses causes; l'appelant vn animal defectueux, produit occasionnellement, plus digne d'estre reputé vn defaut, qu'vn effect de la Nature; comme si elle ne participoit aussi bien de l'essence humaine que l'homme, et n'estoit pas aussi necessaire que luy à la conseruer et prodiguer.[100]

Reynier also mentions a medical thesis submitted at Paris at about this time, entitled 'La femme, est-elle un ouvrage imparfait de la nature?', which is clearly a further reflection of the debate.[101]

---

[97] *Summa theologiae*, 2a 2ae 82, 3. The 'contemplationis defectus' to which Aquinas refers may be associated with Tasso's contention that women should not concern themselves with intellectual virtue (see above, p. 21).

[98] See Jean Chapelain, *La Pucelle*, Paris, 1656, preface ã3ᵛ.

[99] *L'innocence de Chymène*, n.p., 1638, p. 21.

[100] *Theatre françois*, ii. 2. Le Bermen's chapter 'Que la femme est necessaire à la multiplication du genre humain' (*Bouclier des dames*, pp. 9–16) clearly is connected with this debate.

[101] *La femme au XVIIᵉ siècle*, p. 41.

Aristotle's comparison of men to form and women to matter is also commented upon by writers.[102]

The 'imbecillité' and 'infirmité' of women, often referred to in both moralistic and anti-feminist works during this period, are attributes drawn from the traditional beliefs about the physical constitution of women, based partly on the Aristotelian texts mentioned above, and partly on the science of the humours. These attributes are sometimes used to excuse the absence of certain qualities in women,[103] although it is more usual for feminist writers to try to make something more positive out of the evidence available. It is generally accepted at this time that woman is of cold and moist humours, similar to children and criminals, a fact which does not escape the notice of anti-feminist writers.[104] L'Escale stresses the connection between chastity and cold humours, and on the same occasion that between lubricity and man's natural complexion;[105] the author of the *Triomphe des femmes* sees in the coldness of woman's humours a proof of her constancy in love.[106] Because of her moist humours, woman is less prone to frenzy and uncontrollable anger than man, according to Pontayméri,[107] although it is pointed out that the same moist humours indicate a lack of stamina and a tendency to indolence.[108]

The most interesting conclusions drawn from the humours, however, concern the intellectual capacity of women. Le Moyne deduces from the less robust physical constitution of women and

[102] Du Bosc, *L'honneste femme*, i. 224. Grenaille talks of man as the 'sujet' and woman as the 'accident' (*L'honneste mariage*, pp. 206–7).

[103] See Bernier, *Apologie contre l'Alphabeth*, p. 21: 'si les femmes ne sont tousiours tant magnanimes et constantes en aduersitez et prosperitez que les hommes, cela est à cause qu'elles sont plus foibles et moins fortes de corps que les hommes: et pareillement si elles ne sont tousiours tant liberales, et tant promptes à donner que les hommes, c'est à cause qu'elles sont moins fortes pour soustenir les labeurs requis pour acquerir des biens necessaires à subuenir aux indigences: car comme dit Aristote, *Senectus et omnis debilitas illiberales facit* . . .' (see *Nicomachean Ethics*, iv. 1).

[104] See Trousset, *Alphabet*, pp. 74, 186; La Bruyère, *Replique à l'antimalice, passim*.

[105] *Champion des femmes*, f. 33ᵛ: 'la complexion ordinaire de la femme selon tous les hommes, est d'estre froide (à ce que dit Aristote, mesme leur ennemy) et par consequent chaste: au lieu que la constitution naturelle de l'homme le rend luxurieus et paillard.'

[106] *Triomphe des femmes*, pp. 289–90: 'la femme de nature froide, s'émeut plus difficilement que l'homme, mais vne fois attainte elle dure d'auantage en son Amour.'

[107] *Paradoxe apologique*, Paris, 1594, pp. 13–14.

[108] See *La femme genereuse*, p. 126; Grenaille, *Les plaisirs des dames*, Paris, 1641, pp. 183–4; Loryot, *Les secrets moraux*, p. 498.

their cold and moist complexion that they are endowed with greater powers of imagination and memory:

Toutes choses donc sont egales entre les Hommes et les Femmes du costé de l'Ame, qui est la partie Intelligente, et qui fait les Sçauants et les Philosophes: et s'il y a de l'inégalité du costé du Corps, comme on ne peut pas le nier, elle est auantageuse aux Femmes: et perfectionne en elles la capacité dont ie parle [la vraye Philosophie].

On leur reproche l'humidité de leur complexion: mais on ne la leur reprochera point, quand on se souuiendra que l'humidité est la matière dont se forment les images qui seruent aux Sciences: qu'elle est le propre Temperament de la memoire, qui en est la depositaire et la nourrice . . .

Quant à la delicatesse, apparemment ceux qui leur en font vn suiet d'accusation, n'ont pas pris l'auis d'Aristote. Ils sçauroient que le temperament le plus delicat est le moins chargé de matiere: le plus net et le plus propre à estre penetré des lumières de l'Esprit; le mieux preparé aux belles images et à l'impression des sciences.[109]

Loryot and Dinet also point to woman's greater natural powers of memory and imagination, and even writers who make no reference to the humours attribute these qualities to the female sex.[110]

Le Moyne is somewhat embarrassed by the use of such arguments as he employs in the preceding quotation, however, because there is a relationship suggested between intellect and body which runs counter to his dominant contention that the only

---

[109] *Gallerie des femmes fortes*, p. 251. Other feminist writers deny that women are naturally less robust than men: 'quelque delicatesse qu'on attribue à leur corps', writes Suzanne de Nervèze, 'elle est plus à la molesse de leur education qu'à l'imperfection de leur nature' (*Œuvres spirituelles et morales*, p. 86). For such writers, Le Moyne's second argument is unacceptable. The association of moist humours and memory is found in Plato's *Theaetetus* (191B–197A), and is most vividly described in *La femme genereuse*, pp. 91–2: 'l'humide est plus propre à receuoir l'impression, l'empreinte et la graueure des images et pourtrait des choses, qui sont l'objet de la science: sans idée et representation duquel nous ne le pouuons cognoistre. Et il est bien plus aisé de grauer sur vne chose humide qui est tousiours molle, que non pas sur vne seiche qui est d'ordinaire dure. Et estant plus froide (ou moins chaude) que l'homme, le froid en reserrant l'humeur du cerueau, retient en estat et empesche de couler cét humide, et conserue par là la graueure de telles images.'

[110] Loryot, *Fleurs des secrets moraux*, ĕı^v and ĕ4^v; Dinet, *Theatre françois*, ii. 51; see also François Du Soucy, sieur de Gerzan, *Le triomphe des dames*, Paris, 1646, p. 164; Georges de Scudéry, *Les femmes illustres*, Paris, 1642–4, i. 429–31; Gabriel Gilbert, *Panegyrique des dames*, Paris, 1650, pp. 15–16. Ferville manages to interpret these attributes in an anti-feminist manner: 'l'esprit de la femme est comme la toile d'vn Peintre, qui reçoit indifferemment l'impression de toutes couleurs, et n'en a iamais d'asseuree que le noir qui vne fois couché ne s'efface iamais' (*Méchanceté des femmes*, pp. 61–2).

differences between the sexes are corporeal; it is possible to detect here an inconsistency in his argument, of which he is clearly aware, for at one point he writes:

Quant au defaut de chaleur et à l'excez d'humidité qu'on reproche aux Femmes; outre que ce sont des differences superficielles, qui ne vont pas iusques à l'Ame, ny ne peuuent mettre d'inégalité entre les Esprits: on m'aduoüera que ce ne sont pas les chauds et bilieux, mais les froids et les flegmatiques qui sont les Sages.[111]

Le Bermen, who also encounters the problem, talks of 'les diuers temperamens de nos corps qui seruent d'organes et d'instrumens à nos Ames, qui apportent accidentellement quelques diuersitez et difference',[112] but of all who treat this question, the author of *La femme genereuse* presents the most coherent picture:

L'habileté aux sciences vient de la nature et essence, ou du temperament. Celle qui suit la nature est égale aux hommes et aux femmes, puis que l'vn et l'autre sexe est d'vne mesme espece et nature. L'vn et l'autre est defini animal raisonnable. Le sexe ne vient pas de l'essence, ny de l'ame, qui n'est ny masle ny femelle, mais du corps et de la matiere. Pour cela en tous les deux sexes il y a entendement de mesme noblesse et excellence: et de ce costé la mesme disposition à la science en tous. Et toutesfois à cause qu'effectiuement il y a diuersité remarquable en la viuacité des actions de l'esprit tant d'vn homme à vn autre, qu'entre les hommes et les femmes: et telle diuersité ne prouenant pas des principes de la nature, il reste que ce soit à cause des diuers organes diuersement preparez: et de telle preparation suiuant le diuers temperament, il s'ensuit que c'est de luy d'où il faut comme de sa cause rechercher le plus ou le moins d'aptitude aux sciences.[113]

For all this, however, the majority of conclusions drawn from medical evidence and authority are scarcely to the honour of women. It is generally assumed that their passions are less controllable; because of their 'sangs plus subtils', they are said to be more prone than men to anger; in most anti-feminist and moralistic works their lubricious nature is castigated.[114] So great is their weakness considered to be that Loryot can assert in an essay supposedly written to establish the pre-eminence of their intellect:

Disons donc que la femme en son sexe est grandement infirme: qui asseureroit que c'est la mesme defectuosité qui luy donne l'essence de

[111] *Gallerie*, pp. 10–11.   [112] *Bouclier des dames*, p. 124.
[113] *La femme genereuse*, pp. 89–90.
[114] Caillet, *Tableau du mariage*, p. 46; Du Bosc, *L'honneste femme*, ii. 361.

son sexe, ie ne sçay s'il se tromperoit, attendu que retranchant l[e] manquement que la femme a respectiuement à l'homme, il y trouueroit vn homme bien accomply. Tant y a que la femme est le sexe de l'infirmité, ou soit que l'on regarde son corps, ou son esprit. Il y a grandement à rencherir sur ceste besogne de la Nature; si que, qui croiroit qu'elle auoit l'esprit en sequestre quand elle formoit la femme, il ne se mesprendroit de beaucoup . . .[115]

The advantages of physical weakness—beauty and moral qualities associated with gentleness, humility, and compassion—are, however, conceded to women by the same author, although he stresses also that cruelty, hate, and desire for vengeance are more extreme in women than in men.[116] 'Viuacité d'esprit', which results from cold and moist humours, is another characteristic generally associated with women, although it is more often interpreted in an anti-feminist way as 'legereté' or 'caprice', or as the faculty in women's minds which engenders deceit, intrigue, and dissimulation. Feminist writers associate the inventiveness of women with this mental attribute.[117] Patience is a further quality linked by seventeenth-century writers to woman's physical constitution.[118]

It is not easy to classify neatly the remaining fields of evidence adduced by writers of traditional works in the genre; the philological arguments (that the vices are in general masculine in gender, whereas the virtues are feminine), the mentions of muses and goddesses (which, as Trousset points out, should also remind the reader of the Fates and the Furies),[119] the belief that many inventions are attributable to women are examples of such evidence. The assertion that as women are mothers, sisters, and wives, and as they care for men throughout their lives in these capacities, they do not deserve the ingratitude embodied in anti-feminist writing[120] is a commonplace also found in most feminist works.

[115] *Fleurs des secrets moraux*, f4ᵛ. See also Rabelais, *Tiers livre*, 32; Ferrarius in *Commentarii de regulis juris*, p. 47.

[116] *Fleurs des secrets moraux*, p. 20; *Secrets moraux*, p. 89.

[117] Bernier, *Apologie contre l'Alphabeth*, *passim*; Caussin, *Cour sainte*, ii. 258; Du Bosc, *La femme heroïque*, i. 45–6.

[118] Scudéry, *Les femmes illustres*, i. 392; cf. Montaigne, *Essais*, ed. Thibaudet and Rat, iii. 5, p. 863; and above, p. 11.   [119] *Alphabet*, pp. 99–100.

[120] Gaillar, *Bouclier des femmes*, p. 5 : 'quelle impieté de s'addresser à vn sexe de qui nous receuons de l'estre et la vie, sans qui nous ne sçaurions subsister vn moment'; cf. Cyrano de Bergerac, *Lettres*, ed. L. Erba, Milan, 1965, p. 78. Le Moyne, however, argues that women 'seruent moins qu'elles ne sont seruies'. (*Gallerie*, p. 106.)

A further area of evidence which is difficult to define concerns the equation of the peculiar advantages bestowed by nature on the sexes. Machon, quoting Basil, balances man's authority over woman in marriage with female beauty, which woman deploys in turn to exercise authority over her husband, and which is 'vn empire bien plus noble, plus naturel, et plus glorieux';[121] Rampalle produces a more usual equation in his *Discours academiques*:

La Nature qui a refusé aux femmes la force du corps, l'vsage des armes, et toutes ces masles vertus qui accompagnent la gloire des hommes, leur a mis en reuenche sur le visage vne puissance enchanteresse, capable d'ebransler l'austerité d'vn Hermite, et de renuerser la constance d'vn Philosophe.[122]

Scudéry finds it necessary to refute the idea that the equivalent attribute in men to female beauty is intellect and knowledge.[123]
Some feminist writers make both sides of the generally accepted equation (beauty balanced by physical strength) advantageous to their cause: '*la force* du corps qui n'est propre qu'aux valets, et aux païsans . . . seroit mal-seante *aux Dames* . . . incompatible auec *la delicatesse*, qui fait vne des plus agreables parties de l'agrément et de la beauté', writes Gerzan,[124] and Gilbert is even more emphatic in his *Panegyrique des dames*:

Les hommes sont en possession de la force, et les femmes de la beauté: que peut-on conclure de là, sinon que les hommes surpassent les femmes en vne chose, en laquelle ils sont surpassez par les bestes, au lieu que les femmes les surpassent en vne autre, en laquelles elles ne sont surpassées par aucune des choses visibles.[125]

The question of beauty leads naturally to that of neo-Platonist elements in these writings. In the previous century, the *Querelle des amyes* highlighted the relationship of feminist thought and neo-Platonism;[126] the incidence of neo-Platonist elements in the seventeenth century is not as high, but echoes may still be detected. That the external beauty of women is an indication of interior

[121] *Discours ou sermon apologetique*, pp. 93–4; cf. *PG* xxx. 706–7 (Basil, *Liber de virginitate*, xvii).
[122] *Discours academiques*, Paris, 1647, p. 236.
[123] *Les femmes illustres*, i. 424–7; cf. ibid. i. 392.
[124] *Le triomphe des dames*, p. 12.
[125] *Panegyrique des dames*, p. 9; see also ibid., pp. 6–7.
[126] See M. A. Screech, 'La querelle des amyes', *BHR* xxi (1959), 103–30.

virtue is clearly connected with the Ficinian dictum 'omne pulchrum est bonum', and this argument is very often syncretized with theological evidence (especially the argument from *materia*) to produce such passages as the following, taken from Angenoust's *Paranymphe des dames*:

Car outre ce que la femme aussi bien que l'homme a esté formée à l'image et semblance de Dieu, il l'a decorée d'vne beauté nompareille, tant dedans que dehors, à celle fin d'éclairer par le moyen de ses vertus, et tesmoigner à toutes creatures, que Dieu l'a voulu releuer en quelque perfection plus éminente que toutes les autres, et monstrer qu'elle n'emprunte rien de la sagesse de l'homme, la tenant immediatement de Dieu.[127]

To such arguments only the author of the *Discours de l'ennemy d'amour et des femmes* gives a reply, when he cynically asserts:

Ie ne dois pas estre tenu pour impie, si ie dis que les imperfections de nostre iugement forment toutes les perfections que nous trouuons au visage des femmes.[128]

Social and political topics in feminist writing

The body of evidence discussed above indicates the scope for 'extrauagances, fatras et faux raisonnemens' which Du Bosc criticizes in his *Femme heroïque*. There are, however, other, more serious topics discussed by seventeenth-century feminist writers in the traditional genre and others. These are relevant to the social and political dispensation for women at this time; emancipation is not proposed, but limited reforms are suggested within the framework of contemporary French society. It is very common to read passages disclaiming any revolutionary intent, or any attempt to change the structure of society, which rested firmly on the assumption of man's dominance in public affairs and in the family unit, even though any change in the rôle played by

---

[127] *Paranymphe des dames*, p. 37; cf. L'Escale, *Champion des femmes*, ff. 41-2, Le Peletier, *De la chasteté*, p. 51, and Loryot, *Fleurs des secrets moraux*, h4ʳ⁻ᵛ. André Du Chesne's *Figures mystiques du riche et precieux cabinet des dames*, Paris, 1605, is a work devoted to the syncretization of neo-Platonist and biblical conceptions about the role and nature of beauty (see below, p. 162). Cf. also Machon's advice to an erring parishioner: 'si tu connoissois que la beauté des femmes, est vn signe exterieur de la perfection de leurs ames, tu ne la rechercherois pas pour la soüiller et l'abandonner à tes passions insatiables, mais comme un moyen pour esleuer ton esprit à la reconnoissance de son Createur' (*Discours ou sermon apologetique*, pp. 89-90).

[128] *Nouveau recueil des pieces les plus agreables de ce temps*, Paris, 1644, p. 139.

women in these spheres would necessarily modify such structures. Thus there may be seen in retrospect the attempt to appeal to the vast body of conservative thought by means of assurances—probably sincere—that all the reformers wanted to do was to improve woman's lot under the existing dispensation. Only the more enlightened writers had the insight to see the true import of their recommendations.[129]

The topics dealt with fall broadly into three classes: marital and social freedom; the right to be educated and to pursue learning, usually argued on behalf of the leisured middle classes and the lower aristocracy (other sections of society either not having the time, or already possessing the liberty to do this); and finally the question of public office and Salic law. The first of these topics will be treated in separate chapters;[130] the second and third will be discussed here.

The question whether women should be allowed to cultivate their minds is not new; Christine de Pisan adumbrates the issue in her *Livre de la cité des dames*,[131] although she neglects to develop it, and in the sixteenth century there are several eloquent pleas for the right to study.[132] But although the arguments for and against this right are similar in sixteenth- and seventeenth-century texts, the demands of earlier writers are necessarily even more theoretical than those of this period, as the means of educating women are slow to evolve, both in terms of private and public tuition, and books for self-instruction.[133] The debate about female education in the seventeenth century is, however, more vehement in tone and more prolific in texts.

[129] There are found from time to time passages which seem to be claims for emancipation, often in *facetiae*; the author of the pamphlet *La rejouissance des femmes sur la deffence des tavernes et cabarets* writes: 'si quelqu'un pouvoit venir jusques à l'esgalité des biens, ce seroit un grand coup pour nous, parce que nous avons autant d'ambition que les plus huppées, tout le monde seroit vestu esgalement comme à Spartes, l'homme iroit à la femme et les vivres seroient communs: par ainsi personne n'en abuseroit à nostre dam (*Variétés historiques et littéraires*, ed. E. Fournier, Paris, 1855–63, x. 184). It is possible that this is satirical, whereas Lucrezia Marinella's prayer in her *Nobiltà delle donne* (Venice, 1621, p. 47) appears to be sincere: 'o dio volesse, che à questi nostri tempi fosse lecito alle donne l'essercitarsi nelle armi, e nelle lettere. che si vedrebbano cose maravigliose, e non più vdite nel conseruare i Regni, e nell'ampliarli.'

[130] See below, pp. 88 ff. and 119 ff.

[131] *Le Livre de la cité des dames*, quoted in *Le livre de trois vertus*, ed. M. Laigle, Paris, 1912, Introduction, p. 120.

[132] See L. M. Richardson, *Forerunners of feminism*, pp. 73, 76, 108, 110 ff.

[133] See G. Reynier, *La femme au XVIIe siècle*, pp. 133–65.

Nothing could sound more reasonable than Scudéry's assertion in *Les femmes illustres*: 'il est bien iuste ce me semble, puis que nous laissons la domination aux hommes, qu'ils nous laissent du moins la liberté, de connoistre toutes les choses, dont nostre esprit est capable.'[134] D'Aubigné, however, is aware of the disingenuousness of such arguments, for in a letter to his daughters he warns them against using the fruits of learning in discussions with their husbands.[135] The author of *La femme genereuse* is more forthright: 'Les hommes apres s'estre rendu les femmes serues et captiues', she writes, 'leur ont osté la science, comme les seules armes et instrumens à faire la guerre aux hommes et à machiner leur deliurance.'[136] The bastion of those who resist change is 'coustume', 'vsage', 'opinion': Artus Thomas makes this clear in his *Discours . . . qu'il est bien seant que les filles soyent sçavantes* of 1600:

Voicy les maximes de ceux qui s'estiment les plus aduisez. La science et la sagesse se rencontrent rarement en vne fille: elle ne doit auoir autre escole que le mesnage, autre liures que ses ouurages. Leur honneur se conserue mieux par le silence que par la parole. Celle qui a tant de discours, porte ordinairement l'affront dessus le front. Il suffit qu'elles soient conduites sans vouloir conduire. L'authorité est incompatible à leur fragilité. L'vsage commun y repugne, et la croyance vulgaire qui les renoye à la quenouille, est suffisante pour renuerser tout ce qui se peut dire à l'encontre. Nostre siecle plus heureux que cestuy-cy, n'a point esté si curieux, et auec sa simplicité, il s'est conserué en integrité. Bref i'aimerois mieux vne Lucrece qu'vne Cornelie.[137]

The answer, as Erasmus had seen it in the early sixteenth century, is to change 'consuetudo', and to accept the possibility that change is not always to the worse,[138] yet such arguments as

---

[134] *Les femmes illustres*, i. 432.

[135] *Œuvres*, ed. Réaume and Caussade, i. 445: 'Mes filles, vostre frere vous a porté mon abregé de Logique en François, que M. de Bouïllon a nommé la Logique des filles, et laquelle je vous donne à ceste charge que vous n'en userez qu'en vous mesmes, et non envers les personnes qui vous sont compagnes et superieures; car l'usage des elenches des femmes envers leurs maris est trop dangereus . . .'

[136] *La femme genereuse*, pp. 97–8; cf. Marie de Gournay, *Egalité des hommes et des femmes*, ed. Schiff, p. 65.

[137] *Discours*, Paris, 1600, f. 8r–v; see also Charlotte de Brachart, *Harengue . . . qui s'adresse aux hommes qui veuillent deffendre la science aux femmes*, Chalon-sur-Saône, 1604, p. 4.

[138] *Colloquium abbatis et eruditae*, in *Opera omnia*, i. 745:

[Abbas]: Vulgus ita sentit, quia rarum et insolitum est, foeminam scire Latine.
[Erudita]: Quid mihi citas vulgum, pessimum bene gerendae rei auctorem? Quid

'[les filles] n'ont pas grand besoin de cet art qui apprend à parler en public, puis que l'vsage leur en est deffendu',[139] are common in this period. Du Bosc suggests in his *Nouveau Recueil de lettres des dames de ce temps* of 1635 that 'si plusieurs Dames de qualité entreprenoit d'escrire, elles en feroient receuoir la coutume: mais sans cela, celles qui commencent, sont plus en danger d'estre moquées, que d'estre imitées';[140] it would seem that this observation aptly prefigures and describes the process by which educated women became socially acceptable.

Most feminist writers concentrate on proving the capacity of women for study and the advisability of their improving their minds. Their greater powers of imagination and memory, which are deduced from the humours of women, are stressed in nearly all feminist works, with many outstanding examples of female intelligence: 'si l'Oracle d'Apollon declara Socrate pour le plus sage des hommes,' writes Du Bosc, 'Socrate apres confessa librement que sa Diotime luy avoit enseigné cette prudence, que les Dieux mesmes iugeoient incomparable',[141] and this anecdote is often retailed in order to establish the ability of women to understand 'ce qu'il y a de subtil et de Solide dans la plus haute sagesse'. To prove the same point, Le Moyne reproduces in his *Peintures morales* Clement of Alexandria's assertion that the angels gave learning as a dowry to women because of their natural curiosity, because they desire to adorn their mind as well as their body, and for more arcane reasons:

Les Sciences ayant cela de propre, qu'elles éleuent l'Esprit au dessus de la Matiere; les Anges les communiquerent aux Femmes, qu'ils auoient choisies, afin que l'interualle des Esprits estant osté par cette communication, et les Femmes en estant renduës Angeliques en quelque façon, et plus spirituelles qu'elle n'estoient nées, il ne leur fust pas reproché de s'estre alliez bassement, et hors de leur Ordre. Enfin les Anges ayant à communiquer leurs Sciences, s'adresserent aux Femmes

mihi consuetudinem, omnium malarum rerum magistram? Optimis assuescendum: ita fiet solitum, quod erat insolitum: et suave fiet, quod erat insuave: fiet decorum, quod videbatur indecorum.

[139] *Question celebre, s'il est necessaire, ou non, que les filles soient sçavantes. Agités de part et d'autre par Mademoiselle Anne Marie de Schurman Holandoise, et le Sr André Rivet Poitevin*, trad. G. Colletet, Paris, 1646, p. 53; Colletet admits that he is not sure whether Anna Maria van Schurman's position (in favour of changing social attitudes towards female education) 'est vn paradoxe ou non' [*Vies des poètes*, BN N.A. Fr. 3073, f. 431ᵛ]. [140] *Nouveau recueil de lettres*, Paris, 1635, p. 184. [141] *L'honneste femme*, i. 246.

plustost qu'aux Hommes, parce qu'ils les iugerent d'vne matiere plus docile et plus propre à receuoir cette lumiere.[142]

Having established to their satisfaction the capacity of women for study, these writers then move on to the questions whether they should be given the freedom to do so, and what they should be allowed to study. The second of these questions will be examined elsewhere;[143] it is sufficient here to quote Thomas's assertion:

Il est bien vray que ie ne leur desire pas vne science rec[h]erchee, vn sçauoir curieux, friuole et inutile: Ie leur souhaite seulement celle qui peut esclaircir la cognoissance et rendre plus solide le iugement.[144]

As for the advisability of such study, most writers stress that with proper instruction, women would be more able to resist the blandishments of the devil.[145] Du Bosc is eloquent on this subject:

Puisque la Nature ne leur donne pas tant d'auantage pour la vertu, il faut, quoy qu'on die, ou leur permettre de l'estudier, ou leur permettre de pecher impunément. C'est en cecy que la contradiction des medisans doit estre confuse. On dit que leur Sexe est le plus foible, et cependant il y en a qui trouuent estrange, qu'elles aquierent par Art, ce que la Nature leur desnie . . . Et toutesfois, ceux qui disent que le Sexe des femmes est le plus infirme, ne leur permettent point d'estudier, ny de chercher des remedes à leur foiblesse. Ils veulent qu'elles fassent autant de bien que les hommes, quoy qu'elles n'ayent pas comme eux, ny le secours des Sciences, ny les auantages de la Nature.[146]

Against the common accusation that learning tends to corrupt women, Caussin writes:

Pour vne fille instruite aux bonnes lettres, qui auoit manqué à son honneur, on en auoit trouué vne vingtaine d'autres ignorantes, qui auoient choppé d'autant plus lourdement, que moins elles auoient de cognoissance de leur faute . . .[147]

and Thomas points out that in such cases 'la cause de leur folie

[142] *Les peintures morales*, i. 202–3.
[143] See below, pp. 139–40.
[144] *Discours*, f. 17ʳ; cf. Montaigne, *Essais*, ed. Thibaudet and Rat, iii. 3, p. 801.
[145] See Grenaille, *L'honneste fille*, Paris, 1639–40, iii. 72–3; Caussin, *La cour sainte*, ii. 295; Le Moyne, *Gallerie*, pp. 254–5; Bernier, *Apologie contre l'Alphabeth*, p. 29; Thomas, *Discours*, f. 16ʳ.
[146] *L'honneste femme*, iii. 23–5.
[147] *La cour sainte*, ii. 296; for the view that learned women tend to be unchaste see Raynaud, *Dissertatio de sobria alterius sexus frequentatione*, Lyons, 1653, p. 459.

n'a pas procedé de sçauoir, mais de leur desreglé vouloir'.[148]
Philippe d'Angoumois in his *Occupation continuelle* of 1618 even
goes so far as to blame women for not undertaking some form
of study, which suggests that other writers were fighting over
ground already won.[149] Finally, Anna Maria van Schurman argues that learning is not only to a certain extent the birthright
of women, but also in some ways a solution to the problem of
leisure, which preoccupies moralists writing to direct women
of easy circumstances.[150]

A final note should be devoted to the attitude of the Jesuits
towards the issue of female education. English writers of the
early seventeenth century arraign their retrogressive and conservative approach to the problem—Dod, for example, writes of 'the
Jesuits . . . which do so straightly tie women to the wheel and
spindle as they do cut them off and bar them from all confer-
ence touching the word of God, as absurd and far unbeseeming to
their sex'[151]—but at first sight, Jesuits in France seem to favour
the cause of female education: the works of Le Moyne, Caussin,
and Loryot all seem to suggest this conclusion. The conservatism referred to by Dod may be detected, however, in all these
authors, but most markedly in Loryot and Le Moyne.[152] There
are no equivalents in France to the Civil War Sects in England
which encouraged women to acquire the art of writing and reading; the only establishments apart from those destined for the

---

[138] *Discours*, f. 16ᵛ; see also Du Bosc, *Nouveau recueil de lettres*, pp. 180–7.

[149] *Occupation continuelle*, Lyons, 1618, pp. 689–91, quoted by Second de Turin,
'Le capucin Philippe d'Angoumois', *XVIIᵉ siècle*, lxxiv (1967), 15. See also Marie
Crous, *Abbregé recherché pour tirer la solution de toutes propositions d'Aritmetique*, Paris,
1641, who speaks of 'tant de sçauans et sages esprits de mon sexe, qui par leurs
labeurs, triomphent en veüe, et au gré de tous les hommes doctes' (Preface, unsigned
leaf).

[150] *Question celebre*, pp. 17–18; see below, pp. 135–41.

[151] Quoted by K. V. Thomas, 'Women and the Civil War Sects', *Past and present*,
xiii (1958), 55.

[152] *Secrets moraux*, p. 494: 'N'est-ce point encores, que la femme n'a iamais esté
bastie de ceste maistresse Artizane Nature, pour seruir de cabinet aux Sciences?
Sa teste n'a pas les Ressorts assés forts pour loger vn si rare thresor; ell[e] est
destinée ailleurs: ses mains sont pour le fuseau et pour l'aiguille, ses mammelles
luy sont remplies de laict pour nourrir les enfants, et non la teste de grand sçauoir,
pour les instruire'; Le Moyne, *Gallerie*, p. 253: 'Quoy que i'aye dit neantmoins, mon
intention n'est pas d'appeler les Femmes au College. Ie n'en veux pas faire des
Licenciées; ny changer en des Astrolabes et en des Spheres leurs aiguilles et leurs
laines. Ie respecte trop les bornes qui nous separent: et ma question [si les femmes
sont capables de la vraye Philosophie] est seulement de ce qu'elles peuuent, et non
pas de ce qu'elles doiuent, en l'estat où les choses ont esté mises . . .'

leisured classes of society were run by charitable teaching orders,[153] and were very limited in aspiration.

An issue of importance to feminist writing in the latter part of the sixteenth century concerns the involvement of women in public life. The regency of Catherine de Médicis, together with examples of female statecraft abroad (notably Elizabeth of England and Mary Queen of Scots), provokes a debate about the capacity of women to govern.[154] Possibly inspired by Aristophanes' *Parliament of women*, Erasmus wrote a somewhat malicious colloquy entitled *Senatulum foeminarum*, in which the establishment of a female senate to assist in the running of public affairs is discussed; later in the century Henri III Estienne's *Carmen de senatulo foeminarum, magnum senatui virorum levamentum atque adiumentum allaturo*, published in 1596, explores the same idea. The myth of the amazons, and historical accounts of other female rulers also provoke comment and discussion.[155]

Connected with this is the debate about Salic law.[156] François Hotman's *Francogallia*, his brother Antoine's *Traité de la loy Salique* of 1593, David Chambers's *Discours de la legitime succession des femmes aux possessions de leurs parens: et du gouvernement des princesses aux empires et royaumes* of 1579, and the anonymous *Sommaire response à l'examen d'un heretique, sur un discours de la loy Salique*, published in 1587, are all indications of the interest shown in this topic. Montaigne also comments on these matters, and although certain passages seem to suggest a liberal attitude towards woman's involvement in public life, it is more common for him to subscribe to traditional beliefs about the intellectual and moral inferiority of women which disqualifies them in his eyes from such activities.[157] His pronouncements do not go unnoticed.[158]

153 See G. Fagniez, *La femme et la société française dans la première moitié du XVIIᵉ siècle*, pp. 1–48.
154 See John Knox, *First blast of the trumpet against the monstrous regiment of women* (1558); François Hotman, *Francogallia* (1573); anon., *Discours merveilleux de la vie actions et deportemens de Catherine de Médicis roine mere* (1579); John Leslie, *De illustrium foeminarum in republica administranda* (1580).
155 See G. Pistorius, 'Vlasta: le thème légendaire des amazones dans les littératures occidentales: première partie: France, Allemagne, Angleterre', *Comité d'études culturelles franco-tchécoslovaques*, ii (1957), 22–53.
156 For a legal discussion of Salic law, see Denis Godefroy, *Praxis civilis*, Frankfurt, 1591, i. 296–7; D. R. Kelley, *Foundations of modern historical scholarship: language, law and history in the French Renaissance*, New York and London, 1970, pp. 199 ff.
157 The relevant passages are to be found in *Essais*, ed. Thibaudet and Rat, iii. 5, p. 875; ii. 9, p. 379; i. 27, p. 177; ii. 8, p. 376; iii. 3, pp. 800–1.   158 See below, pp. 60 n., 61 n.

In the seventeenth century there are historical works which deal with the question of Salic law: Florentin Du Ruau's *Tableau historial des regences*, written in the regency of Marie de Médicis, and d'Auteuil's *Blanche, Infante de Castille*, which appeared in that of Anne of Austria, are representative of these, and it is significant that both writers feel that in order to be able to discuss such a topic, it is first necessary to establish the capacity of women to govern, although in both cases the conclusions reached are too prudent to be described as feminist. Du Ruau speaks of female regents 'surmontant l'infirmité de leur sexe d'vn courage tout heroïque',[159] and d'Auteuil includes among the reasons why women make better regents the following:

Les Femmes doiuent estre naturellement plus portées à la moderation que les hommes; et . . . elles ne peuuent jamais estre si entreprenantes . . . Si quelquefois il paroist qu'elles le deuiennent à proportion en leur Sexe; . . . au moins par la foiblesse de leur constitution, elles n'ont pas toûjours tant de moyens de satisfaire à leurs desseins ambitieux . . .[160]

The tentativeness of these writers is caused in part by the unprepossessing record of female regents in France, which antifeminists do not fail to exploit. Paul Caillet writes in his *Tableau du mariage*:

Nous n'auons pas besoin de feuilleter l'antiquité pour vous produire des exemples insignes de femmes, qui par leurs mauuais deportements ont perdu non seulement leurs maris et leurs familles; mais aussi des Estats florissans et des Prouinces entieres: la France nous seruira de preuue à nostre grand regret, laquelle autrefois durant la regence des femmes, a eu le malheur de se voir à deux doigts pres de sa ruine, et presque enseuelie dans ses calamités.[161]

Even feminist writers such as Grenaille come out against female participation in government,[162] and others merely dismiss the problem without comment; as Anna Maria van Schurman writes:

Il me souuient d'auoir leu dans Vlpian le Iurisconsulte que les femmes doiuent estre exclues de l'administration des charges publiques. Quelque sens que l'on donne à ceste loy, et de quelque costé que l'on la veüille tourner, on peut tirer d'elle vne preuue assez claire que le

159 *Tableau historial des regences*, Paris and Poitiers, 1615, p. 33.
160 *Blanche, Infante de Castille*, Paris, 1644, ii. 3–4.
161 *Tableau du mariage*, p. 223.
162 *Les amours historiques des princes*, Paris, 1642, pp. 773–80.

repos où nous viuons est louable en ce qu'il nous est ordonné par les loix mesmes.[163]

The exclusion of women from public affairs is said by some to be a concession to the 'delicatesse de leur sexe' rather than a judgement of political abilities.[164] It is rare to find pleas for a new dispensation in feminist works, although *Le triomphe des dames* of the beginning of the century contains the following passage:

Ne s'en trouuera-il point vn ou deux [hommes] capables de raison, et qui me confesseront que participantes à la ruine et desolation, nous deuons iustement participer aux honneurs et commoditez de la chose publique? l'auoüe bien que les loix nous en excluent, mais qui les a faites ces loix? sont les hommes, ils doiuent estre recusables en leur cause . . .[165]

The issue of Salic law is much discussed in the reign of Anne of Austria both in imaginative literature and in pamphlets. Several *mazarinades* deal with this subject; outstanding among these is Sandricourt's *Censeur du temps et du monde*, which appeared in 1652. This writer adduces the following reasons why women should not be entrusted with regencies:

1. Cette grande force d'esprit requise à la conduite des Estats n'est pas le partage du Sexe, *Mulierem fortem quis inueniet?* 2. La constance et l'égalité de la Raison parmy le flux et reflux, et les flottantes passions des Sujets et de la Cour leur est difficile à garder, parce qu'elle n'est point appuyée du sçauoir, ny fortifiée de l'experience au maniement des affaires. Elles épousent plustost l'opiniastreté que la Constance: elles se plaisent le plus où elles ont plus de tort: elles s'irritent contre les coups et la contrainte: tu leur feras plustost mordre dans le fer chaud que de les faire demordre d'vne opinion qu'elles ont conçeu[e] en cholere; quoy que dise le Poëte *Varium et mutabile semper foemina.* 3. En vn mot, la Nature, Aristote, la Politique et l'œconomie les

---

[163] *Question celebre*, pp. 10–12. The parallel between the subjection of women in marriage and in the running of the state is often adduced: see P. Ronzeaud, 'La femme au pouvoir ou le monde à l'envers', *XVIIe siècle*, cviii (1975), 9–33.

[164] Juliard, *Amours de l'amant converty*, p. 347: 'ce n'est pas faute d'entendement qui a fait que l'administration de la chose publique a esté deffendue [aux femmes], c'est plustost pour leur euiter vn si grand rompement de teste, pour la delicatesse de leur sexe'; cf. Grenaille, *Honneste mariage*, pp. 329–30. Marie de Gournay tries to explain Salic law in terms of demographic necessity, 'le sexe feminin estant vraysemblablement d'un corps moins propre aux armes, par la necessité du port et nourriture des enfans' (*Égalité des hommes et des femmes*, ed. Schiff, p. 68).

[165] *Le triomphe des dames*, p. 65; cf. Montaigne, *Essais*, ed. Thibaudet and Rat, iii. 5, p. 832.

rangent à l'interieur, et l'experience de trente contre vne dans nostre
estat me fait conclure et les exclure du maniement des affaires.[166]

D'Audiguier du Mazet was commissioned to write a refutation
of this work,[167] in which he examines in the light of 'la loy, la
raison, l'experience et les exemples' the commonly held opinion
that women are unfit to govern. He argues that Salic law is
'heteroclite', and that no equivalent is found in the constitutions
of other European states; furthermore, if women regents have in
the past relied on the judgement of advisers, scarcely a king of
France had not done so, and the fact that these advisers were men
in the case of female regents, whereas kings often chose female
advisers, are significant points in favour of female rule.[168] Sandricourt published in the same year (1652) an attack on his critic,
in which he does little more than restate his views.[169]

Although in 1627, and again in 1643, the right of women to
become regents, not only during royal absences but also during
minorities, was confirmed by royal ordonnances,[170] the consensus of opinion seems to be against any change in Salic law. The
most convincing argument against such change, in the eyes of
d'Audiguier du Mazet, is the fact that 'les hommes, notamment
les françois, portent plus impatiemment le Gouuernement des
Femmes, et . . . les grands entreprennent plus volontiers sur leur
authorité'.[171] In other spheres of public life, it is generally held
that their participation would be nefarious,; this is not only because of their insufficient abilities, as François Poiré points out
in his *Triple couronne de la bien-heureuse Vierge*:

Les Constitutions humaines auec beaucoup de sagesse ont défendu les
barreaux, et les parquets aux femmes, et n'ont permis qu'elles y fussent

---

[166] *Le censeur du temps et du monde*, Paris, 1652, ii. 24; certain parts of this passage are
near-quotations from Montaigne, *Essais*, ed. Thibaudet and Rat, ii. 8, p. 377 ('elles
s'ayment le mieux où elles ont plus de tort'), and ii. 32, p. 708 ('vous [les] eussiez
plustost faict mordre dans le fer chaut que de leur faire desmordre une opinion
qu'elles eussent conçeue en cholere. Elles s'exasperent à l'encontre des coups et de
la contrainte').

[167] For this commission, see C. Moreau, *Bibliographie des mazarinades*, Paris, 1850,
s.v. *Le censeur censuré*.

[168] *Le censeur censuré*, n.p., 1652, pp. 10–13.

[169] See *La response de Sandricourt . . .*, Paris, 1652.

[170] See J. Portemer, *La femme dans la législation royale des deux derniers siècles de
l'Ancien Régime*, p. 9.

[171] *Le censeur censuré*, p. 13; see also d'Aubignac, *La Pucelle*, Paris, 1642, pp. 81–2,
quoted below, p. 192 n.

admises à plaider les causes. Car outre la foiblesse ordinaire de leurs esprits, outre que ce seroit iamais fait auec elles, leurs attraits, et leurs mignardises auroient trop de pouuoir pour fléchir les cœurs, et mouuoir les affections.[172]

Most feminist writers go no further than asserting that women are worthy of public office 'l'occasion et la necessité s'en offrant';[173] this attitude contrasts with their pronouncements about female education, in which they are far more positive. It is possible that they believed that in the one case their arguments for change might not go unnoticed, whereas there was little hope of altering the legal dispensation for women. It is interesting that at the same time as the involvement of women of the *grande noblesse* in political intrigues of all kinds, there is little written in favour of such activity.

From the fifteenth to the seventeenth centuries feminist and anti-feminist literature is embedded in a rhetorical tradition, in which the material at the disposition of writers is circumscribed, but susceptible of new expression and different arrangement. Throughout the period the same arguments are encountered, the same misuse of logic may be detected, there is the same tendency to speculate facetiously about nature and history and to be biased or even mendacious in references to evidence and sources. Underlying the debate between feminists and anti-feminists is the notion of woman as an inferior being which was examined in the first chapter of this book. Such a notion accounts for the similarity in style and tone between anti-feminist and moralistic works which will be noted further below, as well as the defensive stance of feminist writers, who often write in paradoxes, and who resort to polarity (women better than men) rather than parity (women the equals of men). The defensive stance of feminists may also be discerned in their borrowing of form from anti-feminists (for example, L'Escale's *Alphabet* copies that of Antoninus–Trousset) and in the predominance of refutation in feminist writings. There is much repetition and mimetism in the *Querelle des femmes* not only in form, but also in content: the same historical facts and personages are examined in different lights, the same verses of the

---

[172] *La triple couronne de la bien-heureuse Vierge*, Paris, 1630, ii. 215.
[173] Ménier, *La perfection des femmes*, p. 35; see also Du Bosc, *La femme heroïque*, i. 243.

Bible are glossed, traditional proofs of excellence and inferiority are reversed. By the seventeenth century the derivative and repetitive features of the *Querelle* are very much in evidence.

Nevertheless, the social dimensions of the debate do change. The issue of Salic law becomes topical in the regencies of Catherine de Médicis, Marie de Médicis, and Anne of Austria. The question of female education gains prominence as the possibility of its realization becomes more apparent. Social and marital freedoms, as we shall see, are also discussed with increasing vehemence and topicality. The traditional *Querelle des femmes* is, however, not a suitable vehicle for a serious examination of these issues; these are best explored in the context of enlightened moralistic literature which, after 1630, takes over the rôle of disseminating feminist demands. The traditional *Querelle* is revived, it is true, by Trousset's *Alphabet* of 1617; but in the reign of Louis XIII it is in almost every way an anachronism.

III

The New Feminism and the *Femme Forte*, 1630–1650

In this chapter will be examined the new mode of feminist writing which flourishes during the regency of Anne of Austria (1643–52), and its roots in moralistic and Marian writing. The figure of the heroic woman, the *femme forte*, which is characteristic of the new feminist approach of the 1640s, is conceived as an antithesis to the prevailing notion of woman in moralistic writing; this chapter therefore begins with an account of this notion. The *femme forte* is also related to the portrayal of the Virgin Mary, the most exceptional of all women, and this will also be investigated briefly as a prelude to the description of the *femme forte* herself.

There are four broad categories of moralistic writing which concern women at this time. The first comprises the works of 'compilateurs', and consists of collections of miniature biographies of famous women, dealing in passing with the various moral problems suggested by their lives; in the second class there are single biographies of women, usually religious figures; next come the works which deal with the problems of each state of womankind, unmarried, married, and widowed; and finally there are the tracts written against particular female failings, such as vanity and gambling.[1] Moralistic writing in the early seventeenth century is very derivative, both from the Church Fathers and sixteenth-century works by Vives and Erasmus. It has already been noted that in Renaissance moral philosophy, commonplaces drawn from the ancients which stress woman's domestic rôle, her need to be chaste, obedient, and faithful, her unsuitability for any public office, and her tendency to succumb to temptation are frequently encountered. Vives condemns bodily comfort, fashion-

---

[1] e.g. Pierre Juvernay, *Discours particulier contre la vanité des femmes de ce temps*, Paris, 1635; *Le tableau des piperies des femmes mondaines*; Théotime, *Question Chrestienne touchant le jeu . . . sçavoir si une personne addonnee au jeu se peut sauver, et principalement les femmes*, Paris, 1633.

able dress, cosmetics, dancing, dainty foods, and the reading of novels in his Christian woman, and stresses the need for piety, abstinence, and constant work. Almost all moralists of this period subscribe to the low assessment of the female sex implied in these prescriptions, and it is difficult to see how their view can be distinguished from the following account of typical anti-feminist opinions given by Nicolas Angenoust in 1629:

Ce sont les reproches et blasphemes ordinaires en la bouche de nos haineurs . . . Et quoy (diront-ils) pourroit-on excuser [les femmes] de legereté et inconstance? Chacun ne sçait-il pas que les femmes procedent auec autant de fragilité en leurs opinions et sentences que les enfans, qui considerera l'infirmité de leur sexe? Elles veulent et ne veulent, à mesme temps également toutes choses, prennent autant de formes que Prothée et de couleurs que le Cameleon. Et d'où procede que les enfans se courroucent et hayssent pour legeres occasions, sinon pour autant qu'ils ont l'esprit foible, par lequel ils sont gouuernez? N'est-ce pas l'opinion tenue des Philosophes que la femme n'est qu'vn defaut de l'homme? Que l'esprit de la femme est inepte et incapable des choses bonnes, et prompt à conceuoir les mauuaises, le tout à cause du defaut et priuation, qui semble auoir ie ne sçay quoy de connexe auec le naturel de la femme? Ces animaux iurez de leurs semblables ont dit, que les femmes se delectent plus que les hommes dans l'ornement exterieur de leur corps, à raison que leur nature estant du tout imparfaicte, elles s'estudient plus volontiers à suppléer le defaut de leur condition par le moyen de cet artifice . . . Ils passent plus outre, et disent qu'à cause de l'infirmité et imbecillité de leur sexe, les loix les ont declarées incapables et inhabiles pour aucunes charges ciuiles, moins aussi d'interuenir, ou postuler en iugement pour quelque personne que ce soit, et les mettent au rang des impuberes . . .[2]

For all that Angenoust seems to identify the anti-feminist and moralistic attitudes to woman, moralists claim to set out to be impartial to her: both Jean-Baptiste de Glen and Pierre Crespet speak of 'ce sexe autant digne de louange, quand il suit la vertu; comme il merite de vitupere, quand il s'en desuoye',[3] and the Jesuit Nicolas Caussin writing of the dangers of too high praise and too severe criticism, declares:

Ie suis bien obligé à ma profession, de ce qu'elle m'esloigne de ces deux écueils, où tant de vaisseaux font naufrage. S'il faut blasmer [les

[2] *Paranymphe des dames*, pp. 2–5; cf. Trousset, *Alphabet*, pp. 75–6.
[3] *Du debvoir des filles*, Liège, 1597, p. 1; *Le jardin de plaisir et recreation spirituelle*, Lyons, 1598, i. 500ᵛ.

femmes], ie feray comme celuy qui tua le serpent, sans toucher au corps de son fils, lequel estoit entortillé dans ses replis, ie frapperay le vice, sans médire du sexe, et s'il les faut louer, ie les regarderay comme des idées de Platon, qui n'ont rien de commun auec la matiere.[4]

None the less, it can hardly be said that even the most enlightened of these moralists avoid reference to the fragile basis of virtue in womankind, and in their condemnations they are sometimes even more severe than Angenoust's typical anti-feminist: Le sieur de Vaux writes the following admonition to his reader on the subject of woman:

Remarque le trouble de mille diuerses passions qui l'agitent, la foiblesse du sexe, son inconstance, et son infidelité: n'oublie pas ses tromperies, ses malices, ses cruautez: adiouste à cela, les fards et les artifices, dont les plus naïues cachent leurs vices et leurs defauts.

Leur auarice insatiable, et leurs desirs effrenez, te deuroient donner de la crainte: et ce qui charme tes sens, ayant si peu de durée, te deuroit estre à mespris . . . embrasse donc ceste charongne viuante, ce meslange de tant de deffauts, cet abbregé de toutes les saletez imaginables . . .[5]

Valladier talks of 'le sexe feminin infiniment fragile, craintif, superstitieux, ignorant et lascif';[6] Caussin asserts that 'la complexion d'vn corps [comme celuy d'vne femme] peut distiller en l'ame des inconstances, des infirmitez, et des passions qui prendroient bien de l'essor si elles ne seroient reprimees par la pieté et par la raison',[7] and even Du Bosc makes reference to the fragile basis of virtue in women.[8] L'Archevesque even goes so far as to justify the fact that woman is kept in tutelage throughout her life, 'car si elle chemine seulette, selon ses desirs naturels, la raison et la bien seance la quitteront aussi tost.'[9]

At the base of this distrust of woman's nature lies the assumption that, from the outset, the female sex has a more difficult task in controlling passion because the world, the flesh, and the devil have a greater hold over women than over men. Most writers explain this in terms of their physical constitution, but Le Moyne and others prefer to believe that it is also due to the lack of intel-

[4] *La cour sainte,* ii. 226–7; see also Le Moyne, *Gallerie,* p. 11.
[5] *La Magdeleine au desert,* Paris, 1629, pp. 105–7.
[6] *La sainte philosophie de l'ame,* p. 655.
[7] *La cour sainte,* ii. 251.
[8] *L'honneste femme,* iii. 188; ii. 180; iii. 23–5, quoted above, p. 56.
[9] *Les grandeurs de la mere de Dieu,* p. 418.

lectual training in the right subjects, and most especially in moral
philosophy:

> La Philosophie Morale nous a esté donnée pour gouuerner nos
> Passions; pour distinguer nos deuoirs et nos offices; pour nous ap-
> prendre les exercicés de la Vertu; pour nous conduire comme par la
> main à la Beatitude. Et les Passions des Femmes n'ont-elles pas be-
> soin de gouuernantes aussi bien que les nostres? Ne peuuent-elles se
> méprendre en leurs offices et en leurs deuoirs? Sont-elles nées si in-
> struites et si parfaites, qu'elles puissent apprendre la Vertu sans leçon
> et sans methode? Sont-elles si heureuses qu'elles puissent arriuer à la
> Beatitude de leur seule adresse et sans guide?[10]

Arising out of this belief in the smaller capacity in women for
virtue, whatever its causes, there is the paradox of strength in
weakness to which many writers refer,[11] and which, in the case of
the *femme forte*, encompasses all the failings traditionally associated
with women. This paradox is most explicit in the following
passage from L'Archevesque's *Grandeurs de la mere de Dieu*:

> Ouy la vertu d'vne femme, est plus agreable à Dieu, que n'est pas celle
> des hommes: et la raison qui appuye cette hardie proposition, et l'autho-
> rité qui la fonde, c'est que la vertu se perfectionne, et se rend tres-
> agreable parmy les infirmitez, et les plus grandes contradictions.
> D'autant donc que le sexe feminin est naturellement infirme, foiblet,
> mol et delicat, en cas qu'il s'efforce et triomphe de ses appetits naturels,
> pour acquerir la vertu, sans doute qu'il sera preferable à tous ceux qui
> sans combatre, ou qui sans faire de si grands efforts, paruiendront au
> mesme but, et rapporteront vn mesme prix.[12]

Even Trousset pays tribute to the 'femmes masles' who overcome 'l'inclination de leur sexe' and act with courage and resolution.[13]

While accusing women of the vices mentioned by Angenoust—
vanity, lubricity, inconstancy, indolence, deceit, stubbornness—
moralists also accord to them the qualities which, like their vices,

---

[10] *Gallerie*, p. 254.
[11] Antoine de Nervèze, *La guide des courtisans*, Paris, 1606, f. 105^{r-v}; Dinet,
Theatre françois, ii. 4; Grenaille, *L'honneste fille*, ii. 329; Angenoust, *Paranymphe des
dames*, p. 271; Couvay, *L'honneste maistresse*, Paris, 1654, p. 198.
[12] *Les grandeurs de la mere de Dieu*, p. 569. L'Archevesque acknowledges Abelard
as the source of this passage.
[13] *Alphabet*, p. 333; but cf. p. 334, where Trousset attacks the 'hommasse'.

result from their physical constitution: modesty, clemency, compassion, charity.[14] In this, the position of these writers is different from that of anti-feminists, but although they show more goodwill towards women and are less blatant in their prejudices, the survival in their writings of denunciations of world, flesh, and women, and the fact that, albeit addressed to women, their works are in fact written with a masculine bias, make them appear more retrogressive than those of the adversaries of womankind.

Moralists set out also to give practical advice to women on social behaviour, and here their major preoccupations are infidelity, idleness, and the cult of beauty. The question of infidelity or inconstancy in women had been the subject of a debate at the end of the sixteenth century between *libertin* writers and moralists; following a tradition which may be traced back to Ovid, writers discuss whether, as women are thought to be lustful and changeable by nature, it is unreasonable to expect them to abide by an ethical standard of fidelity which is so alien to their desires. *Libertins* argue that a woman's honour must be preserved intact, as this is necessary for the peace of mind of her husband and the stability of society as a whole; but that her honour is no more than her reputation, and does not lie in the practice of chastity and fidelity.[15] It is natural that moralists should be opposed to this devaluation of the concept of honour in the female sex. Antoine Lemaistre declares in one of his *Plaidoyers* that 'comme Aristote dit elegamment qu'vn homme n'est pas assez genereux lors qu'il n'a que le courage d'vne femme, on peut dire aussi qu'vne fille ou

---

[14] Loryot, *Les secrets moraux*, p. 89: 'ce sexe feminin tant richement doüé de tres-belles parties, et du corps, et de l'ame, par sa beauté, sa pudeur, sa modestie, sa ciuilité, honnesteté, retenuë, prudence, frugalité, chasteté'; cf. also *Fleurs des secrets moraux*, p. 20; Gerzan, *Le triomphe des dames*, p. 210; Du Bosc, *L'honneste femme*, iii. 526–7, where St. Francis of Sales's praise of female charity is quoted; *Première centurie des questions traitees ez conferences du Bureau d'Adresse*, Paris, 1634, p. 205.

[15] The immediate source of this debate seems to have been Marie de Romieu's translation of Alessandro Piccolomini's *Dialogo della bella creanza delle donne*, entitled *Instruction pour les jeunes dames* (1573; reprinted in 1579, 1607, and 1612). Other important contributions are the *Exhortation aux dames vertueuses, en laquelle est demonstré le vray poinct d'honneur*, possibly by Jean Juliard (1596 or 1597); Adrien Turnèbe, *Discours contre un petit traicté intitulé Exhortation aux dames vertueuses* (1598); anon., *Harangue faicte en la defense de l'inconstance* (1598); anon., *Apologie de la constance* (1598); Pierre de Brinon, *Le triomphe des dames* (1599). For a fuller discussion of this debate, see E. Courbet, *La Macette du sieur de l'Espine*, Paris, 1875, Introduction, and my Oxford D.Phil. thesis, 'Feminism and literature in France 1610–52' (1971), pp. 46–53.

vne femme n'est pas assez chaste si elle n'a que la chasteté d'vn homme';[16] this distinction between dominant male and female virtues has already been encountered in Tasso's discussion of female virtue, and is very relevant to the distinction between the heroic woman and her sex as a whole.

Modesty is seen by moralists as the most effective guardian of chastity; its most dangerous enemies are sensuality, ambition, and avarice. Du Bosc, La Mothe Le Vayer, Henri du Lisdam, Claude Maillard, and Paul Caillet all specify these three vices;[17] their common source seems to be a verse in the first Epistle General of John.[18] In the figure of the *femme forte*, the counter-virtues of continence, stoic apathy, and liberality are stressed; again there is an opposition to be detected between the female sex as a whole, in which these vices are thought to be prevalent, and the *femme forte*.

Idleness, too, is a preoccupation of moralists. Du Bosc, in describing its effects on the female character, points to some of the fundamental differences between the *femme forte* and women in general:

La negligence que l'Oisiueté fait naistre, a pour compagnes ordinaires, l'irresolution et l'inconstance. Celles qui en sont infectées, n'ont pas si tost vn dessein, qu'elles le changent: Elles iettent beaucoup de fondements mais elles n'acheuent point d'edifices. Elles n'ont point de resolutions fermes: elles ne disent pas ie veux, mais ie voudrois. Leur volonté tremble sans cesse. Elle n'a point de desirs, mais seulement des souhaits. Elle peuuent deliberer, mais non pas resoudre.[19]

Le Moyne's opposition of the *femme forte* and the seventeenth-century leisured lady in his 'Ode à la Femme Forte' is even more explicit:

> Il se voit de molles Poupées
> Qu'vn masque, vne iuppe, vn miroir,
> Tient du matin iusques au soir,
> Inutilement occupées.

[16] *Les plaidoyez et harangues*, Paris, 1657, p. 293. This idea is taken from Aristotle, *Politics*, iii. 3; see also above, p. 19.

[17] Du Bosc, *L'honneste femme*, iii. 407; La Mothe Le Vayer, *Quatre autres dialogues*, p. 444; Du Lisdam, *L'Ambition, la volupté et l'avarice*, Lyons, 1613; Maillard, *Le bon mariage*, Chs. 13–15; Caillet, *Tableau du mariage*, chs. 2–3.

[18] 1 John 2: 16 ('omne quod est in mundo, concupiscentia carnis est, et concupiscentia oculorum, et superbia vitae').

[19] *L'honneste femme*, iii. 188–9.

Leur esprit se perd dans vn gan;
Il s'embarasse d'vn ruban;
Du bout de leurs cheueux sa sphere est limitée.
Leur plus haute science est le tour d'vn collet;
Toute leur vie est vuide; et leur teste éuentée,
Se remplit d'vne mouche et d'vn point de filet . . .

Loin de ces molles Affetées,
La Femme Forte a ses employs:
Sur les deuoirs et sur les loix,
Ses actions sont concertées.
Tranquille sans oysiueté,
Actiue auec serenité,
Elle sçait allier le Labeur et les Graces.
Et ressemble aux porteurs des celestes flambeaux,
Qui font sans s'abaisser les choses les plus basses;
Qui trauaillent tousiours, et qui sont tousiours beaux.[20]

Beauty is also consistently attacked by moralists as a false
value. Its cult seems in their eyes to be the cause of many of the
vices which they castigate most severely in women. The un-
pleasant physiological realities which constitute beauty are dwelt
upon in several moralistic works,[21] and its ephemerality is everywhere stressed.[22] If beauty itself is criticized, the affectation of
beauty is all the more decried: cosmetics and ornaments, extravagant and unseemly dress all come under heavy attack.[23] It is
perhaps significant that a group of tracts was published in the
1630s condemning female dress and deportment, especially in
church; one writer speaks of a general directive to bishops on

[20] *Gallerie*, ĩi2–3. See also Théotime, *Question Chrestienne touchant le jeu*, pp. 2–3, for
a condemnation of the idleness of seventeenth-century leisured ladies.
[21] See Puget de la Serre, *L'entretien des bons esprits sur les vanitez du monde*, Rouen,
1631, pp. 491–2: 'ceste taille n'est riche qu'en Sapins. Ces cheueux cendrez, ou
noirs, ne sont que les racines à landes, et des forests à poulx. Ce front large et poly,
c'est vn miroir de Cimitiere; car les rides sont autant de chemins qui conduisent au
Tombeau . . . Ces yeux noirs ou bleux sont deux lanternes pleines de suif de chan-
delle, ie veux dire de chassie. Cét en-bon-point, et ce tein deslié, n'est autre chose
qu'vn peu de graisse paistrie delicatement auec le sang . . .'; see also *Le tableau des
piperies des femmes mondaines*, ff. 11ᵛ–22ᵛ.
[22] See Hilarion de Coste, *Les eloges et vies des reynes*, p. 206: 'la vertu est la plus
precieuse bague, la plus riche perle, le vray Soleil et l'ornement des dames, non la
beauté dont elles font tant de cas . . . Car la beauté est vaine et trompeuse: elle
n'est qu'vne qualité passagere qui ne peut subsister, que dans son changement
continuel . . .'
[23] See Jean Polman, *Le chancre ou couvre-sein feminin*, Douai, 1635: Juvernay,
Discours particulier; *Le tableau des piperies des femmes mondaines*.

these subjects, dated 1635.[24] More enlightened moralists, basing themselves on the attitudes of St. Francis of Sales, take a less rigorous standpoint on these issues, and attempt to rehabilitate reasonable use of cosmetics and fashionable dress, but they are very much in a minority.[25] It does not seem to be a generally held opinion among moralistic writers that devoutness is compatible with a proper enjoyment of things of this life.

Moralistic writing at this time is marked by a deep distrust of woman's nature, a belief in her tendency to err, coupled with a critical attitude to her behaviour in society and to her preference of the pleasures of this world to the task of preparing for the next. Because of this low assessment of woman, the qualities of energy, resoluteness, constancy, liberality, to name but a few, take on a paradoxical status when encountered in her, and evoke wonderment. This reaction is based on an assumption of female weakness, which is embodied in moralistic literature; without such a contrast, the figure of the *femme forte* would lose much of its force.

There was a remarkable flourishing of Marian literature after the Council of Trent throughout Catholic Europe; Marracci's bibliography of some three thousand works, published in Rome in 1648, bears ample witness to this. France played an important part in this renaissance, as might be expected from the intense mystical activity prevalent in the country from the end of the sixteenth century to the middle of the seventeenth. Even the vow of Louis XIII, immortalized in the unprepossessing painting by Ingres, may have had some connection with post-tridentine Marianism, although it is no doubt as much a reflection of personal piety as it is of the atmosphere of the age.

The feminism of Marian literature goes beyond the simple statement that Our Lady is 'l'honneur du sexe féminin'. That the female sex is known as 'le sexe dévot' has already been mentioned; in this literature the special relationship of Christ to womankind is described and examined. L'Archevesque is explicit about this in his *Grandeurs de la mere de Dieu*:

Iesus conceu d'vne Mere sans Pere, semble plus appartenir aux femmes de ce costé-là, qu'il ne fait aux hommes desquels il n'est pas conceu: en suitte de quoy il y a eu plus de correspondence de nature, d'humeur

---

[24] See Polman, *Chancre*, pp. 48–53; also H. P. Salomon, *Tartuffe devant l'opinion française*, Paris, 1962, p. 21.   [25] See Du Bosc, *L'honneste femme*, i. 225.

et de sympathie entre luy et ce sexe delicat, qu'entre luy et tous les
hommes . . . Quand les hommes prennent les armes, les pauures
femmes se prennent aux larmes : et le peuple criant qu'il meure, elles
crient de ce qu'on le fait mourir . . . Les hommes l'attachent à vne
Croix, fichants quatre cloux dans ses membres ; et les femmes retirent
ces cloux, les baisent auec vne grande tendresse, les font adorer à leurs
sens, et les portent dans leur sein tout proche de leur pauure coeur
nauré et déchiré de douleur . . . O difference qui fait bien voir que
Nostre Seigneur fut plus aux femmes, par sentiment de pieté et par
sympathie naturelle qu'aux hommes ! Femmes, on vous pouuoit bien
dire à toutes : que Iesus estoit vostre fils, et que vous estiez sa pieuse
Mere.[26]

In a similar vein, Du Bosc remarks that 'on vit trois Maries sous
la Croix, où il n'y auoit qu'vn Disciple'.[27]

The equation that the sin of Eve is balanced by the act of
redemption, in which the Virgin Mary was instrumental, is produced not only in Marian literature, but also by Du Ruau in his
work about female regencies,[28] and Adrien Turnèbe the Younger
in his *Response à un curieux, demandant pourquoy les hommes s'assubiet-
tissent aux femmes*.[29] It is mentioned also in Guerry's *Traicté de
l'excellence du sexe fœminin et des prerogatives de la mere de Dieu* of
1635, the very title of which illustrates the connection between
feminism and the Virgin Mary. When, in the same year, Laurens
Le Peletier writes a litany of her qualities and makes her representative of her sex, he indicates how far the association of feminism
with this cult may be taken :

Par femme toute Iustice est née, par qui est tout rendu, tout donné, que
par femme ? Par qui est le Ciel ouuert, par femme ? par qui vient tout
bien, par femme ? Qui est-ce qui n'a eu, apporté, et receu don de femme ?
Qui est-ce qui a plus seruy au bien de tout le monde que la femme.
Les Anges du Ciel ont par la Vierge Marie receu le fils de Dieu in-
carné, les hommes l'ont receu pour Dieu, Sauueur et Redempteur.

En liberalité, la femme surmonte toutes autres creatures, quand la

---

[26] *Grandeurs de la mere de Dieu*, pp. 479–80.

[27] *L'honneste femme*, i. 214 ; another reflection of this theme is found in the etching
by Jacques Bellange known as 'Les trois Maries' (see Anthony Blunt, *Art and
architecture in France, 1500–1700*, London, 1953, pl. 84).

[28] *Tableau historial des regences*, p. 13.

[29] *Response à un curieux*, Rouen, 1598, 6ʳ : 'car s'il est ainsi que ce monde n'aye
esté creé que pour l'amour de la femme, conserué qu'à cause de la femme, et racheté
en partie que par le moyen de la femme ? Ie penseray vous auoir donné vne raison
suffisante, pourquoy l'homme s'assubietit à la femme.'

Vierge Marie nous a donné le fils de Dieu eternel, reparateur du genre
humain, qui contient toute valeur . . .
    Par femme la Religion Chrestienne est au monde, car de la Vierge
Marie nasquit Iesus-Christ . . . La femme est donc mere de toute
Religion, fontaine de toute deuotion . . .[30]

This honour which accrues to the female sex because of the excellence of Our Lady is, however, coupled with duties, as L'Archevesque and others point out;[31] indeed, Poiré manages to deduce
from the perfections of the Virgin that noblewomen should
breast-feed their offspring.[32]
    The paradox of strength in weakness, of virtue in the female
sex, which has already been noted in the context of moralistic
literature, is a feature also of Marian writing; both Poiré and
L'Archevesque have passages in which the paradox is ampli-
fied,[33] and Guerry writes in his *Traicté*:

En somme ce Sexe a produit au Seigneur des martyres innumerables,
lesquelles et les faits heroïques de tant de Dames d'honneur et hault
courage, comme la mere des Machabées et infinies autres font cognoistre, qu'elles ont concurrence auec les hommes en toutes facultez
d'esprit, vertus morales et cardinales, *virtutes non sex[s]u, sed animo
iudicande, idem fragilior sexus vincit seculum* c'est à dire les vertus ne sont
à juger selon le sexe, mais selon l'ame, le sexe le plus fragile a vaincu
le siecle, l'Eglise l'appelle le sexe deuot, Dieu a choisi la foiblesse pour
confondre la force.[34]

It is significant here that not only are the sexes said to be equal
in virtue, but that female virtue is said to be more striking than
that of man because of the paradox of *foiblesse* and *force*; the
writer allows himself the indulgence of marvelling at moral
strength in the weaker vessel, woman, while at the same time
asserting that sex is no indicator of moral strength. This double

---

[30] *De la chasteté*, pp. 63–4.
[31] See *Les grandeurs de la mere de Dieu*, pp. 469–70.
[32] *Triple couronne*, ii. 41.
[33] *Triple couronne*, ii. 156, quoted below, p. 259; *Les grandeurs de la mere de Dieu*,
quoted above, p. 67.
[34] *Traicté de l'excellence du sexe fœminin*, Paris, 1635, pp. 23–4. The quotation is
attributed in the margin to Jerome; it is in fact a conflation of Jerome (*Epistola
cxxii, PL* xxii. 1016) and Gregory Nazianzenus (*Oratio in laudem sororis suae Gorgo-
niae, PG* xxxv. 806), quoted not from these authors but from Rhodiginus's *Lectiones
antiquae*, xiii. 33, col. 718.

standard or vision, and this emphasis on the paradoxical nature
of virtue in women are fundamental to the new feminism of the
regency of Anne of Austria; but it is not the only characteristic
which Marian literature shares with the writings about the *femme
forte*. The comparison of the Virgin Mary to a warrior is not
uncommon, and stresses the heroic, quasi-military status of Our
Lady in this literature.[35] Furthermore, some theologians see the
depiction of the *femme forte* in the Book of Proverbs as a pre-
figuration of the Virgin herself.[36]

The opening paragraph of Plutarch's *Mulierum virtutes*, which is
the inspiration of much feminist writing, concerns the public
reputation and fame of virtuous women. Where Thucydides
argues that a good woman's name does not pass beyond the
door of her own house, Plutarch, after Gorgias, strongly advocates the public recognition of female virtue, which, in his eyes,
is equal to that of men. From Boccaccio to Du Bosc, feminist
writers show the same concern for the 'gloire des femmes',[37] and
in nearly every case where the writer is male, the tract is dedicated
to a woman, whose prestige the author is most concerned to
promote.

This literature of prestige, which is especially prevalent during
the regency of Anne of Austria, is also related to the perennial
debate about the reasons for the homage paid by men to women.
This is often seen to be incomprehensible, as man occupies the
dominant place in both public and private life. The traditional
explanations—usually based on the conviction that this homage
is an expression of the protection of the weak by the strong, or
a cult of woman in the figure of the 'dame'—were to some extent
replaced in the sixteenth century by the neo-Platonist belief that
the adoration of woman as the object of greatest visible beauty is
a stage towards the achievement of divine love. In the seventeenth
century the debate shifted to more mundane considerations. In
Loryot's *Secrets moraux*, the essay 'Pourquoy le sexe feminin est

[35] See Poiré, *Triple couronne*, ii. 156; Antoine de Balinghem wrote a tract entitled
La toute-puissante guerrière représentée en la personne de la sacrée Vierge Marie, Douai,
1625.
[36] e.g. François Le Roy, *Livre de la femme forte et vertueuse*, Paris, n.d. (*c.* 1500).
[37] See Scudéry, *Les femmes illustres*, i, ã3ʳ⁻ᵛ, and Antoine de Nervèze's 'Avertissement aux jeunes dames', in *La guide des courtisans*, f. 114, for examples of this preoccupation.

fort honoré de l'homme' contains only uncomplimentary reasons, of which the following is representative:

Bien que la femme n'ait pas tousiours l'excellence, qui merite tant d'honneur, comme les hommes luy en font neantmoins, parce que ce sexe est necessaire à l'entretien du genre humain, quoy que d'ailleurs fort incommode: ils ont jugé le deuoir entretenir le plus accortement qu'ils pouuoient, achetant la paix et son secours, au prix de beaucoup d'honneur.[38]

Marguerite de Valois's answer to this essay is characteristically feminist:

Ie ne puis supporter le mespris où vous mettez [mon sexe], voulant qu'il soit honoré de l'homme pour son infirmité et foiblesse; vous me pardonnerez si ie vous dis, que l'infirmité et foiblesse n'engendrent point l'honneur, mais le mespris et la pitié. Et qu'il y a bien plus d'apparence, que les femmes soient honorees des hommes pour leurs excellences.[39]

Nicolas Faret in his *Honneste homme* of 1630 provides perhaps the most complete account of the feminist attitude in this debate:

Et certes ce n'est pas seulement pour les raisons que l'on allegue d'ordinaire, que les femmes sont honorées, comme elles sont, des honnestes gens. Car si ce n'estoit, comme l'on dict, que pour le plaisir que l'on reçoit d'elles, que l'on leur defere tant, les Brutaux seroient ceux qui en feroient le plus d'estat. Si ce n'estoit aussi qu'en consideration de ce qu'elles conservent nostre espece, il n'y auroit guere, que les Philosophes, et ceux qui meditent sur les principes, et les causes universelles des choses, qui les estimeroient; ou bien encore si ce n'estoit que pour reconnoistre la grande peine qu'elles ont de nous porter neuf mois dans leur ventre, de nous mettre au jour, de nourrir et de supporter les defauts de nostre enfance, et quelquefois de tous nos âges, il semble que nous ne devrions les hommages que nous rendent à tout leur sexe, qu'à nos meres particulierement . . . Mais c'est leur vertu que nous respectons, laquelle a d'autant plus de charmes pour se faire admirer, qu'elle est accompagnée des Graces, et comme esclairée des rayons de la Beauté. En effect elle n'est en rien differente de celle des hommes; et Plutarque a raison de s'opiniastrer qu'elle est toute la mesme, et de la prouver, comme il fait, par un grand nombre d'exemples . . .[40]

---

[38] *Secrets moraux*, p. 67; cf. Grenaille, *Amours historiques des princes*, p. 775.

[39] *Fleurs des secrets moraux*, dI[r–v].

[40] *L'honneste homme*, ed. M. Magendie, Paris, 1925, pp. 96–7. Elsewhere, however, Faret writes in a more cynical vein that female demands for homage proceed from women's sense of inferiority, and is an attempt to re-establish equal terms with men (p. 95; cf. *Première centurie des question traitees ez conferences du Bureau d'Adresse*, p. 204).

The brilliant early years of the regency of Anne of Austria were preceded by a decade which saw a steady rise in the prestige of woman. The many writings relating to social behaviour,[41] the power of the salons, and especially of the Hôtel de Rambouillet, the charitable activities of women,[42] inspired by the work of St. Francis of Sales and his successors, create together an atmosphere in which feminism could not but flourish. Even moralistic literature became largely detached from its austere tradition, and where previously dire pictures of vice were found, now there were depictions of virtues, often associated with contemporary figures: both Sébastien de Senlis in his *Epistres morales* (1645) and Rangouze in his *Lettres panegyriques* (1648–50) eulogize female members of the *grande noblesse* in the most inappropriate terms, for the most implausible virtues.[43] The political influence of women, which reaches its apogee during the Fronde,[44] further contributes to the feminism of the regency, which was prepared for by the writings about homage paid to women, discussed above.

An account of the works published between 1640 and 1647 indicates the volume and importance of writing in honour of women. In 1640 Grenaille published (among other things) two parts of his *Honneste fille*, an *Honneste mariage*, a *Bibliothèque des dames*, and an *Honneste veuve*, to which he added in the following year a work entitled *Les plaisirs des dames*. Also in 1641 appeared Machon's *Discours ou sermon apologetique en faveur des femmes*. In 1642 Dinet's *Theatre françois, des seigneurs et dames illustres*, Grenaille's *Nouveau recueil de lettres des dames tant anciennes que modernes*, a reprint of Du Bosc's *Nouveau recueil de lettres des dames de ce temps* (first published in 1635), which is quite different from Grenaille's work, the first part of Scudéry's *Femmes illustres*, and

---

[41] For a detailed study of these, see below, pp. 119–41.

[42] See Fagniez, *La femme et la société française*, pp. 267–397; also contemporary works, such as Gerzan, *Le triomphe des dames*, p. 46.

[43] Hyperbole is very common in feminist works in discussing the virtues of contemporaries; e.g. Gerzan's praise of chastity in Frenchwomen (*Le triomphe des dames*, pp. 63–4): 'sans sortir de la France, ny rechercher les siecles passez, nous pouuons dire à nostre auantage, que nos *Princesses*, nos *Filles*, et nos *Dames* françoises possedent cette vertu en vn si haut degré de perfection, que les anciennes Dames Romaines, de qui les Histoires parlent auec tant d'admiration, ny les *Muzes*, ny les *Vestalles*, ny les *Druydes*, ny les *Sibilles*, n'ont iamais eu nul auantage en cela sur elles.'

[44] See V. Du Bled, *La société française du XVIe au XXe siècle*, iii. 213–58; iv. 203–45.

Suzanne de Nervèze's *Apologie en faveur des femmes* in her *Œuvres spirituelles et morales* were all published. In 1643 appeared perhaps the most virulently feminist work to be published at this time, entitled *La femme genereuse qui monstre que son sexe est plus noble, meilleur politique, plus vaillant, plus sçavant, plus vertueux, et plus œconome que celuy des hommes,* as well as Pierre de Marcassus's *Reine des femmes,*[45] Grenaille's *Galerie des dames illustres,*[46] and a reprint of Du Bosc's *Honneste femme* (first published 1632–6). In 1644 were published the second part of Scudéry's *Femmes illustres,* Puget de la Serre's *Portrait de la reyne,* d'Auteuil's *Blanche de Castille,* and Méat's *Fille heroïque.* In the following year were printed Puget de la Serre's *Temple de la gloire contenant les éloges historiques de treize Annes royales et princesses de France,*[47] le chevalier de L'Hermite's *Princesse heroïque,* and Du Bosc's *Femme heroïque.* Gerzan's *Triomphe des dames* and the *Question celebre, s'il est necessaire, ou non, que les filles soient sçavantes* were published in 1646, and in 1647 appeared Le Moyne's *Gallerie des femmes fortes* as well as a republication of Hilarion de Coste's *Eloges et vies des reynes, princesses, dames et demoiselles* (first printed in 1630). It is noteworthy that at least six of these tracts (together with Sébastien de Senlis's *Epistres morales* and Suzanne de Nervèze's *Genereux mouvemens d'une dame heroïque et pieuse* of 1644) are dedicated to Anne of Austria,[48] and several others to the Grande Mademoiselle.[49]

Although these works deal with historical figures for the most part, there are many references to contemporary or near-contemporary heroines. Dubuisson-Aubenay refers frequently to the *Gazette de Paris,* in which there are many articles concerning heroic deeds by women, and there are also strikingly feminist *mazarinades.*[50] The epithets *généreux, héroïque, illustre, fort* abound

[45] Cited in J. Gay, *Bibliographie des ouvrages relatifs au mariage, aux femmes et à l'amour,* Paris, 1870, s.v. *Reine des femmes.*

[46] Cited in Gay (revised edn., Paris, 1897, ii. 382); possibly a translation of Francesco Pona's *Galeria delle donne celebri,* Rome, 1625.

[47] Cited in Ungherini, *Manuel de bibliographie biographique et d'iconographie des femmes célèbres,* s.v. Anne d'Autriche. Puget de la Serre also wrote *L'histoire et les portraits des imperatrices, des reynes, et des princesses de l'auguste maison d'Austriche, qui ont porté le nom d'Anne* (1648).

[48] viz. *La femme genereuse, La reine des femmes, Le portrait de la reyne, Blanche de Castille, La femme heroïque* (vol. 1 only), *La gallerie des femmes fortes.*

[49] viz. *L'honneste fille* (vol. 1 only), *Le triomphe des dames, Question celebre . . .*

[50] e.g. *L'amazone françoise au secours des Parisiens,* Paris, 1649; *L'illustre conquerante ou la genereuse constance de Madame de Chevreuse,* Paris, 1649.

in titles and texts; these writings express a heightened concept of virtue in women, and an aesthetic delight in the image of the strong, independent female. Coupled with this there is often an implied, if not outspoken, devaluation and denigration of man; the most striking examples of this are found in *La femme genereuse*:

Ayant appris, que toutes les choses naturelles aspirent à ce qui est le plus parfait, i'ay pensé que les femmes sont plus parfaites que les hommes, puis que ceux-cy les prennent pour Iuges, et recherchent si ambitieusement leur approbation . . . Ce qui m'a confirmée en l'opinion que les hommes s'estiment en leur facile conscience beaucoup moins que nous. C'est la remarque ordinaire que ie fais, que mesme leur propre figure leur desplaist; et qu'ils affectent par vne molle et honteuse diligence d'auoir le visage pareil aux nostres. Ils s'ostent la barbe, qui leur donne vne mine austere, et nous retient en crainte d'eux. Ils portent les cheueux longs comme les femmes, pour preparer peu à peu les esprits à les tenir pour femmes; ce qui semble estre le plus hault poinct de leur ambition. Et mesme pour donner plus d'esclat à la blancheur feminine qu'ils affectent d'auoir, ou de faire paroistre sur leur visage, ils y appliquent (comme nous faisons) des mousches et des assassins, esperans de passer pour femmes par ces hypocrites emplastres.[51]

The paradoxical nature of virtue in women, which has been noted as a feature of moralistic writing, is stressed with even greater emphasis in the feminist works of the regency. Again *La femme genereuse* contains an excellent example:

Tousiours ma preuue subsistera, qui fera voir que la femme auec double gloire, est plus genereuse que l'homme, puis qu'elle l'est effectiuement; et que ce n'est pas de nature, mais d'acquisition et de vertu. Et l'homme au contraire, se verifiera estre auec vne double infamie moins courageux qu'elle, puis que pouuant par nature l'estre plus, il se trouue l'estre moins, par lascheté et par foiblesse de cœur, qui s'est amoly dans le vice, et y a enerué ses forces.[52]

Gabriel Gilbert's *Panegyrique des dames* of 1650 provides a different explanation for the superiority of female virtue:

Ie ne puis que ie n'admire icy le soin que la Sagesse diuine a eu de tous les deux sexes, comme les hommes se portent difficilement aux choses honnestes, elle a donné aux femmes la Beauté et la Vertu, elle a mis la

---

[51] *La femme genereuse*, pp. 3–5; see also Gerzan, *Le triomphe des dames*, pp. 215–16.
[52] *La femme genereuse*, pp. 10–11; see also Faret, *L'honneste homme*, quoted above, p. 75.

Vertu au dedans, et la Beauté au dehors pour arrester les hommes, et n'a point voulu separer ces deux choses, afin qu'ayans de l'amour pour l'vne, ils eussent aussi de l'amour pour l'autre. Ainsi la felicité de l'homme dépend de l'amour qu'il doit auoir pour la femme; et il ne doit pas auoir honte de luy rendre de l'obeïssance et du respect.[53]

Although such sentiments did not go altogether unanswered,[54] they appear to be dominant, whereas before anti-feminism prevailed, if not in the traditional genre, then at least in social attitudes and moralistic literature. The writings of the 1640s are filled with a far greater sense of purpose and a deeper conviction than were the productions of the earlier decades of the century, and this is not only because more competent writers deal with the question of feminism, but also that from being defensive, they have taken up the attack, and what was derivative reaction against prevalent anti-feminism has become an active and original assertion of a new social and intellectual climate in which women, if they have little more power, none the less have greater prestige. The *femme forte* is the most striking manifestation of the new approach of these writers.

The conception of the heroic woman in the regency of Anne of Austria is most clear in the two outstanding feminist works of the time, Du Bosc's *Femme heroïque* and Le Moyne's *Gallerie des femmes fortes*. The former consists of eight comparisons between famous men and women, alternatively pagan and Christian, with illustrations and moral reflections; the latter, more ambitious, consists of a frontispiece and a set of twenty engravings (divided into *Fortes Juiues*, *Fortes Barbares*, *Fortes Romaines*, and *Fortes Chrestiennes*), each accompanied by an 'explication', a eulogy, moral reflections, and modern examples of heroines who excelled in the virtues described and discussed in the preceding section.

While these and other feminist works are to some degree moralistic in purpose, and encourage emulation of the heroines described,[55] most authors point out that they are not attempting to alter the marital and legal status of women *vis-à-vis* men. Even

[53] *Panegyrique des dames*, pp. 10–11.

[54] See *Discours de l'ennemy d'amour et des femmes*, in *Nouveau recueil des pieces*, p. 139; and the witty letter which Cyrano de Bergerac wrote 'à Monsieur Gerzan sur son Triomphe des dames' (*Lettres*, ed. Erba, pp. 76–80).

[55] See Du Bosc, *La femme heroïque*, ii. 524; Le Moyne, *Gallerie*, p. 48.

when praising exceptional figures such as Madame de Saint-Balmon, a warrior-poet who flourished in the 1630s and 1640s, writers are at pains to stress their conservatism. Jean-Marie de Vernon, who wrote her biography, justifies her actions by asserting that they were compatible with 'les loix de la bien-séance',[56] and hence socially acceptable; and Le Moyne's eulogy in his *Gallerie* betrays a similar preoccupation:

> Non loin des riues de la Meuse,
> La noble et sage Saint-Balmon,
> Conserue l'exemple et le nom,
> De cette grace courageuse.
> Son épée est à sa pudeur,
> Ce que l'épine est à la fleur;
> Et d'vn double laurier la gloire la couronne.
> Elle a tout ce qui force, elle a tout ce qui plaist;
> Et ioint Muse guerriere et sçauante Bellonne,
> Les arts de la campagne aux arts du cabinet.[57]

It is clear that while most writers are concerned to justify the exception, few seek to make this the general rule; in fact, Le Moyne explicitly denies wishing to do so:

Ie ne dispute pas icy contre l'vsage vniuersel; ny ne pretens faire casser d'authorité priuée, vn Reglement immemorial, et vne Politique aussi ancienne que la Nature. Encore moins est-ce mon dessein, de publier vn ban, par lequel toutes les Femmes soient appellées à la guerre. Elles se doiuent tenir à la distribution que la Nature et le Droit ont faite, et que la Coustume a receuë: et se contenter de la part qui leur a esté assignée dans l'œconomie et dans le ménage.[58]

Although much of this literature of prestige is genuinely concerned with the improvement of woman's social and intellectual lot where this does not necessitate any change in the structure of society, and while its pleas for this are more insistent and more emphatic than those found in the feminist writing of the earlier part of the century, its most original characteristic is its constant play on paradox. Du Bosc assures his reader on the one hand that he is setting out to establish the equality of the sexes,[59]

---

[56] *L'amazone chrestienne, ou les avantures de Madame de S. Balmon*, Paris, 1678, p. 298.
[57] *Gallerie*, ēē3ᵛ; for the image in ll. 5–6, see Le Moyne, *Devises heroiques et morales*, Paris, 1649, p. 19 ('etiam armata placet'), and below, p. 255.
[58] *Gallerie*, pp. 153–4.   [59] *La femme heroïque*, i. 34–5.

and yet, on the other, demonstrates that his heroines surpass his
heroes in the very virtues which are normally considered masculine. This he admits,[60] but argues that heroes may also be shown
to surpass women in what are normally considered to be feminine
virtues: in his work, however, not only is Cyrus surpassed in
courage by Thomyris, but also Joseph is surpassed in chastity by
Susanna.[61] This preference for female virtue, which even a contemporary remarks upon,[62] is an indication of Du Bosc's predilection for paradox. If indeed there is no distinction to be made
between male and female virtue, as Du Bosc argues, then his
examples should demonstrate this: but not only does he paradoxically affirm the equality of the sexes, he goes even further,
and accords to women the advantages peculiar to both sexes.

The *femme forte* takes her name from the first verse of the Alphabet of the Good Woman in the Book of Proverbs (Prov. 31: 10:
'mulierem fortem quis inveniet?'), in which, following the letters
of the Hebrew alphabet, the qualities of a capable wife of good
reputation and sound business sense are outlined. Maillard,
among others, is perfectly aware of the real import of 'fortis' in
this context, even though the Latin translation of the Hebrew
adjective has overtones not compatible with the true sense of the
passage:

Mulierem fortem quis inueniet, heureux le mary qui trouuera vne femme
forte. Voicy les qualitez d'vne femme forte, c'est à dire laborieuse,
diligente, industrieuse: c'est ainsi que se prent souuent le mot de fort
en l'Escriture Sainte Prouerb 10 *manus fortium diuitias parat,* les mains
de ceux qui sont forts amassent les richesses: c'est à dire, qui sont
diligens, laborieux, industrieux . . .[63]

Both Sandricourt and La Mothe Le Vayer assert that this verse
implies that such women are rare, which would appear to
be justified in the context.[64] Rivet furthermore points out that

---

[60] Ibid. i. 46–7.

[61] Ibid. i. 179–265; ii. 611–49.

[62] Saint-Gabriel, *Le mérite des dames*, Paris, 1660 (first printed 1655), p. 107:
'Du Bosc celebre Escriuain de ce temps, duquel sont recueilli[e]s vne bonne partie
de ces pensées, ayant comparé aux heros les Dames heroiques, par vn religieux
scrupule en faueur des hommes, tasche par ses raisons à rendre égaux les deux sexes,
mais il ne laisse pas de faire luy-mesme vne preuue toute contraire, en faisant exceler
celuy des Dames pardessus celuy des plus grands hommes.'

[63] *Le bon mariage*, p. 284.

[64] *Censeur du temps*, ii. 23, quoted above, p. 60; *Quatre autres dialogues*, p. 374; see
also Puget de la Serre, *Le portrait de la reyne*, Paris, 1644, p. 112.

the virtues described in the subsequent verses are scarcely masculine:

> Le sainct Esprit luy mesme faisant par l'organe du Roy Salomon la peinture et la description de la femme forte et genereuse, nous la represente de telle sorte qu'il paroist bien que la pluspart des choses qu'il loüe en elle ne seroient pas louables en la personne des hommes, et que ces deux sexes se rendent ainsi diuersement recommandables.[65]

It is evident that feminist writers do not draw their conception of the *femme forte* from her description in these verses. Le Moyne consistently defines 'fort' in a way which is difficult to reconcile with its use in Proverbs:

> Cette Force armée et robuste [physical strength] n'est que la subalterne d'vne autre Force generale, qui assiste toutes les Vertus; qui est de toutes les grandes actions; qui soustient toutes les bonnes œuures; qui est la directrice de tous les Heros de paix, et tous les Heros de guerre. C'est à cette force que Sainct Ambroise et Sainct Gregoire, attribuent aprez Platon, les victoires de l'esprit sur la chair, celles de la Vertu sur la Fortune, celles de l'honneste sur l'agreable et sur l'vtile. C'est de cette Force que parle le Sage dans cette peinture, où la Femme Forte est tirée auec de si belles couleurs, et couronnée d'vn si magnifique eloge.[66]

It is clear from a later passage in his *Gallerie* that Le Moyne conceives of 'force' as an amalgam of stoic apathy and *fortitudo*,[67] and even le chevalier de L'Hermite's assertion that 'cette femme forte n'a point de prix, pource qu'elle ne donne point de prise à ses passions',[68] has more in common with this interpretation than with the meaning which emerges from the verses in Proverbs. Once removed from the context of the Bible, *femme forte* becomes a description linking pagan and Christian virtues, as does *amazone chrestienne* which is also encountered quite frequently in these works.[69]

Heroic virtue, or *fortitudo*, is, therefore, an essential quality of the *femme forte* or the *femme heroïque*. This is, according to Aquinas,

[65] *Question celebre*, p. 47.　　　　　　　　　　[66] *Gallerie*, ãã4ʳ.

[67] Ibid., p. 60. The four functions of 'force' are said to be justice, stoic apathy ('elle fortifie l'Esprit contre l'vne et l'autre Fortune'), control of the passions, and preparation for death.　　　　[68] *La princesse heroïque*, Paris, 1645, p. 95.

[69] Coste, *Eloges et vies des reynes . . .* , p. 76; L'Hermite, *La princesse heroïque*, p. 3; the title of Jean-Marie de Vernon's biography of Madame de Saint-Balmon also contains these words.

after Aristotle, the virtue by which 'les hommes ont moyen de se rendre comme Dieux';[70] it is not a specific form of courage, but an apotheosis of heroic qualities such as liberality, magnanimity, stoic apathy ('constance').[71] It also implies energy and resoluteness. As it is more often associated with men at this time, it is often identified with the most manly attribute, courage. When applied to women, the question arises whether chastity, which is the most womanly virtue, can be considered a heroic virtue.[72] It is certainly true that chastity is traditionally associated with a form of passive courage; both Le Moyne and the author of *La femme genereuse* point to this fact, and conclude that the virtue required to resist the promptings of the flesh and the blandishments and solicitation of men is no less great than that of men on the battlefield:

La Force est vne vertu necessaire à la Campagne [militaire] . . . mais . . . il y a des combats domestiques, où la victoire est plus difficile, et luy couste dauantage qu'à la Campagne. Les combats de la Chasteté sont de ceux là : quoy qu'ils ne se fassent pas comme ceux de la Vaillance, auec vne montre de terreur et des preparatifs formidables à la vuë; ils ne sont pas moins à craindre, ny moins dangereux. Et si nous mettons à part l'adresse et les fatigues du corps, il ne restera rien qui nous empesche de conclure, que pour faire vn Homme vaillant, il faut moins de force et moins de courage, que pour faire vne Femme chaste.[73]

Other writers, however, suggest that there is only 'quelque image de cette vertu [valeur] dans la chasteté,[74] and Guez de Balzac goes as far as to dismiss any equation of chastity and courage.[75]

I examined above Tasso's proposition that heroic women may be considered to be exempt from the prescription laid on their sex as a whole to be chaste. Le Moyne refutes Tasso's arguments in a section of the *Gallerie des femmes fortes* entitled 'que la chasteté est l'honneur des heroines'. Le Moyne is not only attacking Tasso in this section: he also contests the widely held view that heroic women are often unchaste, and in so doing adds

---

[70] Du Bosc, *La femme heroïque*, i. 8; see also Aquinas, 1a 2ae 68. 1; Aristotle, *Nicomachean Ethics*, vii. 1.

[71] Le Moyne, *Gallerie*, p. 317; see also Tasso, *Discorso della virtù eroica e della carità*, in *Le prose diverse*, ed. Guasti, ii. 190–202.

[72] See Le Moyne, *Gallerie*, pp. 272–7 and 311–17.

[73] Le Moyne, *Gallerie*, p. 273; see also *La femme genereuse*, pp. 138–9, quoted below, p. 259.   [74] Gilbert, *Panegyrique des dames*, p. 36.

[75] *Œuvres*, ed. C. Moreau, Paris, 1854, i. 449–50.

his voice to many others who exonerate Joan of Arc and other such figures from this charge.[76] The case against Tasso is built on the public duties and example of those of high birth, and on the fact that chastity is a virtue 'que la nature elle-mesme a enseignée aux dames'.[77] In attacking Tasso, Le Moyne adds another dimension to his conception of the *femme forte*, at the expense, in places, of honest consideration of Tasso's arguments; nowhere does this writer make the claim which Le Moyne implies that he does in this passage from his refutation:

Si la probité de Caton Censeur et iurongne, n'a pû iustifier l'yurongnerie: ie ne voy pas pourquoy l'impudicité des Dames, sera iustifiée par la valeur de Semiramis conquerante et impudique.[78]

Chastity is also closely allied with female independence, as Du Bosc points out:

L'honneur et la chasteté des Dames font leur veritable liberté. La Dame qui a consenty s'est rendue esclaue, elle ne marche pas la teste leuée: et celuy qui rauit l'honneur à vne femme luy rauit la vraye liberté, mais vne liberté qu'on ne peut rendre; la honte de la seruitude se peut effacer, cette infamie ne s'efface iamais.[79]

Spiritual independence is an essential attribute of the heroic woman, for it allows her the necessary freedom of decision; it is significant that the majority of Du Bosc's and Le Moyne's heroines are either unmarried or widowed, for the constraints of marriage 'ont ie ne sçay quoy d'empeschant, principalement pour les vertus Heroïques'.[80] Le Moyne betrays the same preoccupation with the idea of moral freedom when he writes of Anne of Austria:

Elle garde sa liberté,
Sous le ioug de la Royauté:
Et sans la captiuer le Throsne l'enuironne.[81]

[76] See *Un tournoi de trois pucelles en l'honneur de Jeanne d'Arc. Lettres inédites de Conrart, de Mlle de Scudéry et de Mlle du Moulin*, ed. E. de Barthélemy and R. Kerviler, Paris, 1878 (the letters date from 1646 to 1647); Du Bosc, *La femme heroïque*, i. 242 ff.; Gilbert, *Panegyrique des dames*, p. 37; Scudéry, *Les femmes illustres*, i. 112; René de Ceriziers, *Les trois estats de l'innocence*, Paris, 1659 (first printed 1640), pp. 172–3 (where Joan of Arc is exonerated from accusations of masculinity as well); and by implication in imaginative literature; Béroalde de Verville, *La Pucelle d'Orleans restituee*, Tours, 1599; d'Aubignac, *La Pucelle*, Chapelain, *La Pucelle*. See also N. Edelman, *Attitudes of seventeenth-century France towards the Middle Ages*, New York, 1946, pp. 245–76.
[77] *Gallerie*, p. 172.
[78] Ibid., p. 174.
[79] *La femme heroïque*, ii. 684.
[80] Du Bosc, *L'honneste femme*, ii. 297.
[81] *Gallerie*, ũ4ʳ.

Here chastity is made a positive, almost aggressive, quality, whereas in the eyes of traditional moralists it is passive and introspective; this attitude explains the admiration expressed for such figures as Lucretia, who committed suicide rather than live in dishonour. Du Bosc pays tribute in his *Honneste femme* to those 'qui ont mieux aymé perdre la vie, que l'honneur ou l'innocence',[82] and even Jean-Pierre Camus, in an anecdote in *Les spectacles d'horreur* of 1630, praises one such act.[83]

Moral problems are, however, encountered when praising such figures as Lucretia; as Le Moyne and Du Bosc both have to face these, they are both forced to comment on them. Du Bosc gives a general rule for assessing such cases:

Ie sçay bien qu'entre les Gentils mesmes . . . il y a eu des Dames qui ont monstré tant de constance dans leurs plus grandes infortunes, qu'elles pouuoient faire honte à plusieurs de nostre siècle. Mais quelque force d'esprit que les plus resoluës d'entre elles ayent fait paroistre, ce n'a tousiours esté qu'vne resignation imparfaitte: tant s'en faut qu'elles ayent esté capables de cette genereuse indifference, que la perfection du Christianisme nous demande.[84]

Even such Old Testament figures as Jael present difficulties when used as subjects for emulation, as she is in both Le Moyne's *Gallerie* and Du Bosc's *Femme heroïque*, and both writers are obliged to comment on her action. In a passage entitled 'Loüable façon de violer sa parole', Du Bosc writes:

Il y a plusieurs rencontres où les dames ne sont pas obligées ny à leurs parolles, ny à leurs promesses . . . quelque fidelité que nous ayons iurée aux hommes, nous la pouuons tousiours violer innocemment, pour obseruer celle que nous deuons à Dieu . . .[85]

and Le Moyne's comment is similar: he admits that 'l'Action de Iahel n'est pas de celles qui gagnent d'abord l'approbation; et qui instruisent l'Esprit d'vne simple veuë . . . La mauuaise foy sur tout y semble bien expresse',[85] but then goes on to make the same point about the relative duties to God and to man as Du Bosc.

[82] *L'honneste femme*, ii. 380.
[83] 'La brillante chasteté', in *Les spectacles d'horreur*, Paris, 1630, pp. 207–15.
[84] *L'honneste femme*, iii. 396–7; see also *Gallerie*, pp. 87–8.
[85] *La femme heroïque*, i. 145.
[86] *Gallerie*, p. 32.

The *femme forte* is noted in many cases for her piety and her patriotism. Judith, Deborah, Thomyris, Semiramis, Zenobia, Joan of Arc are all figures outstanding for their services to their country; such service is held to be usually the domain of men, and thus paradox is encountered again. The praise of these figures has also a clear contemporary significance during a regency by a Queen Mother; one may detect in many of the literary productions of the regency disguised (and often overt) compliments to Anne of Austria. For a similar reason, piety is stressed by eulogists such as Puget de la Serre.[87] Apart from features already noted, there are certain minor differences of emphasis in the portrayal of the heroic woman by the various authors: Le Moyne tends to stress energy and resoluteness; Du Bosc, who wrote a work of stoicism entitled *Le philosophe indifferent* (1643), emphasizes stoic apathy; Puget de la Serre stresses religious qualities such as humility and piety. Tasso especially recommends prudence as a heroic virtue in his *Discorso della virtù eroica e della carità*, but none of the French writers seems to make a case for this quality above others.

The contrast between the portrayal of the *femme forte* and of the female sex in general in moralistic literature is clear, but it is worth stressing to what extent it is a polarity. The *femme forte* is attributed with 'constance', 'fidelité', 'résolution', where women are accused of 'inconstance', 'instabilité', 'caprice' by traditional moralists; she is not indolent, but energetic; not 'molle', but 'forte'; not hypocritical and superstitious,[88] but truly devout; she acts with heroic openness,[89] and does not stoop to deceit as her sex in general is said to do. As well as possessing all these qualities, she retains the advantages of the female psyche and physique, for she is both compassionate and beautiful. Again we encounter paradox, well expressed by Le Moyne in his description of spiritual 'force':

Ce n'est pas la hauteur de la taille, ny la force du corps qui fait les Heros: c'est la grandeur et l'éleuation de l'ame; c'est la vigueur et la fermeté de l'Esprit: et il peut y auoir des Ames fort éleuees et de premiere grandeur en de petits Corps; il peut y auoir vn Esprit extremement ferme et d'vne extréme vigueur, dans vne chair fort infirme. De ce costé là donc il n'y a rien qui puisse diminuer les droits des Femmes . . .[90]

---

[87] See especially *Le portrait de la reyne* (1644).
[88] See below, pp. 133–5.
[89] *La femme heroïque*, i. 257, quoted below, p. 246.
[90] *Gallerie*, p. 311.

The constant play on paradox leads to the evocation of surprise and *admiratio* in many of these works: 'lors que ces vertus heroïques esclatent dans le sexe moins robuste', writes the author of *L'amazone françoise au secours des Parisiens* of 1649, 'c'est pour augmenter le nombre des prodiges et faire reuiure le siecle des miracles'.[91] This *admiratio*, which will be the subject of detailed examination in the last chapter, is clearly related to the dramatic emotion described by Corneille in the *Examen de Nicomède*,[92] and therefore not confined to feminist literature, but is rather a manifestation of a far more widespread phenomenon.

[91] *L'amazone françoise*, p. 3.
[92] *Théâtre complet*, ed. P. Lièvre & R. Caillois, Paris, 1961, ii. 392: 'dans l'admiration qu'on a pour sa vertu [that of Nicomède], je trouve une manière de purger les passions dont n'a point parlé Aristote . . . L'amour qu'elle nous donne pour cette vertu que nous admirons, nous imprime de la haine pour le vice contraire . . .'

IV

The Question of Marriage

IT would seem natural to expect marriage to be a prominent topic in feminist discussions in any age; this is certainly the case in the first half of the seventeenth century, in which many tracts about marriage appear. These are usually addressed to the leisured town-dwelling middle classes, to whom references to social behaviour and domestic duties of a certain kind are pertinent; although members of the *grande noblesse* are as much concerned in the theological dimensions of matrimony, little comment is made about their view of the institution as a convenience for political alliance, dowries, and the fulfilment of dynastic duty.

In the fields of social order, law, and religion, marriage was at this time still vested with the importance which it had possessed in the Middle Ages. In the eyes of the state, in France as elsewhere, the family or household (including servants), not the individual, was considered the irreducible unit of society,[1] and from this fact stems the legal and social authority vested in the head of that unit. Furthermore, marriage was important to the state in that it assured the growth of the population, which at this time represented power in a very real way;[2] Louis XIV's exploits would have been inconceivable if France had not been by far the most densely populated country in Europe during his reign. It is therefore not surprising that both men and women were subjected to considerable social pressure to marry. For women, secular celibacy was certainly regarded as eccentric, although much progress was made in the half-century under discussion in converting public opinion to an acceptance of it. For them the only respectable alternative to marriage was the convent, and very often they were not allowed to decide whether they wished

---

[1] See J. Cordier, *La famille saincte; où est traitté des devoirs de toutes les personnes qui composent une famille*, Paris, 1643, in which *famille* is understood to include servants (as in the Latin *familia*).

[2] See Grenaille, *L'honneste mariage*, p. 35.

to enter religious orders or not, just as they were rarely given the choice of partner in marriage. Men also were frequently subjected to the same constraint; *biens* and *lignage* weighed more heavily in the deliberations of parents than the wishes of the unfortunate child. It is only necessary to peruse such authentic accounts of the preoccupations of the age as the *Caquets de l'Accouchée* to see how far down the social scale the problems of marrying off daughters, of dowries, and of heirs were predominant in the minds of parents. Thus marriage was generally thought of not as the consummation of a relationship of intimacy, but as a social convenience where suitability of partner was a minor consideration. This state of affairs gave rise to the discussions about the best sort of emotional attachment between husband and wife, which may appear strangely calculating to modern eyes; it also led to the forming of liaisons outside unsatisfactory marriages, which often may have been adulterous, but which were in most cases probably no more than sentimental compensations for the disillusioned wife or husband.

The legal situation with regard to matrimony was less harsh towards women in practice than is suggested by an account of marriage laws,[3] but the extent of the authority of parents and husband, the laws concerning property in marriage, and, above all else, the legal application of the double standard in cases concerning adultery all weighed heavily against what now would be considered as equitable treatment of the wife. Thus Agrippa's précis of woman's legal status quoted above (p. 16) remained substantially true throughout the period in question. The issue of clandestine marriages, however, which had been prominent in the sixteenth century, and which had been partially resolved by the deliberations of the Council of Trent, is rarely mentioned in the literature of the seventeenth century, and of the writers in question here, only Dinet discusses it at any length.[4]

In the sphere of religion, a distinct difference of approach to the subject between Catholic and Protestant writers may be detected. The latter are more patriarchal in their attitudes, and the few works written by Protestant moralists which deal directly with the institution of marriage are in the main concerned with only the most fundamental issues, such as the marriage of the priesthood, or the natural justification for monogamy or for the prohibition of consanguineous marriages.[5] Catholic writers believe matrimony to be a sacrament, which the Reformed Churches do not, and a divine institution not to be tampered with by man. In an age of at least outward orthodoxy, few writers question the religious authority on which these beliefs rested. Marriage was, moreover, considered as a religious duty to all, with the exception of those who had dedicated their lives to the service of God; Caussin even wrote a tract entitled *La vie neutre des filles dévotes qui font état de n'être ni mariées, ni religieuses* (1644).[6] With this distinction in mind, religious writers divided the female sex into three classes, *vierges*, *épouses*, and *veuves*, and made separate moral provision for each in their treatises.

Much of what has been asserted above might equally well apply to the sixteenth century, and it is indeed striking that there are few new approaches to the subject of marriage to be found in writings which deal with the fields of law, social order, and religion. The beginnings of a comparative study of matrimony may, however, be detected in the works of such writers as Montaigne, who set out to describe the customs and laws of heathen nations and of antiquity relative to this and other states, in order to demonstrate how each system of government produces institutions which are best suited to it, and to show how dangerous it is to change these even in the face of obvious deficiencies and abuses, for fear that the balance of society might be upset. The idea of collections of such *faits divers* appealed also to such writers as Cholières, whose *Forest nuptiale, où est représentée une variété bigarree . . . de divers mariages selon qu'ils sont observez et pratiquez par plusieurs peuples et nations estranges* (1600) is a compendium of anecdotes and details relative to marriage as it is instituted in various civilizations.[7] From such collections of material, moralists

---

[5] See J. Faucher, *Zacharie, ou de la sainteté du mariage, et particulièrement du mariage des ecclésiastiques*, Nîmes, 1627; Moyse Amyraut, *Considerations sur les droits par lesquels la nature a reiglé les mariages*, Saumur, 1648; Guillaume Le Fault, *Petit traicté contre l'abominable vice de paillardise et adultere qui est aujourd'huy en coustume . . .* , The Hague, 1629 (a tract in favour of the marriage of the priesthood). Pierre Du Moulin, however, in his *Premiere decade de sermons* (Geneva, 1642, pp. 116–53) deals with the problems of marriage comprehensively in a sermon based on the text 'maris aimez vos femmes, et ne vous enaigrissez point contre elles' (Col. 3 : 19).

[6] Cited by M. A. Laporte, *Bibliographie clérico-galante*, Paris, 1879.

[7] See also Antoine Du Verdier, *Diverses leçons*, Tournon, 1616, pp. 91–9; Antoine

extracted elements in order to illustrate the rightness of France's indigenous systems by similar practices of heathen nations.[8] Other facets of these alien civilizations, however, such as polygamy, are rarely mentioned, or if they are, it is with the greatest circumspection, especially after the *libertin* trials of the 1620s. There was, however, an accepted framework of hypothesis in which such ideas could be expressed, exemplified in Bernardino Ochino's dialogue of polygamy, where one interlocutor (Ochino himself) expresses the orthodox view throughout.[9] It should also be said here that St. Francis of Sales's writings suggest a new approach to marriage in their assertion that legitimate earthly pleasures, in which he includes the enjoyment of physical love in marriage, are perfectly reconcilable with devotion and religious duty;[10] this attitude is enlightened and modern when seen against the views of traditional religious moralists, who draw extensively on patristic writings on this topic.

There are of course at this time treatises which deal both with the detraction and the apology of marriage; the works of Grenaille (*L'honneste mariage*) and Maillard (*Le bon mariage*) are typical of these,[11] and it can be seen from their titles that their purpose is qualified apology rather than the reverse. These works are set out according to a specific disposition, which it is also convenient to follow in this chapter. They begin with a discussion of the relative merits of religious celibacy and marriage; they next deal with the disadvantages of marriage as a social institution; this is followed by an apology for matrimony; and the works close with a survey of solutions of the problems of marriage. In this chapter three further sections are added: the first deals with the *femme forte* in marriage, as she is portrayed in the works of Du Bosc and

Hotman, *Observationum quae ad veteres nuptiarum ritum pertinent liber singularis*, Paris, 1585; Jean Juliard, *Les amours de l'amant converty*, pp. 211–12 (a list of nations not considering marriage as a sacred institution).

    [8] See *Le tableau des piperies des femmes mondaines*, Ch. 13 ('Des chastiemens et peines ordonnes contre les adulteres'), in which many examples of punishment are taken from the practices of heathen nations to prove the rightness of French laws relating to adultery.

    [9] This dialogue, published in 1563, was attacked by Théodore de Bèze in 1568; E. Auger wrote a refutation of both Ochino and Bèze in his *Discours du sainct sacrement de mariage*, Paris, 1572.   [10] See below, pp. 120–2.

    [11] A possible prototype is Francesco Barbaro's *De re uxoria* (1513), the disposition of which is followed very closely by some (e.g. François Tillier, *Le premier et second livre du Philogame ou amy des nopces*, Paris, 1578), and more loosely by the writers mentioned here.

Le Moyne; the second treats secular solutions to the difficulties of marriage; the last outlines the attitude of the *précieuses* towards matrimony, and the remedies they offer to make it more bearable.

Celibacy and Marriage[12]

'Saincte Catherine de Suede a remporté la gloire d'auoir conserué sa virginité dans le mariage', writes Decret in his *Vraye veuve*, to which he prudently adds, 'où il en est peu qui ne la perdent.'[13] This statement illustrates the importance laid on the physical fact of virginity, the preservation of which is almost in itself an act of devotion. Not all moralists are so unrealistic as to propose such prodigies as models of conduct: Glen asserts that 'si la virginité et les vierges sont en haut degré d'honneur, le Mariage n'en pourra estre reculé loin, lequel engendre les vierges',[14] and Grenaille states in a more down-to-earth manner 'si toutes les femmes eussent fait le vœu de virginité, nous serions encore à naistre'.[15] For all this, religious celibacy is preferable to marriage in the eyes of religious moralists; the commonplace that virginity, widowhood, and matrimony relate to a hundredfold, sixtyfold, and thirtyfold is found in nearly all of the works which deal with this question. The most important biblical source for the belief in the higher status of virginity is Chapter 7 of 1 Corinthians where the situation is quite plainly set out, and to which most of these moralists refer, often adding their own glosses and deductions beyond the text itself.

The first advantage of virginity over marriage is that of spirit over flesh, of the things of the next world over those of this, of eternity over mortality. It is furthermore a sign of grace, as it is a 'don du ciel'. Mystical rights are also attached to this state, described by Poiré as 'conuersation auec les anges',[16] but set out in greater detail by Glen:

1. Les vierges suyent l'Aigneau Iesu-Christ, par tout, comme ses plus intimes courtisans et domestiques.

---

[12] The source of much of the material discussed here is patristic, there being a great number of tracts on virginity by Jerome, Ambrose, Basil, and others; some seventeenth-century works rely very heavily on these (e.g. Joannes Candela, *XIV discours de l'heur et bien de l'estat de virginité et continence*, trans. Antoine Vivieu, Toulouse, 1608; Simon Niclot, *Le petit cabinet des vierges et ames chastes*, Reims, 1649).

[13] *La vraye veuve*, Paris, 1650, p. 448; see also Maillard, *Le bon mariage*, p. 502.

[14] *Le debvoir des filles*, p. 5.   [15] *L'honneste fille*, i. 158.

[16] *Triple couronne*, i. 182.

II. Elles chantent . . . vne chanson, qui leur est propre, et que nul de tous les autres bien-heureux ne peut chanter.

III. Elles ont vn nom propre et particulier, qui est (dict Sainct Bernard) vne excellente gloire, par laquelle elles sont distinguées et separées de tous les autres Saincts; à quoy se conforme le dire des theologiens, que les vierges ont vne couronne speciale, qu'ils nomment AUREOLA . . .[17]

There is, moreover, great strength in virginity, and heroism in the resisting of temptation, in self-denial, and in devotion, which, as has been seen, is the subject of admiration and praise in works of this period. There is 'l'incorruption de la chair', both physical and spiritual integrity, which is highly prized. According to Maillard, virginity is not sterile, as its detractors maintain, for meditation, predication, and good works are engendered of it. Nor is it deprived of companionship, for 'les personnes religieuses sont mariées à Dieu'.[18] It is the chosen state of the 'cresme et mouelle de la Chrestienté, les gens d'Eglise et de religion', as Charron points out in his *De la sagesse*.[19] Finally, it is exempt from the tribulations of marriage, and especially from the punishments laid upon women by God for the 'péché de la pomme', namely labour, child-rearing, and subjection to a husband, and therefore possesses independence and the freedom for self-fulfilment. To this list should be added an advantage rarely referred to in the works of moralists, but undoubtedly important to the women of the time: religious celibacy provided an outlet for female activity and a framework within which women were able to achieve as much as men, both in thought and in action;[20] whence Bremond's tribute to female mystics,[21] and St. Francis of Sales's praise of their charitable activity;[22] whence also perhaps the assertion found in *La femme genereuse* that if men are the rulers of the temporal world, women at least hold sway in the spiritual.[23]

Widowhood, next considered by these moralists, is thought of as a solely female state—'la viduité', writes Grenaille, 'n'appartient proprement qu'aux femmes'[24]—and much space in their

---

[17] *Le debvoir des filles*, pp. 78–9.   [18] Maillard, *Le bon mariage*, p. 61.
[19] *De la sagesse*, Paris, 1613, p. 250.
[20] See N. Z. Davis, *Society and culture in early modern France*, London, 1975, Ch. 3: 'City women and religious change', pp. 65–96.
[21] *Histoire littéraire du sentiment religieux en France*, Paris, 1930, ii. Ch. 2, esp. p. 36.
[22] See Du Bosc, *L'honneste femme*, iii. 526–7.
[23] *La femme genereuse*, pp. 75–7.   [24] *L'honneste veuve*, ã2ᵛ.

works is devoted to dissuading widows from remarriage. As widows, women keep their husband's place in society, they are assured the protection of both God and man, they are exempt from the trials of marriage. More pressing reasons than these are, however, adduced: Du Bosc, glossing a passage in Ephesians, writes:

> L'estat du veufuage des femmes est vne figure de l'estat du veufuage de l'Eglise; et c'est pour cette raison que de grands personnages ont tant crié autrefois contre les secondes nopces, et qu'ils ont quasi nommé adulteres celles qui se sont remariées . . . [25]

Indeed it is almost an unfaithful act to remarry, since the couple had sworn to be 'one flesh'; it is to this which Le Moyne refers when, writing against the suicide of bereaved wives, he asserts:

> C'est vne opinion generalement receuë . . . que les Personnes aimées ont vn estre particulier, et comme vne seconde existence dans l'imagination, dans l'esprit et dans le cœur des Personnes qui les ayment. Elles viuent là intellectuellement et par leurs images: et ces images ne sont pas des figures mortes, ny des impostures d'vn Art qui trompe . . . Or vne Femme qui se tuë par vne fureur aueugle et precipitée, ou qui se consume par vne affliction opiniastre et volontaire, oste à son Mary cette seconde existence, et cét estre intellectuel et d'amour, par lequel il suruiuroit à soy mesme . . . [26]

If the widow needs to find a new master, let her marry God. Like the virgin, the good widow displays a sort of heroism in resisting the temptations of the flesh and of worldly things, and as Grenaille points out, this self-denial is almost more impressive than that of celibates:

> La continence des Veuues semble estre plus genereuse en quelque façon que celle des vierges, en ce qu'il y a plus de difficulté à se passer des contentemens qu'on a experimentez, que de ceux qu'on ignore absolument. [27]

Poiré sees the advantages of the state of widowhood as 'oraison, maceration du corps, bonnes œuures'. This state is further honoured by many saintly women, notably Judith, who is made a figure for the moral strength and the freedom of widowhood. [28]

All writers admit, however, that continence, whether in celibacy

---

[25] *La femme heroïque*, ii. 548; Eph. 5 : 22–33.   [26] *Gallerie*, p. 292.
[27] *L'honneste veuve*, p. 50.   [28] See Du Bosc, *La femme heroïque*, ii. 526.

or in widowhood, is a vocation, and that not all humanity has
been granted the strength to follow it. Thus marriage is considered less 'strong' than the other states, for it is a concession to
incontinence; all these moralists here refer to St. Paul's statement
that 'it is better to marry than to burn'.[29] Grenaille describes the
state of matrimony as 'vne fornication approuuée, vne intem-
perence necessaire'. For all this, marriage has certain things in its
favour: it is a sacrament in the eyes of the Catholic Church,
whereas virginity is no more than a virtue; it was instituted by
God in paradise in the time of innocence, reinstituted after the
flood, further sanctified by the Virgin Mary and by the birth of
Christ, blessed by procreation, and given to man as a means of
achieving a sort of immortality in the flesh. It is a religious commandment, and the fruits of marriage go towards the peopling of
the courts of heaven. It ensures companionship and mutual aid,
and, perhaps most important of all, its union is a mystical figure
for that of Christ and the Church, according to St. Paul. Maillard
finds four mystical figures for marriage, according to the level of
interpretation: 'le sens literal' is the marriage of man and woman;
'le sens allegorique' is that of Christ and the Church; 'le sens
moral' is the union of God and the soul; and finally 'le sens
anagogique' is the marriage of 'le Verbe eternel auec la nature
humaine'.[30] Most religious writers summarize its advantages as
'loyauté, fécondité, sacrement'.[31]

There are, however, many disadvantages. Maillard, glossing on
a verse in Corinthians, points to 'tribulation de la chair', 'seruitude', and 'diuision [of soul and body]';[32] the worldliness and the
physical inconveniences of marriage, the dangers and the suffer-
ings of childbirth, the subjection of women to their husbands,
and of husbands to toil and responsibility, are underlined. Where
virginity has but one master (God), marriage has two (God
and husband).[33] It is a lottery, an 'enfer' or a 'paradis', where
celibacy is not subjected to the same degree of risk. For women
it entails loss of beauty and social freedom, as Grenaille points
out:

Ce que les femmes semblent auoir de plus attrayant leur est venu du

---

[29] 1 Cor. 7: 9.   [30] *Le bon mariage*, i. Ch. 8.
[31] e.g. Poiré, *Triple couronne*, i. 182.
[32] *Le bon mariage*, ii. Chs. 2–4; see 1 Cor. 7: 26–34.
[33] See Grenaille, *L'honneste fille*, i. Ch. 5.

temps qu'elles estoient Filles. En perdant ce nom elles ont fait de grandes pertes; elles ne peuuent plus agreer à tout le monde, ne deuant plus agreer qu'à leurs marys. Le nom de mere qu'elles portent leur fait produire quelquefois de beaux enfans, mais c'est en perdant vne partie de leur beauté. Ces roses commencent à se flestrir si tost qu'on commence à les toucher.[34]

None the less, these writers admit that it is part of the world and comes to grips with the problems of earthly life whereas celibacy is in a sense an escape from those very problems.

Thus while these moralists, as would be expected, show a marked preference for celibacy, they do not condemn marriage; indeed many of them divide their praises equally between the two states, while assessing their theological value differently. For all this, unmarried women are not only praised for their independence, but also for their superior religious state and moral potential, as is clearly indicated by the following passage taken from Du Bosc's *Honneste femme*:

Il faut tousiours auoüer que le mariage a ie ne sçay quoy d'empeschant, principalement pour les vertus Heroïques : parce que c'est comme vn contrepoids qui nous retient et qui nous empesche de nous esleuer à vn plus haut point de perfection. Aussi nous voyons que les Dames qui ont aspiré à se rendre recommandables pour quelque chose d'extra-ordinaire, ont fait profession de Celibat et de virginité. . . . N'ont elles pas toutes renoncé aux embarras du mariage, comme à vne façon de viure qui diminue de beaucoup la liberté qui est necessaire pour les eminentes vertus, et pour les genereuses entreprises?[35]

Detractors of Marriage

After the criticisms of marriage made by religious moralists, the social disadvantages of the institution should next be considered. 'An sit nubendum', 'an vir sapiens ducat uxorem', 'an uxor sit ducenda'—the question is variously phrased—is a humanistic problem, in most cases treated facetiously, expecting the answer no, if any answer at all.[36] Because social celibacy was thought of as sufficiently rare to be considered eccentric in women, the

---

[34] See Grenaille, *L'honneste fille*, i. 28–9.   [35] *L'honneste femme*, ii. 297–9.

[36] It is also a typical subject for demonstrative rhetoric, and is discussed not only in the Renaissance but also in antiquity (see Priscianus Grammaticus, *De praeexercita mentis rhetoricis ex Hermogene*, in Caelius Secundus Curio, *In M. T. Ciceronis oratorias partitiones, explicationum libri tres*, Frankfurt, 1567, p. 146) and in the Middle Ages (see E. R. Curtius, *Europäische Literatur und lateinisches Mittelalter*, Berne, 1948, p. 162).

question is always posed with a masculine bias, and the alternative to marriage is not seen here as religious celibacy, but rather as abstention from permanent liaisons with the opposite sex.

In France, two trends may be traced in the treatment of this question: the first, heavily influenced by Desportes's *Stances du mariage* of 1573, sets out to show the disadvantages of all women as wives, whether they be rich, poor, proud, humble, old, young, beautiful, or ugly. Into this class fall the works of Courval-Sonnet (*Satyre menippee sur les poingnantes traverses et incommoditez du mariage*, 1608), Varin (*Les espines du mariage*, 1604), and several anonymous works in the popular anti-feminist tradition: *La complainte des mal mariez* (1605), *Brief discours pour la reformation des mariages* (1614), *Recueil des exemples de la malice des femmes* (1596), and *Le fantastique repentir des mal mariez* (1623).[37] Other more elevated works draw on this tradition, including those of Grenaille, La Mothe Le Vayer, Rampalle, and Maillard, from whose work the following illustrative passage is taken:

C'est Dieu qui donne la bonne femme, on ne sçait comme proceder au choix; car si vous en prenez vne ieune, elle est dangereuse: si vne vieille, elle est riotteuse: si vne riche, elle est glorieuse: si vne pauure, elle est contemptible: si vne belle, elle est volage: si vne laide, elle fait peur: si vne saine, elle est coureuse: vne malade est ennuyeuse: vne sçauante babillarde: vne idiote est vne beste. Souuent vne noble est superbe: vne roturiere, soubçonneuse: vne mesnagere, auaricieuse: vne liberale, prodigue . . .[38]

The second class of works relating to this question is more elevated in style, and perhaps more insidious in intention; from being 'healthy anti-feminism' it has become 'libertinage'. Here the outstanding works are Rampalle's 's'il se faut marier ou non' in his *Discours academiques* (1647), La Mothe Le Vayer's *Dialogue du mariage* (1631?),[39] and the *Discours de l'ennemi d'amour et des femmes* (1644). Their major sources are the fragment of Theophrastus' *Liber de nuptiis* in Jerome's *Adversus Jovinianum*[40] and

[37] See also Fitelieu, *La contre-mode*, Paris, 1642, pp. 301–27; Sorel, *Francion*, ed. Roy, iii. 19–20; *Recueil general des questions traitées ès conferences du Bureau d'Adresse*, Lyons, 1666, iv. 552–62. [38] *Le bon mariage*, pp. 109–10.
[39] This dialogue belongs to a group published under the title *Quatre autres dialogues faits à l'imitation des anciens par Oratius Tubero*, with the false imprint Frankfurt, 1716.
[40] See C. B. Schmitt, 'Theophrastus in the Middle Ages', *Viator*, ii (1971), 268–9.

Montaigne, whose views on matrimony, although prudently expressed, smack of heterodoxy. In 'Sur des vers de Virgile' (iii. 5) and other essays, he criticizes the institution as an emotional and physical prison, decries its sexual monotony, and seems to favour the idea of divorce.[41] So strong is his influence that Charron, in a chapter entitled *Du mariage* in the first book of *De la sagesse*, reproduces his very words, and Rampalle echoes them in parts of his discourse. In these works, both sides of the question are theoretically examined—indeed La Mothe Le Vayer writes in dialogue form—but fairness is only an illusion, and they are as hostile to marriage as the writings of the popular tradition.

For these writers, there are two major impediments to an easy acceptance of matrimony as it is: the first is the partner with whom it must be undertaken, and the second is the imperfection of the institution itself. On the first subject of grievance, most of these writers display the anti-feminist attitude towards the physiological and psychological weakness of women examined above. Rampalle's sentiments are typical:

Ce n'est pas vne petite suiettion de traisner ses iours aupres d'vn sexe ialoux, inconstant et bigeare, et qui en tout sens est si incommode aux occupations d'vn honneste homme que celuy qui l'apelloit vn mal necessaire ne le connoissoit qu'à demy.[42]

It is not only the inconstancy of women which offends these writers, it is also their perverse nature, their irrationality, and their lubricity: Caillet speaks of husbands who 'se violentent en des exces voluptueux, pour contenter (si possible estoit) les appetits demesurez de ce sexe, qui a moins de bornes en ses passions que l'ocean en ses esmotions'.[43] It seems to most of these writers that women have the wrong motives for marrying; the author of the *Recueil des exemples de la malice des femmes* asks:

Croyriez-vous bien . . . que aucunesfois vne fille prenne vn homme par amitié? Nenny, c'est le plus souuent pour l'argent que le bon homme peut auoir, et aucunesfois elle le prend à faute d'autre, et de crainte de demeurer vieille fille . . .[44]

And La Mothe Le Vayer refers to three vices, 'volupté, ambition, auarice', which have already been seen to be associated with each

[41] See *Essais*, ed. Thibaudet and Rat, ii. 15, p. 599; iii. 5, pp. 827 ff.
[42] *Discours academiques*, pp. 238–9.   [43] *Tableau du mariage*, p. 67.
[44] *Recueil des exemples*, p. 5.

other, as the principal motives for women to marry. What is, however, more serious in the eyes of these writers is the risk of the husband's reputation, which is in the hands of these perverse creatures, as La Mothe Le Vayer points out.[45] Trousset accuses them of more than this:

Elles sont cause des vices et diffamations qui ternissent la splendeur et noblesse des plus genereux courages, et du raualement des hommes dans la turpitude et saleté des pechez, qui vont sans cesse irritant et offençant la Majesté diuine.[46]

The author of the *Discours de l'ennemi d'amour et des femmes* concludes his assessment of women with the remark 'la plus grande commodité que nous puissions retirer d'elles, est qu'elles sont le chemin par où il fait que nous fassions passer nostre posterité',[47] which is the only argument he can find in favour of wives.

If women do so little to enhance the attraction of marriage, then the institution itself is hardly more alluring. The fact that it is indissoluble, and an irrevocable step into the unknown (for who can know his partner's true nature before he marries her?), is the object of much complaint and bitterness. The loss of liberty and the physical and spiritual fetters of the institution are equally decried; 'quel supplice de passer toute sa vie à la chaisne?' writes Rampalle, 'et quelle lascheté d'estouffer dans le sein d'vne femme tant de glorieux desseins, qu'vn ieune courage peut faire, tandis qu'il est affranchy de cét empeschement?'[48] Its lack of diversity causes many of these writers to ask whether man is naturally monogynous. The effect of the institution on the unhappy husband is much lamented; 'sainct Paul mesme parlant de toutes les femmes indifferemment,' writes Trousset, 'dict, qu'elles sont capables de desrober l'estude et le loisir du plus spirituel

---

[45] *Quatre autres Dialogues*, pp. 425–6: 'quelle plus grande stupidité et quel plus grand aveuglement que le nostre, qui preferons en mille rencontres l'honneur à la vie, advoüons que la plus pure partie d'iceluy despend de la bonne conduitte de nos femmes, sçavons leurs infirmitez et inclinations diametralement contraires à nos intentions sur ce subject; et neantmoins les laissons agir en pleine liberté, c'est-à-dire, fouler aux pieds ce pretendu honneur, et faisons un vice de la jalousie, par laquelle seule nous pourrions tesmoigner estre amateurs de nostre reputation.'

[46] *Alphabet*, p. 247.

[47] *Nouveau recueil des pieces*, pp. 137–8.

[48] *Discours academiques*, p. 239; see also Guez de Balzac, *Aristippe*, in *Œuvres*, ed. Moreau, ii. 271: 'une femme et des enfans sont de puissants empeschemens pour arrester un homme qui court à la gloire.'

homme du monde, estant lié auec elles.'⁴⁹ La Mothe Le Vayer
goes further than this and specifies the causes of the husband's
spiritual disintegration:

Un autre plus partial et plus animé que moy contre le mariage, auroit
examiné bien plus par le menu mille autres cuisans soucis ausquels il
nous tient engagez; le soing de la nourriture et entretenement de toute
une famille, laquelle semble ne croistre que pour nous accabler; les
peines que causent les maladies journalieres d'une femme, d'un enfant,
voire d'un serviteur, dont les infirmitez portent necessairement jusques
sur nous; les difficultez qui se trouvent dans l'institution de nos enfans,
souvent pervers, et indisciplinables; les disgraces où nous jettent à
toute heure les mieux nais, par malheur ou autrement, ausquelles il
faut que nous apportions necessairement le remede; l'impossibilité
d'advancer honorablement dans les charges, ou de promouvoir aux
autres conditions de la vie un nombre de garçons et de donner un
doüaire suffisant à plusieurs filles, dont il ne faut esperer de se deffaire
autrement; bref, une infinité de telles amertumes matrimoniales . . .⁵⁰

Grenaille points to an even more dire consequence of the
domestication of man, namely the domination of woman,⁵¹ which
has its origins in the social conventions of courtship, where the
suitor places himself at the feet of his beloved; it is perhaps this
which causes the same writer to describe marriage as 'vne condition qui abbaisse les hommes jusques au dessous des femmes'.⁵²
Du Bosc's comment on the sensual attractions of marriage—'vne
legere volupté qui se termine en vn long deplaisir'⁵³—is reminiscent of another cause of grief, that in marriage the most enjoyable
part of seduction, which is the element of persuasion, is lost.
Rampalle writes that 'il semble mesme que la trop grande facilité
doit emousser la pointe de ce plaisir, luy ostant ce haut goust

⁴⁹ *Alphabet*, p. 14; a thoroughly specious reference to St. Paul (1 Cor. 7: 33),
since the following verse reverses the rôles of wife and husband.

⁵⁰ *Quatre autres dialogues*, pp. 457–8.

⁵¹ *L'honneste mariage*, pp. 189–90, quoted below, p. 217.

⁵² Ibid., p. 106.

⁵³ *L'honneste femme*, ii. 295; this is a commonplace (see Erasmus, *Christiani matri-
monii institutio*, in *Opera omnia*, v. 642, quoted by Screech, 'Rabelais, de Billon and
Erasmus', 257: 'at praepostera res est amor ac temeritas, brevisque voluptatis
lenocinio pertrahunt hominem in perpetuos et inexplicabiles angores'; Alexandre
Hardy, *Panthée*, ll. 351–4, in *Théâtre*, ed. E. Stengel, Marburg and Paris, 1884, i.
113; Corneille, *Mélite*, I: i (Tircis):

> Et l'hymen qui succède à ces folles amours,
> Après quelques douceurs, a bien de mauvais jours).

chatoüilleux que se rencontre aux larcins d'amour et aux conquestes malaisées',[54] and La Mothe Le Vayer asserts:

Le seul mot de mariage vous prive pour tousiours de ce qui est de plus doux en amour; estant certain que sa principale et plus essentielle partie consiste en la connoissance et asseurance que vous prenez d'une affection reciproque, de laquelle les hommes mariez, non plus que par tout ailleurs les rois, et les plus grands princes, ne peuvent jamais avoir que quelques legers ombrages, et jamais aucune certitude, parce que l'ascendant et authorité des uns et des autres sur la chose aimée, luy oste la liberté d'agir volontairement, et fait qu'haïs ou aimés, ils sont tousjours à peu-prés traittez et caressez également.[55]

Thus Melanire, one of the interlocutors in de Pure's *La prétieuse*, is scarcely just when she asserts that 'les hommes sont trop heureux d'estre mariez',[56] and that women alone suffer by it.

That women do also suffer by it is, however, undeniable, and their grievances are voiced in the works of the *précieuses* and in the writings of those favourably disposed towards them. They complain that they have no choice of partner, and that they are at all times legally subjected to the wishes of others. They are unhappy about the punishments meted out to them at the fall: subjection to their husbands, whose tyranny and jealous suspicions could make their existence miserable, care of children, and the pains and dangers of childbirth, which are sometimes reflected upon sympathetically in the works of religious moralists and others.[57] It is significant that there is scarcely a work which extols the joys of motherhood, or the fulfilment of women in marriage, whereas many praise the negative value of non-sterility. Frequency of maternities is often deplored.[58]

[54] *Discours academiques*, p. 267; cf. Montaigne, *Essais*, ed. Thibaudet and Rat, iii. 5, p. 831: 'le mariage a pour sa part l'utilité, la justice, l'honneur et la constance: un plaisir plat, mais plus universel. L'amour se fonde au seul plaisir, et l'a de vray plus chatouillant, plus vif et plus aigu; un plaisir attizé par la difficulté. Il y faut de la piqueure et de la cuison. Ce n'est plus amour s'il est sans fleches et sans feu. La liberalité des dames est trop profuse au mariage et esmousse la poincte de l'affection et du desir.' For a brief summary of the detrimental effects of marriage on men, see Charron, *De la sagesse*, pp. 250–2.   [55] *Quatre autres dialogues*, p. 405.

[56] *La prétieuse*, ed. E. Magne, Paris, 1938–9, ii. 42.

[57] See Robert Angot de L'Esperonnière, 'Lucine ou la femme en couches', a poem published as a pamphlet in 1637 with the title *La consolation des femmes en leurs accouchemens*. See also O. de la Brosse, *Saint François de Sales: les femmes mariées*, Introduction, p. 10, where a relevant *Prière de la femme enceinte* is quoted.

[58] See A. Blum, *Abraham Bosse et la société française au XVIIe siècle*, Paris, 1924; *Les salons littéraires au XVIIe siècle* (Exhibition Catalogue of the Bibliothèque Nationale), Paris, 1968, p. xi.

Lack of freedom in marriage is more unbearable for women than for men, but above all else they feel the injustice of the double standard, which allows marital peccadilloes in husbands, but legislates against the unhappy wife seeking consolation in her sad plight. Even writers well disposed towards women in general, such as Maillard, support this attitude, arguing that adultery is a more serious offence if committed by women because they dishonour their husbands and families as well as themselves, because chastity is the female virtue *par excellence*, because adultery may lead to false heirs, and also because 'd'ordinaire ce peché en vne femme est plus commun et plus scandaleux, et partant plus grand, l'homme peut aysement cacher cette faute, voire quoy qu'il ne la cache on ne s'en scandalise pas beaucoup d'ordinaire'.[59] Other moralists attack this position, among them Du Bosc:

N'est-ce pas vne coustume bien digne de blâme, de voir que les hommes prennent toute sorte de licence sans en donner la moindre? On diroit à voir leur Tyrannie que le Mariage n'a esté institué que pour donner des Geoliers aux femmes. Il y a en cela bien de l'ingratitude aussi bien de l'iniustice, de pretendre vne fidelité qu'on ne veut pas rendre, principalement quand on n'est pas moins obligé à la garder.[60]

The specific grievances and suggestions of the *précieuses* will be discussed more fully below, but it should be said here that they are most vehement about the limitations imposed by marriage on social behaviour and on liaisons formed on the basis of 'amour d'inclination'.

Grenaille summarizes the disadvantages of marriage in female eyes thus:

Bien que [les dames] trouuent vn appuy par le lien du Mariage, elles trouuent d'ailleurs vn ioug qu'il leur faudra tousiours porter. Elles espousent des seruiteurs qui doivent estre leurs Maistres. Quelle peine n'ont-elles point à se voir dans la subiection quoy qu'on les appelle Reines, et à contenter leurs maris quelque bizarres qu'ils soient, comme s'ils n'auoient point de mauuaise humeur. Il faut qu'elles s'attachent à vne maison bien qu'elles doiuent commander à tous les hommes, et qu'elles souffrent leur ialousie aussi bien que leurs caresses. Dauantage, la production des enfans, qui est vne de leurs plus sensibles consolations, est accompagnée de quantité de desplaisirs.[61]

---

[59] *Le bon mariage*, p. 171.   [60] *L'honneste femme*, i. 188–9.
[61] *L'honneste veuve*, p. 22; cf. Corneille, *Polyeucte*, I. iii, ll. 131–7.

Some moralists try to give a fair picture of the difficulties of marriage as they are seen from both sides,[62] but very few give a fair hearing to the case of the wife, because they believe that women gain much more from the institution than their husbands.[63] It offers them protection, social recognition and rank, physical fulfilment in the eyes of men, who see it at this time as little more than a drain on their resources and an uncomfortable formality to be undertaken more out of duty to one's family than for personal contentment: 'Quoy qu'on die', writes Charron, quoting Montaigne, 'l'on ne se marie seulement pour soy, la posterité, la famille, l'alliance, les moyens y pesent beaucoup'.[64] It is therefore not surprising that Grenaille, writing of the 'charges du mariage', devotes fifty-two pages to the masculine case against marriage, and only two to the grievances of wives, and similar figures may be drawn from Maillard's *Bon mariage* and Caillet's *Tableau du mariage*. Nor is it surprising that in their apologies for marriage, these writers are more concerned to convince men than women of its excellence.

Apologies for Marriage

Most writers at this time would agree that marriage is excellent in theory: Caillet can write towards the end of his anti-feminist *Tableau du mariage* 'nous concluons donques que le mariage considéré *in abstracto* est indéfiniment bon';[65] but any meaningful apology for marriage must take into account the difficulties *in concreto* also, which have been outlined above. At the outset the most ardent apologists for marriage admit that it is a lottery: 'à la verité', writes Charron, 'le mariage n'est point chose indifferente, ou mediocre; c'est du tout ou grand bien ou grand mal, vn grand repos ou vn grand trouble, vn paradis ou vn enfer.'[66] This dialectic is apparent also in the approach of such writers as Grenaille and Maillard, who oppose the 'biens' of marriage to its

[62] See Maillard, *Le bon mariage*, pp. 290–1.
[63] See Grenaille, *L'honneste mariage*, pp. 321–34 ('Que l'estat du Mariage est principalement auantageux aux honnestes femmes'), where he shows that the etymology of *matrimonium* (from *mater*) proves the identification of the institution with the interests of women.
[64] *De la sagesse*, p. 254; cf. Montaigne, *Essais*, ed. Thibaudet and Rat, iii. 5, p. 817.
[65] *Tableau du mariage*, p. 242.
[66] *De la sagesse*, p. 254.

'maux', its 'charges' to its 'soulagemens'. They admit that any
realistic appraisal of matrimony must take into account its practical
drawbacks, but they are precise as to what these drawbacks are.
It is argued that the ills of marriage stem not from the institution,
but from its abuse.[67] Such writers would never accept as a weakness of marriage the fact that it involves partnership with women;
all true apologists for this state take for granted the suitability
of the female sex as companions, and some, such as Le Peletier
and Glen, base their whole case for the excellence of marriage on
this assumption.

The apologists for marriage at this time go far beyond the
grudging acceptance of the institution as a cure for incontinence
to be found in Corinthians.[68] As has already been pointed out,
religious moralists underline the fact that it is honoured in the
Bible as a divine institution and a sacrament. They assert also
that it is a religious duty, almost a commandment in the eyes of
the Church, and that its detractors in the name of religion pervert
the message of the Scriptures, as L'Escale points out:

Ce n'est pas que ie n'estime auec toute l'Eglise Catholique le celibat
plus parfaict que le mariage, à qui le peut dignement garder, la chasteté
estant vn don de Dieu, à ce que dict sainct Augustin: Mais, que ie veux
demonstrer que ceste doctrine contre les femmes, est du tout infernale,
inuentée là bas pour corrompre de toute façon le genre humain, et
introduire çà haut vn vilain diuorce entre les deux sexes, source de tous
les maux.[69]

Marriage is honoured by the state, since the institution and
legitimate progeny from it are assurances of the continuing life
of society. The union is made personally desirable by reference to
the neo-Platonist concept of the androgyne, in which man and
woman, conceived of as separated parts of an original whole, by

[67] Maillard, *Le bon mariage*, Preface.
[68] According to most moralists, the love of the husband for the wife should be
a 'saint amour', restrained and not self-indulgent; in this sense, marriage is not a cure
for incontinence, which can only be satisfied by concubines and prostitutes (see
Francesco Barbaro, *De re uxoria libri duo*, Amsterdam, 1639, p. 145: Montaigne,
Essais, ed. Thibaudet and Rat, i. 30, pp. 197–8: 'Aelius Verus, L'Empereur, respondit à sa femme, comme elle se plaignoit dequoy il se laissoit aller à l'amour
d'autres femmes, qu'il le faisoit par occasion conscientieuse, d'autant que le mariage
estoit un nom d'honneur et dignité, non de folastre et lascive concupiscence').
[69] *Champion des femmes*, f. 126[r–v].

reintegration achieve their lost completeness. Grenaille applies this belief to matrimony:

C'est que par cette vnion vn homme ne cherche rien hors de luy, mais il appelle vne autre personne à soy, et se perfectionne en luy donnant sa perfection. Il trouue plustost vn autre soy-mesme, qu'vn principe estranger de felicité. Il participe à toutes les perfections de la femme, non pas par emprunt, mais par vne vraye proprieté. La femme aussi dans ses infirmitez trouue de la force ne faisant qu'vn composé auec celuy dont le sexe semble estre tout puissant au prix du reste des creatures.[70]

The benefits of 'aide, societé, esbattement' mentioned by Pantagruel in the *Tiers Livre* point to the other secular advantages of marriage, to which should be added the benefit of children, through whose existence the parents achieve a sort of temporal immortality. Le Bermen summarized these advantages as 'conjunction, procreation, bienfaict, naturalité, societé',[71] but religious moralists list only four benefits, 'generation, assistance mutuelle, remede à l'incontinence, grace sacramentale'.[72] Grenaille, who considers the 'principe' of marriage to be 'gloire de Dieu et bien de la societé ciuile', names three purposes which honour the institution:

D'estraindre par ce nœud deux personnes de telle sorte qu'elles n'ayent qu'vne ame et qu'vn cœur en vn double corps . . .
    De peupler le monde par deux personnes legitimement assemblés, et de rendre les hommes immortels parmy la mortalité mesme . . .
    D'appaiser la concupiscence par des plaisirs qui ne sont point illicites.[73]

These apologists also try to account for some of the apparent disadvantages and injustices of marriage, although, as has been pointed out, not all. Marie de Gournay offers the following explanation for the subjection of women to men in matrimony, which is not injurious to the former:

Si l'Escripture a declaré le mary, chef de la femme, la plus grande sottise que l'homme peust faire, c'est de prendre cela pour passedroict de dignité. Car veu les exemples, aucthoritez et raisons nottées en ce discours, par où l'egalité des graces et faueurs de Dieu vers les deux

[70] *L'honneste mariage*, pp. 63–4.   [71] *Le bouclier des dames*, Ch. 3.
[72] Maillard, *Le bon mariage*, p. 12. See also Augustine, *De Genesi ad litteram*, ix. 7, PL xxxiv. 397.
[73] *L'honneste mariage*, p. 23.

especes ou sexes est prouvée, voire leur unité mesme, et veu que Dieu
prononce : Les deux ne seront qu'un : et prononce encores : L'homme
quittera pere et mere pour suivre sa femme ; il paroist que cette declaration n'est faicte que par le besoin expres de nourrir paix en mariage.
Lequel besoin requeroit, sans doubte, qu'une des parties cedast à
l'autre, et la prestance des forces du masle ne pouvoit pas souffrir que
la soubmission veint de sa part.[74]

Grenaille explains this in terms of 'l'vnion du sujet et de l'accident', where the 'sujet' (man) takes precedence over the 'accident'
(woman).[75] The same writer argues that the indissolubility of
marriage, which is often regretted in the writings of anti-feminists,
derives not from a religious injunction but rather from man's
nature, which, being 'tousiours miserable', is constantly in need
of support; he also points out that the position of children in
society would be prejudiced if the bonds of matrimony were not
permanent.[76] In a more specious fashion, he establishes that there
is no loss of liberty in marriage :

Il est bien aisé à voir que les hommes ne perdent pas leur liberté quand
ils possedent des femmes, veû qu'elles ne leur ostent pas leurs legitimes
pretensions, mais leur en donnent de nouuelles, et qu'elles ne les em-
peschent pas d'estre à eux-mesmes en leur donnant la compagne des
personnes qui ne font qu'vne mesme chose auec eux.[77]

Dinet, finally, in the steps of St. Francis of Sales, advocates
strongly that the taint of carnality should be removed from
marriage :

Ces Autheurs pensans peut-estre destourner les hommes de l'amour des
femmes, en leur persuadant que leur cohabitation est plus vn appan-
nage du peché originel, et vne suite de la corruption de nostre nature,
qu'vn acte naturel et honneste . . . offencent la nature et le sexe feminin,
que Dieu mesme a honoré de cét auantage par dessus l'homme, qu'il
s'est reuestu de nostre humanité, et l'a prise dans le sein d'vne femme,
sans rien emprunter de l'homme, bien que fait homme.[78]

[74] *Égalité des hommes et des femmes*, ed. Schiff, pp. 76–7 ; see Eph. 5 : 23 ; Gen. 2 : 24 ;
Eph. 5 : 31.
[75] *L'honneste mariage*, pp. 206–7.   [76] Ibid., pp. 90–1.
[77] Ibid., p. 216.
[78] *Theatre françois*, ii. 3 : cf. St. Francis of Sales, *Introduction à la vie dévote*, ed.
F. Henrion, Tours, 1939, pp. 298–303 (Ch. 39 : 'De l'honnêteté du lit nuptial').
St. Francis of Sales draws much of the imagery and content of this chapter from
Barbaro, *De re uxoria*, pp. 141–8 (ii. 6 : 'De coitus ratione').

This attitude towards physical cohabitation is, however, rare at this time, and Grenaille's assertion that 'le Mariage est vn Enfer pour ceux qui veulent viure comme des bestes, mais c'est vn Paradis pour ceux qui dans la chair veulent viure comme des Anges'[79] betrays a more typical attitude.

Even Caillet at the end of his *Tableau du mariage* concludes with a somewhat grudging apology for the institution of matrimony:

Dautant que (suiuant la doctrine des Iurisconsultes) il ne faut jamais iuger par exemples, mais par loix, il n'est pas raisonnable ny iuste de priuer les humains du benefice du mariage pour les inconueniens qui ont esté cy deuant cottés; mais plustost quelque risque et danger qu'on en puisse courir nous faut prester vne obeyssance aueugle à l'ordonnance de Dieu, qui l'a institué dés la fondation du monde, qui l'a renouuelé en la restauration d'iceluy, et finalement qui l'a beni de tant de graces, et confirmé par tant de benedictions.[80]

This indicates how deeply religious conformism affects thought at this time, for after two hundred pages of detractions or at best grudging concessions, Caillet yet concludes on an affirmative note out of keeping with the rest of his work. It is therefore only meaningful to describe writings with a feminist slant as true apologies for marriage.

Moralists' Solutions of the Problems of Marriage

Most of these writers admit that marriage is not an ideal state for the majority of those who undertake it; according to Du Bosc:

Il y a tant de conditions à desirer pour rendre vn mariage parfait, qu'il est quasi impossible de les trouuer ensemble. Theophraste vouloit que la femme fut belle, bonne, et noble; et que le mary fut sain, riche, et sage. Si le Mariage pour estre bon depend de ces trois circonstances, il ne faut pas s'estonner si on n'en voit que fort peu qui reüssissent.[81]

The solutions offered by moralists are all realistic, and are based on the assumptions of mutual concession and duty; once each

---

[79] *L'honneste mariage*, p. 282; cf. *Le tableau des piperies des femmes mondaines*, Paris, 1632, f. 176[r-v]; 'le mariage est vn sacrement institué de Dieu, comme vne chose bonne et salutaire pour la propagation du genre humain, et non pas pour assouuir ses appetits et passions sensuelles, comme les voluptueux, qui en cela ressemblent aux brutes et les imitent: mais pour produire vne saincte et vertueuse lignee qui seruira à repeupler les sieges du Ciel, desertez par la reuolte de Lucifer et de ses complices: aussi ne faut-il vser de l'acte du mariage pour le plaisir que la chair y veut prendre, mais pour ceste fin honneste, saincte et heureuse.'

[80] *Tableau du mariage*, p. 209. [81] *L'honneste femme*, ii. 295-6.

party had its rôle well in mind and the will to fulfil it, then little could go seriously wrong.

The simplest form of matrimonial advice consists of a brief list of such concessions and duties, drawn more often than not from Plutarch's *Conjugalia praecepta*, an example of which is found in Guerry's *Traicté de l'excellence du sexe fæminin*:

L'homme doit à la femme l'instruction, et bon exemple, le giste, la table, l'habit et le support, c'est sa chair, nul n'a sa chair en haine, mais la nourrit et conserue. . . . Et la femme doit à l'homme l'honneur et l'obeyssance, garder la maison et mesnager le bien d'icelle, gouuerner les enfans et la famille.[82]

Religious moralists tend to stress the domestic rôle of women, in accordance both with the teaching of St. Paul and that of Aristotle, who, as has been seen, points to the conservative rôle of women and the acquisitive rôle of men in the state.[83] The duties of the husband are said to be diligence, responsibility, conjugal love and respect, protection, and, above all else, fidelity. If the double standard was accepted in practice as a social reality by these moralists, they none the less condemn it, both because it is no justification for adultery and because the husband, who is the 'head of the wife', should set a good example of behaviour.[84]

To wives, these writers are more astringent. The necessity for obedience is everywhere heavily stressed.[85] With Plutarch, they require that wives should conform to the temperament of their husbands, as the moon takes light from the sun; this is sometimes expressed in the more general injunction 'plaire au mari', which, in terms of social behaviour and dress, soon becomes 'plaire au mari seulement'. Valladier even suggests in his *Speculum sapientiae matronalis* that in describing the husband as the head of the wife, St. Paul meant that wives, 'should not hear, see, taste, feel, want,

[82] *Traicté de l'excellence du sexe fæminin*, p. 45; see Eph. 5: 29.
[83] Maillard, *Le bon mariage*, p. 22: 'comme Dieu a fait l'homme et la femme auec diuersité de sexe, aussi leurs a il donné diuerses habitudes et inclinations, conformement à leur sexe, à l'homme la prudence et la force pour faire les affaires exterieures et plus difficiles: à la femme la vigilance, pour auoir soin des affaires domestiques: à l'homme vne authorité pour maintenir les enfans en leur deuoir: à la femme vne tendresse et douceur pour les nourrir et esleuer: à l'homme l'industrie pour amasser, à la femme la diligence pour conseruer et sagement distribuer.' See above, pp. 20–1.
[84] Le Moyne, *Gallerie*, p. 294.
[85] See Du Bosc, *La femme heroïque*, ii. 447–52.

know, or think about anything without first consulting their husbands'.[86]

Conjugal love is often listed among the duties of a wife to her husband, and in so far as this emotion is definable, it appears to be an amalgam of Christian charity and respect; it is certainly nothing like 'fol amour' or 'amour d'inclination' which all moralists agree are disastrous bases for matrimony, and it is unlike 'amitié' in that it is not founded in equality. Silence, devotion to household duties, and domesticity are recommendations drawn from St. Paul's comments on marriage: 'ne sortir pas souuent dehors, et demeurer en la maison', writes Trousset, 'c'est vn grand signe de la fidelité d'vn mariage, et vne marque tres asseurée d'vne femme sage, vertueuse, discrette, bonne, humble, et obeyssante à son mary.'[87] Maillard lists 'pudicité, pudeur, diligence, obeyssance, modestie ès habits'[88] as the essential qualities of a good wife; Angenoust considers 'chasteté, amour conjugal, diligence et soing qu'elle doit apporter en l'administration de sa famille et instruction de ses enfans en la crainte de Dieu'[89] as her most important assets; the good wife, according to Pierre Mambrun, is 'pudica, casta, viri amans, rei domesticae attenta, et pia',[90] and to these lists of qualities Du Bosc adds 'douceur dans la Conuersation et dans la societé.[91]

If these recommendations fail, however, to make life within marriage bearable, moralists have little more to offer in the way of further consolation and advice. Maillard writes 'nous ne sommes pas à nous, mais à Dieu',[92] and recommends patience and mortification,[93] and Caussin gives similar guidance:

La loy de nature nous donne toute permission de souhaitter de bons maris, mais les loix de mariage nous exhortent à les supporter tant que faire se pourra, tels qu'ils nous sont escheus: si nous aimons pour nous-mesmes, cela est impossible, mais si nous aimons pour Dieu, nous y trouuerons du deuoir et de la facilité.[94]

---

[86] *Speculum sapientiae matronalis*, Paris, 1609, f. 27ʳ. Cioranescu cites a French translation of this work in 1611.

[87] *Alphabet*, pp. 236–7.   [88] *Le bon mariage*, pp. 275–306.
[89] *Paranymphe des dames*, p. 199.   [90] *De epico carmine*, Paris, 1652, p. 115.
[91] *L'honneste femme*, ii. 314.   [92] *Le bon mariage*, p. 14.
[93] As does Adrien de Boufflers, in a chapter in his *Chois de plusieurs histoires*, Paris, 1608 (xlv: 'Le plus souuerain remede que peuuent apporter les prudentes femmes pour ramener leurs maris desbauchez à la raison, est la seule patience').
[94] *La cour sainte*, ii. 300.

There is only a short step between this and Orgon's advice to his daughter: 'mortifiez vos sens auec ce mariage',[95] and the similarity in approach of Molière's misogynist suitors and the moralistic recommendations to women listed above needs hardly to be pointed out.[96] There, as here, heavy stress is laid on duty, and rarely is there any mention of the contentments of matrimony.

The femme forte *in marriage*

As has already been noted in a more general way, a contrast may be detected between the recommendations of traditional moralists to wives and the prescriptions of Du Bosc and Le Moyne to their *femmes fortes.* For Le Moyne, matrimony is not an institution from which to expect pleasure and contentment, but rather hardship and self-abnegation, suffering and duty;[97] Du Bosc also underlines the seriousness of marriage in his *Femme heroïque* in a chapter entitled 'le mariage n'est pas vn commerce enioué, mais respectueux: c'est vne societé serieuse'.[98]

The key to the behaviour of the *femme forte* in marriage is complete commitment, seen in her fidelity and 'amour conjugal'. 'il faut de la force, et pour porter de bonne grace les chaisnes du mariage', asserts Le Moyne in the preface to his *Gallerie des femmes fortes*, 'qui ne sont iamais si bien dorées qu'elles ne blessent; et pour en souffrir le ioug, qui n'est iamais si poly qu'il n'incommode.'[99] The examples of married *femmes fortes* in his work (among them Camma, Arria, Panthea, and Monime) are made the subjects of such searching *questions morales* as 's'il est du deuoir de la femme forte d'exposer sa vie pour donner à son mary le repos de l'esprit', 'du deuoir des femmes enuers leurs maris disgraciez et malheureux', and 's'il est du deuoir et de la fidelité des femmes, de s'exposer à la mort pour leurs marys'. Constancy 'dans l'vne et l'autre fortune' has already been pointed out as one of the central characteristics of the *femme forte*, and it is therefore not surprising that the first and last of these questions expect an affirmative

---

95 *Le Tartuffe*, IV. iii, l. 1305.
96 A connection has been drawn between patristic and moralistic views on marriage and those of Molière's misogynists by G. Lanson, 'Les stances du mariage dans *L'école des femmes*', *Revue politique et littéraire*, IV. xii (1899), 718–20, where these stances are said to be a parody of Desmarets's 'Préceptes de mariage de sainct Gregoire de Nazianze . . . , stances' (*Autres œuvres poetiques*, Paris, 1640, p. 95).
97 *Gallerie*, pp. 231–2.   98 *La femme heroïque*, ii. 453–7.
99 *Gallerie*, āā4ᵛ.

answer. Perhaps the most used example of marital fidelity tested to its extreme limits is the suicide of Arria, to which Du Bosc, Le Moyne, and Grenaille all refer. The fidelity of wives to unfaithful husbands is also praised.[100]

Another of Le Moyne's *questions morales* asks 'pourquoy l'amour coniugal est plus fidele du costé de la femme que du costé de l'homme'. He points to several reasons for this, the dependence of women on their husbands, the greater temperamental capacity of wives for love, the devotion of the accident to the substance, but of the arguments he adduces, the most striking is the following:

Il est du Cœur de la Femme, comme des Riuieres qui sont contraintes et resserrées; et qui n'ont qu'vne pente par où la décharge leur est libre. La Conscience et l'Honneur, la Pudeur et la Crainte, les loix de Dieu et les loix du Monde sont des obstacles qui l'enuironnent de tous costez: et il ne peut se repandre sans les rompre; ny les rompre sans vne violence extraordinaire. Aussi lors que parmy tant d'obstacles, la descharge luy est ouuerte du costé d'vn Mary, il s'épend de ce costé là, auec plus d'impetuosité et moins de reserue, que ne fait le cœur de l'Homme, qui ressemble à ces Riuieres vagues, qui n'ont ny bords ny leuées, et qui ont cent Ruisseaux ouuerts par où elles se déchargent.[101]

Le Moyne does not consider, it would appear, that some other object than a husband could benefit from this emotion, but then, nor would his *femmes fortes*.

Since Du Bosc and Le Moyne undertake serious moral teaching both directly and by example in their works, it should be pointed out here that their heroines are in the great majority not subject to the constraint of marriage, or if they are, they are none the less enabled to display their independence in acts of will permitted by the customs of their time, such as suicide and self-sacrifice. For the artistic design of these writers to work, marriage must be shown not to diminish the grandeur of their *femmes fortes*, and thus they tend to concentrate on those aspects and situations in marriage in which their heroines are made to display their stature. Their moral teaching, therefore, has little to do with everyday marital existence.

[100] See O. de la Brosse, *Saint François de Sales: les femmes mariées*, Introduction, pp. 21 ff.; Du Verdier, *La bergère amoureuse*, Paris, 1622, pp. 162–212 ('histoire de Filenie').
[101] *Gallerie*, p. 107.

Secular Writers on the Reform of Marriage

The idea of any change in the institution of matrimony was, as
has been seen, abhorrent to religious moralists, for the indissolubility and divine institution of marriage were, in their eyes,
tenets of faith too fundamental to be questioned. It i. therefore
at the risk of appearing *libertins* that secular writers undertook to
criticize the state of marriage, and it is scarcely surprising that
after the trials of Théophile and others in the 1620s they display
great prudence in the airing of their heterodox opinions.

Popular anti-feminist literature, drawing on a long tradition of
marriage criticism, proposes no reforms of any substance, con-
tenting itself with complaint and ironic acceptance of the ills of
matrimony. Even the author of the *Brief discours pour la reformation des mariages*, whose work has such a promising title, confines
himself to a catalogue of disadvantages, and ends by advising
those who in spite of his warnings still desire to be married not to
do so unless they are of reasonable age, sound health, and good
eyesight; this advice calls to mind the paintings of Van Eyck and
Cranach the Elder which portray the young wife with the old
husband.[102] Such sentiments are typical of this genre of literature; they are usually coupled with a recommendation to those
already married to exercise stricter control over their wives;
such a suggestion is found in the *Purgatoire des hommes mariez*.

Caillet, Rampalle, and La Mothe Le Vayer show more imagination in the remedies they propose. The first of these writers
stresses the value of the soothing counterweight to the trials of
matrimony occasioned by the wife, namely the dowry:

Encores que la dot ne soit pas de l'essence du mariage, et qu'il puisse
mieux subsister sans elle, qu'elle sans luy, si est-ce qu'il se trouue peu de
gens qui se veuillent embarquer sans biscuir sur cette mer immense,
pour passer le destroit du mesnage, sans l'equipage d'vne dot assignée,
pour fournir à la longueur du voyage, et soustenir les assauts des
pyrates et autres monstres marins, qui sont les charges du mariage
... Les femmes sont de tant plus obligées de contribuer aux charges
de mariage, qu'elles-mesmes en sont les principales et les plus one-
reuses.[103]

---

[102] See also Scudéry, *Le cabinet*, Paris, 1646, p. 196 ('Le portrait d'vne dame qui a
vn vieux mary. De la main de Finzoni').

[103] *Tableau de mariage*, p. 90.

La Mothe Le Vayer regrets that his generation does not have the blessing of divorce, accorded to the fortunate Romans:

[Les Romains] avoient cette jolie porte de derriere qui nous manque aujourd'huy, appellée repudiation, par laquelle avec une feuille de papier en main, intitulée libelle de divorce, ils se tiroient de cet estat calamiteux, là où il n'est pas à present en nostre puissance d'en sortir que par le feu, la corde ou le precipice . . .[104]

Rampalle too evokes the convenience of divorce, or trial marriage, an idea discussed in greater depth by the *précieuses*:

Ce lien tout sacré qu'il est, seroit rompu tres-souuent, presque aussi-tost que noüé, si les diuorces estoient encores en usage, ou qu'il y eût vne année de Nouiciat en cét Ordre comme en tous les autres.[105]

Elsewhere, however, *libertinage* is to be found much nearer the surface, as in the following passage, where the author advocates free love—free, at least, for men:

Ce n'est pas que ie veuille approuuer icy ni le debordement et le vice: quelque volupté qui se trouue dans vne affection secrete, il y a tousiours du blasme en ce qu'elle est illegitime: mais sans faire le Casuiste en ce poinct, ny r'encherir sur la verité de leurs sentimens, i'estimerois que l'offence n'est gueres moindre de ceux qui mescontens de leur mariage chargent leur moitié de maledictions et d'iniures, et vomissant mille[s] blasphemes contre le Sacrement qui les lie, ne cessent d'en maudire les chaisnes; et tous ceux qui s'en sont meslez. Vne licence moderée est quasi moins criminelle qu'vne pareille vie, où l'on ne sorte iamais de la rage et du desespoir.[106]

Elsewhere in these works ideas of a more practicable nature are found. Juliard states that 'la loy, la nature, l' honneur et la coustume . . . veulent que le seul consentement et non autre, fasse le mariage',[107] which may well have been a pertinent reminder in the seventeenth century of what is accepted without question today. One of the interlocutors in La Mothe Le Vayer's *Dialogue du mariage* suggests that equality in marriage might well solve many of the difficulties inherent in that state.[108] Finally, Grenaille gives the following advice about wife-beating:

D'autres vous persuaderont peut-estre de chastier vostre femme afin de

---

[104] *Quatre autres dialogues*, p. 412; cf. Montaigne, *Essais*, ed. Thibaudet and Rat, ii. 15, p. 599.   [105] *Discours aeademiques*, p. 277.

[106] Ibid., pp. 257–8; cf. Sorel, *Francion*, ed. Roy, iv. 159–61.

[107] *Les amours de l'amant converty*, p. 90.

[108] Cassander, in *Quatre autres dialogues*, p. 382.

la rendre sage, et de la tourmenter de telle sorte qu'en fin elle ait de la retenuë apres ses dissolutions. Pour moy ie vous recommande plutost la patience que la iustice, et si vous auez de la force, que ce soit pour souffrir, et non pas pour vous vanger. Puisque vous auez pris vne chaisne pourquoy vous plaignez vous de ce qu'elle vous attache?[109]

If there appears to be a poverty of constructive suggestions on the part of secular thinkers, it is perhaps because they saw scope only for idle speculation, and no real possibility of putting into practice their ideas for reform which, it is safe to suppose, would certainly have included some form of divorce beyond the accepted causes for annulment inside the jurisdiction of the Church. This lack of imaginative remedies is, however, amply made up for in the writings which voice the views of the *précieuses*.

The Précieuses *and Marriage*

The writings dealt with in this section date from between 1653 and 1660, and fall therefore outside the strict chronological scope of this investigation, but it would seem worth while to include an account of them, both because they portray the views of women towards matrimony which neither the religious moralists nor the secular writers set out to do in any detail, and because they represent the culmination of marriage criticism in the half-century under discussion.[110]

In the eyes of the *précieuses* there are two possible ways of reforming marriage, beyond a heroic acceptance of its ills: the first is by altering the institution itself, the second by changing the rôle which women have to play within it. In the first case, there is not the prudence and reticence in their discussions which have been detected in the works of *libertin* writers, but their suggestions were perhaps forgiven by the powers of orthodoxy for their very preposterousness; in the second case, their ideas are far less speculative, and their realism was not opposed to the essential teachings of the Church.

On the reform of the institution of matrimony, the most striking ideas are found in de Pure's *La Prétieuse*, published in the

[109] *L'honneste mariage*, pp. 179–80.
[110] I am much indebted in this section to the articles by P. Hoffmann, 'Préciosité et féminisme dans le roman de Michel de Pure', *Travaux de linguistique et de littérature*, v. 2 (1967), 23–34; B. Treloar, 'Some feminist views in France in the xvɪɪth century', and R. Lathuillère's book, *La préciosité, étude historique et linguistique*, Geneva, 1966 (vol. 1 only).

late 1650s and reputed to be a transcription of conversations among a group of *précieuses* which date from about 1655. In a section entitled 'Remedes aux maux de mariage', this group, which includes one *précieux*, presents its views on marriage reform. All are agreed that under the existing dispensation it is not so much a case of 'se marier à quelqu'vn' as 'se marier contre quelqu'vn'; because of lack of choice of partner, disregard of the rôle of emotional and physical attraction, and the 'iniustice de l'vsage', matrimony for them is irremediably condemned to dissatisfaction, and they are only prepared to see it in this poor light. Thanatime suggests that it would be more bearable if men showed the same respect and submission to women after marrying them as they had done before, and Neosie proposes a similar idea where authority and domination in matrimony would be shared on a yearly rota by husband and wife. Sophronisbe proclaims that marriage should be looked upon as a 'société arbitraire' in which no binding vows are made, and Gésalire (who is generally understood to be Segrais), the sole *précieux*, then advocates free love and an abolition of marriage in favour of the 'douce liberté de faire des conquestes'.

Melanire talks of the necessity to 'se marier et se mettre au dessus du mariage', and suggests that this might be achieved by the institution of a form of trial marriage, renewable every year by both sides.[111] Aracie puts forward a similar proposition to this, which is perhaps the most feminist in implication of all these suggestions:

l'aymerois bien mieux ... borner la durée du mariage, et en prescrire le terme au premier enfant. Apres ce premier ouvrage et cette marque de benediction des honnestes feux dont ils auroient brûlé l'vn pour l'autre, ils partageroient le butin; l'enfant demeureroit au père et la liberté à la femme que le pere reconnoistroit de quelque somme considerable, et qui repondroit au merite de son ouurage.[112]

These ideas are indeed revolutionary, but they lack reference to everyday life, and it would seem that the reading of novels contributed more towards their formation than observation of mundane reality. In a similar way, Mademoiselle de Montpensier, having failed to find a suitor to coincide with her own ideas of rank, proposes the total abolition of marriage in a series of letters to

---

[111] *La prétieuse*, ed. Magne, ii. 27–8.   [112] Ibid. ii. 39.

Madame de Motteville written in 1660, long before her unfortunate affair with Lauzun, inspired perhaps by the equality accorded to women in such institutions as the Abbaye de Thélème, Utopia, and Plato's Republic:

> Ce qui a donné la superiorité aux hommes a été le mariage; et ce qui nous fait nommer le sexe fragile a été cette dépendance, où le sexe nous a assujéties, souvent contre notre volonté, et par des raisons de famille dont nous avons été les victimes. Tirons-nous de l'esclavage; qu'il y ait un coin du monde où l'on puisse dire que les femmes sont maitresses d'elles-mêmes, et qu'elles n'ont pas tous les défauts qu'on leur attribue . . .[113]

The most interesting ideas produced on this subject by the *précieuses*, however, are found in their treatment of the question of changing woman's rôle in marriage as it was traditionally conceived. In this sphere, the legislators of social behaviour, such as Faret, Du Bosc, and Grenaille, whose works really belong to the 1630s, prefigure many of their suggestions. As such writers were concerned to portray the rôle of women in society, and as 'galanterie' is considered as essential quality of the 'honnête homme'—'il faut que chacun sçache', writes Sorel in his *Loix de la galanterie* of 1644, 'que le parfait Courtisan, qu'vn Italien a voulu descrire, et l'Honeste Homme, que l'on nous a despeint en françois, ne sont autre chose qu'vn vray Galand'[114]—traditional attitudes towards female social behaviour became inapplicable, and a new image of woman, which includes the married woman, was proposed, of which Du Bosc writes:

> Il ne faut donc pas s'imaginer qu'en parlant de cette femme accomplie de qui nous faisons l'image, nous entendions de peindre vne mere de famille qui sçait bien commander à ses seruantes, et qui a le soin de peigner ses enfans. Quoy que nous ne blamions point cela, neantmoins il faut auoüer que la Musique, l'histoire, la Philosophie, et d'autres pareils exercices sont plus conuenables à nôtre dessein, que ceux d'vne bonne ménagere . . . le bon naturel et la bonne inclination [des dames] demeurant sans effect, manque de lecture ou de Conuersation, quand la Tyrannie de leurs meres ou de leurs Maris, ou bien quelque autre malheur les empesche d'acquerir les belles qualitez dont elles naissent capables.[115]

[113] Madame de Motteville, *Mémoires*, in *Collection de mémoires relatifs à l'histoire de France*, ed. C.-B. Petitot and L.-J.-N. Monmerqué, Paris, 1820–9, xxxvi. 301.
[114] *Les loix de la galanterie*, ed. L. Lalanne, Paris, 1855, p. 4.
[115] *L'honneste femme*, i. 262–4.

The same writer elsewhere refutes the belief, held by traditional moralists and justified by d'Aubigné in a letter to his daughters already quoted, that this social freedom is only suitable for the ladies of the *grande noblesse*, and that it would interfere with the domestic duties of those of lower station.[116]

This extension of the social rôle of wives is also advocated in the writings of the *précieuses*, notably in those of Madeleine de Scudéry. On a more personal level, in the words of Hoffmann, the *précieuses* wanted to 'décanter l'amour de tout ce qui lui est étranger, la contrainte, l'habitude, la commodité, l'intérêt'. This entailed freedom from the dangers and discomfort of childbirth, freedom from the tyranny of parents and husbands, freedom, moreover, to enter into sentimental liaisons outside marriage without fear of reproach or jealousy. These claims are often over-laid with a deep distrust of men: Eulalie in de Pure's *La Prétieuse* proclaims that it is not the institution of marriage which is at fault, it is the husband, and Scudéry's Sapho in *Le grand Cyrus* says much the same thing:

Il faut donc, sans doute, repliqua Tisandre, que vous ne regardiez pas le Mariage comme vn bien: il est vray, repliqua Sapho, que ie le regarde comme vn long esclauage: vous regardez donc tous les hommes comme des Tirans? reprit Tisandre: ie les regarde du moins comme le pouuant deuenir, repliqua-t'elle, dés que ie les regarde comme pouuant estre Maris.[117]

Eulalie's portrayal of the married *précieuse* adequately summarizes the ideals of such writers as Madeleine de Scudéry:

Elle est mariée comme si elle ne l'estoit pas. Le mariage ny le ménage qui en est vne des plus importantes suites n'en trouble point, ny la quietude de l'ame ny les doux emplois de l'esprit. Elle sçait rendre ses differens deuoirs; elle s'acquite également bien enuers le mary, le monde et soy-mesme. Elle distingue et sépare les choses; elle fait garder les rangs et les espaces à l'amour et à l'amitié. Elle ne confond point ce qui est du deuoir et ce qui est de bonté. Elle considere autrement le mary et le fauory.[118]

It is interesting that this picture has in common with the portrayal of Faret's *Honneste homme* and Du Bosc's *Honneste femme* the fact

[116] d'Aubigné, *Œuvres complètes*, ed. Réaume and Caussade, i. 449–50; see also Du Bosc, *L'honneste femme*, iii. 83.
[117] *Le grand Cyrus*, Paris, 1649–53, x. 577–8.
[118] *La prétieuse*, ed. Magne, ii. 54.

that it is defined by negatives. Here is, however, a realizable project in terms of seventeenth-century society, where the *précieuses'* ideas on marriage reform were not, and here also de Pure ends his discussion of the 'remedes aux maux de mariage'.

The *précieuses*, therefore, would like to extend the concept of marriage so as to include at least spiritual and emotional freedom, and to allow for the figures of both 'mary' and 'fauory'. If this sort of freedom is necessary in practice to make society work, it none the less poses serious moral problems, for it represents the first step on the downward path to coquetry and worse. Du Bosc's *honnête femme*, while a pleasant and agreeable member of society, does not have this added measure of independence; in its place, devotion and piety are stressed, and there can be little doubt that her only consolations, if she is unhappily married, are mortification and patience. The morality of 'galanterie' and the married woman will be discussed more fully, however, in another chapter.

The relevance to feminism of the literature relating to marriage need hardly be stressed further. As is the case with feminist writing, it may be shown to reach an apogee in the middle years of the century, developing out of a tradition of form and content, largely drawn from patristic and sixteenth-century marriage literature on the one hand, and *esprit gaulois* writings on the other. As the century progresses, the influence of enlightened moralists such as St. Francis of Sales, as well as that of sceptical writers who express more searching doubts about the institution of matrimony than are found in the productions of the *esprit gaulois*, alter the tenor of tracts on this subject, and prepare the way for the utterances of the *précieuses*, faithfully recorded by Michel de Pure. As is also the case with feminist writing, it may be shown that texts which discuss marriage and its problems decline in originality and interest at the inception of the personal reign of Louis XIV. A final indication of the close association of feminist writing and that devoted to the problems of marriage is the fact that neither feminism nor marriage is discussed outside the context of the other; questions of matrimony and marital behaviour loom large in feminist literature, and in moralistic tracts which relate to marriage there is frequent reference to such topics as female education and social freedom.

V

Feminist Thought and Society: *Honnêteté* and the *Salons*

WHERE the previous chapter showed the predominantly static attitudes of traditional moralists to marriage which the discussions of *libertins* and *précieuses* fail to influence, here is to be examined a sphere of feminist agitation in which happier results were obtained. The demands for greater social independence and for the freedom to pursue learning may be seen to modify the vision of the lady in society found in treatises on social behaviour in this period. From the traditional moralists' notion, already described in an earlier chapter, there is a development, largely due to the influence of St. Francis of Sales, to the *honnête femme* and *honnête fille* of Du Bosc and Grenaille, and from these, through the freer life of the *salons* and the newly won prerogative of education, to the fully secular ideal of the *précieuse*. This progression in theoretical treatises is matched and preceded by a similar extension of the social rôle of women over the same period.

It may at first glance seem difficult to reconcile this change in attitudes towards women in society with the emergence of the *femme forte* at about the same date. But just as feminist writers, inspired by an increasing appreciation of paradox and the need to evoke wonder or admiration for their artistic creations, had converted the traditional apologies of womankind, which rested on assumptions of female weakness and frailty, into a panegyric of the *femme forte*, so also the religious ideal of woman in society, imbued with piety and attentive to duty and authority, gives way to a secular, more heroic, more independent, more active ideal, the *précieuse*. In both cases the change is due to a reassessment of woman's worth, although the resulting figures have little in common. Their difference may be accounted for by the fact that whereas the *femme forte* is the creation of masculine writers in the main, the *précieuse* represents an ideal conceived of by women.

One might also add, with rather less assurance, that whereas the *femme forte* has overtones of paradox and heroic virtue characteristic of the regency of Anne of Austria, the *précieuse* is most remarkable for her lucidity and sensibility, and belongs more to the period after the Fronde, both as a literary and a social phenomenon.

The importance to literature of this development is incommensurable, for not only do women through the medium of the *salons* become the arbitrators of taste and language, but in those same assemblies they also bring together professional writers and their aristocratic counterparts, and at the same time provide an outlet for female literary productions. Because of its importance to letters in France, this subject has already been investigated widely, and the body of criticism which deals with *honnêteté* and the *salons* is formidable in size. For all this, it has seemed worth while to include this chapter, for not only have some of the writings discussed here not claimed the attention of previous critics, but also no investigation of feminism at this period could be said to be complete without some consideration being paid to the influence of the theory of *honnêteté* and of the *salons* on the remarkable development of the social and literary ascendancy of the female sex.

Before any discussion of *honnêteté* and the *honnête femme* is undertaken, however, the development of the religious ideal of womanhood should be briefly considered.[1] It is in the teaching and works of St. Francis of Sales, and most especially in his *Introduction à la vie dévote*, first published in 1608, that the key to this development may be found. In that work he declares that the devout life is reconcilable with an active rôle in polite, secular society; whereas he does not deny that there will be conflicts, he asserts that these will be no more difficult to surmount than are those of living a life of the spirit in the flesh, which even celibates are constrained to do. Together with this assertion goes the proposition that the devout life should be approached in easy stages, so that the transition from the cares of this world to those of the next will not be too sudden. The first writers to reproduce his ideas in their works include two didactic

[1] Concurrent with the development to be discussed in this chapter, there is also the continuation of the traditional ideal of woman; examples of this may be found in Nicolas Du Sault, *La vie de madamoiselle de Neuvillars, miroir de perfection pour les femmes mariees, et pour les ames devotes*, Paris, 1649 and Simon Martin, *La vie de sainte Ulphe vierge*, Paris, 1648.

novelists: Philippe d'Angoumois, who in 1617 wrote a *Discours sur la conversion d'une dame mondaine à la vie dévote* as part of his Lyons cycle of works, in which the *dame mondaine* is made to see the error of her neglect of family and religion, of her vanity, and of the selfish life of leisure which she has been leading, and turns to God, while remaining a member of secular society;[2] and Jean-Pierre Camus, whose numerous works in the second and third decades of the seventeenth century bear ample witness to this stream of thought.[3]

For all this, the emphasis in these works rests squarely on the *vie dévote*; Du Bosc, who pays frequent tribute to St. Francis of Sales, also begins from this position, as d'Ablancourt points out in his preface to *L'honneste femme*:

J'ay cherché long-temps la cause pourquoy nos Dames viennent si tard à la deuotion et ne la prennent ordinairement que comme vn purgatoire des fautes de leur ieunesse. Ie voyois dans les Histoires, les Payennes en la fleur de leur aage toutes pleines de la crainte de leurs Dieux et de l'amour de la Vertu. Cependant auiourd'huy auec tant de grands Exemples, auec tant de Sermons et de Confessions, elles ne se réforment quasi iamais que sur la fin de leurs iours, et ne changent de vie que sur le poinct de la quitter. J'en ay accusé nostre propre felicité qui nous a amené les delices auec l'abondance et les richesses; ie m'en suis pris à la Decadence des siecles et à la vieillesse du Monde: mais veritablement ie n'en trouue point d'autre raison que celle-cy. Nous les voulons mener d'abord à la perfection Chrestienne, et nous ne considerons pas qu'on ne va que par degrez à vn si haut poinct . . . Il faloit leur apprendre les deuoirs de leur Naissance, deuant ceux de leur Baptesme, et les conduire aux vertus Chrestiennes en les faisant passer par les Morales . . . Enfin apres auoir bien gousté ce liure elles prendront plaisir à celuy de Monsieur de Sales et ce sera icy *L'Introduction de l'Introduction à la vie Deuote*.[4]

Du Bosc, however, progresses from this standpoint, and where in the first part of his treatise he stresses the need for devoutness, in subsequent parts there is a shift of emphasis towards social

[2] See Second de Turin, 'Une apologie littéraire et doctrinale de la dévotion séculière d'après le Capucin Philippe d'Angoumois', *XVIIe siècle*, lxxiv (1967), 3–26 and lxxv (1967), 3–21.

[3] See A. Garreau, *Jean Pierre Camus, Parisien, évêque de Belley, 1584–1652*, Paris, 1968; V. Gastaldi, *Jean Pierre Camus, romanziere barocco e vescovo di Francia*, Pubblicazioni della Facoltà di Lettere e Filosofia, xxi, Università di Catania, 1964.

[4] *L'honneste femme*, i. ẽẽ3ʳ–4ʳ.

graces and qualities. That devoutness is the *sine qua non* of his *honnête femme* is never in question: 'il se peut faire qu'il y en ayt de Deuotes, qui manquent les autres qualitez d'vne honneste femme', he writes in 1636, 'mais il ne se peut faire qu'il y ayt iamais d'honneste femme entre nous, qui ne soit Deuote',[5] and similar statements may be found in the works of moralists of the 1640s; but it is also asserted that the *vertus Chrestiennes* both can be and should be socially acceptable. The *avertissement* to the third and last part of *L'honneste femme* indicates Du Bosc's shift in emphasis:

I'ay voulu monstrer exprez aux Dames, comme les vertus Chrestiennes n'adioustent rien de facheux on d'importun aux Morales; qu'au contraire elles les guident, elles les soulagent, et les embellissent. I'ay voulu leur descouurir l'impertinence aussi bien que la malice de ceux qui leur veulent persuader, que la Deuotion est importune pour la Société, et desagreable pour l'entretien; puis que les infidelles mesmes, ont souhaité la Pieté aux Dames de leurs temps.[6]

If the ideas of St. Francis of Sales find reflection in literature, it is not surprising that their influence may be detected in society, in which sphere he was equally if not more active. Mention has already been made of the tributes paid to the charitable activity of women in the fields of teaching, nursing, and the relief of poverty. It is not necessary to list here the many orders founded for or by women under such directors as St. Francis of Sales, Vincent de Paul, and Coton between 1590 and 1650: their number is as impressive as their scope of activity. They form part of the religious Renaissance, marked also by a resurgence of mysticism in the Church, in which sphere also women played a preponderant rôle. It is not suggested here that these *femmes dévotes* were in any way attached to the doctrines of *honnêteté*; indeed, they probably felt the duality of the *vies mondaine et spiri-tuelle* more sharply than any others of their generation. The clash of the demands of this world with those of the next seems to have caused a divergence of the ideals of devoutness and of secularity at this time, no doubt widened by a desire for commitment to one or the other world, and, in spite of the recommendations of St. Francis of Sales, the spheres of religious activity and of secular society grew apart over the period in question. This divergence may be detected in the continual and violent attacks by clerics on

[5] *L'honneste femme*, iii. 483.   [6] Ibid. iii. ẽ2ᵛ-3ʳ.

the religious hypocrisy of the *femme mondaine*, coupled with an increasing emancipation of women from the strictures of traditional moralists about their rôle in society.

A final prefatory note should be dedicated to the meaning of the epithet 'honnête' when applied to women. Sorel points to the ambiguity of the adjective in his *De la connoissance des bons livres*:

L'Epithete d'Honeste n'avoit force autrefois qu'en disant, *Vn Honeste-Homme*, pour signifier un Homme accomply en toute sorte de perfections, et de vertus; et par *l'Honeste-Femme*, on entendoit seulement celle qui gardoit sa chasteté: mais depuis qu'il y a eu un Livre de ce nom, il a passé avec raison à des significations plus amples, la mesme force estant donnée pour les Femmes que pour les Hommes.[7]

The earlier meaning of 'honnête' when applied to women is, however, never lost, and has in fact survived into modern French where the social rather than moral overtones have disappeared. This would seem to result from traditional moral attitudes to the importance of chastity to women; it is perhaps significant that whereas Faret never mentions the necessity of devoutness or chastity to his *honnête homme*, both Du Bosc and Grenaille in their treatises about the social conduct of women are constrained to underline female continence and piety. While society works on the assumption that men are at all times, and without regard to the niceties of morality, liable to solicit women for their favours, it was generally believed that were women not to make at least public refusals, then anarchy and chaos, both moral and social, would ensue. Thus *galanterie*, as Huet was to point out, was countenanced because it was believed that little immorality would proceed from it.[8]

Honnêteté *and the* Honnête Femme

In his *Connoissance des bons livres* Sorel gives a bibliography of the literature relative to *honnêteté*, which is at first sight impressive in its size, until it is realized that Grenaille alone is responsible for half of the titles.[9] For the purposes of this chapter, the bibliographical landmarks are Faret's *Honneste homme*, first published in 1630, but reprinted many times between that date and 1650; Du

[7] *De la connoissance des bons livres*, Paris, 1671, pp. 5-6, quoted by Lathuillère, *La préciosité*, i. 578.

[8] Huet, *De l'origine des romans*, Paris, 1711, pp. 208 ff., quoted by Magendie, *La politesse mondaine*, i. 89-90.

[9] *La connoissance des bons livres*, pp. 5-6, quoted by Lathuillère, *La preciosité*, i. 578.

Bosc's *Honneste femme*, published in three parts from 1632 to 1636; Grenaille's *Honneste fille*, also in three parts (1639–40), and his *Honneste veuve* (1640); Sorel's *Loix de la galanterie* (1644); and finally Couvay's *Honneste maistresse*, which appeared in 1654, but which has a *Privilège du roi* dated 1648. The last of these works alone lies outside a developing tradition of writing; Du Bosc is clearly inspired by the appearance of Faret's work to write an equivalent treatise for women, Grenaille and Sorel specifically refer to Faret's *Honneste homme*, and the former also pays tribute to Du Bosc's *Honneste femme*.[10] There is some justification, therefore, in approaching these works (with the exception of that of Couvay) as a unified manifestation of attitudes towards social behaviour, even though they were produced over a period of fifteen years.

Honnêteté is a secular ideal of social conduct, combined in the case of women with dominant overtones of chastity, piety, and devoutness. It is an ideal peculiar to the Renaissance, which was first outlined in Castiglione's *Il cortegiano*, where it is instrumental in the refining of society and in making social intercourse agreeable for all who take part in it: prince, ministers, court ladies, and courtiers. In France this ideal is given a national, almost Parisian, character, as it is associated with the *honnête liberté* of French society, which French commentators on the life and customs of other European nations, especially Spain and Italy, find lacking outside the frontiers of their own country. A great deal is written at this time about the different modes of social intercourse of various nations, and it seems to be generally agreed that if the considerable liberty allowed to both men and women in French society has its drawbacks, such as the risk of infidelity on the part of both husbands and wives, nevertheless the less restricted and formalized life which resulted from it is a great advantage, as is a certain *galanterie* in conversation to which Huet was to attribute the emergence of the national character of French literature.[11]

Together with these beliefs go the arguments about climate and its effect on character and society, put forward by Grenaille:

Mais les Filles [en France] principalement ayant les corps les mieux composez, ont les plus belles humeurs; comme elles n'ont point trop de froideur qui fasse croire qu'elles ne sont point bilieuses, elles n'ont

---

[10] Sorel, *Les loix de la galanterie*, ed. Lalanne, p. 4; Grenaille, *L'honneste fille*, i. ẽ2ᵛ–3ʳ. [11] See Magendie, *La politesse mondaine*, i. 88–105.

point aussi de feu qui nous puisse persuader qu'elles sont plus ardantes que temperées. Tenant de chaque extremité elles n'en ont point de vicieuse. Ainsi l'honnesteté leur est plus facile icy qu'ailleurs, dautant qu'elle leur semble aussi naturelle que le vice l'est aux autres. Leur conuersation, qui est l'épreuue des belles humeurs, n'a rien de seuere ny de dissolu; elles sçauent se resioüir et s'affliger à propos, gagner les cœurs, sans perdre rien de leur propre reputation; elles triomphent sans estre touchées de vanité. Elles ne sont ny faciles ny dedaigneuses; elles rebuttent quelquefois sans degouster; elles se font craindre et cherir; on ne les frequente pas pour leur rauir leur honneur, car c'est vne chose impossible moralement, mais seulement pour apprendre l'honnesteté, leur rendant les respects qui sont deus legitimement à leur mérite, aussi bien qu'à leur personne.[12]

Honnêteté is further defined by negatives, by what should not be done; dominating the conversation, wearing inelegant clothes, displaying bad manners, using indecent speech, and so on. It is a middle way between the various extremes of behaviour which are offensive to social intercourse. It is also a definition of duty and function, of how to behave and what to do. With this worldly intelligence goes the need for *bienséance*, which is an aesthetic as well as a moral phenomenon; all that is done should *plaire honnêtement*, and should not exceed the bounds of propriety set by one's place in society, one's sex, one's age, one's quality. The aesthetic element in *bienséance* is very important in the case of women, who are the ornaments of society; both Du Bosc and Grenaille agree, for example, that tears may be seemly in women, whereas anger may not be: 'si les larmes ont quelquefois bonne grace sur vn visage, la cholere n'a pas ce priuilege comme la tristesse', writes Du Bosc; 'quoy qu'on voye souuent de belles melancoliques, ie n'ay iamais ouy parler qu'on ait veu vne belle furieuse.'[13] Grenaille lists three functions of *honnêteté*: to distinguish men from women, to define duty and privilege in society, and to foster elegance in dress, deportment, and expression, thus promoting social grace and the smooth running of society. It is quite clear that such a programme is beyond the capacity of the religious ideal of womanhood, and Du Bosc points in a passage already quoted to the necessity of extending the traditional rôle of women in society.[14]

---

[12] *L'honneste fille*, i. 358–9.
[13] *L'honneste femme*, i. 330; cf. Grenaille, *L'honneste veuve*, p. 71.
[14] See above, p. 116.

The character and attributes of the *honnête femme* (by which name Grenaille's portraits of *fille* and *veuve* will also be referred to) may next be considered. Like Faret's *honnête homme*, she is not necessarily noble, although ideally she may be. Du Bosc includes a chapter entitled 'De la noblesse du sang et de celle de la vertu', in which he defines three nobilities: 'diuine', which depends on the 'puissance de Dieu'; 'mondaine', which arises from 'le bonheur de nostre naissance'; and 'morale', which rests on the 'liberté de nostre esprit'.[15] Of these, the last is open to all those who seek it. In another chapter entitled 'De la naissance et de l'education', he points to the superior rôle of acquired over innate virtue, although admitting that the latter is preferable, as it is natural and unforced.[16] Grenaille talks of moral nobility, and asserts that 'il vaut mieux estre fils d'vn pere fort vicieux, et viure dans la probité, que d'estre meschant estant fils d'vn homme de bien'; but he also praises breeding, and prefers innate to acquired virtue.[17]

Of the physical attributes of the *honnête femme* not a great deal is written. Beauty is, of course, like nobility, an accident of birth, and as Du Bosc and Grenaille talk of moral nobility, so also do they uphold spiritual beauty. Both are against the affectation of youth or beauty, where this is not natural. Du Bosc speaks of beauty as something to be neither adored nor despised, and Grenaille comes to a similar conclusion, balancing the views that beauty is 'vn peu de boue figurée' and, at the same time, 'vne partie du ciel sur la terre'.[18] Du Bosc emphasizes the need for *bonne grâce*, an acquired characteristic which regulates movement, expression, and dress by art; art should, however, not be employed in a way which runs counter to nature, and thus *bonne grâce* does not consist, for example, in wearing *mouches* in such a way as to prevent those displaying them from laughing lest they should fall off.[19] In dress, also, the *honnête femme* should be guided by moderation, and if she is married, she should follow her husband's dictates; it will be impossible to please everyone, but she should have her priorities in the right order. Excess in ornamentation should also be avoided.

It should be pointed out here that these attitudes are enligh-

---

[15] *L'honneste femme*, ii. 235–50.   [16] Ibid. ii. 79–138.
[17] *L'honneste fille*, i. 37–74.   [18] Ibid. iii. 325–44.
[19] *L'honneste femme*, i. 338.

tened for religious moralists. The cult of beauty and youth is attacked vigorously in such works as the *Tableau des piperies des femmes mondaines* (1632), the *Courtisane dechifree* (1642), and the literature relating to royal edicts about the use of foreign lace in clothes.[20] Even Grenaille in his *Plaisirs des dames* reverts to a more traditional attitude in condemning this cult, and in his *Bibliothèque des dames* he includes a translation of Tertullian's violent treatise *De cultu mulierum.* The desire of women to beautify themselves is accepted as a natural and inseparable feature of the female psyche, and, together with the Church Fathers, most religious moralists set out to curb it. Maillard sees in 'la curiosité des femmes à se parer' one of the causes of adultery,[21] although if it is employed to attract only the husband's attention and thus keep him from infidelity, then, according to the author of the *Tableau des piperies des femmes mondaines,* quoting Aquinas, it is excusable.[22] Cosmetics, perfume, and corsetry are perversions of the truth, and, what is more, a wholly extravagant dressing-up of a body which is to serve as 'pâture aux vers'. Since we are for such a short period in this world, time and money spent on the ornamentation of our mortal part is unnecessary and in some cases sinful. Other aspects of ornamentation come under attack: the immorality and inconstancy of fashion; the desire to appear above one's station—'vne bourgeoise ne s'estime pas bien vestue si vne Princesse a de plus beaux habits qu'elle',[23] writes Grenaille; the fact that as inner beauty is reflected in outward attractiveness (here Ficino's 'omne pulchrum est bonum' is quoted), affected beauty tends to hide spiritual ugliness.

With the ever-enlightened St. Francis of Sales, Du Bosc and Grenaille advocate a sane and reasonable attitude to this question, allowing that the desire to appear beautiful may be quite innocent, and permitting a certain degree of ornamentation. Du Bosc, quoting Jerome, writes:

Le sexe [des femmes] est curieux d'ornemens et s'estudie naturellement à la somptuosité des habits, iusques-là mesme qu'on voit beaucoup de Dames tres-chastes qui s'habillent neantmoins auec soin, sans auoir

---

[20] e.g. *Consolation aux dames sur la deffence des passemens, poinct-coupez et dentelles,* 1628; see Magendie, *La politesse mondaine,* i. 31–50.

[21] *Le bon mariage,* p. 167.

[22] *Le tableau des piperies des femmes mondaines,* ff. 64ᵛ–65ʳ; Aquinas, 2a 2ae 169. 2.

[23] *L'honneste mariage,* p. 117.

d'autre but à leurs desseins que leur contentement particulier, par ie ne sçay quelle complaisance ou satisfaction tres-innocente[24]

and Grenaille, in a chapter entitled 'Que le soin du corps n'est pas contraire à l'honnesteté des filles', condemns in a characteristic fashion the two extremes of *affeterie* and neglect of one's appearance, and concludes :

Au reste, l'honnesteté n'est pas tant vne vertu cachée, qu'vne perfection manifeste; elle vient du fond du cœur, et neantmoins elle doit paroistre au dehors. Son essence nous desplaist, quand la figure nous rebute. Nous ne prendrions iamais des filles pour des Anges materiels, si leurs corps estoient plus mal faits, que ceux de plusieurs animaux desraisonnables. Elles ne doiuent estre ny trop materielles, ny trop subtiles.

L'Honnesteté encore estant vne qualité qui rauit l'ame par les yeux, ne sçauroit auoir son effect, si au lieu de leur plaire elle leur estoit desagreable.[25]

It is also pointed out by Anna Maria van Schurman that the fact that women are the ornaments of society makes it one of their duties to 'se parer honnestement'.[26]

As is suggested by the quotation from Grenaille given above, *honnêteté* is thought of as an outward and visible sign of an inward and spiritual quality, and thus it is not surprising that Du Bosc and Grenaille devote the greater part of their portraits to a description of the moral attributes of the *honnête femme*. It should be noted here that these writers, while asserting that women are capable of all the virtues which men can also practise, make it clear that the social pressures on women give them little scope for demonstration of these capacities, and thus advocate the development and enhancement of traditionally female qualities, such as refinement, charitableness, *douceur*, compassion, and so on. Grenaille lists modesty, prudence, discretion, temperance, clemency, and gracefulness as the qualities of the *honnête femme*, and Du Bosc, betraying his own special interest in stoicism, has chapters on 'la crainte et le mespris de la mort , 'la constance et la fidelité', and 'l'esprit esgal dans vne bonne et vne mauuaise fortune'.[27]

---

[24] *L'honneste femme*, i. 281–2; Jerome, *Epistola cxxviii, PL* xxii. 1096.

[25] *L'honneste fille*, iii. 337–8; see also André Du Chesne, *Figures mystiques du riche et precieux cabinet des dames*, ff. 9ᵛ–10ʳ, and *passim*; Lathullière, *La préciosité*, i. 610.

[26] *Question celebre*, p. 8.

[27] *L'honneste femme*, ii. 364–81; i. 215–36; ii. 139–99.

Both writers make a great deal of such Christian virtues as piety, chastity, patience, and humility for reasons already given, and Du Bosc underlines the necessity for 'complaisance', or social adaptability and ease. In his eyes, one of the functions of *honnêteté* is to make virtue socially acceptable, and especially virtue in women, as men emulate them: 'il ne depend que des Dames, de faire beaucoup plus d'honnestes hommes que nous n'en auons', he writes, 'puisque la plus part d'entre nous, mettent toute leur estude à plaire aux femmes : veritablement, si elles temoignoient plus d'inclination à la vertu, les hommes y seroient plus portez.'[28] In a chapter entitled 'De la chasteté et de la complaisance', he declares that these two qualities should go together, one without the other being incomplete. Saintliness is not always earnest and grave, according to this writer; St. Elizabeth of Hungary was, after all, a fine and enthusiastic exponent of dancing, and an example to those who believe that piety and cheerfulness are not reconcilable.[29] A further necessity in society is to 'bien connoistre son humeur affin de la regler'. While the 'humeur gaye' is ideal for social intercourse, it has unfortunate propensities to superficiality, hypocrisy, facility; the more sombre 'humeur melancolique' on the other hand, while less prone to these faults, is far less amenable to social gatherings.[30] Once again there is an opposition of extremes, and a middle course is recommended.

'L'art de plaire à la cour' is one of the major preoccupations of the *honnête homme*, but such expertise is not expected of his female counterpart. Her rôle in the running of society is essentially passive, and her conduct prescribed by more rigid moral dictates than that of the *honnête homme*. Her honour and her reputation, her reaction to *galanterie* and to 'service', are the preoccupations which moralists recommend to her. In discussing the question of the relative value of reputation and 'conscience', both Du Bosc and Grenaille assert that the 'estime de Dieu' is more important than the 'estime du monde', but that reputation may not be dismissed as nugatory, for although it is founded on 'opinion' and sometimes 'medisance', it can obscure the truth and unjustly impugn virtue. 'Ce n'est pas assez . . . que la femme . . . soit innocente', writes Du Bosc, quoting Caesar; 'elle ne doit pas mesme estre soubçonnée.'[31] The full implications of this are

---

[28] *L'honneste femme*, iii. 353–4.   [29] Ibid. i. 171–92.
[30] Ibid. i. 86–126.   [31] Ibid. i. 151–2.

discussed exhaustively in Ceriziers's trilogy of *Innocences,* first published together in 1640.[32]

Galanterie is an integral part of social intercourse in France— Sorel describes Faret's *honnête homme* as a 'vray Galand'[33]—and it clearly consists in great part in homage paid to women. This, according to Faret, is not for the pleasure which we hope to receive from them, nor out of gratitude for their maternities, but because of their inherent excellence; but whether this attitude is representative of public opinion may be doubted, for forty years later Poullain de la Barre was to declare that praise of women is always assumed to be motivated by 'galanterie', by which he seems to mean the tribute paid by the strong to the weak, or 'amour'.[34] *Galanterie* involves all men in the praise and service of all women; this Sorel points out in his *Loix de la galanterie,*[35] and it is not inappropriate to compare this with the feudal attitude that all women should be respected and protected by men: L'Escale, Marie de Gournay, and Du Ruau all refer to this homage as a duty.[36] *Galanterie* as it is conceived of in this period goes further than this, however, and aspires to higher rewards than those tokens of consideration with which suitors in contemporary novels are satisfied. There are grave moral problems in the court- ing of married women, and these are no smaller in the case of the unmarried who are served by gallants who envisage not marriage but physical possession. Du Bosc and Grenaille utter earnest warnings about such 'faux seruiteurs', and recommend to their ideals a 'chaste défiance'.

The question of service is examined in Couvay's *Honneste maistresse,* but only that service which women may claim from those who seek them in marriage. Grenaille deals with a far more general concept of service, by which men in general render them-

---

[32] *Les trois estats de l'innocence, contenant l'histoire de la Pucelle d'Orleans, ou l'innocence affligée, de Geneviefve, ou l'innocence reconnuë, d'Hirlande, ou l'innocence couronnée.* This work is mentioned obliquely by Madeleine de Scudéry in a letter to Conrart (see *Un tour- noi de trois pucelles en l'honneur de Jeanne d'Arc,* ed. Barthélemy and Kerviler, p. 20).
[33] *Les loix de la galanterie,* ed. Lalanne, p. 4.
[34] *De l'égalité des deux sexes,* Paris, 1673, ã2ʳ. Sorel goes further, and sees in *galan- terie* no more than a virtuoso display of good manners (*Histoire amoureuse de Cleagenor et de Doristée,* Paris, 1621, p. 220).
[35] *Les loix de la galanterie,* ed. Lalanne, pp. 25–6.
[36] L'Escale, *Champion des femmes,* ff. 37–8; Marie de Gournay, *L'ombre,* Paris, 1626, p. 200; Du Ruau, *Tableau historial des regences,* pp. 33–4; see also Bronzini, *L'advocat des femmes,* pp. 136–7.

selves subject to women, although for differing motives: 'on respecte les femmes par interest ou par reflexion', he writes, 'les filles par amour.'[37] The paradox of the strong submitting themselves to the weak has already been commented upon; on the one hand, Grenaille points to this:

Nous sommes Superieurs au regard du plus foible sexe, mais nous nous rendons inferieurs volontairement. Nous auons de beaux droicts, mais nous y renonçons; nous auons des richesses pour viure pauures. Le plus grand ennemy que les femmes ayent eu n'a-t-il pas dit autrefois à Rome; c'est vne chose estrange, que nous commandions à tout le monde, et que les femmes nous commandent . . .[38]

yet on the other, he urges his reader to concede that 'en s'assujettissant [aux filles], [les hommes] se soumettent à la Gloire et à l'Equité'.[39] From the masculine point of view, expressed in the works of traditional moralists from Erasmus to Trousset, the practices of service, of courtship, and of wooing are thought to be unmanly, effeminate, and vilifying, and the discomforts and indignities involved are dwelt upon satirically.[40]

For all this, it is clear that the 'empire des femmes' extends beyond the expressions of respect advocated by Grenaille and the legitimate demands on suitors set out by Couvay into the morally questionable sphere of the 'favori'. In Castiglione's *Cortegiano* as in Héroet's *Parfaicte amye*, the difficult subject of the relationship between the unhappily married court lady and her lover is adumbrated, and this is taken up again by the *précieuses*. Du Bosc and Grenaille make no direct reference to this question, and it appears to be assumed in their works that as the *honnête femme* is, will be, or has been also an 'honnête épouse', such relationships would

[37] *L'honneste fille*, i. 215.
[38] *L'honneste mariage*, pp. 167–8. 'Le plus grand ennemy' is Cato (for this anecdote, see Plutarch, *Life of Cato*, viii, and above, p. 22).
[39] *L'honneste fille*, i. 32.
[40] See Erasmus, *Enchiridion militis Christiani*, in *Opera omnia*, v, col. 57, quoted by Screech, 'Rabelais, de Billon and Erasmus', 257: 'propone tibi ante oculos quam indecorum, quam totum hoc insanum sit amare, pallescere, macerari, lacrymari, ac turpiter supplicem esse scorto putidissimo. Occinere ante fores nocturnas, pendere de nutu dominae, pati regnum mulierculae, expostulare, irasci, rursum redire in gratiam . . .'; see also Trousset, *Alphabet*, pp. 140–1, and Bronzini, *L'advocat des femmes*, pp. 99–100, who sees the disadvantages of wooing from their other aspect: 'les pauvres femmes ne se peuuent iamais reueiller la nuict, qu'elles n'oyent des aubades, et des chansons amoureuses, ou qu'elles n'entendent au moins ces esprits sans repos, qui souspirent et se lamentent à l'entour de leurs maisons.'

be unthinkable for her. As was pointed out in the last chapter, mortification and patience are the only remedies to unhappy marriages offered by religious moralists.

A final aspect of the portrayal of the *honnête femme* should here be mentioned. It has already been said that she is defined to a large extent by negatives, and Du Bosc systematizes these into four antiportraits, which he calls respectively 'la scandaleuse', 'la desbauchee', 'la superstitieuse', and 'la coquette'.[41] The first is characterized by malicious gossip, and the second is the female equivalent of the 'libertin des mœurs'; the other two deserve rather fuller descriptions. The 'coquette' is unlike the *honnête femme* in that she is 'affetée', where Du Bosc's ideal is modest, natural, and at all times mindful of her honour, even at the expense of social grace. The 'coquette' is ever trying to appear to be something which she is not: if old and plain, she strives to seem young and beautiful; if low-born, she strives without success to appear noble:

Les Femmes de grande fortune, mais de petite naissance, ont vne certaine Coquetterie plus insuportable que toutes les autres. Comme elles ont moins de generosité, elles ont plus d'insolence et d'affeterie. Elles sont tousiours empeschées de leur contenance; elles ressemblent à celles qui sont braues depuis peu, et qui n'ont pas de coustume d'estre pompeusement habillées. Ce ne sont que mines contraintes : ce ne sont que regards et que sousris estudiez...Mais tout cela ne reüssit point; l'on reconnoit en elles, que comme les personnes nées riches, sont les moins auares : aussi celles qui sont nées grandes, sont les moins vaines. Elles ressemblent à ces Reynes de Theatre, qui n'ont qu'vne Maiesté forcée...[42]

They do not dress to please their husbands, but their 'favoris'; they are full of vanity and pretension, and even go so far as to judge works of literature (both Grenaille and Du Bosc mention this, and disclaim seeking their approbation); they are 'molles, lasches, delicates'. They are, in fact, the antitheses of Le Moyne's *femme forte*. It is not, however, clear how profligate they are; certainly in the eyes of these moralists they set too great store by the things of this world, but whether they correspond to the 'femme mondaines' of Trousset and other anti-feminist writers (who are the 'meretrices' of patristic literature) is not altogether

---

[41] *L'honneste femme*, i. 348–64; iii. 91–172, 241–82, 333–72.
[42] Ibid. iii. 136–7.

clear. D'Alibray's sonnet on the subject would seem to suggest
that they do:

> Qu'vne femme coquette est vn fardeau pesant,
> Encor qu'elle ait tousiours la teste fort legere!
> Aux amants de dehors rien n'est si complaisant,
> Mais à son poûre Espoux, c'est pis qu'vne Megere.
>
> A t'elle des enfans de quelque fauory?
> Des maux qu'elle ressent son Espoux est coupable:
> N'a-t-elle point d'enfans? elle en blasme vn mary
> Qui de la contenter ne fut iamais capable.
>
> Chez elle, elle est malade et ne prend goust à rien,
> Elle perd la parole, et manque d'entretien;
> Faut-il suiure vn Galant? elle est gaillarde et saine:
>
> Elle entre en appetit, elle a de la vigueur,
> A force de vomir ne se rompt plus la veine,
> Car c'est son seul mary qui luy fait mal au cœur.[43]

Certain attributes of the 'coquette' (pretension to literary and
linguistic arbitration, the accommodation of 'mary' and 'fauory',
affectedness of manner) appear to be prefigurations of features of
the *précieuses*, but the 'coquette' lacks distinction and seriousness
of purpose, and appears not to be a 'janséniste de l'amour'.

'La superstitieuse' is a portrait of an altogether different nature,
and is characterized by insufficient or imperfect religious practice.
The hypocrisy of women in church had been one of the themes of
the preaching of the Franciscans, and it is therefore not surprising
to find it in the work of Trousset, who was one of their order:

Vous verrez quelquefois [des femmes impudiques] à l'Eglise deux et
trois heures, les genoux en terre, feindre vne extase meditatiue, en
monstrant le blanc des yeux aux voûtes du temple, sans sourciller, et
faire tous les signes d'vne ame religieuse et deuote, pour receuoir le
guerdon de l'honneur du monde, et en receuoir loüange d'estime et de
reputation, couuant en cependant vn escadron de desirs lascifs, vne
armée de mauuais desseins, et vn bataillon de folies, de vanitez, et
d'impertinences en affection . . .[44]

The *Tableau des piperies des femmes mondaines* has an even more
lengthy description of the behaviour of women in church,[42] Du

---

[43] *Œuvres*, Paris, 1653, ii. 26.   [44] *Alphabet*, pp. 154–5.
[45] *Tableau des piperies des femmes mondaines*, ff. 44ʳ–46ʳ.

Bosc writes an equally forceful denunciation,[46] and Grenaille
points out that such women do not go to church to worship, but
to be worshipped.[47] Guez de Balzac even declares:

Les dames sont aujourd'huy obligées de se confesser d'avoir esté à la
messe, et le desir qu'elles ont de se faire regarder est la profanation
ordinaire du lieu où elles sont regardées.[48]

Of the confessions of women, Trousset writes that they are 'in-
fructueuses pour n'estre entieres et parfaictes',[49] and Théotime
in addressing the 'dames de Paris' is equally scathing:

Estes vous aux pieds d'vn Confesseur ou il vous tarde que vous n'en
soyez dehors, ou si vous y demeurez longtemps, c'est pour leur dire
milles choses dont ils n'ont que faire . . .[50]

Perhaps the most prominent issue concerning women and the
practice of religion at this time is the worldliness of their dress
and deportment inside churches. As has already been mentioned,
a directive was sent out by the Archidiacre of Arras regarding
female attire in church,[51] and two priests, no doubt inspired by
this, produced treatises in which they debate whether the exposure of breasts in public, let alone in church, is a mortal or a
venial sin, both concluding that if the sinner realizes the effect of
her manner of dress on men, then she has sinned mortally. These
works—Polman's *Chancre, ou couvre-sein feminin* and Juvernay's
Discours particulier sur la vanité des femmes de ce temps—were both
published in 1635, the latter being reproduced in an enlarged
form in 1637, and again in 1640; they belong to a tradition of such
admonishments: Antoine Estienne's *Remonstrance charitable aux
dames et damoyselles de France, sur leurs ornemens dissolus* of 1585, the
preaching of Sufrin and Valladier in the second decade of the
seventeenth century,[52] the anonymous *Paraenese aux filles et
femmes, pour la modestie et honnesteté Chrestienne* published at about
this time, and, for that matter, Jacques Boileau's *De l'abus des
nuditez de gorge*, published at Brussels in 1675 and at Paris twelve

---

[46] *L'honneste femme*, i. 338-9; iii. 241 ff.   [47] *L'honneste fille*, ii. 122.
[48] *Œuvres*, ed. Moreau, i. 448.   [49] *Alphabet*, p. 97.
[50] *Question Chrestienne touchant le jeu*, p. 9.
[51] See also H. P. Salomon, *Tartuffe devant l'opinion française*, p. 21, where the part
played by the Compagnie du Saint Sacrement in the control of female dress in
churches is examined for the same period (1634).
[52] See *Tableau des piperies des femmes mondaines*, ed. P. Lacroix, Paris, 1879, Introduction, p. xiii, and Valladier, *La saincte philosophie de l'ame*, p. 814.

years later,[53] all bear witness to the same preoccupations. As well as the danger to the spiritual well-being of both sexes occasioned by low-cut dresses, their profanity and inappositeness in places of worship and their evil social effects are dwelt upon, as is indicated by the following passage from the *Courtisane dechifree*:

Que fait la Courtisane venant au lieu sacré, la gorge et la poictrine nue, sinon, pour faire vn change detestable, sçauoir l'échange de son mary, qui sera Homme de bien, chaste, modeste et pretieux en vertus comme l'or, à quelque paillard et lascif muguet qui luy plaist? C'est aussi pour y vendre de la chair viue; car elle met son[t] sein et ses mammelles à découuert, c'est estaler sa marchandise de chair viue, et se vendre elle-meme . . .[54]

No excuse is accepted for this exposure: Coste, answering the most obvious line of defence, writes, 'vous dirés que c'est la mode: mauuaise mode, qui mene et qui conduit si aisement à la damnation.'[55]

If the ideal of the *honnête femme* seems unattractive and un-remarkable, it is perhaps because those virtues are attributed to her which tend to place women in the background of society, such as discretion, modesty, quiet taste in dress and ornaments, silence. It is striking that there are few female characters in the imaginative literature of the time which equate closely to the depictions of the *honnête femme* discussed here; while there are many figures similar to the *femme forte*, and, later, to the *précieuse* also, and while the heroine of the novel is omnipresent, it is only this last depiction of woman which shares many characteristics with the *honnête femme*, and it may be argued that she is too adventurous and outgoing to qualify for this description. Du Ryer's Lucretia is a figure exceptionally close to the feminine ideal of Du Bosc and of Grenaille; but she is almost unique in her day (1638). Until the *honnêtes femmes* of Molière's comedies, there is little to suggest that this predominantly bourgeois ideal made any deep literary impact.

Education and the Use of Leisure

Throughout the sixteenth and seventeenth centuries there was a steady growth in the numbers of the leisured middle classes and

[53] Salomon challenges the attribution of this work to Jacques Boileau (*Tartuffe devant l'opinion française*, pp. 24–5 n.).

[54] *La courtisane dechifree*, Paris, 1642, p. 227.

[55] *Eloges et vies des reynes*, p. 78.

the lower aristocracy,[56] and consequently an increase in the number of women for whom the household was no longer a necessary preoccupation, yet for whom the range of pastimes was limited and unsatisfactory. In confronting this problem in perhaps the first age in which it had become critical, moralists of this period, instead of advocating the creation of reasonable outlets for worthwhile activities outside the context of religion, are concerned with one question alone: how should leisured women fill their spare time without prejudicing their salvation, and without offending against *bienséance*? This preoccupation is common to both secular and religious writers at this time; Anna Maria van Schurman points out that the essential problem behind the *Question celebre, s'il est necessaire, ou non, que les filles soient sçavantes* concerns the 'veritable deuoir et le iuste employ d'vne fille bien née',[57] and Du Bosc writes in his *Honneste femme*:

Cependant que les hommes passent leur vie, à combattre, à estudier, à gouuerner, et à voyager; si on demande ce que font la pluspart des femmes, on ne peut rien respondre, si non qu'elles employent tout leur temps, à se parer, à se promener, à caqueter, ou à iouer. Ne sont-elles nées que pour cela?[58]

It is quite clear that few moralists approve of the pastimes followed by the leisured women of their day. In 1633 a writer calling himself 'Théotime' published a *Question Chrestienne touchant le jeu, addressee aux dames de Paris, sçavoir si une personne addonnee au jeu se peut sauver, et principallement les femmes*, in which he gives a description of a day in the life of a leisured woman; rising late in the morning, she spends two hours dressing, skimps her religious duties, enjoys a long lunch consisting of delicacies, consecrates her afternoon to card-playing and gambling, partakes of another sumptuous meal, and then retires. After this account he declares:

Ie trouue vostre façon de viure excellente, vous ne parlez que de rire, que de iouër, que de passer le temps, vous ne craignez ny les tentations, bien que vous soyez continuellement parmy les hommes, ny la pauureté, bien que vous ioüiez les pistoles à douzaines, ny l'orgueil et la vanité, bien que vous soyez superbement vestuës, ny le desreiglement en paroles, bien que vous disiez tout ce qui vous vient en pensée, ny les moindres atteintes contre la chasteté, car vous estes

---

[56] See R. Mandrou, *Classes et luttes de classes en France au début du XVIIᵉ siècle*, Florence, 1965, pp. 49–62; V. L. Tapié, *La France de Louis XIII et de Richelieu*, Paris, 1967, pp. 42–8.   [57] *Question celebre*, p. 4.

[58] *L'honneste femme*, iii. 175–6.

toutes pures, ayant la gorge descouuerte au milieu des Bals, et des
Comedies, et des festins . . . . Sans mentir, ceste façon de viure est
excellente, comme ie vous disois, mais neantmoins apres auoir faict
beaucoup de reflexion dessus, ie ne pense point qu'elle soit Chrestienne,
et qu'on se puisse sauuer sans miracle, viuant d'vne telle façon.[59]

This treatise further demonstrates how card-playing and gambling
can endanger the sanctity of marriage, one's reputation, and, of
course, one's salvation, and another anonymous writer, 'le sieur
la Franchise', saw fit to write an answer to this part of Théotime's
work. In his *Deffence des dames* he takes up an attitude similar to
that of St. Francis of Sales, which is also faithfully reproduced
in Du Bosc's *Honneste femme* : those who only play cards 'par
recreation et par diuertissement' are in no way sinning, since
card-playing is 'indifferent' in the theological sense of that word.
This author does, however, venture on to more dangerous ground
when he suggests that 'l'oisiueté et la feneantise porteroient
peut-estre les femmes à de plus grands maux et plus dangereux,
dont ceste occupation les diuertist'.[60]

Grenaille, in a work entitled *Les plaisirs des dames*, published in
1641, describes seven pastimes ('bouquet', 'cours', 'miroir', 'pro-
menade', 'collation', 'concert', and 'bal') and, with a characteristically violent dialectic, first eulogizes, then condemns them in turn,
the condemnation carrying the greater force. In this work he
attacks the 'delicatesse' of women in their choice of food, the
frivolous attitude of women to walking—'les Dames', he writes,
'n'entrent pas dans les bois pour s'instruire, mais pour y deuenir
plus ignorantes'[61]—the profanity of dancing, the sensuality of
music, and suggests that the only suitable mirrors for women are
the lives of the saints and the 'plaies de Iesus-Christ'. In this work,
in that of Théotime, in the *Tableau des piperies des femmes mondaines*,
there may be detected a moralistic attitude to 'diuertissement'
similar in many ways to that of Pascal; leisured women fill their
days with worthless occupations to postpone or banish the hour
when they will be faced with the realization of the vanity of their
existence, and of the error in their priorities, in putting this world
before the next, and themselves before God; thus such occupations take on an almost obsessive character.

[59] *Question Chrestienne touchant le jeu*, pp. 5–7.
[60] *La deffence des dames*, Paris, 1634, p. 38.
[61] *Les plaisirs des dames*, Paris, 1641, p. 214.

If such pastimes are thought to be unsuitable for reasons of morality or religion, others are attacked for reasons of decorum and *bienséance*. Balzac, in a letter to Madame Desloges, mentions two types, the 'femme caualier' and the 'femme docteur', which he thinks are unseemly:

Ie . . . ne sçaurois estimer les dames qui veulent faire les caualiers. Il y a des bornes qui nous séparent, et qui marquent nos deuoirs et nos conditions. Ny vous ny nous pouvons les passer legitimement, et les loix de la bien-séance sont si anciennes, qu'elles font mesmes partie de l'ancienne religion . . . Il faut que les femmes soient tout à fait femmes. Les vertus de nostre sexe ne sont pas celles du leur, et plus elles veulent imiter les hommes, plus elles s'eloignent de leur fin . . . La pedanterie n'est pas supportable en vn maistre és ars, comment le sera-t'elle en vne femme? Et quel moyen de l'ouyr parler vn jour durant metamorphose et philosophie; méler ensemble les Idées de Platon, et les cinq voix de Porphyre; ne faire pas vn compliment, où elle n'employe vne douzeine d'orizons et d'hemispheres. Et finalement quand elle est au fonds des autres matieres, me dire des injures en grec, et m'accuser d'hyperbole et de cacozele. Elle veut qu'en deux vers il y ait pour le moins quatre pointes. Elle a dessein de remettre sur pié les strophes et les antistrophes. Elle regle la poësie Epique, et la dramatique, et dit qu'elle n'a point assez de patience pour souffrir vne comédie qui n'est pas dans la loy des vint-quatre heures, qu'elle s'en va publier par toute la France. Si j'auois vn ennemy mortel, voila la femme que ie luy souhaiterois pour me bien venger de luy.[62]

These sentiments are deeply impregnated with a conservatism to be expected from a writer who belonged to the world of erudition as well as to that of the *salons*, and Le Moyne, in his *Gallerie des femmes fortes*, makes an indirect reference to this letter and answers it by pointing out that if women were shown to be capable both of strenuous physical exercise and of deep learning, then the 'bornes qui nous séparent' should fade away, and 'vsage' be made to change.[63]

All these moralists conclude from their assessment of the daily round of leisured women that suitable and useful employment must be found for them. Caussin declares:

Les Romains ont gardé plusieurs siècles ainsi qu'vne relique, la quenoüille de la Reyne Tanaquil, beaucoup plus cherement que la lance ou l'espee de Romulus, estimans qu'il estoit plus necessaire de donner

---

[62] *Lettres, seconde partie,* ii. 869–79.   [63] *Gallerie,* pp. 209–13.

aux femmes des exemples de trauail, que de fournir aux hommes des idées de la guerre.[64]

Théotime asks 'pour estre Dames de qualité, pensez vous estre exemptes de trauailler? C'est à ces iours là, mes Dames, qu'il faut que vous imitiez la femme forte, dont il est parlé dans l'escriture, Il faut prendre l'aiguille et le fuzeau en main . . .',[65] but these admonishments to economically unnecessary and, by their very nature, boring and routine occupations are scarcely attractive or persuasive; Du Bosc's suggestion is more sensible:

> Platon veut au septiesme de ses Loix qu'on employe [les femmes] aux mesmes exercices que les hommes, et tache de prouuer qu'elles n'en sont pas moins capables . . . mais si son opinion ne semble pas si iuste pource qui est des armes, et qu'il nous fasche de faire reuenir ce regne des Amazones: au moins on ne peut desauoüer, qu'elle ne soit fort raisonnable pour plusieurs autres employs, où les Dames pourroient se rendre vtiles au public, au lieu de viure comme elles font, dans l'oisiueté. Si elles ne naissent pas auec un corps assez robuste pour la guerre, au moins elles naissent auec vn esprit capable de bonnes instructions, aussi bien que nous.[66]

Some form of occupation of the mind is therefore advocated, but exactly what is suitable is a matter of some contention. The existing education offered to young ladies before entering society incurs the scorn of Madeleine de Scudéry's Sapho in *Le grand Cyrus*:

> Y a-t'il rien de plus bizarre, que de voir comment on agit pour l'ordinaire, en l'education des Femmes? On ne veut point qu'elles soient coquettes, ny galantes; et on leur permet pourtant d'aprendre soigneusement, tout ce qui est propre à la galanterie, sans leur permettre de sçauoir rien qui puisse fortifier leur vertu, ny occuper leur esprit.[67]

In Du Bosc's view, women should be encouraged to study both that which is 'agreable' and that which is 'vtile', although care must be taken to avoid 'des sciences qui portent à la dissolution'. Home economics seems to him a very suitable subject for study, since it will silence those critics of female education who assert that learning will divert attention from household duties, in spite of the fact that these household duties take up a negligible amount of time.[68]

---

[64] *La cour sainte*, ii. 297.   [65] *Question Chrestienne touchant le jeu*, p. 51.
[66] *L'honneste femme*, iii. 176–8.   [67] *Le grand Cyrus*, x. 671–2.
[68] *L'honneste femme*, iii. 54–5; 83.

The range of subjects suitable for study is far from agreed among these moralists. Rivet echoes Vives's prescription of Cicero, Jerome, Seneca, and the Bible;[69] Le Moyne recommends moral philosophy,[70] as does Du Bosc, although this writer adds medicine, jurisprudence, and economics, is uncertain about eloquence, and actively dissuades women from the study of poetry, astrology, and military history.[71] Anna Maria van Schurman proposes theology (here all writers are in disagreement), natural history, modern history, and languages;[72] Marie de Gournay favours poetry, history, and moral philosophy.[73] All these writers, together with a long line of moralists from Vives through La Noue to the period in question, condemn the reading of novels and *libertin* works; the *approbation* of Grenaille's *Honneste fille* specifically states that it is judged to be 'tres-vtile pour porter les filles bien nées à toutes sortes de vertus conuenables à leur sexe, et les rendre maistresses des vices que la lecture des liures prophanes de ce temps peut allumer en leur cœur',[74] and in his text Grenaille roundly condemns such writings, among which he includes the works of Ovid and Tasso.[75] The misuse of learning to challenge the authority of the husband is also universally decried.

L'Espine, in his *Parure des dames* published in 1606, points out, however, that little literature is produced which is suitable reading for women:

L'on voit auiourd'huy (mes tres-honorées Dames et Damoiselles) le monde remply d'vng nombre infini de liures et beaux discours: ou pour le faict de la guerre: ou de la doctrine et lettres: ou de la police et regime de l'estat: matieres ou les Dames ne sont receues n'y desireuses (comme ie croy) d'en auoir cognoissance ou instruction. Et peu s'en treuue ordinairement, qui s'employent à donner quelque goust et exercice à elles.[76]

For all the agitation for female education of the 1630s and 1640s, it

---

[69] *Question celebre*, pp. 41–68. [70] *Gallerie*, pp. 252–3.
[71] *L'honneste femme*, iii. 1–90. [72] *Question celebre*, pp. 1–40.
[73] *Advis ou presens*, Paris, 1641, p. 294; cf. Montaigne, *Essais*, ed. Thibaudet and Rat, iii. 3, p. 801. [74] *L'honneste fille*, ii. ĕ4ʳ.
[75] Ibid. iii. 230–1; Béroalde de Verville's *Le moyen de parvenir* and the *Parnasse satyrique* are attacked specifically in *La courtisane dechifree*, in a chapter entitled 'La lecture mauuaise des liures lascifs' (pp. 186–207), and in the anonymous *Méchanceté des filles* (n.p., n.d.), p. 17, quoted by C. Nisard, *Histoire des livres populaires ou de la littérature de colportage*, Paris, 1864, i. 432.
[76] *La parure des dames*, Liège, 1606, f. 9ʳ⁻ᵛ.

is only some twenty years later that works are produced which take into account the deficiencies and limitations imposed on women readers by their traditional upbringing; of such works, the writings of Louis de Lesclache and Bary's *Fine philosophie accommodée à l'intelligence des dames* are examples.[77]

The acceptance of study as a suitable occupation for women is, therefore, the outcome of a crisis in moralistic thought, which was caused both by the terms of reference of religious moralists, which did not admit social change, and by the historical fact of the growth in importance of the leisured middle classes. Where traditional moralists such as Puget de la Serre attempt to cure the social *malaise* arising from the problem of leisure by more strict prescriptions and entrenched attitudes, the more enlightened writers make concessions to modernity, following in the footsteps of St. Francis of Sales. The question of female education, which is primarily social, has an important literary aspect, for not only does it affect the composition of the reading public, but it also is directly related to the rise of the *salons*, which in turn provoke a reaction seen in the republication of such anti-feminist works as Trousset's *Alphabet*, and in the debate about the value of female conversation, discussed below. As has already been noted in the context of feminist and anti-feminist literature and writing about marriage, traditional attitudes coexist with new approaches, and social and literary phenomena are closely related.

The Salons

The practice of assemblies of men and women interested in literature and polite conversation has always been assumed to begin in earnest at the Hôtel de Rambouillet at about the same time as the publication of the first part of *L'Astrée*. Such assemblies must, however, have been common in Italy in the early sixteenth century, and probably also in Lyons in the 1550s; it is to be supposed that the religious troubles which broke the tradition of art and culture fostered in the courts of the last Valois

---

[77] See Reynier, *La femme au XVIIe siècle*, pp. 133–65 ('Comment les femmes ont pu s'instruire'). Bary's work dates from 1660, Lesclache's writings from 1667. Before this, according to Sorel, women had only novels as a means of educating themselves (*L'anti-roman*, Paris, 1633–4, iv. 889, quoted by Magendie, *Le roman français au XVIIe siècle*, Paris, 1932, p. 334, and below, pp. 202–3).

kings were also responsible for the cessation of these gatherings. In the years of Henri IV's official reign an atmosphere of masculinity and mild anti-feminism seems to have been predominant at court, but it is perhaps significant that there is a revival in literary agitation for the freedom for women to study.[78] Such agitation preceded and accompanied the proliferation of *ruelles* in the 1640s and 1650s, and although little evidence of the formation of cultured circles at the beginning of the century has been uncovered, it would nevertheless seem reasonable to suppose that they existed, and that their obscurity is due to their being centred in the provinces and to their bourgeois tone and class. The Chambre Bleue, on the other hand, owes its fame to the fact that it was at Paris, and remained at all times aristocratic, even to the extent of giving *particules* to the Voitures, Benserades, and Chapelains who frequented it.

It should not be assumed that all the *ruelles* (to give them their contemporary title) were alike in character: the Vicomtesse d'Auchy presided over gatherings of *pédantes*, surrounded by astrolabes and mathematical instruments, to which Balzac is probably referring in a letter to Chapelain denouncing 'la pedanterie de l'autre sexe', dated 1638;[79] Madeleine de Scudéry's assemblies were at once more literary and more feminist in tone than those of the Hôtel de Rambouillet, which preserved throughout its aristocratic character, and which was praised above all the others for its good taste and moderation. There are certain common traits, however; the most striking, and the most significant here, is that in all these assemblies women set the tone; it is generally agreed that in the teaching of worldly manners they are the touchstone of what is in good taste and what is not. A second common feature of the *ruelles* (with the exception of the 'sénat féminin' of the Vicomtesse d'Auchy) is their attempt to recreate the escapist world of the *romans de chevalerie* and the pastoral tradition inside the confines of their meeting-places. In this 'romanesque' world, sensibility and refinement are sovereign qualities, and there is a universal preoccupation with love and heroism, 'service' and dangers, where consummation and marriage

[78] See *Le triomphe des dames* (1599), *Discours en la faveur des dames* (1600), Artus Thomas, *Qu'il est bien seant que les filles soyent sçavantes*, *Discours* (1600), Charlotte de Brachart, *Harengue . . . qui s'adresse aux hommes qui veuillent deffendre la science aux femmes* (1604).

[79] *Œuvres*, ed. Moreau, i. 250-1.

are asymptotes which, if reached, would herald the return of
everyday reality.

In all cases, the fundamental rules laid down by traditional
moralists to govern female behaviour are broken: avoidance of
contact with men; the preoccupation with household duties;
'le peu parler'. What is more, the formation of assemblies in
which the conversation turns continually on questions of love
and *galanterie*, and where the 'mary' and the 'fauory' are both
accommodated, runs counter to the precepts of even enlightened
moralists. It is not surprising, therefore, that there is a literary
debate about the 'conversation des femmes' at this time.

The 'conversation des femmes'

Of the documents which relate to this question, two are manuscripts of what appear to have been speeches given before all-
male assemblies, which may be tentatively placed in the 1640s,[80]
and a third is a printed account of a *Conférence du Bureau d'Adresse*,
entitled 'Si la conuersation des femmes est vtile aux hommes' and
dated October 1641. The works of Faret, Du Bosc, and Grenaille
naturally deal with this question, as do certain anti-feminist
works, among them the *Discours de l'ennemy d'amour et des femmes*.
As was the case in the discussion of marriage, it is most convenient to deal with the religious and anti-feminist attitudes to
mixed conversation before examining the apologies.

The religious moralists' attitudes to mixed assemblies is
naturally hostile. On the one hand, women, according to St. Paul,
are bound to remain in the background and to say little, and then
only as wives: 'si les femmes veulent encore se rendre loüables',
writes L'Archevesque, 'qu'elles se separent tout à fait des hommes,
ou à tout le moins qu'elles ne s'en approchent qu'en cas de pure
necessité.'[81] On the other hand, Lambert, author of the remarkable
*Discours du danger et peril qu'il y a de converser et hanter trop familiare-
ment auec femmes, tant seculieres que religieuses*, points to the dangers
to men of contact with women, whose very presence is incitement
to concupiscence and lust. For these moralists, it is in the interest
of both sexes to keep well apart except in marriage, and where they

---

[80] BN N.A. Fr. 124, ff. 177–210 (entitled *De la conversation des femmes ou il est
traité sçavoir s'il est utile aux jeunes gens de les hanter, et de converser avec elles*); BN N.A.
Fr. 1554, ff. 1–10 (Miramion, *Discours de la conversation des femmes sçavoir si cest une
chose utille à la jeunesse*).

[81] *Les grandeurs de la mere de Dieu*, p. 557.

are constrained to meet in public, such as in places of worship, these writers underline incessantly the danger of infidelity and the risk to the sanctity of marriage. In uttering these warnings, they quote frequently from patristic texts which are even more violent in tone than their own asseverations.

The anti-feminist case against mixed conversation is similar to the anti-feminist case against marriage. In the *Conférence du Bureau d'Adresse*, social intercourse with women is condemned because it is 'vn charme qui rend les hommes incapables de tous les bons emplois et exercices plus honnestes'.[82] For unmarried men it is unnecessary, since in marriage they are going to suffer from a surfeit of it; as for those already married, they have enough of the bickering of their wives not to seek for more of it; for celibates it is a 'frequentation insupportable'. In the manuscript discourse *De la conversation des femmes ou il est traicté sçavoir s'il est utile aux jeunes gens de les hanter, et de converser avec elles*, conversation as such is praised as both 'vtile' and 'agreable', but the author, who claims to be impartial, sets out to ask whether 'la conuersation des femmes' has either of these qualities, and further examines whether it is 'incompatible auec la pureté des mœurs'. Its utility is set at nought by this writer: 'ie ne sçache personne de bon sens qui l'ose asseurer, que la conuersation des femmes soit fort vtile pour les sciences ou pour les arts. Ce n'est pas la qu'il faut chercher l'Erudition ou la profondeur des choses.'[83] This is not only because women are not educated, but also because, even when furnished with knowledge, they have no understanding of it. As for the question of the moral effect of such frequentation, the mere choice of subjects in the 'cercles des dames' leads to a *galanterie* especially dangerous to the passionate nature of the young, not to speak of the deleterious effect on character and courage:

[N'est-ce pas] une chose deplorable que tant de personnes perdent la uigueur de leur Ieunesse florissante dans des occupations indignes d'eux et de leur condition, qu'ils passent les années a hanter les cercles des Dames ou aux pieds d'une idole de beauté qu'ils adorent, ne songeans pas que cette beauté du corps se passe comme une fleur . . . tirant uanité de la complaisance qu'à pour eux le sexe le plus fragile, et de la gloire de la chose la plus legere du monde . . .[84]

---

[82] *Cinquiesme tome des questions traittées és conferences . . .* , p. 47.
[83] N.A. Fr. 124, f. 182r.   [84] Ibid., ff. 196–7.

If there is any pleasure in such conversation, then it arises not from the 'force de la vertu', but from the 'infirmité de l'esprit'; in any contact with women, enjoyment is tempered by the effects of the social vices to which they are prone, which this writer lists as 'malignité, enuie, curiosité, indiscretion, médisance'. Miramion, whose *Discours de la conversation des femmes sçavoir si cest une chose utile à la jeunesse* is an apology for mixed social intercourse, begins with an account of the case against such frequentation, in which he mentions the assumption of the low worth of women as companions, the evil effect of contact with women on so many great men, the pernicious character and the effeminacy of those who frequent women as opposed to the masculinity and upright nature of those who shun them.

It should be pointed out that from the female point of view, or more precisely from one female's point of view, all is not perfect; not only does this writer complain that men prefer young female interlocutors to 'celles qui passent trente ou trente-cinq ans, quelque agréable conuersation qu'elles ayent, et quelque fade que l'ayent ces premières . . .',[85] but also that the views of women (or more particularly Marie de Gournay) do not get a fair hearing :

Mais afin de taire pour ce coup les autres griefs [du sexe]; de quelle insolente façon est-il ordinairement traicté, je vous prie aux conferances, autant qu'il s'y mesle? Et suis si peu, ou pour mieux dire, si fort glorieuse, que je ne crains pas d'advoüer, que ie le sçay de ma propre experience. Eussent les Dames ces puissans argumens de Carneades, il n'y a si chetif, qui ne les rembarre auec approbation de la pluspart des assistans, quand avec un sousris seulement, ou quelque petit branslement de teste, son eloquence muette aura dit : C'est vne femme qui parle.[86]

Although Du Bosc points out in his *Femme heroïque* that 'quelque bons que soient les sentimens des femmes, ils sont suspects à plusieurs, seulement par ce qu'ils viennent d'vne femme',[87] it cannot be assumed either that this attitude was widespread other than among *érudits*, or that Marie de Gournay's hurt feelings were shared by many women.

The apologists for mixed conversation do not face as difficult a task as the apologists for marriage, and they acquit themselves

[85] Marie de Gournay, *Advis ou presens*, p. 374, quoted by Magendie, *La politesse mondaine*, i. 91.
[86] *Grief des dames*, ed. Schiff, pp. 90-1.   [87] *La femme heroïque*, i. 151-2.

of their arguments and opinions honourably. The proposer of the utility of such conversation in the *Conférence du Bureau d'Adresse* classifies conversation into three categories: all male (which too often leads to 'contestation'); all female (prone to become no more than 'caquet'); and mixed, which is 'pleine d'vn respect et d'vne douceur et d'vne defference mutuelle'. Its utility for men is evident; 'comparez-moy la rusticité honteuse d'vn païsan qui n'ose leuer les yeux deuant vne fille auec la gentillesse d'vn courtisan accoustumé à cajoler les dames, et vous connoistrez par là si leur conuersation est inutile aux hommes.'[88] Miramion contrasts the pedant and the frequenter of *salons*, and emphasizes the art of conversation which is learnt in such places:

La science de parler apropos, de ne point mesler une Langue auec un[e] autre pour en faire un lengage de barbare, scauoir louer ce qu'un autre condamne, et de scauoir condamner ce qu'un autre louë, sans paroistre un esprit de contradiction, le discernement du pedentisme dauec la veritable science des honnestes gens, le moyen de trouuer le millieu entre l'affectation des sciences et l'ignorance grossiere, toutes ces choses quoy qu'on en dize, ne se trouuent point autre part que dans la conuersation des femmes spirituelles . . .[89]

He also declares that the *honnête homme* is a product of such conversation. Faret declares that of all the manners of social intercourse, that with women is the most difficult, if the most agreeable:

[La conuersation] des hommes est plus vigoureuse et plus libre; et pource qu'elle est ordinairement remplie de matieres plus solides et plus serieuses, ils prennent moins garde aux fautes qui s'y commettent que les femmes, qui ayant l'esprit plus prompt, et ne l'ayant pas chargé de tant de choses qu'eux, s'apercoiuent aussi plustost de ces petits manquements, et sont plus prontes à les releuer.[90]

However, he too points to the civilizing force of female company.

Both Du Bosc and Grenaille, after St. Francis of Sales,[91] naturally do not deny to women the pleasures of conversation, but they are both restrictive in their prescriptions. When in public they must maintain a balance between naïvety and 'subtilité', between too great 'complaisance' and austerity, between silence and 'babil'; discretion and modesty are recommended above all

[88] *Cinquiesme tome des questions traittees és conferences . . .* , p. 46.
[89] N.A. Fr. 1554, ff. 6–7.
[90] *L'honneste homme*, ed. Magendie, p. 89.
[91] See St. Francis of Sales, *Introduction à la vie dévote*, ed. Henrion, pp. 241–5.

other qualities. Pedantry in social intercourse is impugned by Du Bosc with particular force. Grenaille displays an ambivalent attitude; on the one hand, he asserts of his works that 'c'est dans le commerce des hommes que i'ay appris ces veritez instruisantes, et non pas en la compagnie des femmes',[92] and yet, on the other, he undertakes to refute perhaps the most common argument about the danger to men of the company of women, that is, the loss of courage and initiative:

Comme les fables nous ont representé vn Dieu de la guerre, qui va auec plus de fureur contre les ennemis, venant de salüer la Deesse de l'Amour, on a veû sans fiction des hommes illustres qui triomphent tousiours, allant de la presence des Dames à la conduite de leur armée, et de la conduite de leur armée à la conuersation des Dames.[93]

What has so far been discussed concerns the moral advisability and the utility of the 'conuersation des femmes'; about its subject-matter, religious moralists and anti-feminists write even more scathingly. Its frivolity and lack of solid learning are obvious targets for those who write as *érudits*: 'les sublimes discours leur escorchent les oreilles', asserts the author of the *Discours de l'en-nemy d'amour et des femmes*, 'et font donner le nom de Pedant à celuy qui en est l'autheur. Leur entretien ne passe point la cuisine ou l'equipage de l'amour.'[94] Religious writers rail constantly against the dangers of the discussion of profane love, as would be expected, just as they rail against the novels in which such love is a cult. No apologies for the subjects of *salon* debates are made, probably because they found widespread acceptance, and because such subject-matter is thought to be inseparable from social intercourse with women.

Of *salon* conversations, Ascoli writes:

Ces conversations n'ont point un objet très varié; on y parle surtout du sentiment, et si l'on s'y occupe des livres et de toutes les productions littéraires, c'est surtout parce que c'est encore un moyen de revenir à l'analyse du sentiment. Les femmes, douées naturellement de beaucoup de pénétration, de finesse et de délicatesse, sont préparées à merveille pour ces discussions à demi tendres; au XVIIe siècle, elles y brillent, elles en prennent la direction, elles habituent les hommes eux-mêmes à limiter là l'effort de leur pensée : et certes c'est une victoire féminine, mais ce n'est pas de l'ordre de celles que les «féministes» désirent.[95]

---

[92] *L'honneste marriage*, p. 260.
[93] Ibid., p. 280.   [94] *Nouveau recueil des pieces*, p. 147.
[95] 'Essai sur l'histoire des idées féministes en France . . .', *RSH* xiii (1906), 52.

As is suggested here, the discussion of the subtleties of the 'vie du cœur' is eminently suited to the particular gifts of insight and understanding of women at this time, and contemporaries are also aware of this. Even the author of the anti-feminist discourse *De la conversation des femmes* confesses that 'finesse' is a quality peculiar to women, and includes this with 'politesse' and 'ciuilité' among those features which enhance female conversation.[96] Scudéry wrote *Les femmes illustres*, if his preface is to be believed, to illustrate the natural eloquence of women;[97] Grenaille refers especially to their 'grace du langage'.[98] 'Finesse', eloquence, elegant speech: a combination of qualities which would banish pedantry and instil lightness of touch, piquancy, perhaps even an edge of malice to give point to incisive psychological investigations into persons and emotions.

'Paris est maintenant tout remply de Dames, soit à la Cour ou d'ailleurs', writes Gerzan in 1646, 'qui accordent tres-iudicieusement et delicatement, la science auec l'eloquence, les Muses auec les Graces, et l'Art auec la Nature.'[99] In an atmosphere created by the fostering of these female qualities, it is not surprising that *galanterie* should flourish; nor should the proliferation of *salon* games—metamorphoses, portraits, paradoxes, maxims, epigrams, 'guirlandes', anagrams, and most especially 'questions d'amour'—be wondered at. Where levity and piquancy are touchstones, it is to be expected that literary productions would be short and pointed, both because this is a form suited to pungency, and because these can be produced at speed, which, as novelty is an addictive need for the *salons*, especially as their membership grew more fixed, is a very necessary quality. The choice of subject-matter—always personal, often to do with the passion of love—is also dictated by the composition of these assemblies, whose motive spirits are women both expert and passionately interested in amateur psychology. Love became ennobled by these discussions, then sanctified, and finally raised to level of a cult, against which there was a predictably sharp reaction in the writings of *libertins* and moralists; the *Tableau des piperies des femmes mondaines*, Fitelieu's *Contre-mode*, Chapelain's *Discours contre l'amour*, the

[96] N.A. Fr. 124, f. 182^v.

[97] *Les femmes illustres*, i. ã4^v–ẽ1^r. He is not the first to have done this; cf. Ortensio Landi, *Lettere di molte valorose donne nelle quali chiaramente appare non esser ne di eloquentia ne di dottrina alli huomini inferiori*, Venice, 1548.

[98] *L'honneste fille*, iii. 75.   [99] *Le triomphe des dames*, pp. 134–5.

Discours de l'ennemy d'amour et des femmes, the realistic novels, the
Parnasse satyrique, and the *Cabinet secret,* at a later date the works of
literary opponents of the *précieuses,* especially d'Aubignac, are all
in their own way directed against this cult.

Just as these assemblies lived on their literary games and their
personalities, so also did they feed on literature, as this was both
fare for their addiction to novelty, and, in the form of novels
and love poetry, material for discussion and analysis. From the
authors' point of view the reception of their work in the *salons*
was crucial to its failure or success; as early as 1632, long before
the court had any literary interests or pretensions (Chapelain
writes to Marie de Gournay in that year to say that at court 'poet'
was considered the synonym of 'chantre, balladin, caymand,
bouffon, et parasite'[100]), Du Bosc declares:

I'en connoy plusieurs [Dames de grande science] qui sçauent si bien
juger des bonnes choses, et qui les possedent si parfaitement, que leur
conuersation sert d'Ecolle aux meilleurs Esprits; que les plus excellens
Auteurs les consultent comme des Oracles, et qu'on s'estime glorieux
de leur approbation et de leurs loüanges.[101]

and Gerzan, in 1646, inquires 'les plus grands esprits de ce temps
font-ils imprimer leurs ouurages sans auoir l'approbation [des
dames]?'[102] But it will be remembered that one of the features of
Du Bosc's 'coquette' also was the judging of literary productions,
and her approval is expressly not sought by writers: 'comme ie
n'ay trauaillé qu'en faueur des honnestes femmes, ie serois bien
marry d'auoir l'approbation des Coquettes,' declares Grenaille;
'mon liure seroit bien mauuais, si elles en faisoient vn bon iugement.'[103] Where authors at this time seek the opinion of the more
respected *salons,* and especially that of the Marquise de Rambouillet,
they are not concerned with soliciting what are presumably the
forerunners of the 'précieuses ridicules' for their advice.

Literature, therefore, owed as much to the *salons* as the *salons*
owed to literature. This mutually convenient arrangement was
highly productive, but it may legitimately be asked whether much
that was produced by it is now worthy of consideration. These

---

[100] Quoted by Magendie, *La politesse mondaine,* i. 55.
[101] *L'honneste femme,* i. 273.
[102] *Le triomphe des dames,* p. 133. See also Chapelain, *Opuscules critiques,* ed. A. C.
Hunter, Paris, 1936, pp. 404, 421, 449.
[103] *La bibliothèque des dames,* Paris, 1640, ẽ3ᵛ.

'bagatelles' are at once the strength of the *salons*, displaying their most brilliant and fertile aspect, and their weakness, for there is a constant danger of thinly disguised repetition and superficiality, for all their pretensions to 'pénétration'. While also the *salons* provided an acceptable outlet for female literary creativity, and while women who belong to them are urged to write by Madeleine de Scudéry and others,[104] not all were accommodated inside their framework; Marie de Gournay complains of the disrespect shown to the 'Œuures des femmes' by the 'vulgaire des Lettrez',[105] but, as before, it is safe to assume that these sentiments were not universally felt.

In questions of language and vocabulary also, the *salons* exerted a considerable influence:[106] 'c'est parmy les femmes que l'on apprend veritablement la langue françoise', writes Miramion.[107] The author of the *Femme genereuse* is more emphatic:

Le ciel par ses nouuelles influences . . . reduisant les hommes à l'ABC, mesme de leur propre langue . . . les a raualez à ce poinct honteux, de venir à l'escole des femmes apprendre les mots de la mode, dont elles tiennent la regence (auec quelques hommes instruits par elles) et dont elles sont iugées capables par l'aueu vniversel des hommes de la mode.[108]

It is impossible to assess exactly how far the influence of the *salons*, and of their female members in particular, may be traced: Vaugelas writes in 1647 that his guide to usage in the *Remarques sur la langue françoise* had been 'la plus saine partie des auteurs de ce temps' and the court, 'et quand je dis la cour, j'y comprends les femmes comme les hommes'.[109] The emphasis here on women is significant, as a later comment shows:

Dans les doutes de la langue, il vaut mieux pour l'ordinaire consulter les femmes et ceux qui n'ont point étudié, que ceux qui sont bien savants en la langue grecque et en la latine; les premiers ne connaissant point d'autre langue, ils vont tout droit à ce qu'ils ont coutume de dire ou d'entendre dire.[110]

---

[104] See *Les femmes illustres*, i. 422, Preface to the harangue of Sapho to Erinne: 'ie luy fais prendre l'occasion, d'exorter son amie de faire des vers comme elle, afin de faire voir que les Dames en sont capables: et qu'elles ont tort de negliger vne si agreable [o]ccupation.' [105] *Grief des dames*, ed. Schiff, p. 94.
[106] See Y. Fukui, *Le raffinement précieux dans la poésie du XVIIᵉ siècle*, Paris, 1964, pp. 58–61 ('Le rôle des femmes dans la purification du langage').
[107] N.A. Fr. 1554, f. 7ᵛ. [108] *La femme genereuse*, pp. 97–8.
[109] Quoted by L.-F. Flutre, 'Du rôle des femmes dans l'élaboration des *Remarques* de Vaugelas', *Neophilologus*, xxxviii (1954), 241–8. [110] Ibid.

As might be expected, there is a reaction of grammarians and *érudits* against the authority of women in matters of language, in which may be detected the seeds of one of the issues of the 'querelle des anciens et des modernes'.[111] Scipion Dupleix, in a work entitled *Liberté de la langue françoise dans sa pureté*, written to refute Vaugelas's *Remarques* and published in 1651, puts the case for the 'ancients':

Quant à ce que nostre Auteur [Vaugelas] comprend les femmes, comme les hommes (ce sont ses termes) sous la plus saine partie de la Cour, cela, sous son respect, est ridicule: si ce n'est qu'il nous produise en tout temps des femmes, qui aient deux conditions principalement, voire necessairement requises pour discerner le bon Vsage d'auec le mauuais. L'vne qu'elles soient bien instruites aux regles de la Grammaire, pour sçauoir sa congruité; et aux preceptes de la Rhetorique, pour juger de l'elegance et de la pureté des termes et des phrases. L'autre qu'elles soient bien versées en la langue Latine et mesmes en la Greque, afin de sçauoir la force de l'expression d'vne infinité de mots que la nostre emprunte de l'vne, et de bon nombre qu'elle a tiré de l'autre. Cela estant ainsi, où se trouveront des femmes qui aient ces deux conditions? et s'il y en a quelques-vnes aujourd'huy (dont ie n'ay pas la cognoissance) qui nous asseurera de la succession d'autres de pareille capacité?[112]

Géname's (or Ménage's) speech in de Pure's *La prétieuse* may be seen as an answer to such a position:

Ie ne doute point que les femmes ne soient capables de plus d'invention que les hommes, par la raison mesme de leur ignorance; car comme elles n'ont point d'embarras des notions estrangeres, ny l'esprit usé des principes de sçavoir qu'on peut y avoir fait glisser, elle agit avec liberté et au gré de son essort: si bien que la Nature abandonnée à elle-mesme, s'éleve tout autrement dans cette fougue qu'alors qu'elle est dans les contraintes de l'art, et embarrassée dans les principes du sçavoir.[113]

The debate about the 'conuersation des femmes' is undoubtedly won by the feminist faction, and after 1650 little is written to question the value and agreeableness of mixed social intercourse

[111] For the connection between feminism and the position of the 'modernes' see A. Adam, 'Baroque et préciosité', *Revue des sciences humaines* (July–Dec. 1949), 213.
[112] *Liberté de la langue françoise*, pp. 24–5; see also La Mothe le Vayer, *Considerations sur l'eloquence françoise de ce temps*, Paris, 1638, pp. 110–12.
[113] *La prétieuse*, ed. Magne, i. 169–70.

presided over by women. The literary and linguistic rôles of the *salons* are also established by that date, and their catalytic action on literature confirmed by the productions of the 1650s, both in style and content. It is difficult to assess the rôle of study and of the freedom for women to educate themselves in the growth in number and prestige of the *ruelles*, but it may safely be assumed to be associated with this phenomenon, although the study undertaken is perhaps very different from that proposed by the protagonists of female education. The recurrent description of cultivated women, 'sçauantes sans la paroistre', is indication enough of the importance of learning to the *salons*.

It would seem safe to assume, therefore, that for female members of the leisured bourgeoisie and the higher classes, the social atmosphere and the range of activities and outlets changed considerably for the better between 1620 and 1650, largely as a result of feminist agitation in society and literature. For all this, however, in the words of Mlle Gueudre, 'les salons n'élaborent aucun humanisme'.[114] Their members were a self-confessed élite, separated from the 'vulgaire' by a bastion of purified language and by a barrier of allusions, unconcerned with the problems of the society of their day, fiercely intent on the preservation of their self-created world of refinement, taste, and sensibility. It is quite clear that the *honnête femme*, as she is described by Du Bosc and Grenaille, is not a suitable member of this world, because of her all-pervading piety, her reticent and subservient obedience, her emotional commitment to her husband. There is also lacking a quality of wit, of levity, of delight in intrigue; if the *honnête femme* had taken part in these gatherings, observation rather than active participation would have been her rôle.

The ideal of the *ruelles* is the *précieuse*. *Préciosité* offered women a system of existence conceived of as an antidote to their plight as wards and wives, but that this is its sole facet is clearly not the case. The preoccupation with love in terms of a cult, the purification and enrichment of language, the creation of a self-conscious intellectual élite, are other manifestations of this movement, which precede its emergence. The *précieuse* develops essentially feminine qualities, such as 'finesse', elegance, sensibility; she is neither pedantic nor unlearned, but 'sçauante sans le paroistre';

[114] 'La femme et la vie spirituelle au XVIIᵉ siècle', *XVIIᵉ siècle*, lxii–lxiii (1964), 47.

she exists in a universe in which love is deified, but only that love
which has been purified from constraint, from considerations of
convenience and financial gain, from the dangers of habit and
monotony. It is, in fact, the love of the world of the novel,
where the lover displays infinite patience, where adventures and
dangers serve to keep passion alive, where marriage is always
just out of sight; the world of *Le roman de Mélusine* and *Le
grand Cyrus.*

There are many literary portraits of the *précieuse,* and as many
anti-portraits; the earliest of these is perhaps that to be found in
Scudéry's *Femmes illustres* of 1642, in a harangue addressed by
Sapho to Erinne. Ten years later, in *Le grand Cyrus,* Madeleine de
Scudéry depicted another and more famous Sapho, which contemporaries took for a self-portrait, and contrasted this with a
figure called Damophile:

Damophile s'estant mis dans la teste d'imiter Sapho, n'entreprit de
l'imiter en destail, mais seulement d'estre sçauante comme elle: et
croyant mesme auoir trouué vn grand secret pour acquerir encore
plus de reputation qu'elle n'en auoit, elle fit tout ce que l'autre ne
faisoit pas. Premierement elle auoit tousiours cinq ou six Maistres,
dont le moins sçauant luy enseignoit ie pense l'Astrologie: elle escriuoit
continuellement à des hommes qui faisoient profession de science: elle
ne pouuoit se resoudre à parler à des Gens qui ne sçeussent rien: on
voyoit tousiours sur sa Table quinze ou vingt Liures, dont elle tenoit
tousiours quelqu'un quand on arriuoit dans sa Chambre, et qu'elle y
estoit seule: et ie suis assuré qu'on pouuoit dire sans mensonge, qu'on
voyoit plus de Liures dans son Cabinet, qu'elle n'en auoit leû: et
qu'on en voyoit bien moins chez Sapho, qu'elle ne lisoit. De plus,
Damophile ne disoit que de grands mots qu'elle prononçoit d'vn ton
graue, et imperieux; quoy qu'elle ne dist que de petites choses: et
Sapho au contraire ne se seruoit que de paroles ordinaires, pour en
dire d'admirables . . .[115]

Other portraits may be found in de Pure's *La prétieuse,* and two of
Saint-Evremond's minor writings, *Le Cercle,* and *L'idée de la
femme qui ne se trouve pas et qui ne se trouvera jamais.* The most
famous of the anti-portraits is of course Molière's *Précieuses
ridicules.*

Madeleine de Scudéry also points to two types of women who

[115] *Le grand Cyrus,* x, 590–1; cf. Guez de Balzac's comparison of Madame Desloges and 'la femme docteur' of 1628 (*Lettres, seconde partie,* ii. 875–7).

were opposed to the *précieuses*. The first is remarkably similar to Du Bosc's 'coquette':

Il y auoit encore des Femmes . . . qui fuyoient Sapho et ses Amies: et qui en faisoient des railleries à leur mode. Il est vray que c'estoient de ces Femmes qui ne pensent qu'elles doiuent iamais rien sçauoir, sinon qu'elles sont belles: et qu'elles ne doiuent iamais rien apprendre, qu'à se bien coiffer: de ces Femmes, dis-ie, qui ne peuuent iamais parler que d'habillemens et qui font consister toute le galanterie, à bien manger les Colations que leurs Galans leur donnent . . .[116]

This attack on such women is interesting, since more than one contemporary wrote satires of *préciosité* in which *précieuses* are described as 'coquettes': of these Juvénel's *Portrait de la coquette* is perhaps the best known. The second type described by Madeleine de Scudéry is somewhat similar to Du Bosc's description of the *honnête femme*:

Il y auoit encore aussi d'vne autre espece de Femmes, qui pensant que la vertu scrupuleuse vouloit qu'vne Dame ne sçeust rien faire autre chose, qu'estre Femme de son Mary; Mere de ses Enfans; et Maistresse de ses Esclaues; trouuoient que Sapho et ses Amies, donnoient trop de temps à la conuersation: et qu'elles s'amusoient à parler de trop de choses qui n'estoient pas d'vne necessité absolue.[117]

The development of the notion of the *précieuse* illustrates the efficacy of feminist agitation over the period in question; it is inconceivable that such an ideal of social conduct could have been proposed without the social advances of the 1630s and 1640s, which themselves owe much to the influence of feminist thought. In order that a balanced picture be given, however, it should be pointed out that the educational programmes proposed for girls by Jacqueline Pascal in her *Reglement pour les enfans* of 1657,[118] and later by Madame de Maintenon and Fénelon, do not reflect this change in society and social attitudes, and while in the second half of the seventeenth century women were able to acquire learning and culture in adult life, little action was taken to provide for girls the same education as their brothers. This cherished hope of even the earliest feminists[119] was not to be fulfilled until the late nineteenth century.

[116] *Le grand Cyrus*, x. 586–7. [117] Ibid. x. 587.

[118] Reprinted in P. Faugère, *Lettres, opuscules et mémoires de Madame Périer et de Jacqueline, sœurs de Pascal . . .* , Paris, 1845, pp. 228–300.

[119] See Christine de Pisan, *Livre de la cité des dames*, quoted in her *Livre des trois vertus*, ed. M. Laigle, Introduction, p. 120.

VI

Feminism in Imaginative Literature

HAVING undertaken in earlier chapters an investigation into feminist writing as such, one may now turn to imaginative literature, and attempt to identify elements of feminism in the various genres. From the examination of feminist writings three broad manifestations of feminism have emerged: the first is typified by the rhetorical treatise on the excellence of women, and is traditional in argumentation and content; the second relates to the institution of marriage and to woman's rôle in society; the third is embodied in the depiction of the heroic woman, and arises out of the reversal of moralistic commonplaces about the female sex in general. Little evidence may be expected of the first manifestation, as this was already old-fashioned at the beginning of the century, and is not easily adaptable to imaginative literature.

Genres have been preferred to authors or themes as a means of approach, because there is a convenient division of subject-matter between comedy and serious drama, the pastoral, the novel, and lyric poetry; because they afford the possibility of an analysis which takes form into account; and because the more general framework of the argument will allow for a survey from which the elements of period style which are the subject of the last two chapters of this study will emerge most clearly. *L'Astrée* and the pastoral tradition with its preponderant interest in the relationship between the sexes is examined first in this chapter; after this there is a survey of lyric poetry, tragedy and tragicomedy, comedy, and the novel. Absent from this list of genres is the epic; although there is much evidence of feminist thought which is touched upon in other contexts,[1] the works of Saint-Amant, Chapelain, and Le Moyne are all published after 1652, and a comprehensive study of them falls outside the scope of this book.[2]

---

[1] See above, p. 46, and below, p. 228.

[2] For indications of feminist influences see R. A. Sayce, *The French biblical epic in the seventeenth century*, pp. 78–9, 112–13, 225–6.

L'Astrée *and the Pastoral Tradition*

It appears to be generally agreed that *L'Astrée* is a work rich in feminism: Maurice Magendie and Roger Lathuillère point out that there is an element of gynaecocracy,[3] for the government of fifth-century Forez is in the hands of women; Jean Rousset associates the heroine Astrée with the *précieuse* of the middle of the century, of which she is said to be a 'première esquisse';[4] Jacques Ehrmann has more recently set out to investigate the nature of sexuality and the relationship of men and women to each other in the novel, and many of his conclusions are relevant to the present study.[5]

In this section feminist elements in *L'Astrée* will be explored by means of reference to and comparison with the tradition of pastoral literature roughly contemporary with the novel. *L'Astrée* is, of course, a work of sufficient stature and influence to merit separate treatment, but the pastoral drama of Tasso and Guarini, Racan and Mairet can throw interesting and pertinent light on the issues to be dealt with here. As a novel, it has obvious connections both with its precursors in the same genre, Montemayor's *Diana* and Montreux's *Bergeries de Juliette* (these have been admirably elucidated by Magendie[6]), and with the class of composition described by Reynier, perhaps too restrictively, as the *roman sentimental*.[7] In the latter, the preoccupation with love and fidelity, the birth of love in the soul of young, unmarried women, the clash of inclination with social or moral conventions (often represented by oracles in the pastoral tradition), the predilection for conversations, letters, and verses, the *terminus ad quem* of marriage, and, perhaps most strikingly, the evocation of a pathos tinged with a delight in the afflictions of the heroine are common features which indicate, according to Reynier, the preponderance of female taste in the reading public of the age.[8]

The distinguishing features of the pastoral tradition are well known. Encompassed by idyllic and varied landscapes, shepherds, shepherdesses, huntsmen, priests, and sorcerers engage in rustic

[3] M. Magendie, *Du nouveau sur l'Astrée*, Paris, 1927, p. 328; Lathuillère, *La préciosité*, i. 333.

[4] J. Rousset, *La littérature de l'âge baroque en France*, Paris, 1954, p. 33.

[5] J. Ehrmann, *Un paradis désespéré : l'amour et l'illusion dans L'Astrée*, Paris and New Haven, 1963, esp. pp. 7–27.   [6] *Du nouveau sur L'Astrée*, pp. 92–231.

[7] See *Le roman sentimental avant L'Astrée*, Paris, 1908.

[8] Ibid., pp. 39 and 237.

pursuits and in interminable conversations; their destinies are guided by pre-Christian or non-Christian gods who occasionally make themselves heard by oracles. In the case of *L'Astrée*, the central characters are the descendants of refugees from court life, in which human relationships, and especially love, are contaminated by contact with ambition, flattery, and dissimulation. It is only possible in the innocent society of the pastoral to strive after true fidelity and love.[9] It would not be true, however, to say that social conventions are completely absent from the pastoral tradition; *L'Astrée*, and even French pastoral drama, are rich in reflections on society which arise from social problems encountered in the course of the action. The concept of female honour, the problems of marriage and of the tyranny of parents over their daughters' fates, are examples of such difficulties.[10]

These elements of social discussion contributed in large part towards the popularity of *L'Astrée*, considered as the breviary of correct behaviour and manners by contemporary readers; but the pastoral is also remarkable for the attempt made by its authors to investigate the nature of men and women and their relationship in a natural setting, as free as possible from traditional beliefs and conventions. This milieu leads to a preponderance of nature imagery and similes, and accounts for the predilection for analogies drawn from natural science, such as the magnet theory of love propounded in *L'Astrée*;[11] in order to be consistent with the 'uneducated' state of the shepherd, technical philosophical language in the description of love must be avoided, and, by this process, the mysteries of neo-Platonism are given popular expression so as not to appear incongruous in the story. Nature herself is often evoked, and her beauty and creative force lead to an implied analogy of women to nature, which, if not feminist, is at least a sign of the dominant strain of femininity in the pastoral tradition.[12] Thus it is possible to detect the prerequisites of a glorification of the female sex, for not only is their close relationship to the dominant forces in the pastoral implied, but also they

[9] In Mairet's *Sylvie* (ed. J. Marsan, Paris, 1932, p. 85) the adjective *courtisan* is used on one occasion as a synonym of *déloyal*.
[10] For two harangues against the tyranny of parents see *L'Astrée*, ed. H. Vaganay, Lyons, 1925–8, iii. 245–6 and iv. 147–56; see also Ehrmann, *Un paradis désespéré*, p. 88.
[11] *L'Astrée*, ed. Vaganay, i. 387–9.
[12] e.g. *L'Astrée*, ed. Vaganay, i. 9; ii. 175–6; iii. 5–7; iii. 509.

are in no way excluded from the understanding of mysteries by default of education.[13]

As social conventions are impugned and nature in all its forms is promoted, we may expect to find in the pastoral an emphasis on the sensual and the erotic, set against the arid demands of an unnatural code of honour. This is especially true of *L'Aminta*, in which the false god Honour is vigorously attacked by the chorus, and the passing of the Golden Age, in which maidens did not refuse their lovers the assuagements of love, is regretted.[14] The presence in pastoral of aggressive shepherdesses who 'sacrifice' their honour to their love and pursue their lovers is also relevant to this emphasis on natural desires as opposed to artificial restraint. *L'Astrée* is somewhat different from pastoral drama in this, for the female characters in that work are governed by a personal sense of honour, more demanding than that of the heroines of pastoral drama. There are, however, many erotic elements in d'Urfé's novel, especially in the interchanges between the transvestite Céladon and Astrée;[15] the aggressive female lover is also in evidence in this novel,[16] but she is shamed out of her behaviour by her more virtuous and modest companions.

One expression, therefore, of the predominance of nature is the omnipresence of love and the sensual pleasures attached to it. Their opposites, however—virginity and the destructive pleasures of the chase—also play a considerable part, as in *L'Aminta*. Here may be detected the intimate involvement of the pagan gods in the fabric of the pastoral. Diana, as goddess of the hunt and of chastity, dwelling in shady woods, appears prominently in all these works: she is explicitly the figurehead of a cult in *L'Astrée*,[17] and such names as *Silv*ia, *Silv*io, and *Silv*andre are indicative of her connection with these figures, who are themselves at some time or other associated with the pursuit of hunting and the rejection of love. The power of primitive nature over these figures even leads others to question their very humanity,[18] and here may be

[13] Cf. A. Adam, *Histoire de la littérature française au XVIIe siècle*, Paris, 1962, i. 129 n.: 'Roland Desmarets caractérisait en 1650 les développements philosophiques de *l'Astrée*: "Doctrina summa eaque tanta cum facilitate et perspicuitate tradita, ut difficiles philosophiae locos etiam feminis intellectu faciles reddiderit."'

[14] *L'Aminta*, i, chorus.   [15] *L'Astrée*, ed. Vaganay, iv. 38 ff.

[16] Ibid. i. 391–420 ('Histoire de Célion et Bellinde'); also, i. 196–236; i. 457 ff.

[17] Ibid. iii. 519.

[18] *L'Aminta*, ii. ii.

sensed a further facet of the opposition of nature to civilization in
the pastoral.

The division of pastimes between the pursuit of love and
hunting, similar to the distinction between acquisitive male and
conservative female rôles in society, is of interest here, since it
poses the question whether hunting is considered as a male preserve. Many of the female characters in the pastoral tradition
hunt, but this fact rarely goes uncommented: to one of these
huntresses, motherhood is proposed as an alternative,[19] which
would seem to indicate that hunting is indeed a male occupation;
but nowhere is this explicitly stated. The undoubted association
of the hunt with a flight from love (and perhaps from humanity,
where this is understood as sensibility to beauty), is found also
in the figure of the satyr. He may be said to represent the ultra-
masculine attitude to women and to life in general (whereas the
perfect lover, in the admission of Céladon, 'n'est pas homme');[20]
he reacts vigorously against respectful solicitation of women
and against matrimony; he considers love, women, and marriage
to be vilifying and adulterating in their effects on men.[21] Perfect
lovers, in his opinion, are effeminate 'mignons', and the truly
masculine attitude to love is to take, not to beg, favours. He is a
prominent figure in the Italian pastoral drama, but less extrava-
gantly portrayed in French writings, appearing as a 'chevalier
monstrueux' in *L'Astrée*,[22] as a predatory wolf in Mairet's *Sylvie*,[23] and, in Racan's *Bergeries*, dressed up as a 'mignon', although
he is too 'robuste, pelu, nerveux' to carry off this disguise.[24]

Some of the satyr's attitudes may be detected in huntsmen—
Silvio, for example, describes love as 'pensieri effeminati'[25]—but
they are rarely satyric in behaviour. More striking is the contrast
made between the satyr and the perfect lover. The former rejects
the practices of humility, service, and fidelity, whereas the latter
suffers the humours of his mistress and prides himself on his
complete devotion and receptive sensibility. This beautiful youth
(contrasted in appearance with the older and repugnant satyr), is

[19] Ibid. I. i.
[20] *L'Astrée*, ed. Vaganay, ii. 282–3, quoted below, p. 166.
[21] Ehrmann points out that the satyr, a figure for the animal nature of man, is
contrasted with the nymph, who represents spirituality (*Un paradis désespéré*, p. 58).
[22] *L'Astrée*, ed. Vaganay, i. 232.
[23] *Sylvie*, ed. Marsan, p. 20.   [24] *Les bergeries*, ed. P. Camo, Paris, 1929, p. 42.
[25] *Il pastor fido*, I. i.

the lover of the Golden Age, whose service never ceases, and in whom are merged the two figures of *mari* and *amant*. The problems caused by the association of the spiritual and unassuaged love of the lover and the more sensual affection of the husband are considerable, and will be touched upon in another context.

Connected with the satyr figure, although no huntsman, is Hylas, the witty and charming *inconstant* of d'Urfé's novel. Like the satyr, he rejects female domination, but for very different reasons: he sets out to show that inconstancy is a principle of the sublunary world, and that, as a result, inconstancy in love is both natural and praiseworthy. The arguments rehearsed by this 'athée en amour' are related to those found in the literature about the 'faux honneur des dames',[26] and are thus connected with the *libertinage* of the early seventeenth century. Together with such beliefs goes a rather different portrait of women from that encountered in moralistic or panegyrical writing: womankind is essentially endowed with 'bellezza' and 'leggiadria', attracting men by fleeing before them (another image of the hunt); such a description may be found in the mouth of Hylas, in a quatrain based on a speech in *L'Aminta*:

> Elle fuit, et fuyant elle veut qu'on l'attaigne:
> Refuse, et refusant veut qu'on l'ait par effort:
> Combat, et combattant veut qu'on soit le plus fort:
> Car ainsi son honneur ordonne qu'elle feigne.[27]

This attitude to female virtue is not obviously related to the behaviour of Astrée and her companions of equal stature, who are governed by a strict sense of personal honour which does not seem to allow for any implication of such coquettishness;[28] its appropriateness in Hylas's mouth is, however, obvious.

The dominance of feminine forms and attributes (emanating from the principle of Mother Nature) conduces greatly to the prestige and authority of women in these works; this applies especially to the high premium laid on the possession of sensibility and sensitivity, both 'feminine', or at least non-satyric, features. In the theories of love propounded in the pastoral, the glorification of the beauty and virtue of women adds yet further to this

[26] See above, p. 68.
[27] *L'Astrée*, ed. Vaganay, ii. 116.
[28] The heroines do, however, possess feminine guile (see *L'Astreé*, ed. Vaganay iv. 278).

prestige. Love, the immanent force in the universe (in *L'Aminta*, nature herself is described as being in love), is a mystery, whose cult is reserved for druids and druidesses; it is eternal, and hence, to be perfect, requires that lovers be constant; it is, as Reynier points out, the overriding preoccupation of the inhabitants of fifth-century Forez: 'ils sont persuadés que l'amour est l'unique affaire de la vie.'[29] Only druids, perfect lovers, and women are admitted to a full knowledge of its subtleties and cult.

The neo-Platonist and other sources of love-theory in *L'Astrée* have already been investigated,[30] and it is only necessary here to point to what is relevant to the prestige of women. The relationship between lover and beloved is that of the courtly-love tradition, in which service is undertaken to win the esteem and heart of the lady by gratitude or pity; this service has as its end the moral elevation of the soul rather than the hope of physical reward. The true lover has no greater concern than the preservation of his lady's honour; and yet he serves in the hope of eventual assuagement for his physical passion. The battle between spiritual and physical love is waged therefore not only between lover and beloved, but also in the soul of the lover himself. Through the trials of love, either self-imposed or prescribed by his lady, the lover may hope for moral regeneration and purification, and thus in its disinterestedness and its immortality the love aspired to is in some degree comparable to divine love. The imperiousness of the lady stems from this fact: the lover humbles himself before her as before a deity. As in the Middle Ages anti-feminist writers had reacted against this unreal self-abasement, so also does the satyr in the pastoral tradition, and the arguments used are essentially the same in both cases.

Many of the ideas about love in *L'Astrée* are clearly neo-Platonist: the commonplace 'mourir en soy pour revivre en autruy',[31] the hierarchy of physical passion and spiritual love,[32] the connection between beauty and goodness,[33] may all be found

[29] *Le roman sentimental*, p. 346; cf. *L'Astrée*, ed. Vaganay, ii. 52.
[30] See A. Adam, 'La théorie mystique de l'amour dans *L'Astrée* et ses sources italiennes', *Revue d'histoire et de philosophie*, iv (1936), 193–206; *Histoire de la littérature française au XVII*ᵉ *siècle*, i. 129–31.   [31] *L'Astrée*, ed. Vaganay, i. 290.
[32] Ibid. ii. 61: (Célidée) 'j'ay ouy dire . . . qu'on peut aymer en deux sortes: l'une selon la raison, l'autre selon le desir. Celle qui a pour sa reigle la raison, on me l'a nommée amitié honneste et vertueuse, et celle qui se laisse emporter à ses desirs, amour.'
[33] Ibid. iii. 502–20 ('Harangue de Silvandre').

in the novel, and some of these ideas are given interpretations which contribute greatly to the prestige of women: Silvandre, in one of the more important debates about love, asserts that men love more perfectly than women (against the generally accepted belief[34]) because they have as objects of their affection more perfect beings than themselves.[35] The reciprocity of true love is also very much stressed,[36] and the idea of the interchange and mirroring of souls, by which the lovers can survive even death, is an important admission of the equality of the sexes on this level of personality. The rôle which beauty plays in inspiring love is also indicative of neo-Platonist influences: because the appreciation of the beauty of the body leads to the higher appreciation of the beauty of the soul, it is possible for two women (or for that matter, two beautiful youths, although this eventuality is not investigated) to fall in love with each other, as in fact occurs *in simulacro* in the relationship between Alexis-Céladon and Astrée.[37]

The theory of the power of beauty is, however, taken well beyond the limits of neo-Platonism, and just as 'mourir en soy pour revivre en autruy' is by implication syncretized with Romans, Chapter 6 (the resurrection of the new man in Christ), so also a connection is made between the neo-Platonist beliefs about goodness and beauty, and about the uplifting effect of its contemplation, and the biblical treatment of these themes, notably in the Song of Songs. The currency of such ideas at this time may be traced in Du Chesne's *Figures mystiques du riche et precieux cabinet des dames* of 1605, in which pagan and biblical ideas on this subject are brought together. Beauty itself is a perfection, a sign of goodness, and a force emanating from God, by which women equal and even surpass men, and by which they approach the 'divine intelligences' (angels). This last notion will be discussed more fully below, but it is relevant to point out here that Du Chesne also offers for this a connection with Christian thought, for he recounts that St. Bonaventura, surprised in the contemplation of a beautiful woman during a meal, excused his conduct by declaring that he was communicating with the divine mysteries

---

[34] See below, p. 47.

[35] *L'Astrée*, ed. Vaganay, iii. 505–20; iv. 113.

[36] Ibid. ii. 179–80.

[37] See also Benserade's play *Iphis et Iante* (1636), and W. Gibson, 'Women and the notion of propriety in the French theatre (1628–43)', *FMLS*, xi (1975), 1–14, esp. 8–10.

through the medium of the beauty of the woman in question.[38]
Physical beauty is, however, also a bridge to spiritual love, as is
exemplified in the story of Célidée in *L'Astrée*.[39]

Important too for the theory of love is the connection drawn
between 'amour' and 'raison' in d'Urfé's novel. The famous
definition of love as 'un acte de la volonté qui se porte à ce que
l'entendement juge bon'[40] indicates the effect of love on the
intellect, which, in turn, should instil constancy and fidelity in
the lover. Women, especially in *L'Astrée*, are given to examining
their affections in the light of reason, and their deliberations often
appear excessively calculating.[41] This rational love is, according
to Ehrmann, a sign of the predominant influence of woman on
man, for by rejecting the masculine domain of sensuality, and
attracting man to a spiritual world of purified emotion in which
she is mistress, 'elle arrive ainsi à renverser les valeurs convenues
selon lesquelles c'est l'homme qui, par sa supériorité physique,
domine et la femme, qui par sa faiblesse, se soumet. Son inferio-
rité devient principe de supériorité, dès que l'homme accepte de
jouer son jeu à elle.'[42] Thus here, as elsewhere, love-theory
enhances the dignity and prestige of woman.

The superiority of women is even more apparent in the practice
of love in the pastoral. This is similar to that found in the chivalric
novel, in which it is the function of the knight to fight and to serve
his lady, and that of the lady to be served and adored.[43] The
partition of action and passivity is not found in the pastoral,
however, in which the mistress is a more positive and more
overtly dominant figure. Her superiority finds expression in her
froideur and in her sense of honour. Coldness to suitors is dictated in part by woman's perennial distrust of male motives, and
it is at once a weapon against the importunate suitor and a test

---

[38] *Figures mystiques*, f. 51ʳ⁻ᵛ. [39] *L'Astrée*, ed. Vaganay, ii. 435–53.
[40] Ibid. ii. 386.
[41] e.g. Cryséide to Arimant (ibid. iii. 383): 'ne croyez point, Arimant, que j'aye
faict quelque chose à la volée ou sans une meure deliberation. Quand j'ay commencé de recevoir vostre bonne volonté, j'avoue que ç'a esté sans dessein et seulement parce que vostre recherche m'y convioit, mais quand je vous ay donné la
mienne, croyez aussi, si vous ne voulez avoir mauvaise opinion de moy, que ç'a
n'a point esté sans avoir longuement debatu en moy-mesme si je le devois faire, et si
je ne serois point blasmée d'une telle election. J'ay consideré vostre maison . . . j'ay
regardé vostre personne . . . j'ay recherché vostre vie . . .'
[42] *Un paradis désespéré*, p. 26.
[43] Stated explicitly in *L'Astrée*, ed. Vaganay, iii. 530.

of the fidelity and sincerity of the true lover.[44] From the male point of view it may be seen as an indication of arrogance in the mistress. The *froideur* of female characters is also connected with the cold and moist humours of their sex, which enable them to control their passions, in contrast to the male characters, who give way to them in a flagrant fashion. It is further associated with modesty, which is seen in the seventeenth century as an essential part of beauty.

The sense of personal honour displayed by such characters as Astrée and Diane is intimately connected with social questions and with *bienséance*. In the Golden Age, as Tasso and Racan point out, women were not restricted by externally imposed restraints; in the Age of Iron, their rôle is different, and their behaviour subjected to stricter control. Men may avow their love, but women may not; according to Célidée, to be known as a 'fille amoureuse' is a dishonour,[45] and another heroine, Bellinde, reproving a friend who had declared her love to a shepherd, asserts 'il semble que nostre sexe ne permette pas une si entière authorité à l'amour'.[46] Here may be detected one of the fundamental points of difference between the pastoral drama and *L'Astrée*; in the former, shepherdesses who are aggressive in love are tolerated, whereas in the latter, they are not. The most striking clash of honour and love in *L'Astrée* (admittedly not written by d'Urfé) is the recognition scene of Alexis-Céladon and Astrée,[47] in which it is made clear that the slightest shadow cast upon female honour is sufficient to tarnish it irremediably. For this reason perhaps the shepherdesses of Forez are so demanding of their suitors; in a letter to Céladon, Astrée writes:

Je suis soupçonneuse, je suis jalouse, je suis difficile à gaigner, et facile à perdre, et plus aisée à offenser et tres malaisée à rapaiser. Le moindre doute est en moy une asseurance: il faut que mes volontés soient des destinées, mes opinions des raisons, et mes commandemens des loix inviolables.[48]

Family duty, and especially obedience to parents, is another part of female honour, which, in the course of d'Urfé's novel, is never offended against overtly by any of the principal female

[44] Cf. *Les antitheses des dames de Cypre*, Paris, 1621, p. 41: 'quelque recompense que recoiue vn Amant de sa Maistresse, elle est tousiours plus grande qu'il ne merite.'
[45] *L'Astrée*, ed. Vaganay, ii. 58.
[46] Ibid. i. 396.   [47] Ibid. v. 244–60.   [48] Ibid. i. 67.

characters. It is sufficient for Bellinde to say to her disappointed
suitor Célion that 'ce sont des commandemens de mon pere
ausquels mon honneur ne permet que je contrarie',[49] as she explains to him the necessity of her marriage to Ergaste. Honour as
it is conceived here is thought to run counter to natural law and
desires; its validity is questioned in *L'Astrée* on several occasions,
especially over the feminist question of the right of women to
choose their marital partners,[50] but its authority remains all-
powerful.

In matters of service, the initiative is in the hands of women.
The lover is completely under the direction of his mistress; the
only command he must not obey is that to cease serving her.
To be admitted as a 'serviteur' is itself an honour: Astrée says of
Céladon, 'il fallut que je luy permisse d'estre mon serviteur.'[51]
Service is a voluntary humiliation, a renunciation of all masculine
prerogatives (hence the often-noted analogy of *service/esclavage*
and *inconstance/liberté*).[52] The admission 'ne pas haïr' on the part
of the mistress to her suitor marks a great step forward in service,
for *froideur* and disdain are in part dictated by woman's vulnera-
bility, and to have gained the trust of his mistress is very important to the lover. While the imperfect lover may admit that physical
possession of his lady is the end of his service (as does Alcidor
in Racan's *Bergeries*[53]), the true lover must strive after spiritual
love, by which he may achieve himself his own spiritual elevation.[54] Sensual desires may, even in a neo-Platonist system, be
consistent with the pursuit of this higher love; the caresses
which the transvestite Céladon receives and gives not only
indicate the complexity of his love but also add to the novel an
important erotic element, centred on the theme of stolen favours.
The struggle of passion and respect is connected with the more
difficult question of the moral effects of love; traditionally, love
of women is associated with the adulteration of virtue (this will
be discussed more fully in the context of tragedy), but it is also
held at this time that sensual passion may have a more positive
effect, and is not altogether to be condemned.[55]

The suitor, by means of tears, sighs, humility, patience, and

[49] Ibid. i. 404.
[50] Ibid. iii. 245–6 and iv. 147–56.
[51] Ibid. i. 120.
[52] See Ehrmann, *Un paradis désespéré*, p. 47.
[53] *Les bergeries*, I. i.
[54] *L'Astrée*, ed. Vaganay, ii. 389.
[55] See A. H. T. Levi, 'The neoplatonist calculus', in *Humanism in France*, ed.
A. H. T. Levi, Manchester, 1970, pp. 229–48.

complaints of cruel and ungrateful treatment, hopes to appeal to his mistress's pity and gratitude, out of which there might develop an affection for him. This appeal to her *misericordia* may be tentatively compared with the contemporary cult of the Virgin Mary, as exemplified in such works as the *Esclavage des devots de la B. V. Marie, empérière du monde* (1629), in which Our Lady is asked to take pity on her servant as he languishes in a state of deprivation (not, as in the pastoral, of carnal love, but of Christian grace). This emphasis on pity and gratitude adds to the *hauteur* of the mistress, for although it is everywhere stated that love can only be complete if it is reciprocal, the suitor's affection is balanced not by one equal to it, but by 'le desir d'estre aimee'.[56]

In both the theory and practice of love, women are, therefore, the dominant parties with whom the initiative rests, and men are self-humiliated adjuncts of the female will. This state of affairs is but one indication of the reversal of male and female rôles and attributes in *L'Astrée* as in the whole pastoral tradition; this reversal is essentially feminist in inspiration and expression, for women are raised to the level of men and men reduced to that of women. The debased status of the lover is quite explicitly pointed to by Céladon in a conversation with Léonide:

— Et quoy, dit la nymphe, laisse-t-on d'estre homme quand on devient amant?

— Si vous appelez estre homme, dit-il, que d'estre subjet à toutes sortes de peines et d'inquietudes, j'avoue que l'amant demeure homme; mais si cest homme a une propre volonté, et juge toutes choses telles qu'elles sont, et non pas selon l'opinion d'autruy, je nie que l'amant soit homme, puis que dés l'heure qu'il commence de devenir tel, il se despouille tellement de toute volonté et de tout jugement, qu'il ne veut ny ne juge plus que comme veut et juge celle à qui son affection l'a donné.[57]

If *homme* is used here with the sense of the Latin *homo*, then women may be said to be *homines*, for they are attributed with both will and 'jugement',[58] and furthermore with the power to apply these faculties ('résolution'). The notion that 'résolution' is a female

[56] See Ehrmann, *Un paradis désespéré*, p. 57; Madeleine de Scudéry, *Le grand Cyrus*, iv. 113, quoted by V. Cousin, *La société française du XVIIe siècle, d'après Le grand Cyrus de Mlle de Scudéry*, Paris, 1858, ii. 6: 'pour les dames, la coutume ne les oblige pas nécessairement à aimer, mais à souffrir seulement d'être aimées'.

[57] *L'Astrée*, ed. Vaganay, ii. 282–3.

[58] Ibid. i. 65.

attribute is prominent in the feminist texts of the regency of Anne of Austria, as has been seen; it contradicts the commonplace about women's irresoluteness. Throughout *L'Astrée*, women's resoluteness is associated with the controlling of passions and the control of their external signs; when Léonide, who loves Céladon, hears of his love for Astrée, '[elle] ne peut cacher ses larmes. Toutefois, comme sage qu'elle estoit . . . elle resolut d'estre maistresse de ses volontez.'[59] An even more striking example of 'résolution' is Bellinde, who, by self-control and determination, asks Célion, whom she loves, to transfer his service to Amaranthe, and later, when betrothed by her father to Ergaste, does not break down in front of the weeping and fainting Célion, but shows 'grande constance et extreme resolution'.[60] Elsewhere she is described as an 'orgueilleuse beauté, qui aimoit mieux estre jugée avec peu d'amour qu'avec peu de resolution'.[61] Here is a clear example of the stoic feminism which was to be so popular as a literary theme in the 1640s. Thus women both think and decide for themselves, in contrast to the male characters, who in the face of adversity sink into lethargy and despair.

If *homme*, however, as used by Céladon, is the equivalent of *vir*, then the reversal of rôles and attributes is complete. Just as the traditional attributes of men are transferred to women (resolution, self-control, initiative, and independence of mind), so also are the traditional physical weaknesses of women found in male characters, and especially lovers (those who accept most readily the demands made upon them by women): sighs, trembling, tears, fainting fits, and with these external signs of weakness go the concomitant moral characteristics: timidity, fearfulness, humility, long-suffering. Not robustness but beauty is further-more praised in the lover: Céladon in *L'Astrée*, and Silvio in *Il pastor fido*, are both described in terms of feminine beauty. Thus the triumph of female traits is complete in the lover, and only the satyr resists them altogether. Even inconstancy, usually ascribed more readily to women than to men, is more strikingly present in the figure of a man (Hylas in *L'Astrée*) than in any female character.

The reversal referred to above has a kind of counterpart in the frequent examples of transvestism.[62] This is, of course, prohibited

[59] Ibid. i. 385.   [60] Ibid. i. 411.   [61] Ibid. i. 404.
[62] See J. D. Charron, 'Le thème de la "métamorphose" dans l'Astrée', *XVIIᵉ siècle*, ci (1973), 3–14.

by the law of Moses, but 'tous les Acoutremens et Habits propres aux femmes; desquels les hommes ne peuvent honnestement et sans reproche se servir'[63] are worn on more than one
occasion, and by more than one character in *L'Astrée*, and it is
not impossible that Trousset's diatribe against transvestism is
occasioned by his reaction to the pastoral tradition.[64] Women who
dress up as men and fight as men are clearly feminist figures,
abundant in Tasso's and Ariosto's epics, and frequently encountered in the novel of this period; it is also not uncommon
to find women in male attire pursuing their lovers, a motif often
found in Spanish *novelas*, marking yet another reversal (the
mistress pursuing the 'serviteur'). There are examples of the
latter sort in *L'Astrée*.[65] Men who dress up in women's clothes
are, however, most frequently found in the pastoral tradition,
and they testify to the preponderant femininity of the genre.
The effeminacy of Céladon is specifically referred to on several
occasions: not only is his beauty feminine (he does not wear a
beard), but he, as Alexis, 'sçavoit si bien contrefaire la fille, qu'une
seule de ses actions n'en dementoit point le nom'.[66] This passage
is, however, contradicted later in the same book, when d'Urfé
stresses the masculinity of Alexis-Céladon's character and sexual
drives. The transvestite theme in the pastoral is connected also
with the theme of the stolen favour, and, at one point in *L'Astrée*,
with clothes fetishism.[67]

That this reversal of female and male attributes is conscious on
the part of d'Urfé is indicated by the use he makes of it in the
fourth part of his novel. Here, Alexis-Céladon, having given
himself up to Polémas in the hope of securing the release of
Astrée, who had been taken prisoner in his place (it was a day on
which they had exchanged clothes), is exhorted to suffer 'her'
fate according to the dictates of female honour and virtues:
'Genereuse fille . . . ton courage doit paroistre en supportant
cette mort qui t'est preparée, constamment et non pas avec
fureur.'[68] The occasion of this admonition was the attack by
Céladon on the guards who are tying up Astrée, an action worthy

---

[63] Du Chesne, *Figures mystiques*, f. 16ʳ.   [64] *Alphabet*, pp. 331–2.
[65] *L'Astrée*, ed. Vaganay, iv. 753–76; i. 196 ff; i. 457 ff.
[66] Ibid. iv. 160; but cf. iv. 213: 'Alexis . . . encore que revestue en fille, ne pouvoit
se despouiller du personnage d'homme que la nature luy avoit donné . . .'
[67] Ibid. iii. 596.   [68] Ibid. iv. 797.

of a man but not of a woman. Elsewhere, during the battle which ensues, Céladon, still dressed in Astrée's clothes, draws attention to himself: 'tous demeuroient ravis de voir ce que Celadon faisoit, car l'habit de Bergere qu'il portoit rendoit toutes ses actions plus admirables.'[69] This, of course, is strictly not feminist, but the *admiratio* evoked by Alexis-Céladon's actions adds, whether justifiably or not, to the general impression of the glorification of female virtue.

A final aspect of the pastoral to be discussed here is the mystical and divine rôle attributed to women in the works of this genre. It is striking that the two principal heroines of *L'Astrée*—Astrée and Diane—have names paralleled by those of two goddesses, Astraea and Diana, the first the goddess of justice, the second of chastity. This analogy may be developed further: the honour and glory of the two shepherdesses being the triumph over *impudicité* and *médisance*,[70] their innocence and chastity are therefore particularly stressed. The perfect lovers, Silvandre and Céladon, make the analogy between their mistress and the respective goddess explicit: Silvandre at one point kneels before Diane, and makes the following prayer to her:

O Diane! l'honneur non seulement de ces Forests et de ces rivages, mais la gloire de tous les hommes, et l'ornement de tout l'univers, vous voyez devant vous un berger, qui non seulement vous ayme, et vous offre son service et sa vie, mais vous adore, et vous sacrifie et son cœur et son ame, avec une si entiere affection, ou plustost devotion, que tout ainsi que la nature ne peut plus rien faire qui se puisse esgaler a vous, aussi l'amour ne sçauroit plus allumer une si grande ny si parfaicte affection dans quelque cœur ce soit.[71]

Céladon, for his part, raises a temple to his beloved Astrée, in which the syncretism of the figures Astraea and Astrée is made even more clear, for the goddess's image is a portrait of Astrée herself.[72] The association of pagan mysteries with women, especially in the figures of Diana and Venus, has been noted elsewhere as a feature of Renaissance thought and art,[73] and this association survives in the pastoral, in which it is strengthened by

---

[69] Ibid. iv. 802.
[70] In Racan's *Bergeries* (IV: chorus, ed. Camo, p. 110) the identification of Astraea and innocence is explicit.
[71] *L'Astrée*, ed. Vaganay, iii. 519.   [72] Ibid. ii. 180–201, esp. 193.
[73] See E. Wind, *Pagan mysteries in the Renaissance*, London, 1967, pp. 75 ff.; E. H. Gombrich, *Symbolic images: studies in the art of the Renaissance*, London, 1972, pp. 66 ff.

the presence of mistresses, assimilated with goddesses, who are worshipped in terms of gynaecocentric, sacrificial love.

Women are also said to be in closer harmony with angels than men; this notion may be linked both with the neo-Platonist theories of beauty and the traditional feminist argument that women, being of a 'matière plus subtile', are more spiritual by nature. Although these ideas are not original (Le Moyne, from quite different sources, refers to the mystical relationship between women and knowledge in terms of a dowry given to them by angels[74]), they are rarely so powerfully expressed as in a speech of Sylvandre in *L'Astrée*:

> Les femmes sont veritablement plus pleines de merite que les hommes, voire de telle sorte que, s'il est permis de mettre quelque creature entre ces pures et immortelles intelligences, et nous, je croy que les femmes y doivent estre, parce qu'elles nous surpassent de tant de perfection, que c'est en quelque sorte leur faire tort que de les mettre en un mesme rang avec les hommes, outre que nous pouvons avec raison les estimer un juste milieu pour parvenir à ces pures pensées (c'est ainsi que les plus sçavans les nomment presque ordinairement), puisque nous apprenons par l'experience que c'est d'elles que toutes les belles pensées que les hommes ont, prennent leur naissance, et que c'est vers elles qu'elles courent, et en elles se terminent. Et qui doutera qu'elles ne soient le vray moyen pour parvenir à ces pures pensées, et que Dieu ne nous les ait proposées en terre pour nous attirer par elles au Ciel, où nos druides nous disent devoir estre nostre eternel contentement?[75]

The medial position of women between men and the divine mysteries is demonstrated in *L'Astrée* in terms of the comprehension of the mysteries of love, in which field women are superior to men.[76] The debates about questions to do with love are usually arbitrated by women; occasionally a druid or a perfect lover fulfils this rôle, but this is rare. This comprehension of the subtleties of love is connected with the figure of the *femme-prophète*, the sibyl, again an important figure in Renaissance mysteries; the gift of interpretation and prophecy is connected with both the cult of Diana and Christian beliefs about the prerogatives of virginity.

The association of the female sex with expiatory sacrifice is also

---

[74] *Les peintures morales*, i. 202–3, quoted above, pp. 55–6. Le Moyne's source is Clement of Alexandria.

[75] *L'Astrée*, ed. Vaganay, iii. 512–13.

[76] Ibid. ii. 385.

present in pastoral. This is found in the *Bergeries* of Racan, in *Il pastor fido*, and in the fifth part of *L'Astrée*. Like the Iphigenia theme, it is associated with innocence and metamorphosis; the motif of the maiden who expiates the ineluctable, supervoluntary sin of her people may also be tentatively compared with the theme of the redemption of the sin of Eve by the Virgin Mary, found in Marian literature. In both cases, the honour incurred by the whole sex is dwelt upon at some length.

A significant element of feminism may, therefore, be found in the pastoral tradition in this period: by the playing down of the importance of traditional social values, which in general reflect the conventional beliefs about women's inferiority, and by the concomitant stress on sensibility and beauty, in which spheres the female sex is superior to the male, women are made the dominant force in the pastoral universe, and their dominance is further asserted in both the theoretical and practical expression of codes of love. The abdication of men from their natural prerogatives leads to a sort of mystical transference of attributes, manifested in the reversals pointed to above and in the theme of transvestism. Finally, the element of female spirituality and mystical powers, perhaps comparable to the rôle played by the female mystics in the religious Renaissance, serves to underline woman's superiority in the sphere of the spirit. Although there may be said to be elements of social feminism—the emphasis on social manners, the place given to conversations dominated or arbitrated by women, the discussion of social freedoms—it would seem that these are outweighed in importance by the aspects listed above, which postulate a feminine universe, built around feminine sensibility and subservient to feminine discipline.

Lyric Poetry

Since the first publication of Desportes's 'Stances du mariage' (1573), *stances* and alexandrines are not infrequent media for feminist and anti-feminist tracts: Marie de Romieu, Jacqueline de Miremont, Courval-Sonnet, Jean Deplanches, Mme Liebaut, Pierre Motin, and Jacques Du Lorens all write in verse.[77]

Although it is usual to write satires such as those of Courval-Sonnet in rhyming couplets, it is difficult to see why some of these authors write in this medium rather than prose, unless it is to bestow on their productions the status of literary works, in the cases where a feminist tract of the same length in prose would be considered as little more than a *facétie*.

After the debate caused by Trousset's *Alphabet*, there are few poetical works which are feminist in the strictest sense. Some of the poems in Scudéry's *Cabinet* of 1646 might be considered as such,[78] but Marino's *Galeria*, which is Scudéry's inspiration for much of his *Cabinet*, contains poems which are outstandingly feminist,[79] and it is interesting that his imitator leaves these on one side. In a more general sense, the association of women with power of one form or another is more commonly encountered. Some political poetry, especially in praise of the queen regents Marie de Médicis and Anne of Austria, may be described as feminist;[80] there are also poems which treat heroic women, of which Corneille's liminary verses for André Mareschal's play *La sœur valeureuse* are a good example:

> Rendez-vous, Amants et Guerriers,
> Craignez ses attraits et ses armes;
> Sa Valeur égale à ses charmes
> Vnit les myrthes aux lauriers:
> Miracle d'Amour et de Guerre,
> Tu vas domter toute la terre;
> A l'éclat de tes yeux, on voit de toutes parts
> Mille cœurs à l'enuy voller sous ta puissance:
> Et s'il est vn mortel rebelle à tes regards,
> Ton bras soudain le range à ton obeissance.

Lorens, *Les satyres*, Paris, 1624, pp. 29 ff., satyre v 'mariage'. The influence of Juvenal's sixth satire is strong in all these works: see E. Hobert, *Die französische Frauensatire*, pp. 22 ff.

[78] *Le cabinet*, Paris, 1646, pp. 5–7, 11–16, 33, 81, 141–3, 185, 196. The scenes described in these pages include Dido's death, Joan of Arc, Hercules and Omphale, Rinaldo and Armida, and Thalestris. See below, p. 217.

[79] An interesting comparison between Marino's and Scudéry's approach is afforded by the subject of Hercules and Omphale (*Cabinet*, p. 33; *La Galeria*, Venice, 1635, pp. 43–7). Marino discusses the feminist implications of the incident at length; Scudéry dwells only on the force of love, not that of women over men.

[80] See, for example, Malherbe, *Œuvres complètes*, ed. Lalanne, Paris, 1862–9, i. 182–8, 205, 213; and the outstandingly feminist 'Ode à la Reyne' in Le Moyne's *Gallerie*.

Telle contre le Roy d'Arger
Courut autre-fois Bradamante :
Telle fut cette pauure Amante
A la queste de son Roger :
Telle, mais auec moins d'adresse,
Venus s'arma contre la Grece :
Telle contre son Fils pour le Roy des Latins
Camille dans le chocq se jettoit animée :
Et telle du cerueau du Maistre des Destins
Son mary fit sortir Minerue toute armée.[81]

Le Moyne's 'Ode à la Femme Forte' in his *Gallerie* is of course strikingly feminist, embodying many of the ideas expressed in the body of the text, and deploying with great skill the techniques of repetition, enumeration, antithesis, and chiasmus;[82] in the same work there are sonnets for each of the illustrated heroines. The *Recueil de diverses inscriptions proposées pour remplir les tables d'attente étans sous les statues du roi Charles VII et de la Pucelle d'Orleans* of 1613 also illustrates amply this aspect of feminist writing in verse.[83]

Love poetry is also said to be written in honour of women, and as a tribute to the power of their beauty. Some writers at this time argue that for this reason it should be considered feminist, since it enhances the prestige of women in general. L'Escale seems to suggest this when attacking Desportes's 'Stances du mariage', in his *Champion des femmes* :

Desportes, les autres poëtes, et tous les hommes ensemble, tandis qu'ils esperent quelque chose des bonnes graces de leurs maistresses, qu'ils s'en croyent cheris, et bien-voulus, que ne font-ils pour les loüer et exalter? Elles ne sont rien moins que des Deesses, leurs yeux des Soleils, leur bouche du coral, leurs dents d'yuoire, leur sein fait honte à la neige, et semblables hyberboles. Mais croyent-ils avoir vn riual, ou quelque ombrage de desdain entre t'il en leurs ames, adieu tous ces beaux epithetes, adieu tant de louanges, et en mesme temps les voilà sur la mesdisance. Telle est l'inconstance et legereté des ceruelles des hommes : et qui n'en voudra plus douter, qu'il prenne la peine de lire tant de beaux et inimitables vers, que le mesme sieur Desportes a

---

[81] *La sœur valeureuse*, Paris, 1634, ã6ᵛ–7ʳ. Rotrou's liminary poem is also strikingly feminist (ã6ʳ).

[82] See the passage quoted above, pp. 69–70.

[83] Another edition in 1628; cited by Lalanne in Malherbe, *Œuvres complètes*, i. 205.

composés à la gloire immortelle des femmes, et il trouuera que ceux-cy surpassent de beaucoup en quantité ceux-là que nostre desnaturé [Trousset] cite contre le mariage.[84]

Cyrano de Bergerac, writing in 1646 to Gerzan 'sur son *Triomphe des dames*', implies a similar conclusion when he asserts that Gerzan's feminism is original because 'vous [Gerzan] n'avez point dressé des montagnes de neiges à la place de leur sein; l'or, l'yvoir, l'azur, le corail, les roses et les lys, n'ont point esté les materiaux de vostre bastiment'.[85]

Although in both of these quotations there is a clear association of feminism with the commonplace imagery of love poetry, it is difficult to accept without severe qualification the conclusion that all love poetry which employs this imagery is feminist. The comments of L'Escale and Cyrano are not totally reliable as evidence, since they are respectively polemical and satirical in context; furthermore, the imagery referred to is a commonplace of love poetry of all periods, and does not seem to alter in the same way that feminist writing as such alters over the period in question. It is also pertinent to point out that the love poem is as much, if not more, about self-knowledge and self-investigation as about the love object; although she often appears as a dominant force, endowed with cruelty and coldness of heart, it is her effect on her adorer which is stressed. Moreover, as she is often married, her behaviour may be determined by *bienséance* more than by her natural inclinations; whence the deluge of Ovidian denunciation of false standards of honour, and the validity of 'natural' desires.

Another aspect of lyric poetry in this period which is relevant to this inquiry is the fact that it appears to have been overshadowed as a genre by dramatic productions, and seems often to take second place to these even in its manner of publication.[86] Love poetry itself is derivative to a considerable degree, relying not only on the native tradition of imagery and subject remotely derived from Petrarch, but also on such poets as Ovid, whose *Ars amatoria*, *Heroides*, and *Metamorphoses* were translated and adapted at the beginning of the century, and Marino, who influenced

---

84 *Champion des femmes*, ff. 39–40.
85 *Lettres*, ed. L. Erba, p. 78.
86 See Y. Fukui, *Raffinement précieux dans la poésie française du XVIIe siècle*, Paris, 1964, p. 135; here it is asserted that in many cases in the early seventeenth century poetry did not seem to merit separate printing, but was published in appendices to plays.

Saint-Amant, Tristan, Scudéry, and others.[87] What feminism may
be detected in poets of this period is often difficult to distinguish
for this reason from similar manifestations of feminism in earlier
writings.

In this examination of love poetry, the erotic verse of the early
years of the century may first be considered. This, far from being
all obscene, stretches across quite a wide spectrum; at the one end,
the productions of Du Perron, Vauquelin des Yveteaux, and Malherbe on the theme of 'la victoire de la constance', where the
woman accedes to the solicitations of her lover;[88] at the other,
the *Parnasse satyrique*, with its undisguised and brutal sensuality.
It is interesting to note that several of the postulates of these
poems are those put forward by anti-feminist works of the period:
the validity of *voluptas*, set against the nullity of the concept of
female honour:

> Ces vieux contes d'honneur, invisibles chimères,
> Qui naissent aux cerveaux des maris et des mères,
> Etoient-ce impressions qui pussent aveugler
>   Un jugement si clair?[89]

the virtue of inconstancy, and the consequent praise of 'athées en
amour'; the doubts about the possibility of felicity in marriage;
the depiction of the *femme lubrique*, of the fragility of female
virtue, which persistent solicitation will overcome:

> Je l'invitois au doux esbat
> Où jamais femme ne se lasse.[90]

Together with this goes a distinct lack of social respect for women,
perhaps arising out of the fact that the love object, being both
accessible and frail, is used rather than worshipped. Yet it would
be wrong to assign all this poetry to the anti-feminist camp; it
lacks the element of physical disgust for women which is a
feature of much clerical misogyny, and it does not pretend to
assess their spiritual worth. Furthermore, while deeply reliant on
moralistic commonplaces about the female sex—its frailty, lubricity, inconstancy—it none the less bestows a curious equality on
it, for both man and woman are dependent on and dominated by

[87] Ibid., pp. 66 ff., 112 ff.   [88] Ibid., pp. 66 ff.
[89] Malherbe, *Œuvres complètes*, ed. Lalanne, i. 30; cf. also Théophile de Viau,
Œuvres poétiques, ed. J. Streicher, Geneva, Paris, and Lille, 1951–8, ii. 16–26.
[90] Saint-Amant, *Œuvres*, ed. J. Bailbé, Paris, 1971, i. 167; see also ibid. i. 142–6.

love, and since she is associated with the passion of the lover in this more intimate way, the love object comes to life in some poems, if only on a sensual and affective plane:

> Quand tu me vois baiser tes bras . . .
> Quand tu sens ma bruslante main
> Se pourmener dessus ton sein,
> Tu sens bien Cloris que je t'aime.[91]

This obviously does not apply to many of the contributions to the *Parnasse satyrique*, in which preoccupation with psychology is minimal, but it would seem to be true of poems written on the theme of *jouissance* at this time.[92]

A different combination of elements typifies the contributions of Monfuron and Boisrobert to the *Recueil Malherbien* of 1627.[93] The moralistic portrait of womankind, used as a basis for the understanding of their psychology in erotic poetry, is still to be found here, but in conjunction with a mock-respectful attitude to the love object. There is also a shift in emphasis from the physique of women to their psyche, and a concomitant change in the concept of *amabilité*; now the whole woman becomes attractive, and the poet celebrates not only her physical beauty, but also her mental capriciousness, her moods, and her failings. In a genre of poetry given over to the discussion of the emotional relationship between the sexes, there is, as should be expected, no serious appraisal of the intellectual gifts and capacities of women, but rather an amused and mildly satirical investigation of female wiles. The attitude of the poet is no longer one of adoration and worship, but it remains affectionate and gallant.

From these beginnings developed the more famous *salon* poetry, of which the outstanding exponent is Voiture. Here, in sharp contrast to previous conventions of love poetry, in which *toucher* is at least as important as *plaire*, there is an emphasis on light-heartedness, on wit, on conceits—unsuitable adjuncts to the expression of serious feminist intellectual pretensions, or to the techniques associated with the aesthetic feminism of Le Moyne and Du Bosc (paralipsis, hyperbole, repetition, to name but a few). In a milieu in which, as has been shown,[94] women were the

---

[91] Théophile de Viau, *Œuvres poétiques*, ed. Streicher, i. 150.

[92] e.g. ibid. ii. 202–3; Saint-Amant, *Œuvres*, ed. Bailbé, i. 163–71.

[93] See Fukui, *Raffinement précieux dans la poésie française*, pp. 91 ff.

[94] See above, pp. 149–52.

arbiters of taste, the popularity of Voiture's bantering poems may appear paradoxical. Y. Fukui declares that the disrespect shown to women is an indication of their growing prestige;[95] it is possible also that female interest in the psychology of the passions and in mild flirtation within the bounds of *bienséance* and *galanterie* influenced the development of *salon* poetry in this way. In Voiture's poetry there is little mystique surrounding the passion of love; wit takes the place of psychological analysis. An indication of the preponderance of female taste is the fact that love is often expressed in gynaecocentric terms.

Voiture's denunciation of female vices may at first sight appear susceptible of shocking its *salon* audience; he writes in his 'Elegie pour une Coquette':

> La nouveauté vous plaist, et ne se passe jour,
> Que vous ne fassiez naistre, ou mourir quelque amour.
> Vous estes sans arrest, foible, vaine et legere,
> Inconstante, bizare, ingratte et mensongere,
> Pleine de trahisons, sans ame et sans pitié,
> Et capable de tout, hormis une amitié . . .[96]

If one should be tempted to see in such verses a severe castigation of female shortcomings, it is well to remember that at least one *précieuse* (Mme de Brégy) wrote harsher criticism in her *Sphere de la lune, composée de la teste de la femme*,[97] which is certainly a *facétie*.

A different aspect of this ironic tendency may be found in one of Tristan's love poems. We have already encountered in feminist literature the opposition of élite (the *femme forte*) and mass (the female sex in general); Tristan's sonnet 'Les vaines imprecations' is a witty development of this:

> Sexe ingrat et leger, deffaut de la Nature
> Sans foy, sans iugement, et sans election,
> Qui changes en vn jour cent fois d'affection,
> N'aimant que par caprice et que par auanture.

---

[95] *Raffinement précieux dans la poésie française*, p. 191: 'le respect de [la] poésie envers la femme n'est . . . pas le signe de l'émancipation féminine. Au Moyen-Age, les femmes étaient divinisées par les poètes; or la condition sociale de ces femmes nous semble peu enviable. Cette divinisation apparaît même comme une compensation. La "désacralisation" de l'amour ne signifie nullement un mépris des poètes pour la femme: au contraire, les femmes sont plus que jamais convoitées, cajolées. En dépit du paradoxe apparent, il faut affirmer que c'est une étape vers l'émancipation féminine.'

[96] *Œuvres*, ed. H. Lafay, Paris, 1971, i. 12.   [97] Paris, 1652.

Afin que ma vengeance égale mon iniure
Ie veux ainsi que toy suiure ma passion,
Et décrier si fort ton imperfection
Qu'elle soit detestable à la Race future.

Mais quel transport t'égare? vne rare Beauté
Que tu nommes ta Reine et ta Diuinité,
T'impose la douceur dans le sang et la flamme.

Vn Romain dont l'Histoire a ses traits embellis
Fit grace à tout vn peuple en faueur d'vne femme,
Fais grace à tout vn sexe en faueur de Philis.[98]

Salon poetry was practised not only by men but also by women, and one result of the development of both poetry and the *salons* is the emergence of the woman poet, who, like the woman playwright, the woman novelist, and the female writer of epics, appears as a literary figure of some importance in the decades after the Fronde. Outstanding among women poets at this time is the Comtesse de la Suze.[99] Although such figures emerge at that time, literary activity on the part of women is of course a natural extension of the interest shown in writing by the *salons* in earlier decades, mentioned above.[100]

It would seem fair to conclude that lyric poetry at this time reflects only in peripheral ways current modes of feminism. There is evidence of the growing influence of female taste in its development, and in it may also be traced the growing involvement of women in literature through the *salons*; but it is rare to find poetry in this period which voices feminist intellectual or social pretensions (nearly all the poets mentioned in the first paragraph of this section wrote their relevant works before the beginning of the reign of Louis XIII), and it does not seem that this medium was as well suited as drama or the novel to the depiction of the heroic woman and the paradox which she embodies.

Tragedy and Tragi-comedy

It is convenient to consider together dramatic genres which are centred on heroic and dangerous action, whether calamity ensues or not; the portrayal of the heroine and other female figures is not

---

[98] *Les plaintes d'Acante et autres œuvres*, ed. J. Madeleine, Paris, 1909, pp. 105–6.
[99] See Fukui, *Raffinement précieux dans la poésie française*, pp. 289 ff.
[100] See pp. 141 ff.

fundamentally different in tragedies, tragi-comedies of the more serious sort, and heroic comedies of the period. The interpretation of all drama is, however, fraught with difficulties which make this investigation especially tenuous in this sphere of writing: the influence of sources and subject on the production of the play; the deliberately inconsistent use of vocabulary from character to character, reflecting their different moral priorities (this applies especially to such words as 'généreux', 'magnanime', 'fidèle');[101] the fact that contradictory opinions are expressed by different characters, and sometimes by the same character (Mark Antony, for example, denounces female frailty during certain peripeteias, yet voices feminist sentiments at other times in the dramas in which he plays a part); the influence of changing concepts of *bienséance*. To these difficulties must be added that occasioned by the development of dramatic theory and taste during this period.[102]

We have already associated the *admiratio* evoked by playwrights such as Corneille with the expressions of horror, surprise, and wonderment found in the feminist writings of the regency of Anne of Austria;[103] there are also parallels to be drawn between the subject-matter of drama and of feminist literature of this period. Cleopatra, Mary Queen of Scots, Zenobia, Joan of Arc, Porcia, Semiramis—to name but a few—all are eponymous heroines of tragedies and tragi-comedies, and religious drama of the time also bears witness to the influence of feminism in its portrayal of Judith and St. Catherine. Heroines who evoke pathos are also represented in both drama and feminist works: Sophonisbe, Lucretia, Mariamne, Esther, and Artemisia are examples. It is not uncommon to find pathos mixed with *admiratio* in these heroines, as is indicated by the 'Argument' for the third act of Tristan's *Mariane*:

Herode accuse Mariane, et produit l'Eschançon, qui la charge de l'empoisonnement supposeé. Elle tesmoigne en se defendant sur ce crime, plus de courage que d'esprit. Mais tandis qu'elle braue la

---

[101] An example of this may be found in Gabriel Gilbert, *Semiramis*, Paris, 1647, II. iii, p. 46.
[102] On the development of drama and the changing concepts of *bienséance* see H. C. Lancaster, *A history of French dramatic literature in the seventeenth century*, Baltimore and Paris, 1929–42, i. 2. 753–9; ii. 2. 762–75.
[103] See above, p. 87.

Fortune et la mort, auec vne constance digne d'vne grande Princesse, elle ne se peut empescher de donner quelques larmes aux sentiments de la Nature; se representant l'estat où ses enfants se trouueront, estant priuez de son example et son support . . . Herode est touché de ses pleurs, et l'amour qui estoit sortie de son cœur par la porte de la crainte et de la cholere, y r'entre aussi-tost par celle de la pitié . . .[104]

Such an association of dramatic emotions should not be surprising, for as well as being heroines, these women are nearly all involved in the love intrigue, which often ends tragically.[105]

Certain rôles and attributes are consistently ascribed to women in serious drama. Their prophetic and mystical powers, already mentioned in the context of the pastoral, are reflected in the premonitory dreams which they recount in many of the dramas of this period, and the presence of these clairvoyant women may also be associated with the current predilection for the motif of the dream. The revengeful woman, a prominent figure in both the Bible and in antique drama, is encountered often in such figures as Medea, Cleopatra, and Vashti. The depiction of the afflicted and often innocent female, connected with the evocation of the sort of pathos tinged with cruelty which seems to be characteristic of the period, is equally common, and sometimes associated with the theme of sacrifice; Dido, Mary Queen of Scots, even Mairet's Cleopatra, and, more strikingly, Sophonisbe are examples of this. Lastly, the rôle of advocacy ascribed to women should perhaps be mentioned; this is connected with the commonplace about female clemency and *misericordia*, and with the physical inferiority of women, who, unable to act, are reduced to pleading. Porcia in Boyer's *La Porcie Romaine*, Octavie in Mairet's *Le Marc-Antoine*, and Pauline in *Polyeucte* may be mentioned in this context.

Most outstanding, however, is the identification of the power of women and that of love in the drama of the period, and the opposition of the resultant force with courage ('virtus'), which may be described as 'heroic misogyny'. In a few cases this identification is not made: treatment of the Dido theme leads more often to an opposition of love and destiny, although this may involve a discussion of the adulterating force of love, and hence of women, on heroes; Théophile's *Pyrame et Thisbé* portrays love

---

[104] Tristan L'Hermite, *La Mariane*, Paris, 1644, p. 51.
[105] Corneille's Cléopâtre and Médée are notable exceptions.

as a force to which both men and women are independently subject; *amour-estime* is said to be an affection which strengthens the sense of honour of hero and heroines, but even in Corneille's tragedies it coexists with *amour-faiblesse*. These exceptions aside, however, the association of love and women is a feature of many plays at this time (and probably of most heroic drama of any era), and, furthermore, a point of discussion in moralistic and religious treatises, as has already been pointed out.[106] It is interesting to note that the same arguments are adduced against women by anti-feminists, and against marriage by misogamists, as are adduced in this context against love by heroic misogynists.

While in popular literature it is often asserted that 'les gens de courage sont plus enclins à l'amour' (here the examples of Samson, Mark Antony, and Aeneas are adduced),[107] and while such writers as Grenaille (possibly as a compliment to Condé) deny that the company of women is in any way adulterating,[108] and proclaim the compatibility of Mars and Venus, it is none the less far more common to find asseverated in the drama of the time that heroic virtue is weakened by love. The episode of Hercules and Omphale is used on more than one occasion as an emblem to describe this debasing process.[109] It is man's duty and privilege to prefer the pursuit of 'gloire' to that of women; this is explicitly stated by Du Ryer's Lucretia,[110] and is implicit in the attitude of Gilbert's Semiramis, who declares that 'la soif de régner' is a more noble passion than love.[111]

The power of love is associated with the force of beauty, which is the endowment of nature on the female sex to compensate for man's greater physical strength. Beauty is female arms and armour; indeed it is so powerful that women may even feel the beauty of other women (this idea has been met before in the context of the pastoral; such plays as Mareschal's *Sœur valeureuse* make great

---

[106] See above, pp. 143 ff.

[107] Anon., *Meslanges de divers problemes*, Paris, 1647, pp. 307–14; 'Probleme XLIX: Pourquoy est-ce, selon le dire ordinaire des poetes, et celuy d'Aristote mesme au second liure de sa Politique, les gens de courage sont plus sujets à l'amour?'

[108] *L'honneste mariage*, p. 260, quoted above, p. 147.

[109] e.g. Hardy, *Didon se sacrifiant*, IV. chorus (*Théatre*, ed. Stengel, iii. 55); Mairet, *Le Marc-Antoine*, Paris, 1637, IV. i, p. 55.

[110] *Lucrece*, Paris, 1638, II. vi, p. 36: 'L'homme est fait pour la gloire et non pas pour les femmes.' See also Rodeline in *Pertharite*, III. iii, quoted below, p. 248; Venda in Gillet de la Tessonerie, *Sigismond*, Paris, 1646, II. iv, p. 46.

[111] *Semiramis*, III. ii, p. 51: 'Au trône laschement préferer vne femme'.

play on it). In some cases, too, men are praised by their wives or mistresses for their beauty.[112]

But the force of beauty is only half the dangerous armoury of women which can 'renuerser la constance d'vn philosophe': their *finesse* and their ability to control the expression of their emotions combine with it to form a weapon so powerful that only the man who is virtue itself is not seduced by it. This power is referred to in Du Ryer's *Esther* and *Lucrece*[113] and Benserade's *Cleopatre*,[114] and its calculatedness is exposed in Boyer's *Sœur genereuse*, in which one princess describes to her sister how she forced the king, who is her captor, into complete submission to her:

> I'attens donc ce tyran, s'il flate ie menace;
> S'il paroist tout de feu, ie suis toute de glace;
> Et tousiours insensible à ses folles ardeurs,
> Ie les voy tout d'vn coup croistre par mes froideurs.
> Vn dépit furieux enflamme son visage,
> Il murmure, il fremit, ses yeux brillent de rage;
> Alors iettant sur luy des regards assez doux,
> Son espoir se rallume, et flate son courroux.
> Puis i'arme mes regards d'vn éclat plus seuere;
> Enfin le regardant d'vn œil plein de colere,
> Ie voy que la fureur de cet audacieux
> Cede insensiblement au pouuoir de mes yeux.
> Là pour ne laisser point la victoire imparfaite,
> Par vn puissant discours i'acheuay sa deffaite,
> Et ce lasche brutal se voyant abatu
> Reconnut bien alors ce que peut la vertu:
> Cette Reine des cœurs, qui sur mon front preside
> Meslant auec ses traits d'vne pudeur timide
> L'éclat esblouïssant d'vne noble fierté
> Deuient mesme adorable à sa brutalité.
> Iamais vn feu pareil, et si plein d'esperance
> Ne fit si peu d'effet et moins de resistance;
> Alors pour s'affermir dans ce prompt changement
> Par l'immobilité d'vn fidele serment
> Il iure, et me promet que sa flamme effacée
> Par le seul repentir viuroit dans sa pensee.[115]

[112] e.g. Prince by Princesse in Gilbert, *Marguerite de France*, Paris, 1641, IV. v, p. 82; Mairet, *La Sophonisbe*, Paris, 1635, IV. i, p. 65, where the heroine recounts to Massinisse how she fell in love with him.
[113] *Lucrece*, II. i, p. 17 and III. iv, p. 51; *Esther*, Paris, 1644, IV. i, p. 80.
[114] *La Cleopatre*, Paris, 1636, v. iii, f. 44ᵛ.
[115] *La sœur genereuse*, Paris, 1647, III. iii, pp. 63–4.

A similar force in women is that held by mothers over their children; this is mentioned in Corneille's *Rodogune*.[116] These powers are all referred back by moralists to the *topos* about the power of women found in Plutarch's *Life of Cato*.[117]

The hero, therefore, must resist the authority of women if he is to remain independent. Brutus in *Lucrece*[118] and Scipio in *Sophonisbe*[119] speak proudly of their commitment to stern virtue and insensitivity, as do Corneille's aged male characters in the cast of the elder Horace and Don Diègue. These figures associate women and love with 'oisiueté' and 'volupté'—associations which have been noted elsewhere[120]—and underline the hero's commitment to honour above all else: 'nous n'avons qu'un honneur, il est tant de maitresses.'[121] Like the pastoral satyr, they consider women to be playthings, but unlike him, they act according to *bienséance*, and are often gallant. Their low assessment of women accounts in large part for their sense of dishonour if defeated or outwitted by one of them; Porcia, Zenobia, and Sophonisbe[122] by their suicide bring glory to themselves and draw grudging admiration from their captors in this way.

There is only one sure way of combating the power of love and woman, that is, by flight from it: such heroes as Horace, Cinna, Polyeucte, Mark Antony, and Aeneas[123] all have recourse to this expedient at some point or other in the action, and make specific reference to its sole effectiveness:

> Aux combats où l'amour attaque, et presse vn cœur,
> La palme est au plus lâche, et qui fuit est vainqueur.[124]

---

[116] *Rodogune*, II. v: 'Elle sera sa mère, et pourra tout sur lui.'

[117] See above, p. 22, and Caelius Rhodiginus, *Lectiones antiquae*, Geneva, 1620, xiv. 14, vol. 756. This whole section is relevant here, as it contains references to Hercules and Omphale and to classical texts relating to the *fraudes* of women, and their identification with *voluptas*.   [118] Du Ryer, *Lucrece*, I. ii, pp. 5–14.

[119] Mairet, *Sophonisbe*, IV. iii, p. 74:
> Ce n'est pas que mon sein soutienne vn cœur de roche,
> Impenetrable aux traits que l'amour nous descoche:
> La main qui fit le vostre a fait le mien aussi,
> Et la seule vertu me le rend endurcy.

[120] See above, p. 69, and below, p. 246.

[121] Don Diègue in *Le Cid*, III. vi.

[122] Guérin de Bouscal, *La mort de Brute et de Porcie*, Paris, 1637, v. vii, p. 99; d'Aubignac, *Zenobie*, Paris, 1647, p. 140; Mairet, *Sophonisbe*, v. vii, p. 108.

[123] *Horace*, II. vi, vii, viii; *Cinna*, III. iv; *Polyeucte*, I. ii; Benserade, *La Cleopatre*, v. iii; Scudéry, *Didon*, Paris, 1637, IV. ii.

[124] Benserade, *La Cleopatre*, v. iii, f. 45ʳ. Sometimes heroines also flee from love; e.g. Venda in Gillet de la Tessonerie, *Sigismond*, II. iv, pp. 46–7; IV. ii, p. 55.

Pauline's lament about the waning influence of women on men in *Polyeucte* may also be associated with this flight from female persuasiveness.[125]

It follows naturally that heroic misogyny is connected with a low assessment of womankind, approaching that of the religious moralists. This assessment is extended by most characters (even including heroines themselves) to the mass of women, and is reflected in the action of the plays by the passive rôle often assigned to female characters: even such a heroine as Porcia is forced to act through an agent,[126] and Rodogune must offer herself as a prize for the deeds of others in order to be influential.[127] The commonplaces about the female sex already discussed in a previous chapter are very much in evidence, and just as the *femme forte* is thrown into relief by the frailty of her sex in general, so also is the heroine in the drama by comparison with the ideas expressed about womankind as a whole.

The most common of the *topoi* relating to women—their frailty—is often encountered. Pauline's admission 'Je suis femme, et je sais ma faiblesse'[128] is clearly connected with it, and similar statements may be found in almost every other drama of this period. This belief in frailty is coupled in Hardy's *Didon se sacrifiant* with a distrust in female chastity,[129] and in Du Ryer's *Lucrece* with a conviction that women are of inferior intellect.[130] Their subjugation to passion and consequent irrationality or loss of lucidity are exemplified in many of the dramas of this period in scenes where a female character loses control of her emotions or verges on insanity. In *Horace*, however, it is suggested by Sabine that the control and consequent dissimulation of one's passions is hypocritical, and that she is happy to leave 'un tel art' to men, preferring the greater honesty of the behaviour of women.[131] Certain passions are particularly difficult to control for women:

[125] *Polyeucte*, I. iii.
[126] Boyer, *La Porcie Romaine*, Paris, 1646, IV. i, pp. 73–4: (Porcie)
  Car enfin pensez-vous qu'auec les seules larmes
  Ie puisse retablir la gloire de mes armes?
  Nos malheurs sont trop grands, et pour borner leurs cours,
  Vne femme, Seigneur, est vn foible secours.
[127] *Rodogune*, III. iv. There are of course exceptions; Oronte in Mareschal's *Sœur valeureuse* fights four times and wins all her combats, but it is rare to find such an active rôle assigned to a woman at this time.
[128] *Polyeucte*, I. iv.   [129] *Didon se sacrifiant*, III. i, and *passim*.
[130] *Lucrece*, III. i.   [131] *Horace*, III. vi.

anger, curiosity, jealousy, and, above all else, fear. Here the heroine is most clearly differentiated from the mass of her sex, since the only fears to which she is susceptible are for the fate of her husband or lover (this being a 'genereuse crainte'[132]) or for personal dishonour. The female sex is also accused of inconstancy and garrulousness, and, in the sphere of politics, of ambition and imperious behaviour; these last accusations will be dealt with more fully below.

The more attractive side to this failure to resist passion is the propensity of women to feel pity for the plight of others. Such pity may sometimes be transformed into a proclivity to hate and a desire for vengeance when their sympathy is not requited or returned, and this inverted compassion or love provides a psychological basis, as has already been pointed out, for one of the stock of rôles ascribed to them. It is perhaps the traditional association of women with clemency (explicitly referred to in Mairet's *Marc-Antoine*[133]) which leads Du Ryer to change the tenor of the biblical story and make Esther plead for the life of Haman.[134] Their sensitivity to the feeling of others is also connected with the commonplace about the civilizing force of women on men and the humanization of *virtus*, made explicit in Gilbert's *Marguerite de France*.[135] A further extension of this belief is the assertion found in Rotrou's *Deux Pucelles* that women are more perfect lovers than men.[136]

It is in the light of these attitudes to the female sex as a whole,

---

[132] Boyer, *La Porcie Romaine*, II. ii; cf. Mairet, *Le Marc-Antoine*, v. vi.

[133] *Le Marc-Antoine*, v. iv.

[134] *Esther*, v. v.

[135] *Marguerite de France*, III. iii, p. 65: (Prince)

> . . . La femme adoucit nostre sort rigoureux,
> Et l'on ne la forma, que pour nous rendre heureux:
> Si la vie est vn mal, elle en est le remede;
> La nature voulut qu'elle nous fût vne ayde,
> Que sa douce presence allegeast nos trauaux,
> Dissipast nos ennuis, et charmast tous nos maux.

[136] *Les deux pucelles*, I. iii (*Œuvres complètes*, Paris, 1820, iii. 473): (Léocadie)

> Hélas! qu'il est bien vrai, chétives que nous sommes,
> Que nos affections passent celles des hommes,
> Que nous souffrons plus qu'eux leur offrent du secours,
> Et que leur passion est toute en leurs discours!
> Ils parlent de la bouche, et nous parlons de l'âme;
> Ils ne sont qu'éloquents, et nous sommes de flamme;
> Ils feignent seulement ce que nous recélons,
> Et ne sont qu'échauffés alors que nous brûlons.

unexceptional in their time, that the depiction of the heroine must be seen. Here the great feminist figures of the works of Du Bosc and Le Moyne—Zenobia, Judith, Semiramis, Joan of Arc, Panthea—are encountered: indeed, the portrait of the 'Illustre Amazone' in the play of that name may derive to some extent from her description in Le Moyne's *Gallerie*.[137] As in the works of these moralists, the nature of female virtue is investigated through these figures. At its most mundane level this is defined as resistance to attacks on chastity (the attacks are necessary to prove the existence of the chastity, as is pointed out in Du Ryer's *Lucrece*[138]). The question whether this resistance constitutes heroic virtue finds a place in drama as well as in moralistic writings;[139] its most extensive discussion is in Du Ryer's *Lucrece*.[140] Tasso's argument that unchaste behaviour is tolerable in women who are endowed with heroic virtue finds echoes in the drama of this period; d'Aubignac's *La Pucelle* contains an exoneration from the often-levelled charge of lubricity against its heroine.[141]

Constance is perhaps the most frequently encountered abstract virtue attributed to the heroines of drama; this quality is admirably described in its two facets in Mairet's *Marc-Antoine*:

> Receuoir et le bien et le mal
> D'vn visage pareil et d'vn esprit esgal.[142]

In Regnault's *Marie Stuard* it is associated with a 'mepris des choses terrestres' with Christian and stoic overtones, further indicated by such phrases as 'estre au-dessus du malheur' and 'vaincre sa douleur'.[143] Its acquisition by the fortifying discipline of moral philosophy, one of the reasons in favour of female education adduced by Le Moyne, is also found asserted in the drama,[144] and it is associated on the one hand with stoic apathy,

---

[137] Rotrou, *Œuvres complètes*, v. 575–658; the play is not certainly the work of this author, however; cf. Le Moyne, *Gallerie*, pp. 264 ff.

[138] *Lucrece*, II. i, p. 18: (Tarquin)

> Mais peut elle [la femme] estre sainte et chaste reputée
> Si jamais sa beauté ne fut sollicitée?
> La femme n'est pudique et ne s'en peut venter,
> Que lors qu'elle a dompté ce qui la put dompter.

[139] See above, p. 83.

[140] *Lucrece*, II. i, ii.   [141] *La Pucelle*, p. 116; see also above, pp. 83–4.

[142] *Le Marc-Antoine*, I. iii, p. 9.

[143] *Marie Stuard*, Paris, 1639, III. vii and IV. vi.

[144] Mairet, *Le Marc-Antoine*, III. i, p. 40.

and on the other with male virtue ('asseurance plus que masle', 'resolution masle', 'courage plus que viril').

As the above quotation suggests, it implies both the possession of virtue and the outward control of the passions, and is often contrasted with female irresoluteness and fluctuating emotions. Its most striking portrayal is in death scenes, in which the fear and irresolution which the doomed heroine might be expected to show is transferred to the onlookers, and she herself, in this reversal of emotions, left impassive; this technique is often employed in book illustration, and is closely connected with the evocation of *admiratio*: the deaths of Mary Queen of Scots,[145] Mariamne,[146] and Saint Catherine are all excellent examples of this, and the reversal of male and female virtue is made especially clear in the last case.[147] There are two levels of *constance*, one more sublime than the other, which subdivide these heroines: the outward control of the passions, while suffering their internal revolt (Pauline in *Polyeucte*, and Camille in *Horace* provide excellent examples of this), and the control of the passions both outwardly and inwardly; Corneille's Théodore fulfils these conditions, and it is perhaps this fact which induces her author to declare that 'une vierge et martyre sur un théâtre n'est autre chose qu'un Terme qui n'a ni jambes ni bras, et par conséquent point d'action'. Heroines exempt from ambition are most highly placed in this respect.

A further element of female virtue is fidelity, and the toleration of the husband's infidelity. This is the subject of several of Le Moyne's 'questions morales' in his *Gallerie*, and is exemplified in the drama by such figures as Lucretia, Panthea, and especially Octavia. It is to some degree related to the praise of independence and the freedom of the spirit, even in the captivity or degradation of the body. The theme of 'death before dishonour' is a feature of several of the plays under consideration: Boyer's *La sœur genereuse*, d'Aubignac's *La Pucelle*, Tristan's *La Mariane*, and, of course, Du Ryer's *Lucrece*.

We have seen that the possession of such virtue by heroines is contrasted with their assumed absence in the female sex as a whole, and this may be considered to be feminist, as it postulates the

---

[145] Regnault, *Marie Stuard*, v. iv.   [146] Tristan, *La Mariane*, v. ii.
[147] Anon., *Le martire de ste Catherine*, Caen, 1649, v. vi, p. 90, quoted below, p. 252.

possibility of women overcoming their inherent weakness. The source of the virtues is, however, rarely attributed to the fulfilment by the heroine of her innate capacities. In a few cases, 'vertu' and its female possessor are described as separate entities, as in *L'Illustre Amazone*; when Sigismond asks Ebroin who has murdered the duke, Ebroin replies: 'Elle-même [L'Illustre Amazone], Seigneur, ou plutôt sa vertu',[148] and this division may be found also in Du Ryer's *Lucrece*,[149] and less explicitly in Boyer's *La Porcie Romaine*.[150] This may be seen as an extension of the patristic assertion 'virtutes non sexu, sed animo judicande', quoted by Guerry.[151] In Mairet's *Sylvie* the social *bassesse* of the heroine is said to be compensated for by her 'vertu',[152] but such equations are rare. It may be further compared with the asseveration found in Du Ryer's *Lucrece* that women are responsible for their own frailty,[153] and with the implication in the writings of Du Bosc and Le Moyne that virtue may be acquired through judicious reading and education.[154]

It is more usual to find virtue associated with the motif of reversal already mentioned (for example, Esther is described as being endowed with 'vertu masle'[155]), or with the prerogative of high birth or divine grace. As has already been shown in another context, the literature relating to virgin martyrs and, to a lesser extent, to the cult of the Virgin Mary embodies this association of heavenly inspiration with heroic virtue or religious zeal in women, which makes them equal or even superior to men; in the prayer of the heroine of *L'Illustre Amazone* as she prepares herself to commit suicide to save her honour, this association is specifically referred to:

> Dieu, qui des chastes corps avez formés vos temples,
> Présentez à mes yeux ces généreux exemples
> Et ces mâles esprits qu'une chrétienne ardeur

---

[148] Rotrou, *Œuvres complètes*, v. 646 (*L'Illustre Amazone*, v. iii).
[149] *Lucrece*, II. v, p. 33: (Tarquin) I'ay cru voir vne femme, et i'ay veu la vertu.
[150] *La Porcie Romaine*, v. ii, p. 86: (Porcie's prayer to the Roman people)
        Affranchissez ce cœur des foiblesses du corps.
[151] See above, p. 73.   [152] *Sylvie*, ed. Marsan, pp. 156 and 158.
[153] *Lucrece*, IV. i, p. 63: (Lucrece)
        Si la femme est fragile, elle l'est par sa faute,
        Le bien qu'elle a du Ciel, elle mesme se l'oste,
        Et l'on ne trouue point cette fragilité,
        Où l'on veut conseruer de la fidelité.
[154] See above, pp. 56 ff.   [155] Du Ryer, *Esther*, I. ii, p. 12.

Obligea d'immoler leur vie à leur pudeur;
Et si l'on me contraint de l'immoler au crime,
Permettez que j'en sois le prêtre et la victime.[156]

In this case, as in the case of Joan of Arc, it is necessary that virtue should be heaven-inspired, as the heroines are not of high birth; Saint Catherine and Theodora combine the advantages of virtue by blood with that of heavenly grace. Such words as 'miraculeux', 'prodigieux' used of these Christian heroines are more than hyperbolic epithets, as there are theological overtones to them. In all these cases, the virtue with which the heroine is imbued is referred to explicitly as male virtue.

In secular drama, the heroine's strength is almost exclusively attributed to her high birth; here the contrast between the élite and the mass of women takes on its most social and hierarchical aspect. At the head of this élite is placed the queen or the princess —Esther, Marguerite de France, Zenobia; her rôle is to 'viure et mourir en Reine'.[157] This class of heroine is further differentiated from the coquettish woman consort:

En seruant vne autre Reine, il suffiroit de luy fuser les cheueux, ou tenir vn miroir deuant elle: la suiure au bal, et dans les vaines pompes de la Cour. Mais Zenobie doit receuoir de nous des seruices plus conuenables à sa vertu. Il faudroit prendre les armes auec elle, il la faudroit suiure dans le combat auec autant de zele qu'elle a de generosité.[158]

The political rôle of such women will be dealt with more fully below.

After queens and princesses come the Roman heroines of Corneille, of Boyer, of Du Ryer, inheritors of the virtue for which their nation is famous. It is interesting that they are compared on more than one occasion to the Marquise de Rambouillet and her daughter, equating them therefore to the *grande noblesse*.[159] Connected with these Roman heroines is the idea of *gloire*, of fame and posterity. Just as by their example the whole female sex is glorified, so also, by the example of the Rambouillet family, Le Moyne

[156] Rotrou, *Œuvres complètes*, v. 639–40 (*L'Illustre Amazone*, IV. ii).
[157] Tristan, *La Mariane*, II. i, p. 24.   [158] d'Aubignac, *Zenobie*, III. i, p. 56.
[159] Boyer, *La Porcie Romaine*, Epistre à Madame la Marquise de Rambouillet, ã2ʳ; Le Moyne, *Gallerie*, p. 253.

can postulate the capacity of all women for education. Their example furthermore leads to the moral elevation associated with *admiratio*; what Du Bosc writes of Judith is equally applicable to them: 'au seul recit de ses victoires, toutes les femmes sont conquerantes dans leur ame, toutes voudroient luy ressembler, toutes voudroient iouyr de sa gloire'.[160] This preoccupation with immortality by reputation is explicit in Zenobie's dying speech:

> Et ie veux estre vn example en faueur de nostre sexe. Ouy, ouy, la Reine de Palmire sera mise au rang de ces Illustres Femmes dont les charbons ardents et le poignard [i.e. Porcia and Lucretia] ont eternisé la memoire. I'auray pourtant cet aduantage en mourant comme les Romaines, qu'elles n'auroient iamais vaincu les Romains comme moy.[161]

Corneille's use of the substantive 'Romaine' is clearly associated with this idea of *gloire*,[162] as is the 'noble refus de suiure un char' in a Roman triumph of Zenobia[163] and Sophonisbe.[164]

Virtue is closely allied to the sense of honour, which, for heroines, encompasses not only their chastity but also rank-consciousness and family or personal pride, leading them into conflict with state, and, in some cases, even husband. The clash of personal honour and 'inclination' in such figures as Pauline and Venda becomes a struggle between a self-imposed masculine sense of honour and promptings of their feminine nature; the struggle, while providing dramatic interest and glorifying the will of the heroine, at the same time detracts from her *constance* and stoic apathy.

The concept of female virtue in drama, however acquired, is above all else pleasing, and almost invariably associated with the

---

[160] *La femme heroïque*, i. 226-7.   [161] d'Aubignac, *Zenobie*, p. 132.
[162] e.g. *Cinna*, ii. v; *Horace*, i. i; *Pompée*, iii. iv.
[163] d'Aubignac, *Zenobie*, p. 125.
[164] Mairet, *Sophonisbe*, v. iii, p. 95; see also Mairet, *Le Marc-Antoine*, v. vii, p. 90, where there is the following discussion of Sophonisbe's suicide:

> Caesar: La mort la moins difforme, est vn monstre d'horreur,
> Qui dans les plus grands cœurs imprime la terreur,
> Et se rauir par elle aux triomphes de Romme,
> Plutost que d'vne fâme est l'ouurage d'vn homme.
> Maecene: Sophonisbe pourtant ne le fit pas trop mal.
> Caesar: Mais toutes ne sont pas la fille d'Astrubal.

Here the identification of virtue and high birth is clearly seen. Cleopatra herself provides in this play another example of a heroine preferring suicide to dishonour.

beauty of the heroine, thereby forming the sublime combination of 'masle generosité' and 'feminine douceur'. This adds to the dramatic effect of death or suicide scenes or *récits*, especially when combined with a stress on the innocence and powerlessness of the victim, as it is in the cases of Lucretia, Panthea, Mary Queen of Scots, and Portia. Here is an enriching of the traditional sacrifice theme, for the demise of these figures evokes *admiratio* as well as pathos, and a 'crudeltà che piace' as well as a sense of injustice.

In this brief survey, it has been shown how closely the portrayal of heroines is related to that of the *femmes fortes* of moralistic literature both in content and technique. An aspect of these plays which highlights this relationship is the involvement of women in politics, and discussions of the case for and against government by women.[165] One effect of high birth is to instil in heroines ambition and 'la soif de régner'. As has been previously noted, ambition is an un-Christian attribute which writers at this time do not attempt to justify, but simply accept as the result of *générosité*; this uncritical attitude is well reflected in a speech of Cleopatra in Corneille's *Pompée*:

> J'ai de l'ambition, et soit vice ou vertu,
> Mon cœur sous son fardeau veut bien être abattu;
> J'en aime la chaleur et la nomme sans cesse
> La seule passion digne d'une princesse.[166]

Female characters play active parts in the politics of many plays of this period, and often display a developed political consciousness; the Countess of Warwick in *La Pucelle*, in attempting to dissuade her husband from his love for Joan of Arc, says:

Tandis que vous m'auez seule offensée dans cette folle inclination i'ay souffert auec patience, mais maintenant que vous blessez les interests de l'Estat, et que vous engagez toute vostre maison dans la ruyne, ie serois mauuaise Angloise, mauuaise femme, et mauuaise mere, si ie ne m'efforcois d'y apporter quelque remede.[167]

The order of priorities *Angloise–femme–mere* is here significant.

---

[165] See M. Baudin, 'The statesman in seventeenth-century French tragedy', *MLN* liii (1938), 319–27, for an account of some aspects of this question.
[166] *Pompée*, II. i.
[167] d'Aubignac, *La Pucelle*, III. v, pp. 98–9.

The association of women with power leads to a consideration of the ability of women to rule; the question of Salic law is specifically referred to in *La Pucelle*;[168] and in *Zenobie*,[169] *Semiramis*,[170] *Sigismond*,[171] and *Don Sanche d'Aragon*,[172] all of which were published in Anne of Austria's regency, there is treatment of the more general issue in similar terms to those already examined in Chapter II. It is perhaps possible to see in the following speech

[168] Ibid. II. i, pp. 81–2: (La Pucelle) 'Dieu qui pourueut les François d'vn cœur absolument incapable de souffrir la domination des femmes, leur inspira cette fameuse loy Salicque . . . Ne iugez pas de la generosité des François par vostre foiblesse; il n'appartient qu'à vous de pouuoir estre les esclaues d'vne femme, et de porter le ioug d'vne insolente domination, où d'ordinaire la passion fait toute la suffisance, le caprice toutes les regles du gouuernement . . .'

[169] d'Aubignac, *Zenobie*, IV. iii, pp. 99–100, quoted below, p. 193. It is interesting that the same author should, in 1642, give his heroine anti-feminist sentiments on this subject, and in 1647 strongly feminist views.

[170] Gilbert, *Semiramis*, v. iv, p. 115: (Semiramis) 'Monstrons . . . qu'vn trône est dignement remply d'vne femme.'

[171] Gillet de la Tessonerie, *Sigismond*, v. i, pp. 101–2: (Sifroy)

L'Empire d'vne Femme est d'autant plus Auguste
Qu'on trouue en luy cedant, comme en obeïssant,
Vne necessité qu'on apporte en naissant.
  Le droit de la Couronne et celuy du visage
Font en se confondant vn parfait assemblage,
Qui meslant la Puissance auecque la Beauté,
Accordent la douceur auec la Majesté . . .
  Sçachant se commander beaucoup mieux que nous autres,
Leurs desirs sont tousiours plus nobles que les nostres,
Et la sage froideur de leur emotions
Accordent la raison auec leurs Passions.
  En vain nous auons fait d'iniustes Ordonnances
Pour priuer leurs Esprits des belles connoissances,
Puis qu'vn beau Naturel leur donne par hazard
Vn brillant qui preuault nostre Estude et nostre Art.
  Aussi nous confessons que de pareilles flammes
Composent les esprits des Hommes et des Femmes
Qu'vn mesme Dieu forma les nostres et les leurs
Sans qu'il ait fait les vns plus foibles ou meilleurs;
  Ouÿ l'Ame ce rayon de la grandeur Suprème,
Par sa propre vertu fait son genre elle-mesme,
Elle n'a point de Sexe, ou n'est masle qu'alors
Que la Gloire la porte à de nobles efforts.

For other implications of this very feminist speech, see above, pp. 47 ff. and below, pp. 249 ff.

[172] *Don Sanche d'Aragon*, I. ii: (Dona Isabelle)

Que c'est un sort fâcheux et triste que le nôtre,
De ne pouvoir régner que sous les lois d'un autre;
Et qu'un sceptre soit cru d'un si grand poids pour nous,
Que pour le soutenir il nous faille un époux!

by Zenobia in favour of female rule an allusion to Anne's regency:

La Souueraineté des Femmes est d'autant plus juste que la nature leur en a donné les caracteres sur le visage, et les commencemens dans le respect de tous les hommes. La valeur seule est le tiltre pour commander, et si vous n'en auez point fait de loix, nous en auons fait des exemples. La vaillante Victorine regne encore sur les Gaules.[173]

The involvement of women in politics is often associated with the commonplace about their *superbia* and imperiousness, and heroic misogynists identify the *pouvoir politique* of women with their *pouvoir amoureux*, since both are insidious and may only be defeated by flight. It is also asserted that their ambition is not a pure 'soif de régner', but rather a mixture of emotions of revenge and hate. Their intriguing is sometimes seen as a manifestation of their perverse nature straining against male domination—hence the use of such words as 'braver', 'audace', 'défiance' to describe their political behaviour.[174] This low assessment is explicit in *Nicomède*:

La fourbe [in politics] n'est le jeu que des petites âmes,
Et c'est là proprement le partage des femmes.[175]

Like the most heroic male characters, the greatest heroines act without dissimulation, with 'force ouverte': for this Joan of Arc is especially commended.[176] But providence or divine protection is necessary to save figures of such integrity from the wiles of dissimulators and flatterers; political *fourberie* by women is only countered by romanesque strokes of good fortune, as in *Nicomède* and *Rodogune*.

This survey of heroic drama may be said to show the importance of feminism and feminist thought to the genre and the intimate connection between the portrayal of the dramatic heroine and that of the *femme forte*: in both cases these figures are contrasted with the mass of their own sex, and associated with male attributes and rôles. Whereas the social aspect of feminism is most clearly reflected in the novel of the period, as will be seen, the aesthetic use of female figures which is the distinguishing feature of feminist literature at this time finds most complete expression

[173] d'Aubignac, *Zenobie*, IV. iii, pp. 99–100; see also Baudin, 'The stateswoman in French Tragedy', *MLN* liii. 324. [174] See below, p. 248.
[175] *Nicomède*, IV. ii. [176] d'Aubignac, *La Pucelle*, pp. 115–16.

in the heroic drama, to which many of the stylistic techniques deployed in feminist writings, which will be discussed in a later chapter, are most successfully adapted. The dramatic, dialectical nature of the *femme forte* may also account in part for her close assimilation with the heroine of tragedy and tragi-comedy.

Comedy

This genre may be said to be one of the least developed in this period; apart from the comedies of Corneille, which will form the basis of this inquiry, there are few outstanding works of any originality. Antoine Adam offers for this the following explanation:

Il semble que les écrivains et le public aient quelque peine à concevoir un comique détaché des traditions de la comédie latine et de la farce. Ce qui semblerait l'indiquer, c'est la présence d'éléments comiques excellents dans la pastorale et la tragi-comédie. Le public les goûtait sans doute. Mais il était à ce point accoutumé à lier l'idée de comédie aux rôles traditionnels de pédants, de valets, de soldats fanfarons, de nourrices et d'entremetteuses que lorsqu'il assistait à une scène d'observation plaisante et délicate, il ne comprenait pas que la comédie, c'était précisément cela.[177]

Comedy at this time, as is suggested here, is a combination of stock characters and situations with social comment and observation, and from this emphasis on the unheroic and the real, one may expect to encounter both interesting social reflections germane to feminism and satire of feminist pretensions (most clearly seen in Desmarets's *Visionnaires*, and in Saint-Evremond's depiction of Mlle de Gournay in *La comédie des académistes*). As Corneille points out in one of his *Epîtres*, the deceit and intrigue of the comedy are more important than the maintenance of credible psychology in the characters.[178] This fact makes it difficult to draw conclusions about comic characters, but certain general tendencies in the portrayal of women may be noted.

One factor which should be borne in mind in comedy as in more serious drama is the changing notion of *bienséance*. In the

---

[177] *Histoire de la littérature française au XVIIᵉ siècle*, i. 554.

[178] *La Suivante*, Epître, in *Théâtre*, ed. Lièvre and Caillois, i. 414: 'les fourbes et les intrigues sont principalement du jeu de la comédie; les passions n'y entrent que par accident.'

early years of the seventeenth century, Hardy's tragedies and tragi-comedies contain irreverent discussions of marriage and women (which find their way in an attenuated form into the comedies of this period) as well as explicit scenes of passion and adultery.[179] As has recently been shown,[180] the practice of including such material in drama does not end with the open return to theatrical performances of *honnêtes femmes*; irregular dramatists, preferring action to narration, include such scenes in their plays, and portray heroines who lose their honour. The removal from the stage of over-eager female lovers, prostitutes, and unmarried mothers may be attributed in great part to the *Querelle du Cid*. The heroines of the 1640s are in fact more moral than those of the 1630s, but the latter, for all their actions, retain an 'aura of innocence' which permits us here not to differentiate between the portrayal of female figures in earlier and later comedies.

It is convenient to consider first the stock female characters of comedy, mentioned by Adam above. The *nourrice*, or *suivante*, or in some cases *servante*, performs the function of exonerating the heroine from responsibility for the more dishonest tricks which are employed on her behalf, and of advising her on the best ways to win a man's heart. The advice of an aged woman to a young maiden or wife is a feature of such writings as *La Celestina* and Piccolomini's *Dialogo della bella creanza delle donne*, and is nearly always associated with worldly, if not immoral, counsel about the art and wiles of love; in the comedy of this period it is usually less pernicious, and more directly related to the intriguing and deceit which form the basis of the action. The *servante*, from her base social position, is privileged in the same way as the fool and the madman in being free from the dictates of social convention; she is at liberty to say precisely what she likes. Her overriding traits are *finesse* and insolence.

The heroine herself is a paradoxical combination of apparent innocence with innate female guile.[181] She is not heroic in the sense that the heroine of tragedy is heroic: Clarice in *Le Menteur* is not prepared, as her tragic counterpart might be, to 'mourir de constance'[182] when crossed in love, and her namesake in *La*

---

[179] e.g. *Panthée*, II. ii (*Théatre*, ed. Stengel, i. 112); *Cornélie*, III. i (ibid. ii. 110).
[180] See W. Gibson, 'Women and the notion of propriety in the French theatre'.
[181] The heroines of Mairet's *Galanteries du duc d'Ossonne* (Paris, 1636) are notable exceptions; they are scarcely innocent.   [182] *Le Menteur*, III. ii.

Veuve confesses that she is not resolute enough to act as a mistress should:

> Refuser d'un amant ce doux nom de maîtresse!
> N'avoir que des mepris pour les vœux qu'il m'adresse!
> Le voir toujours languir dessous ma dure loi!
> Cette vertu, Nourrice, est trop haute pour moi.[183]

It is true that there is much profusion of good filial and obedient sentiments by comic heroines, but these are in general only expressed when they coincide with their desires: this is made very clear in *Le Menteur*.[184] Thus self-satisfaction and non-renunciation take precedence over *devoir*, *honneur*, *famille*, in sharp contrast to the behaviour of female characters in heroic drama. To some degree, the heroines of comedy may be seen as satires on their counterparts in tragedy, who represent the unattainable ideal of womanhood to which female characters in comedy do not aspire; this satirical aspect is explicit in *Les Visionnaires* in the figure of Mélisse.[185]

Because they are resolved not to suffer their fate, but to work for the fulfilment of their own desires, comic heroines make great use of female guile, both on their own account and through the agency of other female figures. This is their dominant trait in some cases, and they are quite unashamed of it: Cloris says almost boastfully 'nostre sexe a le don de tromper finement'.[186] This guile is of course related to the *pouvoir amoureux* so reviled by heroic misogynists. The fulfilment of their hopes nearly always involves marriage, and it is rare that the paths of courtship are trodden alone or without misunderstanding: hence the many scenes of female jealousy.[187] All this unprincipled intriguing sets off diatribes of anti-feminist sentiments in the slighted lover and the disappointed father: *La Veuve*[188] and *L'Illusion*[189] bear witness to this. Thus when Lucrèce urges Sabine to give an account of 'le naturel des femmes' to Dorante in *Le Menteur*,[190] one may expect no discourse on *constance*, fidelity, and moral elevation in the style of Le Moyne, but rather an Ovidian treatise on seduction.

---

[183] *La Veuve*, II. ii.
[184] *Le Menteur*, V. vii:
> Clarice : Mon père a sur mes vœux une entière puissance.
> Lucrèce : Le devoir d'une fille est dans l'obéissance.
[185] Desmarets, *Les visionnaires*, ed. Gaston Hall, Paris, 1963, p. 97.
[186] *Mélite*, III. iv; cf. III. ii.
[187] e.g. Mairet, *Galanteries du duc d'Ossonne*, IV. i, ii.   [188] *La Veuve*, III. iii.
[189] *L'Illusion*, V. iii.   [190] *Le Menteur*, IV. viii.

Marriage or betrothal plays an integral part in many of the comedies of the period, and it is natural that the institution should draw much comment. The standard arguments against marriage from the male point of view are rehearsed in *Mélite*,[191] in *La Place Royale*,[192] and in *La Suite du Menteur*;[193] especial emphasis is given to the restrictions which it imposes. Woman's case against matrimony is also to be found expressed, albeit satirically, in *Les Visionnaires*, by the three female characters.[194] It is rare, however, that heroines do not want to marry, unless they are being forced to marry the wrong person. This eventuality leads to the ineluctable denunciation of parental authority in this sphere, and of the marrying off of daughters for financial considerations alone.[195] In the context of comedy, however, these arguments may not be given too much weight, for very often daughters are used as chattels to make the plot work out (this is the case with Florise in *La Suivante*). The financial aspect of marriage is frequently discussed: the question whether women should consider merit above solid income in their prospective husbands is debated in *Mélite*[196] and *La Veuve*,[197] and fulsome praise of dowries may be found in the mouths of more than one suitor.[198] A certain amount of practical advice and good sense is proffered on the subject of marriage, although this is probably incidental: the advantages of similar social backgrounds are mentioned in *La Suivante*,[199] and an enlightened view about the freedom to choose one's partner is propounded in *La Galerie du Palais*.[200] In *La Veuve*, the social and marital advantages of widowhood are exemplified.[201]

As would be expected in a genre given over to social observation and contemporary issues, the questions of *galanterie* and of

---

[191] *Mélite*, I. i.   [192] *La Place Royale*, I. iv.   [193] *La suite du Menteur*, I. i.

[194] *Visionnaires*, v. iii, iv, v.

[195] See Du Ryer, *Les vendanges de Suresne*, Paris, 1636, IV. vi.

[196] *Mélite*, IV. i.   [197] *La Veuve*, I. iv.

[198] Notably Eraste in *Mélite*, I. i, and Octave in *Galanteries du duc d'Ossonne*, IV. iii, p. 77:

> O qu'vne femme pauure est vn fardeau pesant !
> Ma foy ie veux du bien, et du bien tout present.
> La fille pauure et belle, à mon auis est née
> Pour la resoüissance, et non pour l'hymenée ;
> Qui selon le prouerbe est pire que l'enfer,
> Quand au lieu d'estre d'or ses chaines sont de fer.

[199] *La suivante*, III. vi.

[200] *La Galerie du Paris*, v. viii; see also Du Ryer, *Les vendanges de Suresne*, IV. vi, vii.

[201] See also Mairet, *Galanteries du duc d'Ossonne*, v. ix.

social behaviour both by and towards women are prominent.[202] This is especially true of *Les Visionnaires*, in which different manners of female behaviour are satirized in the three sisters; Mélisse is caught up in romanesque fantasies about heroic lovers, Sestiane, the amateur of the theatre, is remarkable as a *précieuse avant la lettre* and Hesperie believes that all men love her, and behaves coquettishly. Anti-feminist denunciation of female social vices may also be detected in some of the comedies of the period, as, for example, in Cliton's eulogy of the silent woman in *Le Menteur*:

> Quand une femme a le don de se taire,
> Elle a des qualités au dessus du vulgaire;
> C'est un effort du ciel qu'on a peine à trouver;
> Sans un petit miracle il ne peut l'achever;
> Et la nature souffre extrême violence
> Lorsqu'il en fait d'humeur à garder le silence.[203]

On more than one occasion criticism is made of the demands of *bienséance*, and the restrictions imposed by convention on female behaviour: 'Quelle importune loi que cette modestie!' exclaims one heroine.[204] Also relevant to this element of contemporary social comment is the description of Paris by Lyse in *La suite du Menteur*:

> Où des dames, dit-on, est le vrai paradis . . .
> Les maris y sont bons, et les femmes maîtresses.[205]

This may be associated with the *topos* about female domination attributed to Cato, referred to above, and perhaps also with the strikingly feminist *Epître* to *La Place Royale*, quoted below.

The commonplaces about respect and passion, service and recompense, already examined elsewhere, are found in great profusion in the mouths of the male characters of comedy.[206] These figures are typified by their combination of *galanterie* with anti-matrimonial attitudes, similar to that of Hylas: Alcidor of *La Place Royale*, Dorante of *Le Menteur*, and initially Eraste in

[202] See Du Ryer, *Les vendanges de Suresne*, I. i.
[203] *Le Menteur*, I. iv; see also Du Ryer, *Les vendanges de Suresne*, I. i and II. v.
[204] Daphnis in *La Suivante*, II. vi; see also Du Ryer, *Les vendanges de Suresne*, I. iii, p. 13:
> Dorimene: Triste condition d'vne fille amoureuse
> Qui pour n'oser le dire est souuent malheureuse.
[205] *La suite du Menteur*, II. i.
[206] These are parodied in *La suite du Menteur*, IV. i and V. i.

Mélite all reproduce the arguments which have become familiar through the writings of Rampalle, La Mothe Le Vayer, and others :

> L'Hymen de soi-même est un si lourd fardeau,
> Qu'il faut l'appréhender à l'égal du tombeau.
> S'attacher pour jamais aux côtés d'une femme !
> Perdre pour des enfants le repos de son âme !
> Voir leur nombre importun remplir la maison !
> Ah ! Qu'on aime ce joug avec peu de raison ![207]

Yet their behaviour is consistently gallant in the company of women, and their objection to the institution of marriage is not in any way associated with a low assessment of the female sex, but rather with an obsession about personal liberty, verging on solipsism in the case of Alcidor, who sees love as an infringement on his independence :

> Impuissant ennemi de mon indifférence,
> Je brave, vain Amour, ton débile pouvoir :
> Ta force ne venait que de mon espérance,
> Et c'est ce qu'aujourd'hui m'ôte son désespoir.
>
> Je cesse d'espérer et commence de vivre ;
> Je vis dorénavant, puisque je vis à moi . . .[208]

This combination of inconstancy and *galanterie* leads inevitably to the expression of the perennial female distrust in male motives, seen most clearly in the monologue of Angélique in Act IV of *La Place Royale*.[209]

The status of love in comedy should finally be considered. This has already been treated in detail in Octave Nadal's book,[210] and it is only necessary here to show the connection between feminism and the different theories of love to be found in this

---

[207] *Mélite*, I. i; see also Mairet, *Galanteries du duc d'Ossonne*, IV. iii, p. 77, quoted above, p. 197 n.

[208] *La Place Royale*, V. viii; cf. Montaigne, *Essais*, ed. Thibaudet and Rat, i. 39, pp. 234–5 : 'or, puis que nous entreprenons de vivre seuls et de nous passer de compagnie, faisons que nostre contentement despende de nous; desprenons nous de toutes les liaisons qui nous attachent à autruy, gaignons sur nous le pouvoir à bon escient vivre seuls et y vivre à nostr' aise . . .'

[209] *La Place Royale*, IV. viii. In Du Ryer's *Les vendanges de Suresne*, there is an inconstant female character, reminiscent of Guarini's Corisca (Lisette), who expresses her philosophy of love in II. iv, p. 45 :
> L'on iuge qu'vne fille à beaucoup de merite
> Par le nombre d'amans que l'on void à sa suite.

[210] *Le sentiment de l'amour dans l'œuvre de Pierre Corneille*, Paris, 1948, deuxième partie.

context. As has already been suggested, scant respect is paid in comedy to the maintenance of strict psychology; when this fact is combined with the functional rôle played by marriage in many cases—as in the novel, the asymptote of comedy is matrimony, and its achievement is as much a mechanical part of the intrigue as an expression of the desires of the characters—the status of love may be seen to be much reduced, for it does little more than provide the rudimentary psychological explanation for the action. It is looked upon by characters of the stamp of Alcidor as a weapon in the armoury of women by which they try to get their own way, and references to the 'débile pouvoir de l'Amour' may be seen also as allusions to the 'débile pouvoir des femmes'. There are, however, interesting discussions on the subject of love, and this may be seen as an accurate reflection of the demand of contemporary taste.[211] The two extremes of this passion—*amour-fureur* and *amour-raison*—are both given feminist slants in the comedy, the first, as suggested above, because it subjugates men to women, the second, more interestingly, because it is a compliment to their qualities of mind as well as of body. This is made explicit in the *Epître* to *La Place Royale*:

L'amour d'un honnête homme doit être toujours volontaire; . . . on ne doit jamais aimer en un point qu'on ne puisse n'aimer pas; . . . si on en vient jusque-là, c'est une tyrannie dont il faut secouer le joug; et . . . enfin la personne aimée nous a beaucoup plus d'obligation de notre amour, alors qu'elle est toujours l'effet de notre choix et de son mérite, que quand elle vient d'une inclination aveugle, et forcée par quelque ascendant de naissance à qui nous ne pouvons résister.[212]

Comedy, therefore, is a genre in which there is satire of feminism and quite faithful reflections of current discussions about love, about social behaviour, and about marriage, but few indications of aesthetic feminism, and little serious treatment of the questions of the moral prestige of women. In the years which follow the limits of this inquiry, and especially in the plays of Molière, discussions of feminist topics are very much more prominent and less incidental; such questions as the right of women to be educated, which appears only peripherally in *Les Visionnaires*, are given extensive treatment,[213] and the whole

---

[211] e.g. Mairet, *Galanterie du duc d'Ossonne*, II. i (a discussion of *amour-folie*).

[212] *Théâtre*, ed. Lièvre and Caillois, i. 493.

[213] See F. Baumal, *Le féminisme au temps de Molière*, Paris, 1923; G. Reynier, *La femme au XVIIe siècle*, esp. Ch. 8.

range of *précieux* demands represented. The fact that this does not appear to be the case in this period may be ascribed to the current misconception about the genre mentioned by Adam in the quotation which opened this section.

The Novel

In earlier chapters, and in an earlier section of this chapter,[214] mention has already been made of the important rôle played by the novel in the development and diffusion of feminist ideas; this is also attested by Magendie in his monumental thesis on *honnêteté* and in his account of the French novel in the first half of the seventeenth century.[215] Contemporaries also are aware of the close connection between the glorification of women and this genre; Sorel, in his *Connoissance des bons livres* of 1671, attacks the novel for the very elements which are of interest to this inquiry:

En ce qui est des Femmes et des Filles, elles n'ont garde qu'elles ne cherissent cette sorte de Livres [novels], puisqu'outre la recreation qu'elles prennent à voir leur diversitez, elles trouvent qu'ils sont faits principalement pour leur gloire, et qu'à proprement parler, c'est le Triomphe de leur sexe. C'est là qu'on pretend monstrer que les Femmes sont les Reynes des Hommes et de tout l'Vnivers, et qu'on doit mesmes les reconnoistre pour Deesses; il n'y a point de lieu où leur merite soit eslevé plus haut. On y parle de quelques Filles qui n'ont que la beauté pour partage avec quelque agréement d'humeur, lesquelles sont plus estimées que celles qui sont riches et de haute condition, et l'on y trouve quelquefois des Princes humiliez devant une petite Bergere. Quelle esperance cela ne donne-t'il point aux Filles de bas lieu ou de mediocre? Ne croyent-elles pas qu'elles pourront estre un jour la plus chere conqueste de quelque Prince aventurier, et que leur beauté ne leur doit guere moins promettre qu'une couronne? Les Femmes mariées n'y trouvent-elles pas encore quelque avantage et quelque satisfaction? Ne se divertissent-elles pas au moins des avantures que l'on y raconte, et ne leur est-ce point un doux apas pour quelques plaisirs mondains? Enfin ces belles imaginations ne cessent de les charmer toutes, et il faut croire que la puissance en est tres grande, puis qu'encore que de tels recits ne soient pleins en quelques endroits que d'avantures de guerre dont la cruauté devroit estonner, elles ne laissent

[214] See above, pp. 156 ff.
[215] See *La politesse mondaine et les théories de l'honnêteté en France au XVIIᵉ siècle, de 1600 a 1660*, esp. vol. i; *Le roman français au XVIIᵉ siècle de* L'Astrée *au* Grand Cyrus.

pas de les cherir, et de rechercher ce qui les fascheroit autre part, tellement qu'on peut dire que ces Livres leur plaisent par le seul nom de Roman.[216]

It is interesting that Sorel neglects to deploy the traditional arguments against the novel, which attack its immorality and eroticism,[217] but rather concentrates on sociological aspects. One may detect here the assumption that the genre is directed at a female or female-dominated audience or readership, and the many dedications to women in general are a further indication of this.[218] When a genre is wholly dedicated to pleasing them, the cult of women may be expected to be as pronounced as Sorel declares it to be.

Another of Sorel's implied criticisms, that women hold greater prerogatives in literature than in society at this time, suggests that the novel provided an escape from mundane reality into a fictional world which compensated the social impotence of its readers, and in this the genre fulfils a similar function to the *salons*. Yet for all the escapist element, there is a great deal of social comment in the novels of this period, as has already been noted in other chapters: discussions on the subject of marriage and parental authority over the unmarried; debates about the possibilities of divorce; investigations into the nature of woman's social rôle, which often include apologies for the homage paid to women by the gallant; harangues on female education; speeches about the civilizing force of women on men, and about their contribution to refined society. It is interesting that Amarylle in Sorel's *Berger extravagant*, in a debate about the value of novels, defends them for their social usefulness:

Nous autres femmes qui n'allons point au college, et qui n'avons point de precepteurs comme les hommes pour nous apprendre les diuerses

---

[216] *De la connoissance des bons livres*, pp. 136–7.

[217] e.g. Vives, *Institutio foeminae Christianae*, i. 3; François de la Noue, *Discours politiques et militaires*, Basle, 1597, pp. 133–46 (vi: 'Que la lecture des livres d'Amadis n'est moins pernicieuse aux jeunes gens, que celle des livres de Machiavel aux vieux'); Jean-Pierre Camus, *L'Autheur au pelerin Alexis*, cited by Magendie, *Le roman français au XVIIe siècle*, p. 143.

[218] e.g. Du Verdier, *Le roman des dames*, Paris, 1630–2; Jean Baptiste Du Pont, *Le miroir des dames*, Lyons, 1605; Desmarets, *L'Ariane*, Paris, 1639, ã2^r: 'Beau sexe, a qui la Nature a donné ce qu'elle auoit de plus riche et de plus aimable; source des plus agreables delices; qui tenez dans vos belles mains l'Empire de l'Vnivers, puisque vous commandez aux hommes, et que vous leur distribuez comme il vous plaist, ou l'infortune ou le bon-heur . . . c'est à vous . . . à qui ie desire plaire le plus.'

choses qui se passent au monde, c'est seulement dans les Romans que nous auons le moyen de nous rendre sçauantes. Si l'on nous les oste l'on nous rendra toutes stupides et toutes sauuages : car nos esprits n'estans pas propres aux liures de Philosophie ny aux autres ouurages serieux, ce n'est pas là que nous ne pouuons apprendre ny la vertu ny l'Eloquence.[219]

The cult of women to which Sorel refers in the passage from *De la connoissance des bons livres* quoted above is, as has been seen, very marked in *L'Astrée*, which, together with the Greek novel, sets the pattern for the large-scale, many-volumed novels of the period, such as Gomberville's *Polexandre*, La Calprenède's *Cléopâtre* and *Cassandre*, Le Maire's *Prazimène*, and the works of Scudéry and Desmarets. With or without pastoral elements, the novel of this period is in the main the more or less complicated story of a long and faithful suit, ending usually, after many difficulties and misunderstandings, in a happy marriage. The perfection of the heroine is implicit, setting numerous rivals at loggerheads; even when she is not presented, like Alcidiane in *Polexandre*, as an inaccessible goddess for whom the idea of marriage with a mortal is an insult,[220] she is worshipped by the hero as devoutly as Céladon worshipped Astrée. From the point of view of the plot, the respectful hero and the admirable heroine, Desmaret's *l'Ariane*, to take a single example, may appear typical of the genre, illustrating particularly well the influence of *L'Astrée* and of feminist ideas.[221]

The hero of Desmaret's novel, Mélinte, like Silvandre and Céladon, proves himself at all times to be respectful of women, and a defender of their honour. His debate with Garamante, an importunate suitor of Ariane, is a good example of the way in which traditional feminist arguments are reproduced in modified form in such contexts. Garamante decries the submission of men to women in service, and advocates a more aggressive and direct expression of love :

Mélinte . . . luy demanda, sur quel fondement il appuya cette vanité; sur ce, dit-il, que pour vn aduantage qu'ont les femmes par dessus nous,

[219] Sorel, *L'Anti-roman*, iv. 889, referred to by Magendie, *Le roman français au XVIIe siècle*, p. 334.
[220] See Adam, *Histoire de la littérature française au XVIIe siècle*, i. 414–16.
[221] See Magendie, *Le roman français au XVIIe siècle*, pp. 96–117 (Ch. 3 : 'Influence de l'Astrée').

qui est la beauté, les hommes en ont mille sur elles, qui sont bien de plus grande consequence; comme la grandeur de courage, la prudence, la force et l'adresse de corps, auec vne infinité d'autres. Mélinte luy respondit: quand mesmes nous aurions ces aduantages, ie les trouue bien foibles, puis qu'il faut que nous les soubmettions tous au pouuoir de leur beauté: mais nous sommes bien esloignez de les auoir, car vne Dame tesmoigne plus de courage en la conseruation de son honneur, et plus de prudence en sa conduitte, que nous ne pouuons faire en aucune action: elles ont de bien plus rudes espreuues à souffrir que nous, et plus de consequences à preuoir. Il faut qu'elles soient incessamment en garde, sans que dans vne si grande attention il paroisse aucune contrainte, et soit que cela se fasse auec peine ou auec facilité, elles sont loüables, ou d'vn grand soin, ou d'vne grande dextérité d'esprit. Au contraire nous laissons aller mille paroles, et faisons mille actions, qui seroient autant de crimes aux Dames, ce qui tesmoigne en elles vne nature bien plus parfaite que la nostre, et vne plus grande pureté de vertu, en qui la moindre faute feroit vne grande tache. Il ne nous reste que la force du corps, qui est vn aduantage bien petit pour s'en preualoir: comme si le Lion deuoit estre plus estimé que l'homme pource qu'il est plus fort . . . Aussi n'est-il point d'homme si puissant qu'vne Dame ne domine: il ne faut qu'vn regard ou vne parole, nous voila abbatus, alors il faut venir aux prieres et aux soumissions, ce qui est vne marque infaillible de leur aduantage . . .[222]

Here may be detected the essence of a feminist tract such as that by Gilbert,[223] but reduced in scale, purged of example and extravagant arguments, and rendered not in highly rhetorical prose, but in a more natural, if still latinate, style. This passage is doubtless not unique among the novels of the period,[224] and it may be

---

[222] Desmarets, *L'Ariane*, pp. 163–4; for the implications of Garamante's argument, see below, pp. 249 ff.; for examples of arguments similar to those deployed by Mélinte, see above, pp. 51–2.   [223] *Panegyrique des dames.*

[224] See Magendie, *Le roman français au XVIIe siècle*, pp. 92 ff.; le sieur de Mousé, *Les larmes de Floride essuyees par Minerve*, Paris, 1627, pp. 186–7: (Minerva to Floride) 'ne te flatte point sur la foiblesse de ton sexe, disant qu'il n'est pas assez fort pour resister à des assauts si violents: car proposer telle chose, c'est vouloir se desarmer soy-mesme, pour prendre subiet de fuir laschement, au lieu de combattre auec vne resolution genereuse.

Non, non, Floride, nous ne sommes pas naturellement moins capables d'actions, de vertu que les hommes, et nostre sexe est susceptible des mesmes qualitez dont ils font gloire et trophée tous les iours: ce qu'eux-mesmes ont esté contraints de confesser.' There follows from this four pages of traditional proofs of feminine superiority, based on example and authority, constituting a feminist document similar in scope to Marie de Gournay's *Egalité des hommes et des femmes*, but proving the superiority of women in this case.

supposed that such speeches were far from displeasing to the
female reading public.

The influence of *L'Astrée* is clearly seen in the portrayal of
female characters in the novel. In *L'Ariane*, the eponymous
heroine is, like Astrée, of a 'humeur desdaigneuse naturelle'; she
has a deep sense of personal honour; her presence of mind and
capacity for action are demonstrated on several occasions, and her
qualities are such that at one point they are equated with those of
the hero Mélinte:

Ils auoient tous deux vne grandeur de courage si parfaite, vn esprit si
sage, vne viuacité si brillante dans la conuersation, et vne modestie si
maiestueuse, entre les beautez dont la Nature les auoit si liberalement
partagez, que iamais couple ne se rencontra auec tant de perfection et
d'égalité . . .[225]

She is also modest, and expresses at one point her feelings of
inadequacy as a woman:

Il faut que nous confessions . . . que les hommes ont bien plus de force
que nous aux resolutions: car lors qu'ils ont conceu vn dessein qui
importe au bien de toute leur vie, ils le maintiennent iusques au dernier
souspir . . . au contraire nostre esprit se relasche au moindre obstacle;
nous ne sçauons plus deuenir; et nostre foiblesse nous empesche de
franchir le moindre passage, pour paruenir aux supremes felicitez.[226]

In spite of such assertions, she is able to assassinate her Scythian
captors, and her account of this bears witness to the same modesty
as may be detected in the above quotation.[227] It is interesting that
she, in the same way as the author of *La femme genereuse*, is rendered
courageous by male cowardice.[228] In her moral and intellectual
qualities, as well as in her heroic attitude to life, she may be compared to the *précieuse*.

Ariane's defence of her person is, of course, no more than one
would expect of a descendant of Chariclea. This is a commonplace of fiction, and there are many examples, notably in the
novels of Jean-Pierre Camus, of the heroine who resists an
aggressor either by employing violence against him or against

[225] Desmarets, *L'Ariane*, p. 366.   [226] Ibid., p. 421.
[227] See below, p. 227.
[228] Desmarets, *L'Ariane*, p. 713: 'l'autre Scythe ayant entendu siffler [la fleche] . . .
a commencé de fuir. Sa lascheté m'a rendüe courageuse, et je me suis sentie em-
portée par vne certaine ardeur de gloire, pour auoir l'honneur de tuer le dernier
des Scythes'; cf. *La femme genereuse*, pp. 3–5, quoted above, p. 78.

herself: the latter alternative is also a theme of moralistic and
feminist writing, as has been shown.[229] Incidentally, we may also
note as recurrent, especially perhaps in novels where the Amadis tradition survives, the counterpart of this theme: the man
who, like Joseph or Theagenes, resists the overtures of forward
females.[230]

This last point recalls the reversal of rôles which was discussed
in connection with *L'Astrée*, sometimes accompanied by change
of costume. After Magendie,[231] there is no need to demonstrate
how often in the novel of the period men disguise themselves as
women and vice versa.[232] Most striking perhaps from the point
of view of this study is the part played in this literature by the
warlike woman in male garb. The number of heroines who are
brought up to fight, hunt, shoot, and ride is prodigious;[233] these
are not only professional warriors and amazons such as Thalestris
in *Cassandre* and Telesmane in *Polexandre*, but also heroines such
as Menalippe in *Cléopâtre* and Clarice in Du Verdier's *La Parténice
de la cour*, whose involvement in violent action is incidental.
Epicharis, sister of the hero of *L'Ariane*, appears on several
occasions in the course of the story dressed as a man or as a
soldier, and in such disguises she performs heroic deeds, while
deploring the fact that she should be forced to be so dressed:

Ie sçay bien que ce desguisement est estimé vn crime, pource qu'il y
a eu de mon sexe qui ont caché leur infamie sous cét habit, et s'en sont
seruies pour continuer auec plus de liberté des actions indignes d'elles;
mais [i'ay] esté contrainte de la prendre pour conseruer mon honneur.[234]

This association of *infamie* and transvestism has been met before
in the context of the pastoral;[235] it may also be found in the
drama.[236] Du Verdier goes much further than Desmarets in the
portrayal of female warriors, for in his *Roman des dames* the two

[229] See above, p. 85; Camus, *Spectacles d'horreur*, pp. 207–15; Sorel, *Le
palais d'Angelie*, Paris, 1622, p. 157; and Célidée in *L'Astrée*, ed. Vaganay, ii. 435–53.
[230] See Magendie, *Le roman français au XVIIe siècle*, pp. 307–8.
[231] Ibid., pp. 226–9.
[232] For Sorel's critique of this feature of the novel, see *L'anti-roman*, iii. 601–2.
[233] See Magendie, *Le roman français au XVIIe siècle*, pp. 47–8.
[234] Desmarets, *L'Ariane*, p. 723.
[235] See above, pp. 167–9.
[236] e.g. d'Aubignac, *Zenobie*, iv. iii, p. 99; (Aurelian) 'où trouuez-vous que [les
loix] authorisent dans la conduite de la guerre vn sexe à qui la nature n'a permis de
faire des conquestes qu'auec les yeux?'

heroines, Astrabelle and Claridanie, bored by their pampered existence, embrace the career of a soldier, and revel in violence:

Que le contentement estoit grand de leur voir desplier le bras sur ces cheualiers estonnez de leur valeur incomparable? Quelques vns couppez en deux pieces tomboient sous le foudre des coups de Claridanie, Astrabelle les fendoit constumierement iusques aux espaules, icy l'on voyoit voller vn bras sur la terre, vne teste sautoit d'vn autre costé . . .[237]

Such heroines retain all of the beauty of their sex, and their remarkable combination of qualities gives rise to such speculations as the following, which are those of the warrior Clarofilant in Du Verdier's *Roman des dames*:

Si ie m'arreste à son habit et si ie me souuiens de la force prodigieuse auec laquelle ie luy ay veu mettre en pieces deux geans horribles ie croiray que le bras d'vne femme n'est pas capable de si grandes choses, mais aussi si ie considere ses actions, le ton de sa voix, ce teint delicat et cette incomparable beauté que les hommes n'ont que rarement ie songeray que c'est vne femme qui cherche des diuertissemens honorables au trauail des armes.[238]

There are many examples of such unusual combinations of attributes in novels at this time;[239] the implications of such depiction are examined in detail below.[240] It is sufficient here to point to the presence in this genre of transvestite female soldiers and adventurers, as a further reflection of the current predilection for paradox and surprise which has already been noted in the portrayal of the *femme forte*.[241]

From Magendie's exhaustive account, and from the novels which have been cited in this section, there is every indication that feminism plays an important rôle in the novel, both because the genre was principally directed at a female or female-dominated reading public, and because in terms of characterization and episode, heroines, like the *femme forte*, are compared favourably with men, and often surpass them. As is the case with drama, it is difficult to assess how far sources influence the depiction of heroines, but the popularity of independent, enterprising women

[237] Du Verdier, *Le roman des dames*, ii. 406–7.
[238] Du Verdier, *Le roman des dames*, i. 163–4.
[239] See Magendie, *Le roman français au XVIIe siècle*, pp. 47–8.
[240] p. 244.
[241] See above, pp. 79 ff.

in novels is in itself an adequate testimony of contemporary taste. At the same time, the lover's service to the heroine reflects the more traditional deference paid to women. Sorel's remarks about the feminine bias of the genre would seem then to be totally justified.

It is possible, therefore, to assert with some confidence that feminism is a significant feature of the imaginative literature of this period. It is reflected in the current debates about the social rôle of women and about marriage which find their way into most genres at this time, and in these discussions certain arguments drawn from feminist and anti-feminist writings may be detected. These concern the domination of men by women and the source of this purely moral authority, which is usually ascribed to the power of beauty and to its mystical associations. Examples and theological argumentation, as well as most medical evidence, which form a large part of feminist tracts as such, are rarely encountered in imaginative literature, and this fact strengthens the conviction expressed in Chapter II that such material really belongs to previous centuries, and is not easily reconcilable with the sensibility of the period under review here.

In the pastoral, the preoccupation with the relationship between the sexes in an Arcadian setting in which the male-dominated pursuits of politics and war are out of place leads to a concentration on aspects of thought and behaviour—sensibility, spirituality, peace—in which women are the equals or the superiors of men. The notion that women are the source of all social virtues and of civilization is also reflected in the novel, in which the romanesque exploits of heroines and the power over their suitors are further indications of the appeal of this genre to its female readership. In drama, the reversal of male and female rôles and attributes, the contrast drawn between the heroine and the female sex as a whole, the paradoxical concept of female *amabilité* are facets of style and thought which the feminism of imaginative literature shares with that of Du Bosc and Le Moyne, and which reflect mid seventeenth-century sensibility in France; the remaining chapters will be devoted to their examination.

1. 'Fortitudo', from Ripa, *Iconologia* (1611)

2. Frontispiece of L'Hermite, *La princesse heroïque* (1645), engraved by Esmé de Boulonnois

3. The emblem 'custodiendas virgines', from Alciati, *Emblemata* (1591)

Left: 4. 'La vertu', engraved by Abraham Bosse (1637)

Right: 5. Frontispiece of Mareschal, *La sœur valeureuse* (1634), engraved by Michel Lasne

ANIMOS, CVRASQVE INDVTA VIRILES

BLANCHE INFANTE DE CASTILLE.

Os ſuum aperuit ſapientiæ; et lex clementiæ in lingua eius. Prouerb. 31. in Muliere forti

5. Frontispiece of d'Auteuil, *Blanche de Castile* (1644), engraved by Grégoire Huret

ALPHABET
DE L'IMPERFECTION
ET MALICE
des femmes.

Virum de mille vnum reperi : mulierem
omnibus non inueni. Ecclef. cap.7.

De mil hommes i'en ay trouué vn bon,
& de toutes les femmes pas vne,

Dedié à la plus mauuaife du monde.

A PARIS,
Chez IEAN PETIT-PAS, ruë Sainct
Iacques à l'Efcu de Venife prés
les Mathurins.

M. DC. XVII.
Auec Priuilege du Roy.

7.

7. Title-page of Trousset, *Alphabet de l'imperfection et malice des femmes* (1617)

8. The emblem 'rex animo non sexu', from Le Moyne, *Gallerie des femmes fortes* (1647)

9. The emblem 'mares haec foemina vincit', from Flamen, *Devises et emblesmes d'amour moralisez* (1648)

10. The emblem 'semper aliquid', from Flamen, *Devises et emblesmes d'amour moralisez* (1648)

8.

9.

97 *Cette femefle l'emporte fur le mafle*

10.

37 *Jamais oifif.*

Te clauam inutare colô cum cerneret, Heros,
Hæc matri referam ludicra: dixit Amor.

S. Vouet pinxit   cum priuileg. Regis   M. Dorigny Sc. 164

1. 'Hercules and Omphale', engraved by Michel Dorigny after Vouet (1643)

13. 'The death of Lais', from Le Moyne, *Les peintures morales* (1642), engraved by Grégoire Huret

DISCOVRS PARTICVLIER

CONTRE LES FEMMES

DESBRAILLÉES DE ce temps.

Par PIERRE IVVERNAY Preftre, Parifien.

TROISIESME EDITION.

A PARIS,
De l'Imprimerie de PIERRE LE-MVR,
dans la grand-Salle du Palais.

M. DC. XXXVII.

12. Title-page of Juvernay, *Discours particulier contre les femmes desbraillées de ce temps* (1637)

15. Frontispiece of Niceron, *Thaumaturgus opticus* (1646), engraved by Charles Audran after Vouet

14. Frontispiece of Le Moyne, *Gallerie des femmes fortes* (1647), engraved by Charles Audran after Pietro da Cortona

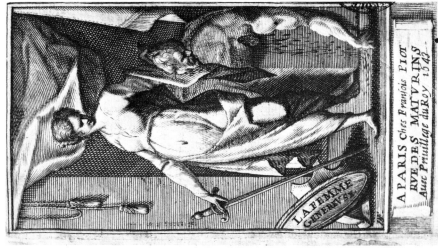

Left: 16. 'Judith', from
Lescalopier, *Les predica-*
tions (1645), engraved by
Abraham Bosse

Right: 17. Frontispiece of
La femme genereuse (1643)

IVDITH VICTORIEVSE D'HOLOFERNE

F.C. in et fe.

*Vne femme Iuifue a ietté la Confusion
dans la maison du Roy Nabuchodonosor*
au·1· de Iudith·

8. 'Judith', from Du Bosc, *La femme heroïque* (1645), engraved by François Chauveau

SALOMONE MERE DES SET MACABÉES.

Mère tout afait admirable, et digne de la memoire de tous les Siecles . Macab. I. 2. chap. 7.

19. 'Salomone', from Du Bosc, *La femme heroïque* (1645), engraved by François Chauveau

20. 'Jael', from Le Moyne, *Gallerie des femmes fortes* (1647), engraved by Abraham Bosse after Vignon

21. 'Zenobia', from Le Moyne, *Gallerie des femmes fortes* (1647), engraved by Abraham Bosse after Vignon

THOMYRIS VICTORIEVSE DE CYRVS.

Œ. in et fe.

*Boy maintenant a ton ayse du sang humain,
dont tu as esté si alteré.*

Herodote. l. 1.

2. 'Thomyris', from Du Bosc, *La femme heroïque* (1645), engraved by François
Chauveau

23. 'Joan of Arc', from Le Moyne, *Gallerie des femmes fortes* (1647), engraved by Abraham Bosse after Vignon

4. Illustration for Book 15 of Desmarets, *L'Ariane* (1639), engraved by Abraham
Bosse after Vignon

26. Frontispiece of Saint-Amant, *Moyse sauvé* (1653), engraved by Abraham Bosse after Vignon

25. Illustration for Book 8 of Desmarets, *L'Ariane* (1639), engraved by Abraham Bosse after Vignon

VII

Feminist Literature and the Visual Arts

IN this chapter a preliminary inquiry will be undertaken into the relationship between feminism and the taste and sensibility of this period through a comparison of the visual arts with feminist literature. Such an approach to the question of baroque is of course in no way novel, and rests to a large degree on the work of previous scholars and critics. In the case of feminist literature the comparison is particularly relevant, since two of the most important feminist productions of the regency of Anne of Austria—those of Du Bosc and Le Moyne—contain engravings which form an integral part of the conception of the works themselves. Also pertinent to this study are emblem books and iconologies, as these often shed light on the meaning of paintings and engravings, and may in themselves be feminist.

It is interesting to note to what extent feminist painting of this period is associated with the production of galleries of heroic figures. Outstanding among these galleries is that of Rubens, executed between 1622 and 1625 for Marie de Médicis, which is now in the Louvre, but was originally painted for the Palais du Luxembourg. Described by Sir Anthony Blunt as the most important event in the early part of the seventeenth century in Paris,[1] this series of paintings depicts the life and career of Marie de Médicis, and is in many ways strikingly feminist. According to Jacques Thuillier,[2] Marie wanted to commemorate herself more as a heroine than as a queen; for this reason, the romanesque episode of the escape from Blois is included, whereas acts of the regency, such as the founding of hospitals, are not. The portrait of Marie de Médicis in the guise of Bellona which was placed in the same gallery, and the inclusion of the battle of Juliers with the Queen Regent in the foreground on a horse (although she

[1] *Art and architecture in France, 1500–1700*, p. 129.
[2] J. Thuillier and J. Foucart, *Rubens' life of Marie de' Medici*, New York, 1967, pp. 27 ff.

H

was in fact not present at the battle), are further indications of her desire for worldly apotheosis as a heroine during her own life-time.[3] The glorification of women is present also in other forms: three of the paintings depict the royal marriages of Marie's daughters; in the episode of the coming of age of Louis XIII there is a galley, representing the ship of state, manned not by oarsmen, but by bare-breasted females who also embody the virtues of a monarch, the emblems of which are seen on the shields at their sides; furthermore, in such female personifications as *La France*, it is possible to detect traces of the pedagogical and mystical rôle often assigned to women in Renaissance painting.[4] Blunt asserts that these paintings exerted little or no influence, 'so contrary were they to the current conventions of late manner-ism, and the new canons of classicism which were about to be imposed'.[5] It is possible, however, that they influenced certain book illustrators, among them Grégoire Huret, and that they contributed to the popularity of galleries of related paintings in France at this time. From a letter of 1622, written by Peiresc to Rubens, it is known that Marie de Médicis planned a similar series of paintings to decorate the dome of the entrance portal at the Palais du Luxembourg. This series was to illustrate eight famous women, most of whom were queens and the mothers or wives of famous men.[6] Between 1633 and 1636 Champaigne, Vouet, and others produced a gallery of famous French heroes and heroines for the Palais Cardinal (later to become the Palais Royal), which included Marie de Médicis, Anne of Austria, and Joan of Arc;[7] in 1637 Vouet, with the aid of pupils, painted a gallery of heroic women for the Maréchale de la Meilleraye at the Hôtel de l'Arsenal,[8] and the same artist was invited in 1645 to

---

[3] For a slightly different interpretation see O. von Simson, *Zur Genealogie der weltlichen Apotheose im Barock*, Strasburg, 1936. Thuillier points to literary parallels which describe Marie as a heroine, not only pamphlets but also poems by Malherbe and Marino (*Rubens' life of Marie de' Medici*, pp. 27 ff.).

[4] See Wind, *Pagan mysteries of the Renaissance*, pp. 75 ff.

[5] *Art and architecture in France*, p. 130. See also Thuillier and Foucart, *Rubens' life of Marie de' Medici*, pp. 39–40.

[6] See O. von Simson, *Zur Genealogie der weltlichen Apotheose im Barock*, p. 290; W. R. Crelly, *The painting of Simon Vouet*, New Haven and London, 1962, p. 110 n. Blanche de Castille is included among the eight.

[7] See Y. Picart, *La vie et l'œuvre de Simon Vouet*, ii: 'Simon Vouet premier peintre de Louis XIII', Paris, 1959, p. 14.

[8] See J.-P. Babelon, 'L'Hôtel de l'Arsenal au XVIIIe siècle', *L'Œil*, cxliii (1966), 26–35, 55–8.

produce three paintings of the actions of famous women for the apartments of Anne of Austria at the Palais Royal.[9]

In literature, too, the idea of the gallery was popular at this time. Marino's *Galeria*, first published in 1619, is a collection of poems describing paintings and sculptures, among which are many subjects which could be considered feminist. This work inspired Georges de Scudéry to produce his *Cabinet* in 1646, in which may also be traced a certain feminist influence.[10] In prose writing, the practice of grouping together biographies of feminist figures is in no way new; compilations of such subject-matter had been current since Boccaccio's *De claris mulieribus*, and had been widely used to press the feminist case by means of argument from example. The idea of a gallery of feminist figures, which appears to be peculiar to this period, is exploited by Francesco Pona in his *Galeria delle donne celebri* (1625); Grenaille produces a *Gallerie des dames illustres* in 1643, four years before Le Moyne's *Gallerie des femmes fortes*; Puget de la Serre published two 'galleries' in 1645 and 1648, both in honour of Anne of Austria;[11] Vulson de la Colombière adapts the gallery of the Palais Cardinal to book form in 1650.[12] Another possible adaptation of the concept

---

[9] See R.-A. Weigert, 'Deux marchés passés par Simon Vouet pour les décorations de l'appartement d'Anne d'Autriche au Palais-Royal', *BSHAF* (1951), 101–5. One might also mention that in 1646–7 Romanelli came to Paris at the request of Mazarin to paint the ceiling of the Galerie Mazarine (now in the Bibliothèque Nationale in Paris), for which he chose mythological subjects, including Apollo and the Muses, who are portrayed with the faces of leading *salon* women (see L. Hautecœur, *L'histoire des châteaux du Louvre et des Tuileries*, Paris and Brussels, 1927, p. 39). There are also two further galleries of famous women painted in France in the 1650s: one in the Louvre, consisting of Judith, Esther, and the cardinal virtues, painted for Anne of Austria's apartments ('cette décoration était habituelle dans les chambres des souveraines', according to Hautecœur, *L'histoire des châteaux du Louvre et des Tuileries*, p. 43); and another, also painted for Anne of Austria's apartments, in the Château de Richelieu, consisting of Judith, Esther, Artemisia, Cleopatra, the wife of Astrubal, Sophonisbe, Dido, Thomyris, Semiramis, and Bathsheba (see C. de Grandmaison (ed.), 'Description du Château de Richelieu par un anonyme du milieu du XVIIIe siècle', *Nouvelles archives de l'art français*, 2e série, iii (Paris, 1882), 211–37, esp. 221).

[10] See above, p. 172; *Les salons littéraires au XVIIe siècle*, pp. xi, 23–6.

[11] *Temple de la gloire contenant les éloges historiques de treize Annes royales et princesses de France* (1645); *L'isthoire et les portraits des imperatrices, des reynes et des illustres princesses de l'auguste maison d'Austriche, qui ont porté le nom d'Anne* (1648).

[12] *Les portraits des hommes illustres françois qui sont peints dans la Gallerie du Palais Cardinal de Richelieu . . . ensemble les abregez historiques de leurs vies* (1650). A collection of poems based on the portraits in the Palais Cardinal was produced by B. Griguette (*Eloges des hommes illustres peints en la Gallerie du Palais Roial*, 1646). Du Bosc's *Femme heroïque* (1645) may also be included in this list, since the illustrations give the work a gallery-like quality.

of a gallery may be found in Desmarets's *Jeux des reynes renommées* of 1644, a pack of playing-cards illustrating fifty-two famous queens for the benefit of the Dauphin's education. The subjects of these painted and literary galleries range quite widely, but certain figures recur: biblical heroines such as Deborah, Jael, and Judith; amazons and queens of antiquity such as Semiramis, Thomyris, and Zenobia; Roman women, and especially Lucretia, Panthea, and Paulina; finally, modern heroines and rulers associated with France, notably Joan of Arc, Mary Queen of Scots, Marie de Médicis, and Anne of Austria. The galleries are usually contributions to the prestige of contemporary figures, and the commonplace of the past paying tribute to the brilliant present is found in several of the literary galleries.[13]

It is necessary to mention at this point the relationship of iconologies and emblem books to book illustration as a preface to the discussion of the works of Du Bosc and Le Moyne. The connection of emblems and iconology with the visual arts is seen in Rubens's Gallery of 1622–5, in which female figures are often iconological depictions of virtues, and in the Gallery of the Palais Cardinal, the paintings of which were surrounded by emblems which bear on the life of the hero or heroine. There are also emblems in Le Moyne's *Gallerie des femmes fortes*.[14]

The problem posed by iconology is of interest here. It would appear that the depiction of virtues as male or female figures depends on the Latin gender of the virtue in question (*virtus heroica* is an exception),[15] and that it is therefore inappropriate to describe such depiction as feminist. This is traditional, however,[16] just as the association of furies and fates with anti-feminism is traditional.[17] One image of *virtus* is described in Cesare Ripa's *Iconologia* as a 'donna bella, armata e d'aspetto virile';[18] this description is almost identical with that of *fortitudo* (Plate 1), an armed woman with a lance or a sword, sometimes also bearing

[13] e.g. Le Moyne, *Gallerie*, ã3r: ('A la Reyne Regente') 'les Femmes Fortes assemblées en cette Galerie, sont venuës de tous les endroits de l'Histoire, pour mettre leurs Couronnes aux pieds de Vostre Maiesté: et se réiouyr en commun, de l'honneur que vous faites à vostre Sexe.'

[14] Ibid., ãã1r-v.

[15] Cesare Ripa, *Iconologia*, Padua, 1611, pp. 537–9.

[16] e.g. Pontus de Tyard, *Solitaire premier*, ed. S. F. Baridon, Geneva and Lille, 1950, pp. 46–7.

[17] e.g. Trousset, *Alphabet*, pp. 99–100; Grenaille, *L'honneste mariage*, pp. 140–1.

[18] *Iconologia*, p. 540.

a shield.[19] These iconological depictions (it is often difficult to be certain whether *virtus* or *fortitudo* is in question) are adapted for the purpose of historical, fictional, and even contemporary portraiture. The frontispiece of *La princesse heroïque* (an account of the life of Mathilda, Marchesa of Mantua published in 1645) exemplifies the use of the conventional image of *fortitudo* or *virtus* in a feminist work. Here (Plate 2) is a female figure with helmet, sword, and shield, and, on the right, a broken pillar (another indication of force, alluding to Samson's destruction of the Philistine temple).[20] On the shield are papal insignia to indicate the religious and pious enterprises of the Marchesa; the face, *d'aspetto virile* as prescribed by Ripa, is perhaps intended to express the heroic qualities of resoluteness, calmness, and integrity. There is also the common device of amoretti bearing the arms of the heroine, to indicate her 'générosité' and probably also that of the holder of this title at the time of the publication of the book, who was a feminist figure in her own right.[21] This portrait was executed by Esmé de Boulonnois.

The iconological depiction of *virtus* is sometimes confused with the emblematic or mythical representation of Minerva (*Pallas armata*). Alciati's emblem entitled 'custodiendas virgines' (Plate 3) depicts Phidias's statue of Minerva as a young woman with a helmet, lance, and shield, on which there is a Medusa's head. At her feet there is a dragon.[22] This same figure, used by Alciati as a representative of chastity, is portrayed as 'La vertu' by Abraham Bosse in an engraving published in 1637 (Plate 4), to which the following text is appended:

> Ce sexe doit rauir les Esprits mecontents,
> Pour montrer que la famme est extente de blame.
> Ils apprendront que de tout temps
> On donne a la vertu les habitz d'vne famme.[23]

[19] Ibid., pp. 179–82.
[20] Cf. Titian's statuette of *fortitudo* in the Victoria and Albert Museum (a female figure holding a broken column); and Bosse's engraving of *fortitudo* in his series of theological and cardinal virtues.
[21] Marie-Louise de Gonzague, later to become Queen of Poland. Saint-Amant's *Moyse sauvé* (see below, p. 228) is dedicated to her.
[22] See A. Henkel and A. Schöne, *Emblemata: Handbuch zur Sinnbildkunst des XVI. and XVII. Jahrhunderts*, Stuttgart, 1967, col. 1732.
[23] This engraving forms the frontispiece of Reynier's *La femme au XVIIe siècle*. There is a copy in the Cabinet des Estampes of the Bibliothèque Nationale. The same confusion of the iconological representation of abstract virtue with the reality of the

The confusion of *virtus*, *Pallas armata*, and feminism is here clearly exposed. Similar confusions can be found in other illustrations at this time: the unsigned frontispiece of Puget de la Serre's tragi-comedy *Climene* of 1643 portrays a *Pallas armata* who is both the heroine of the play and an iconological depiction of *virtus* (the sub-title of the play is 'le triomphe de la vertu');[24] Mareschal's tragi-comedy *La sœur valeureuse* has a similar illustration of the heroine as Minerva holding a shield on which is depicted the portrait of a man (Plate 5). The man's head fulfils a triple function, for not only is a shield bearing a portrait carried by the heroine in the play itself, but also it may portray the Duc de Vendôme, to whom the play is dedicated, and further alludes to Hercules, whose head sometimes appears on *fortitudo*'s shield as an indication of strength. *La sœur valeureuse* was published in 1634; the same engraving without the man's head, but with the inscription 'La Dorinde' on the shield, was previously used as the frontispiece of Auvray's play of that name which appeared in 1631. It subsequently served, with appropriate adaptations, as the frontispiece of Le Maire's novel *La Prazimène* (1638). The engraving was executed by Michel Lasne.

It seems to have been fashionable among ladies of the *grande noblesse* in the 1640s to be painted as *fortitudo* or *Pallas armata*. Mlle de Scudéry refers to this vogue in a letter to Conrart in 1646:

Je serois peut estre assez adroite pour broder une escharpe avec de l'or et de la soye, et mesme assez heureuse, sy vous le voulés, pour trouver dans ma mémoire quelque devise espagnole ou italienne assez galante pour mettre sur un bouclier; mais je ne seray jamais assez courageuse ny assez desraisonnable pour conseiller à une personne de mon sexe de se servir de l'une ny de l'autre sy ce n'est pour se faire peindre en Pallas.[25]

As evidence of this fashion there are portraits of the duchesse de Longueville engraved by Nicolas Poilly and the Grande Made-

image (a woman) may be found in Sarasin's dialogue *S'il faut qu'un jeune homme soit amoureux* (1649) (*Œuvres*, ed. P. Festugière, Paris, 1926, ii. 156). Bosse also executes an engraving of Deborah dressed as *Pallas armata* for Le Moyne's *Gallerie*.

[24] The same frontispiece, suitably adapted, is used for Puget de la Serre's play *Le martyre de sainte Catherine* (1643), and signed DF (cf. below, Plate 17).

[25] *Un tournoi de trois pucelles en l'honneur de Jeanne d'Arc*, ed. Barthélemy and Kerviler, Paris, 1878, p. 23. This vogue may be connected with the practice of some seventeenth-century portraitists, who prepainted the costume and figure and filled in the face on demand (see Mme de La Fayette, *Romans et nouvelles*, ed. E. Magne, Paris, 1970, pp. 231–4).

moiselle painted by Pierre Mignard.[26] The vogue extends to historical portraiture: in d'Auteuil's *Blanche de Castille* of 1644, the frontispiece (Plate 6), one of two depictions of the Queen Regent, shows her as *Pallas armata*, yet surrounded by emblems of peace—the olive branch in her hand, the caduceus at her feet, the musical instrument and books lying beside her.[27] The Medusa's head is usually placed on Pallas's shield: here its position beneath her foot may relate to the quelling of discord in France.[28] Her martial exploits are indicated by the trophies and shields in the background; her fame is symbolized by the laurel wreath which an amoretto holds above her head. The light-source emanating from the top left-hand corner is probably a conventional image for divine inspiration, often encountered in such illustrations (cf. Plate 23). Both the motto above her head and the quotation from the Alphabet of the Good Woman at the foot of the portrait are feminist. As in the case of Plate 2, the facial expression indicates heroic qualities such as courage, impassivity, and resoluteness, and as in Boulonnois's engraving of *La princesse heroïque*, there is a striking suppression of feminine characteristics.

Iconological or mythical depictions of armed women are therefore used in this period with a feminist slant; I have mentioned *fortitudo*, *virtus*, and *Pallas armata*, and to this list *Bellona* (in which guise Marie de Médicis is portrayed by Rubens), *victoria*, and *Venus armata* should be added.[29] In the case of abstract virtues, the link with Latin gender is disregarded, and the female figure is taken to represent her sex as a whole, or an individual of her sex. It is rare to find vices such as *invidia* or *ira* used to illustrate anti-feminist arguments; emblems, on the other hand, being commonly regarded as didactic at this time, offer more scope for writers hostile to women. The ecphrasis, or description, of paintings or statues of the ancient world forms the basis of a good number of these. The interpretations made of Phidias's statue of Minerva has already been discussed; on the anti-feminist

[26] Poilly's portrait, and an engraving of that by Mignard, are to be found in the Cabinet des Estampes of the Bibliothèque Nationale.

[27] The olive branch is associated with Pallas in Alciati's emblem 'vino prudentiam augeri' (see Alciati, *Emblemata*, ed. Claude Mignault, Leyden, 1591, p. 123).

[28] The cutting off of a head may symbolize the quelling of civil strife or the defeat of tyranny: cf. L'Escale, *Champion des femmes*, ff. 133–42.

[29] See Blunt, *Art and architecture in France*, Plate 111a, for a reproduction of Vouet's painting of *victoria*; for an account of *Venus armata*, see Lilio Giraldo, *Historiae deorum syntagma XIII*, in *Opera omnia*, Leyden, 1696, i. 394.

side there is the 'hieroglyph' on the title-page of Trousset's *Alphabet* (Plate 7), which depicts a harpy,

portan[t] visage de belles filles, vn ventre puant et pourry, des mains crochuës, infectant toutes choses par leurs attouchements, deschirant les viandes des banquetans, les tetasses pendillantes, pleines de laict mortifere, succées par des chattons, vestuë de plumes, pasle de faim, auec des pieds de Poule.[30]

Trousset's moralistic interpretation of this figure, based on an ecphrasis in the *Aeneid* (iii. 216–19), is characteristic of the violent misogyny of his work:

Ce beau visage humain et ce corps brutal monstrent que tes attraicts [ô femme], tes allechements, et tes ruses feminines ne tendent qu'à des actions lasciues et brutales, et à des comportemens plus de brutes que de creatures raisonnables.

Ce ventre putride et fetide, declare les saletez et les puanteurs qui sortent de ta charogne, exposée et prostituée aux exclaues de ton impudicité . . .

Ce visage pasle de faim descouure en toy deux appetits insatiables, l'vn des richesses et l'autre des voluptez . . .

Les chattons sucçans le laict mortifere de tes tetasses, font entendre, que les effeminez chassans au parterre de tes mondanitez, la proye de leurs voluptez succent en goustant la douceur, vn laict empostumé, si amer, et si desgoustant, que le repentir funeste s'en ensuit fort promtement.[31]

Alciati's emblem 'mulieris famam non formam vulgatam esse oportere', which is reproduced in many of the emblem books of this period, is another example of an emblem with implications which lend it more easily to an anti-feminist interpretation.[32]

If one sets aside emblems of statecraft, courage, and glory adapted to feminist ends, few emblems can be described as indis-

---

[30] *Alphabet*, pp. 6–7. [31] Ibid., pp. 7–9.

[32] See A. Henkel and A. Schöne, *Emblemata : Handbuch zur Sinnbildkunst des XVI. und XVII. Jahrhunderts*, cols. 1749–52. This emblem is referred to by Le Bermen, *Le bouclier des dames*, pp. 94–5 : 'les Egyptiens nous figurant, quelle deuoit estre vne femme pudique, nous depeignoient vne Venus tenant vne clef deuant la bouche, et ayant vn pied sur vne Tortuë, nous signifiant par cest hieroglifique, que la femme ne doit parler qu'en temps et lieu, et qu'elle ne doit non plus que la Tortuë (qui porte sa maison sur son dos) gueres sortir d'icelle.' Maillard gives a different interpretation (*Le bon mariage*, p. 124) : 'comme la tortue n'a point de cœur, ainsi ceux qui se laissent emporter à la volupté sont sans cœur, ou s'ils en ont, elle leurs rauit'; Maillard attributes this emblem to Phidias, and its interpretation to Pausanias and Plutarch, as does Lilio Giraldo, *Historiae deorum syntagma XIII*, in *Opera omnia*, i. 387.

putably feminist. The 'devise' in Le Moyne's *Gallerie*,[33] 'rex animo non sexu' (Plate 8), which is a depiction of a beehive, is a reference not only to the supremacy of the female in the republic of bees, but also to the value of industriousness. More obviously feminist, the depiction of two falcons, entitled 'mares haec foemina vincit', by Flamen in his *Devises et emblesmes d'amour moralisez* (Plate 9), is said by him to indicate the superiority of women in the power of love,[34] although Vulson de la Colombière, after Guisse, gives it a more mundane interpretation.[35] Perhaps of greatest interest here is the emblem depicting Hercules with Omphale, which is accorded several interpretations. Flamen entitles this emblem 'semper aliquid' ('jamais oisif') (Plate 10), and sees in it an encouragement to industry;[36] the episode is generally assumed in drama to illustrate the power of love,[37] and Scudéry in his *Cabinet* draws the same conclusion;[38] Grenaille, however, finds a more militantly feminist implication in the incident:

Si tost que [les femmes] ont changé l'ordre de la Providence, at qu'au lieu que les desirs de la femme doiuent estre subordonnez à la puissance du mary, ceux du mary le sont à ceux de la femme, on void vn homme qui deuient femme, et vne femme qui deuient homme. Omphale tient la massuë et Hercule tient le fuseau.[39]

Vouet's painting of Hercules and Omphale, published as an engraving by Dorigny in 1643[40] (Plate 11), stresses the reversal of

---

[33] *Gallerie*, ãã1ᵛ; cf. Le Moyne, *Devises heroiques et morales*, p. 9.

[34] *Devises et emblesmes d'amour moralisez*, Paris, 1648, pp. 106–7: 'dans le vol, les Faucons femelles sont plus estimées que les masles, et dans l'amour les femmes l'emportent sur les hommes; car soit que nous considerions la tendresse, soit que nous regardions la violence, soit que nous examinions les delices dont elles assaisonnent cette passion, il faut auoüer qu'elles y excellent.' Flamen continues in a more traditionally feminist vein: 'pour ce qui est de l'Ame, l'homme n'a point de preéminence sur la femme, ils partagent également les merites et le Paradis; mais la femme l'emporte dans les graces speciales qu'elle a obtenuës au dessus de l'homme dans le premier ordre de la creation: elle a esté creée la derniere comme la plus parfaicte; c'est elle qui commence le repos de Dieu, car il cessa de créer apres la perfection de la femme.'

[35] *Portraits des hommes illustres françois*, Paris, 1650, G2ʳ. The emblem is said to indicate that Joan of Arc had greater courage than the men of her generation. Jean Guisse provided the emblems for the Gallery of the Palais Cardinal (see Picart, *Simon Vouet premier peintre de Louis XIII*, p. 13 n.).

[36] *Emblesmes d'amour*, p. 36.

[37] e.g. Hardy, *Didon se sacrifiant*, in *Théâtre*, ed. Stengel, iii. 55; Mairet, *Le Marc-Antoine*, p. 55.

[38] *Le cabinet*, p. 33.   [39] Grenaille, *L'honneste mariage*, p. 189.

[40] Illustrated in *Les salons littéraires au XVIIᵉ siècle*, p. 26. Vouet probably painted this subject for Marie de Médicis c. 1627 for inclusion in the Palais de Luxembourg

occupations; here is an abasement of man and a glorification of the power of woman, which have already been noted as a feature of feminist texts of this period. Vouet's depiction of Mars and Venus, also engraved by Dorigny, may have similar overtones.[41]

Related to emblems, but less oblique, are the illustrations found in moralistic works, some of which deal with subjects of interest here. The decoration of churches in the Middle Ages with illustrations of the fate of the sinner is well known, and this medieval admonitory trend may be detected in the engravings for such works as Juvernay's *Discours particulier contre la vanité des femmes de ce temps*, first published in 1635, and reprinted in 1637 in an expanded form with two illustrations. The frontispiece (Plate 12) portrays the fate of women who wear low-cut dresses. The grotesque fiends, the coquettish woman with her bovine expression, and the *topos* of the mouth of hell (found also in such works as El Greco's *Dream of Philip*) are all features indicative of the medieval atmosphere of the engraving. A second illustration of similar quality, also unsigned, depicts Mary Magdalene rejecting the artefacts of beautification—cosmetics, perfumes, toiletry—which lie before her on a table, with an expression of pious spirituality.[42] In both cases the message is clear. It is interesting to note that although in such moralistic works as these, the baring of breasts is attacked as a sin, the conventions of heroic portraiture allow the representation of women half-naked; nor is such representation only permitted for pagan women, for in Chapelain's *Pucelle*, Agnès Sorel appears in this manner.

A second, more advanced, didactic illustration may be found in Le Moyne's *Peintures morales* of 1643,[43] the work of Huret (Plate 13). Here it may be possible to detect the influence of Rubens and the Flemish baroque. Depicted is the death of Lais,

(Crelly, *The painting of Simon Vouet*, p. 83). For interpretations of this emblem in the sixteenth century, see M.-R. Jung, *Hercule dans la littérature française du XVI* siècle, Geneva, 1966, pp. 137–57. He associates the incident with Omphale with the encounter with Deianira, which also is mentioned in our period (e.g. Benserade, *La Cleopatre*, f. 50).

[41] This engraving, dated 1638, may be found in the Cabinet des Estampes of the Bibliothèque Nationale. On Mars and Venus, and their relationship to feminism, see E. H. Gombrich, *Symbolic images*, pp. 66–8.

[42] For other examples of the very common theme of penitence, often associated with Mary Magdalene, see Jacques Callot, *Les penitents et penitentes* (n.p., n.d.), and Jean Baudoin, *Les penitentes illustres*, Paris, 1647.

[43] *Les peintures morales*, ii. 320.

a Corinthian courtesan who was torn to pieces by jealous bac-
chantes. The grandiose setting, the violence and movement of the
group of women which forms an oval in the composition,[44] the
cruelty and horror of mutilation, as well as the implicit paradox
of female gentleness set against the fanatical strength of the
women depicted here, all bespeak a strong baroque element. On
the left in the background Cupid is being expelled by a figure
with a whip, while on the right Venus protects another Cupid
figure and makes a gesture of moderation. This illustration is
intended to convey, according to the poem written by Le Moyne
to accompany it, 'la fin tragique des amours deshonnestes', and
the paradox pointed to above is referred to at some length in the
text.[45]

The many illustrations of social life in this period by Abraham
Bosse may also be said to have a didactic, perhaps also satirical
purpose, and may be mentioned in passing in this context as
relevant to social history and to the evaluation of the place of
women in society.[46] There are also the traditional and more
satirical illustrations of husband-beating, cuckoldry, and marital
discord executed by Bosse and Pierre Brebiette, which are very
reminiscent of the tracts written against marriage in the *esprit
gaulois* tradition, discussed above.[47]

Claude Vignon and François Chauveau, respectively the illustrators of Le Moyne's *Gallerie* and Du Bosc's *Femme heroïque*,
are highly versatile artists, and one may expect to find in their

[44] For the connection between baroque and oval form, see Rousset, *La littérature
de l'âge baroque en France*, pp. 169–74.

[45] *Les peintures morales*, ii. 326–7:

> Mais quoy, pourrions nous bien auoir la dureté
> D'assister de la veuë à cette cruauté?
> Des Femmes à nos yeux assouuiront leur rage
> Et feront à leur Sexe vn si barbare outrage?
> Nous les verrons fouler la Nature et ses Loix,
> Sans luy donner secours des mains ny de la voix?
> Respectez vostre Sexe inhumaines Riuales,
> Vos forces ne sont pas à ces armes égales:
> Rappellez la douceur et la honte en vos yeux,
> Ostez vous ces regars sanglans et furieux . . .

[46] See A. Blum, *Abraham Bosse et la société française au XVIIe siècle*.

[47] See above, pp. 96 ff.; Bosse's 'femme fouettant son mari' (which also portrays a sister beating her brother and a hen pecking a cock) and Brebiette's engraving
'le pauvre Badin', to which is appended a long anti-feminist poem, are examples of
this genre of illustration to be found in the Cabinet des Estampes of the Bibliothèque Nationale.

work elements in common with contemporary engraving in spheres other than heroic portraiture[48] and iconology. One area of obvious relevance to the depiction of Old Testament heroines is biblical illustration. For Jael, Judith, and Deborah there are traditional dispositions of figures and conventional clothing and background: the stylization of the dress of the hero or heroine (plumed helmet, loose tunic or flowing robes, and sandals) and of the landscape has already been elucidated elsewhere.[49] The predilection for scenes of violent action, especially battles, which is a feature of Antonio Tempesta's illustrations for the Bible, may also be traced in the engravings of Vignon and Chauveau.[50] One point of difference, however, is the degree of technical skill, which is to some extent determined by the scale of the engraving. Perspective and detail are more precise in the illustrations of Vignon and Chauveau; where the medium is wood-cut and not engraving, as in the case of Le Clerc's *Figures de la saincte Bible*, published in 1633, the difference in execution and style is even more marked, although the composition of the illustration may remain the same.[51]

Du Bosc's *Femme heroïque* consists of eight comparisons of heroes and heroines, each accompanied by a double-page pair of engravings, one depicting the hero, the other the heroine. In Le Moyne's *Gallerie* there are twenty-one plates in all; a frontispiece depicting Anne of Austria, a commentary on which is found in the dedicatory epistle, followed by four sets of engravings ('fortes Juives', 'fortes Barbares', 'fortes Romaines', and 'fortes Chrestiennes').[52] A full account of these illustrations is

[48] On the question of historical and heroic portraiture, see J. Duportal, *Etude sur les livres à figures en France de 1600 à 1660*, Paris, 1914, pp. 275-6, where it is claimed that Scudéry's assertion that he provided accurate portraits of his long-dead heroines in his *Femmes illustres* indicates that 'le public avait dû manifester des préférences en faveur des images exactes et fidèles ou tenues pour telles'. The 1654 edition of Caussin's *La cour sainte* also contains such engravings 'tirées des médailles antiques', and it would seem more likely that the representation of heroines on medallions is conventional. Certainly iconological factors seem to weigh more heavily than accuracy in dress or facial resemblance in Plates 2 and 6.

[49] See Sayce, *The French biblical epic*, pp. 32-4. 225-46.

[50] See Antonio Tempesta, *Figurae biblicae* (n.p., n.d.); Sayce, *The French biblical epic*, p. 33.

[51] Jean III Le Clerc, *Figures de la saincte Bible*, Paris, 1633; p. 144 has an illustration of Judith which in many ways resembles Chauveau's engraving of Judith (Plate 18), and which suggests that the subject was treated almost as a set piece.

[52] Le Moyne was possibly inspired to set out his book in this way by Thomas

beyond the scope of this inquiry; for this reason the actively heroic woman is best represented in the discussion which follows, as she evokes most clearly the aspects of taste and sensibility which are of interest here.[53]

The portrait of Anne of Austria in Le Moyne's *Gallerie* (Plate 14) was executed by the Italian baroque painter Pietro da Cortona and engraved by Charles Audran; the composition bears a close resemblance to Audran's engraving after Vouet for the frontispiece of Jean-François Niceron's *Thaumaturgus opticus*, published in the previous year (Plate 15). As well as indicating the popularity of the gallery motif at this time, this resemblance may suggest that da Cortona's contribution resides principally in the depiction of Anne herself, and that Audran is responsible for the context. The Queen Regent is placed in a grandiose alfresco 'gallery' beset with niches containing the statues of the outstanding women treated by Le Moyne in this work, and superimposed by female figures perhaps representing abstract excellences, such as learning and temperance, although this is not made clear. The cornucopia and the phrase 'mere du peuple' betray the date of the engraving, which was completed before the advent of civil strife and the Fronde; as has already been pointed out, the regency was indeed ostensibly glorious up to 1648. The engraver and the

Heywood's *The exemplary lives and memorable acts of nine the most worthy women of the world: three Jewes, three Gentiles, three Christians,* London, 1640; this book also contains a series of engravings.

[53] One aspect of these illustrations not treated here deserves passing mention, as it is important also to literature: the evocation of a sort of pathos tinged with cruelty inherent in the dramatic treatment of such figures as Dido, Mary Queen of Scots, and Sophonisbe may be traced also in the depictions of Lucretia and Monima in Le Moyne's *Gallerie*. The elegiac atmosphere of these portraits, evoked by the heavenward cast of the eyes, the pleading gestures of hands and body, the expression of despair, is tempered by the dagger which, in one case, a slave is about to plunge into the breast of the victim, and in the other, is the instrument of self-immolation. Mourning groups replace the admiring individuals of the other, more robust, illustrations. For a literary parallel see Hilarion de Coste, *Eloges et vies des reynes*, pp. 480–1, where there is the following description of Zenobia being dragged along by a chariot in a Roman triumph: 'obiect lamentable, de voir ce corps delicat chargé de liens: ces yeux, qui ne perçoient les cœurs que de compassion: et on ne pouuoit considerer sans souspirs et sans larmes, que cet esprit enfermé dans ce beau corps, et capable de tant de genereuses entreprises, ne s'employoit plus qu'à rechercher de fortes considerations pour s'armer contre l'impatience et le desespoir.' Cf. Montaigne, *Essais*, ed. Thibaudet and Rat, III. i, p. 768: 'au milieu de la compassion, nous sentons au-dedans je ne sçay quelle aigre-douce pointe de volupté maligne à voir souffrir autruy.'

masons depicted here are representations of abstract virtues, as is made clear by Le Moyne in his *Epistre panegyrique*:

Ces vertus [force, pieté, prudence, iustice, les graces, magnificence, souueraineté, moderation], MADAME, qui sont toutes Heroïques et toutes Royales, ont trauaillé en commun à la Statuë, qui vous est erigée au milieu de cette Gallerie. La Magnificence a fourny la matiere, qui est precieuse et digne du merite et de la reputation de l'ouurage. Les Graces, ie dis les Graces industrieuses et sçauantes, l'ont taillée: et luy ont donné tous les traits, qu'vne Figure acheuée peut auoir d'vn parfait Modele. La Force l'a receuë de leurs mains, et l'a éleuée sur sa baze. La Iustice a graué l'inscription: et la Pieté a esté l'Intendante et la directrice de toute la besongne.[54]

The connection between iconology and feminism may again be noted, the more striking here because the female figures are performing tasks so uncharacteristic of women. Also noteworthy are the play on illusion—it is not immediately clear whether the 'masons' are supporting figures or masons, nor whether the group is static or in movement—and the conceit ('placer dans une galerie') embodied in the composition. The statue of Anne, naturalistically portrayed, looks down with an expression of mildness and piety: her right hand holds the sceptre of regency, while her left makes a gesture of modesty. The dedicatory epistle stresses the contrast between the humility of the Queen Regent as she is depicted here and her high virtue, indicated by the subordination to her in the gallery of so many illustrious heroines.[55]

Judith is illustrated in both Du Bosc's and Le Moyne's works, as one might expect from such a popular subject at this time: this biblical heroine appears in a Spanish emblem book in 1610;[56] Rubens painted at least three depictions of her beheading of Holofernes;[57] François Garasse's *Doctrine curieuse des beaux esprits de ce temps* of 1623 has a frontispiece on which she is portrayed,

[54] *Gallerie*, ẽ4ʳ.

[55] See above, p. 84; cf. also Simon Martin, *La vie de sainte Ulphe vierge*, *3ʳ⁻ᵛ: (Epistre à la Reyne Regente) 'par vn miracle inconnu de son temps, (Vostre Maiesté) conserue la saincteté dans les délices: l'humilité dans les grandeurs: la liberté d'esprit dans le gouuernement d'vn estat, et la deuotion parmy le bruit de la Cour, et dans le maniment des plus grandes affaires du monde.' This might well be a paraphrase of part of Le Moyne's 'Ode à la Reyne' (Gallerie, ũ4ʳ).

[56] See Henkel and Schöne, *Emblemata*, col. 1855, where this emblem, from Sebastián de Covarrubias Orozco's *Emblemas morales* (Madrid, 1610) is reproduced. The emblem is entitled 'dux foemina facti' (*Aeneid*, i. 364).

[57] See M. Rosse, *L'œuvre de P. P. Rubens*, Antwerp, 1886, i. 154–8.

no doubt as a symbol of the triumph of good over evil; Bosse executed at least three engravings of Judith, one of which is intended as an illustration for Lescalopier's *Predications* of 1645 (Plate 16). Here she is shown wielding a sword on which is inscribed 'la femme forte'; superimposed on the light-source emanating from the top left-hand corner of the engraving are the words 'viriliter age'. Similarly militant feminist sentiments are implied in her depiction on the frontispiece of *La femme genereuse* of 1643 (Plate 17). The whole composition of this engraving is what Blunt describes as 'mannerist',[58] and is very reminiscent of Bellange: the small, carefully posed hands, feet, and head, the stance and movement of the body. The swanlike head looks down with scorn on the corpse of the victim. Blood flows abundantly from Holofernes' body. This engraving is very expressive of the anti-male theme which is prominent in *La femme genereuse*. The engraving is signed 'DF'; there are no prominent engravers at this time with these initials in Duportal's list or in the Cabinet des Estampes in Paris.[59]

Chauveau's engraving for Du Bosc's *La femme heroïque* (Plate 18) depicts two events which in fact took place at different times: the beheading of Holofernes, and the sortie of the Israelites from the beleaguered city. Noteworthy here is the contrast between the serenity of Judith's expression and the horror of the action: this she has just performed, for she still holds a sword in her left hand, and blood gushes from the decapitated corpse. The servant betrays the admiration for the deed in her stance and face, and it is this reaction which Du Bosc evokes in his text.

In Vignon's illustration for Le Moyne's *Gallerie*[60] different moments of time are again depicted in background and foreground (indeed, this diachronism is a feature of many of these engravings[61]): behind the figure of Judith, who is holding an enormous severed head of Holofernes, the angel of God is seen in the act of giving the praying heroine a sword, while at the foot of Holofernes' bed two winged cherubs are breaking and scattering his

---

[58] *Art and architecture in France*, p. 125; cf. ibid., Plate 82, 'the three Marys', by Jacques Bellange.

[59] *Études sur les livres à figures*, Appendix 1; R. A. Weigert, B.N. *Cabinet des Estampes inventaire du fonds français; graveurs du XVIIe siècle* also gives no clue as to the identity of the engraver in question.   [60] *Gallerie*, p. 38.

[61] J. Simpson (*Le Tasse et la littérature et l'art baroques en France*, Paris, 1962, p. 63) describes diachronism as both a gothic and a mannerist feature.

armour, no doubt to indicate the victory of piety over brute force. Another angel lights the tent in which the unfortunate commander sleeps. The element of piety and divine inspiration in the action of Judith is therefore given greater emphasis in Vignon's illustration; whereas Du Bosc's text emphasizes the achievements of Judith, Le Moyne dwells on the mystery of the divine plan, which confounds the strong by the agency of the weak, and evokes admiration by this 'prodige'.[62]

Salomone, mother of the Machabees, is also illustrated in both Du Bosc's and Le Moyne's works: the former praises her for her constancy in suffering, the latter for her religious feeling and piety. In Chauveau's engraving (Plate 19),[63] We may detect an appeal to our pity as well as an exaltation of female strength of purpose. Du Bosc's eulogy underlines both this and Chauveau's tactful dishonesty about the age of the heroine.[64]

Vignon's illustration is more honest about her age, and no less full of horror, although one is spared the mutilation of Salomone, reminiscent of illustrations of martyrdoms.[65] Vignon confines himself to depicting two sons being boiled alive, two burning at the stake, and a small child, presumably the youngest son, being led away to his death. Both Le Moyne and Du Bosc attenuate in their texts the fanaticism of the biblical Salomone.

Jael is illustrated only in Le Moyne's *Gallerie*, and thus no comparison may be made, although one is tempted to surmise that had Chauveau executed a drawing of this figure, he would, as Vouet had done in the gallery of heroic women at the Hôtel de l'Arsenal, have chosen to depict her in the process of hammering the nail into the head of Sisera. Vignon (Plate 20)[66] is scarcely less violent, although the act itself is not illustrated; the recumbent figure of Sisera and the protruding nail cause surprise and horror among the small group of warriors, one of whom is an amazon, whose presence is not explained. Here, as in the illustrations for Judith and Salomone, the influence of contemporary

---

[62] Bouvot's Judith (*Judith, ou l'amour de la patrie, tragœdie*, Langres, 1649, III. v, pp. 28–9) prays in a similar way that she should become an agent of the glory of the Almighty in the divine plan.

[63] *La femme heroïque*, i. 271.

[64] Ibid. i. 305 : 'pour son âge, elle a quatre-vingt dix ans, et dans vne vieillesse si extréme n'est plus en estat de resister ny à la douleur ny à l'amour . . .'

[65] Cf. Antonio Tempesta, *Imagini di molte SS vergini Romane nel martirio* (c. 1600).

[66] *Gallerie*, p. 26.

illustrations for the Bible may be detected in the mixture of the classical and the biblical; the armour, the tent, the lances contrast with the setting and subject. The calm serenity of the face of the heroine as she demonstrates how she accomplished her action contrasts with the expressions on the faces of the onlookers, and this technique of transferring admiration to a spectator or a group of spectators had already been noted as a feature of the drama of the period. In choosing this subject, Le Moyne was courting difficulty, and his *Question morale* treats the problem 's'il y eut de l'infidelité dans l'action de Jahel': the very choice of subject, however, betrays his predilection for episodes susceptible of evoking surprise and horror.

Vignon's illustration of Zenobia (Plate 21)[67] is perhaps the most strikingly feminist of the engravings in Le Moyne's work. This figure has considerable panache: she strides forward, recognizably feminine in face (in contrast to Plates 2 and 6), with a finely plumed helmet and much ornamentation on her robes. With her left hand she makes a commanding gesture. In the background she is seen, bare-breasted and brandishing a spear, resolutely set on the slaughter of an inexpertly drawn lion: also in the background three amazons look on as two winged amoretti tend an unidentifiable victim of the hunt (perhaps a leopard). On the left, another amazon rides a slavering horse. This picture abounds in energy and activity, and is expressive of Zenobia's authority and presence of mind. The traditional passive and frontal depiction of women is replaced here by a profile of a heroine in movement. Le Moyne's *Question morale* concerns the problem 'si les femmes sont capables de la vertu militaire'. If a man were to replace Zenobia in this engraving, it might become a glorification of male leadership: and yet, as well as this equation of Zenobia with a heroic leader, there is a feminine quality about her which indicates the peculiar attraction of such figures to the sensibility of this period, as they combine 'douceur feminine' with 'masle generosité'.[68]

The engraving of Thomyris in Du Bosc's *Femme heroïque* (Plate 22)[69] is one of two executed by Chauveau on the same

[67] *Gallerie*, p. 144.
[68] Cf. Gilbert, *Semiramis*, a3ʳ: (Epistre à Madame la duchesse de Rohan) 'vostre Genie est adrait et judicieux, et possede toute la delicatesse de vostre sexe, et toute la force du nostre.'
[69] *La femme heroïque*, i. 183.

subject; the other appears as an illustration for the tenth volume of *Le grand Cyrus*, which appeared in 1653.[70] Here, in a characteristically diachronic composition, is a combination of movement and stillness, and presumably of silence and noise. In the background there is a conventional representation of a battle; in the foreground Thomyris, commanding with a gesture a servant to immerse the head of the fallen Cyrus in an urn of blood, utters the words of vengeance recorded at the foot of the engraving. The figure of Thomyris is only recognizable as feminine by the convention of clothing all men with beards and moustaches. In the later version of the same scene tents form the background (thus making background and foreground synchronic), and from one of these issues a group of women, making gestures of surprise and horror; there are more spectators, and the figure of Thomyris is not as prominent as here.

All the illustrations of Vignon for Le Moyne's *Gallerie* consist of two planes, one so far in advance of the other that the heroine who occupies it towers over the figures in the background. This simple device of perspective adds considerably to the grandeur of the heroines, even though in diachronic compositions they themselves may be one of the figures dwarfed by the colossus of the foreground. In the case of Joan of Arc (Plate 23)[71] this effect heightens the impression of rusticity and noble simplicity. Although totally encased in armour in the background, she does not wear a helmet, associated with nobility, but a bonnet in the foreground, and there is less arrogance in her face and demeanour than may be detected in those of her fellow heroines. Although Le Moyne describes her as a combination of Deborah and Judith, and treats the *Question morale* 'si les femmes peuuent pretendre à la vertu heroïque' in connection with her, the illustration for once does not convey the strength and conviction of the text, but dwells on the rusticity of the heroine.[72]

While the engravings in the works of Du Bosc and Le Moyne offer the most striking examples of feminist book illustration,

---

[70] *Le grand Cyrus*, x. 515. This illustration of Thomyris is conventional, and appears in woodcuts for Boccaccio's *De claris mulieribus* in early sixteenth-century editions (see Estienne Pasquier, *Le monophile*, ed. E. H. Balmas, Milan, 1957, where such woodcuts are reproduced).

[71] *Gallerie*, p. 302.

[72] In the Gallery of the Palais Cardinal, Joan of Arc also wears a bonnet with armour: see Vulson de la Colombière, *Portraits des hommes illustres françois*, G2[r].

this is not confined to such productions. Illustrations for novels may also betray the same glorification of the female sex, and the same delight in paradox, surprise, and horror: indeed, Furetière asserts that the subjects of such illustrations always tend to be drawn from the most violent and extravagant episodes in the novels.[73] The examples given here are taken from the 1639 edition of Desmaret's *Ariane*, illustrated by Vignon and engraved by Bosse, the same combination that produced many of the plates for Le Moyne's *Gallerie*. Plate 24[74] depicts an incident in book fifteen, in which Ariane, accosted by two Scythians who intend to carry her off, but cannot decide to whom she belongs, takes advantage of their quarrel and kills them both with one arrow. Other Scythians, who are watching from a distance, believing her to be a goddess, then bear her in triumph to their camp. The elements of this picture—the stance of Ariane, her shooting of the arrow, the surrounding woods—all call to mind a depiction of Diana the huntress, and it is clear that this association is intended. The importance of the figure of Diana to feminism has already been discussed in the context of the pastoral tradition, and needs no further underlining here. The calmness and heroism displayed by Ariane in this engraving are belied by her own account of these events in the text, and it is of interest to compare the two versions.[75]

A second illustration from Ariane (Plate 25)[76] shows Mélinte, the hero, declaring his true identity as the son of a nobleman of ancient lineage at the Syracusan games. Ariane presides over this festival as its elected queen, and is attended by her female companions; Mélinte stands below her, but on a raised platform, and his declaration is causing consternation in the assembly below. This engraving may be said to be feminist in that it portrays the celebration of the beauty of woman and the deference shown to her sex by the men in attendance at lower levels; Ariane is not, however, the centre of attention, if she is queen of the games, and there is no strength, moral or otherwise, expressed in her passively

---

[73] See R. Picard, 'Racine and Chauveau', *Journal of the Warburg and Courtauld Institutes*, xiv (1951), 271.

[74] *L'Ariane*, p. 702.

[75] Ibid., pp. 708–9: 'ie pris alors courage, et croyant estre assistée d'vne inspiration diuine, ie me saisis d'vn de leurs arcs . . . et courbant l'arc auec le plus de force que ie pus, ie laissay aller la flesche . . .'

[76] Ibid., p. 352.

seated figure. It is interesting to compare this illustration with the frontispiece for Saint-Amant's *Moyse sauvé* (Plate 26), executed by the same artist and the same engraver some fourteen years later.[77] Here, in spite of the differences, the general plan of the engraving is the same, for the Egyptian princess towers above the other figures as does Ariane, and is similarly placed on the left of the picture. Whereas, however, Ariane is a passive figure, expressing 'douce maiesté', and is not even the centre of attention, the princess subordinates all the action in the frontispiece to *Moyse sauvé* to her commanding gesture, and is very much the focus of attention. The heroic grandeur of the helmeted princess, as well as the presence of an amazon as a chariot-driver, are additional points of contrast.[78]

Having completed the consideration of these book illustrations, we may now progress to some suggestions about the sensibility and taste of this period. There is a remarkable tolerance to anachronisms in engraving at this time: Roman armour appears among the tents of Israel, mannerist gardens by classical temples,[79] Renaissance dress on thirteenth-century English princesses.[80] This may be accounted for to some degree by the stylization and conventions which govern certain fields of illustration, notably the biblical, at this time. The same conventions affect the representation of battles and landscapes. The airborne amoretti, the miraculous light-sources, and the pose of many of the heroines are also conventional, and have been described as features of baroque painting.[81]

Underlying many of these illustrations, and explicit in some, is a didactic purpose; as has already been pointed out, there is a development in moralistic teaching in this period, which is characterized by a change in emphasis from an account of the dangers inherent in the path of sin to a eulogy of the felicities to be won from the pursuit of virtue. The same development may be traced in didactic illustration: Juvernay's bovine woman about to suffer the pains of hell becomes the triumphant Zenobia,

[77] *Moyse sauvé, idyle heroïque* (1653).

[78] For a fuller account of this engraving, see Sayce, *The French biblical epic*, pp. 225–6.

[79] e.g. Vignon's illustration of Lucretia (Le Moyne, *Gallerie*, p. 162).

[80] e.g. Vignon's illustration of Isabelle de Castille, princesse de Galles (ibid., p. 282).

[81] Blunt, *Art and architecture in France*, p. 174.

or the enterprising Judith, or the chaste Lucretia. These figures are proposed as subjects for emulation on a domestic level.[82]

Connected with this affirmative approach to moral teaching is the sense of the glorious present which may be detected in many of the illustrations and writings of the period. Contemporary figures are clothed and arrayed as abstract virtues,[83] the heroines of the past pay tribute to the heroines of the present, the 'siècle des miracles' is reborn.[84] The concept of the gallery in honour of living women is also involved in this glorification.

Such a disproportion between past and present in an age when antiquity was still venerated is a symptom of a greater phenomenon, the unsettling of the universe, the *renversement du monde*, the upsetting of all accepted opinion. The play on perspective and the diachronism of many of these engravings have been mentioned, and betray an interference with the scales of time and space, involving the mixture of different and sometimes contradictory elements, the contrast between background and foreground, the enriching of the illustration from the status of a simple portrait into a combination of this and the depiction of an historical incident. Such a mixture also juxtaposes active and passive states, and emphasizes the immobility of the one and the movement of the other. Paradox and the mixing of opposites, which are two features of this *monde renversé*, may also be detected in the suppression of female characteristics in many of the illustrations, the dual nature of the heroines both as women and as men, the reversal inherent in depictions of female victories over males, the implied metamorphosis of such figures as Zenobia, who in the foreground are feminine, and in the background are behaving in a masculine manner. Distortion is naturally involved in such illustration.

Where these engravings and feminist literature have most in common is, however, in the evocation of *admiratio* or *maraviglia*: the latter term is perhaps preferable, for it preserves the religious

---

[82] Cf. Du Bosc, *La femme heroïque*, ii. 524: 'ie m'asseure qu'au seul recit de ses [Judith's] victoires, toutes les Dames sont conquerantes dans leur ame, toutes voudroient luy ressembler, toutes voudroient iouyr de sa gloire; mais voicy le rabat-joye. Et quoy, est-ce assez de ces premieres esmotions, et de ces transports? Non sans doute, ce n'est rien d'estre touchez de sa gloire, si nous n'en venons iusques aux effets pour la meriter; tous ces souhaits ne sont que des auortons.'

[83] See above, pp. 212–15, and *Les salons littéraires au XVIIe siècle*, pp. 50–9.

[84] See above, pp. 76 ff.

connotations inherent in such evocation. Just as in literature writers insist on the grandeur of the undertakings and achievements of the heroines, so also is this grandeur present in the visual arts in the magnificence of the settings, the physical scale of the heroines, the grandiose nature of the action. To achieve the greatest effect, the subjects chosen often involve the representation of violence, cruelty, or mutilation. The paradox of women caught up in violent action, and of such violent action being 'agréable',[85] is associated with the shock caused to the reader or spectator by cruelty practised by or on women. It is easy to see in the predilection for scenes of mutilation, especially when associated with an anti-male theme, a concern with the idea of emasculation; the movement and action involved in mutilation (spurting blood, the wielding of the instrument of execution) as well as its irrevocability and horror are, however, sufficient grounds for it to have appealed to the writers and artists of this period. As has been seen in the case of *L'Ariane*, there is a tendency in writing to attenuate the shock of feminine violence by reference to divine inspiration and opportunism, but such attenuation is not common to all literature.[86]

Surprise is also evoked by the representation of women in armour or in military situations. This, as has been seen, is a feature of iconology, at first sight unconnected with feminism; its involvement with the glorification of women is an important aspect of the visual arts of this period. Underlying such depiction is the paradoxical premiss that women are equal to men in heroic or martial virtue.

Maraviglia works on two levels: within the work or picture, and on the reader or spectator. By the use of diachronic compositions, and by the exploitation of perspective and widely different space scales, the actor is separated from the action, and her impassivity (or stoic apathy) is contrasted with the reaction of her servant, or of an admiring group of smaller figures. Here is encountered a technique also found in drama, in which the description of executions or deaths of heroines, or of their great deeds, includes mention of the reaction of those present at such

---

[85] Best expressed by Marino in his poem on Tempesta's engraving of 'la battaglia de' Lapiti', quoted by Sayce, *The French biblical epic*, p. 243, and echoed by many French writers.

[86] Cf. Du Verdier, *Le roman des dames*, ii. 406–7, quoted above, p. 208.

incidents, who, like the admiring servant or group, betray the emotion which is evoked in the reader or spectator. The second level (the effect of the whole composition or *récit* on reader or spectator) will be discussed in greater detail in the context of the rhetorical devices associated with it.[87]

The impassivity of the heroine implies another important paradox, embodied in the description *femme forte*. The idea of constancy in the inconstant sex, of strength in the *femme faible*, is expressed in the visual arts by the *aspetto virile* of which Ripa speaks, the set of the features, sometimes even by the robustness of the limbs and the suppression or disguising of female characteristics. The calm of the heroine also contrasts with the horror or violence of the action she has just undertaken,[88] and the antithesis of movement and stillness is again dwelt upon.

The combination of virtue and beauty, which is said to evoke admiration,[89] is also inherent in both feminist literature and the visual arts, and is sometimes enriched with divine inspiration. Then, in terms of the *Nicomachean Ethics*, referred to by Du Bosc, there may occur an apotheosis of the agent of such virtue, and it is to this climax that many feminist writers aspire.[90]

The visual arts, therefore, afford an interesting approach to the features of period style in feminist literature which will be

[87] See below, pp. 260 ff.
[88] Cf. *La femme genereuse*, p. 45 : 'sur le trouble et estonnement de la mort du Roy, cette princesse [Semiramis] se fait voir en public sans émotion: et d'vn plus que masle fermeté de cœur, de visage, de parole et d'action, remonstre au peuple qu'elle estoit autrice du meurtre . . .'
[89] See d'Urfé, *L'Astrée*, ed. Vaganay, i. 390, quoted below, p. 235.
[90] See Du Bosc, *La femme heroïque*, p. 8, and above, p. 83 ; cf. the plan of Grenaille's *Honneste fille* (never completed), in *L'honneste fille*, i. īī^r–2^v: 'la troisesme Partie [de *L'honneste fille*] establira l'Empire des Filles, et ne les fera pas seulement passer pour honnestes, mais encore nous les produira triomphantes. Au premier Chapitre ie décriray le pouuoir que les Filles semblent auoir sur Dieu mesme, et montreray combien les Graces terrestres ont de credit dans le Ciel . . . Dans le quatrieme Chapitre ie les feray commander aux Roys et aux Empereurs, et apres ie les rendray victorieuses des Tyrans aussi bien que de tous les Sages . . . le septiesme prouuera que tous les grands Guerriers cedent leurs palmes à ces belles Conquerantes . . .
La quatrieme Partie contiendra les modeles de l'honneste Fille [la Saincte, la Vierge, la Maistresse ou l'Amante, la Sçauante, la Sage] . . . Au sixiesme [Chapitre] *l'Amazonne* paroistra, sans que pour la produire i'aye besoin de recourir aux anciennes Fables. Nous verrons des Filles qui d'vn courage viril ont fait de grandes conquestes, et qui par vn nouueau prodige ont assemblé en elles deux extremitez bien differentes : à sçauoir, la foiblesse et la force, la vaillance et la beauté de leur sexe. *La Princesse* composera le tiltre suiuant, où les Filles qui ont regné dans le monde auec autant de iustice que de douceur, seront mises dans leur veritable éleuation.'

examined in the following chapter. The popularity of the theme of feminism is related to sociological considerations, especially the importance of such patrons of the arts as Marie de Médicis and Anne of Austria; but feminism is also attractive to contemporary artists and writers because of the ease with which it may be manipulated to evoke horror or surprise. The final chapter will investigate how far texts containing feminist elements reflect the taste for *admiratio* which impregnates much of the book illustration of this period.

VIII

Feminism and Baroque

THE question of seventeenth-century period style in France has been the subject of a protracted debate around the words 'mannerism', 'baroque', and 'classicism'. There is no need here to give a full account of this debate, for its fortunes are well known, but as the term 'baroque' appears in the title of this chapter, a preliminary note about its use is necessary. The word was first applied in a critical context to Roman architecture, but its usage was soon extended to encompass all the visual arts, and now implies a concordance of style and taste across the whole spectrum of artistic production for an ill-defined period of time. 'Baroque' has been used to describe a recurrent phase in the cycle of style (in the same way as Bray uses the word 'préciosité'); it has been applied to almost every country in Europe, and to several beyond; it has been divided into sub-styles ('pré-baroque' and 'plein-baroque'); it has been associated both with the Counter-Reformation and with Lutheran poets such as Gryphius; there is scarcely an age, from prehistoric times to the present day, which has not witnessed its flowering, according to one critic.[1] As for its ideological and stylistic characteristics, the divergence of opinion could hardly be more pronounced. In all this confusion, the most useful purpose which the term 'baroque' has served is to have drawn attention to those aspects of literature which a post-classical critical tradition has consigned to artistic failure or dismissed as baffling. For the purposes of this study, the features of style which emerged from a study of book illustration and the visual arts in the preceding chapter may provide us with an adequate starting-point for the examination of written works.

The association of feminism with baroque is not new. In his *French biblical epic* of 1955, R. A. Sayce suggests that feminism may be looked upon as a feature of baroque in a similar way to the

---

[1] Eugenio d'Ors, *Lo barocco*, Madrid, 1945 (first published 1934).

theme of inconstancy, or metamorphosis, or theatricality, or the preoccupation with death:

It may also be suggested, with rather less assurance, that the feminism of the epic, eloquently summarized in the frontispiece of the *Moyse* but equally present in all the Susanna, Judith, and Esther poems, is a baroque characteristic. At any rate the Renaissance shows in the *Querelle des femmes* two positions, which are later reflected on the one hand in the works of Du Bosc and Le Moyne as well as in the poems, where no distinction is made between masculine and feminine virtues, on the other in Molière and in Boileau's satire, where the differences are vigorously maintained. We may see here again the baroque tendency to break down barriers and mix opposites, the classical attachment to firm divisions and the rule of common sense.[2]

More than twenty years before the appearance of these lines, Eugenio d'Ors suggested that the *Ewig-Weibliches* is the essence of baroque, which he describes as a recurrent style in civilization. The evidence which he adduces to support his theory (the rites of Eleusis, the Song of Songs, a suggestive phrase from Michelet's *Bible de l'humanité*) is, however, elusive and unconvincing.[3] A further asseveration, that the baroque is represented in the 'derrota y triunfo de la mujer' (Mary Magdalene is given as an example), finds echoes in this period, not only in the visual arts but also in literature.[4] This last idea is taken up by Madeleine Maurel, who describes woman in the eyes of baroque writers as 'une créature privilégiée, qui appelle l'hommage ou l'exécration',[5] suggesting that both feminism and anti-feminism contribute to this style. It might also be possible to consider Jean Rousset's choice of Circe as a symbol of baroque as an indication of the privileged rôle played by woman in the art of this period;[6] the association of baroque with preciosity may also be mentioned in this context.[7]

In the search for common denominators of style, one is hindered by the heterogeneous nature of feminist writing at this time, which is made up of both prose and verse, both fiction and

---

[2] *The French biblical epic*, p. 245.   [3] *Lo barocco*, pp. 32–5.

[4] Ibid., pp. 36–9; see also above, p. 218.

[5] 'Esquisse d'un anteros baroque', *XVIIᵉ siècle*, lxxxiv–lxxxv (1969), 3–20. This dualistic attitude is also a feature of some patristic texts; Raynaud points out that 'S. Chrysostomus . . . agnoscit mulierem et ad bonum et ad malum posse quamplurimum' (*Dissertatio de sobria alterius sexus frequentatione*, p. 76).

[6] *La littérature de l'âge baroque en France: Circe et le paon*.

[7] See Antoine Adam, 'Baroque et préciosité'.

non-fiction. The task is made more difficult by the virtuosity of some writers who set out to match their style to their intended audiences.[8] One unifying factor may be the aesthetic purpose of the writer. It is generally accepted that most literature in the seventeenth century sets out to 'plaire et instruire', and the combination of *prodesse* and *delectare* is, as has been indicated, a marked feature of feminist writing.[9] A more lofty aspiration of many such writings is the evocation of *admiratio*, which is associated with morality and pleasure in a sort of hierarchy by Céladon in *L'Astrée*:

Il est tout certain . . . que la vertu despouillée de tout autre agencement, ne laisse pas d'estre d'elle-mesme agreable, ayant des aymants tant attirans, qu'aussi tost qu'une ame en est touchée, il faut qu'elle l'aime et la suive. Mais quand cette vertu se rencontre en un corps qui est beau, elle n'est pas seulement agreable, mais admirable, d'autant que les yeux et l'esprit demeurent ravis en la contemplation et en la vision du beau.[10]

Associated with *admiratio* is the rhetoric of persuasion, by which its effects may be evoked. In this chapter, baroque features, and especially *admiratio*, will be investigated through the vocabulary, syntax, and imagery of feminist works, or works in which there is evidence of feminist thought.

It is relevant to point out at this stage that while the examples of style are all drawn from texts which are in some way or other germane to feminism, no claim is made for the existence of a 'feminist style'. Nor is it possible to assert that what is discussed here applies exclusively to this period; indeed, it would seem very possible that much of it is relevant to a far wider field of literature, both in terms of geography and chronology.

A preliminary note should be devoted to writings about women in the earlier part of the period (*c.* 1610–30). Here certain difficulties arise from the republication of sixteenth-century, fifteenth-century, and even patristic texts as integral parts of a literary debate about the female sex. This gives rise not only to a high incidence of disguised quotation and surreptitious plagiarism,

---

[8] Grenaille says in the *Avertissement* of his *Honneste veuve* that he is writing in a 'stile plus serré que celuy des autres de ma façon . . . i'ay creu que parlant à des personnes desolées ie deuois dire peu de mots, mais qui eussent beaucoup d'efficace' (ẽ1ʳ). See also Le Moyne, *Gallerie*, ãã2ᵛ.

[9] See above, pp. 76 ff.   [10] *L'Astrée*, ed. Vaganay, i. 390

but also leaves a deep impression on style. It is difficult to determine whether the resurrection of these texts is a symptom of antiquarianism, or a reflection of their social immediacy, or a deliberate revival of a literary tradition which stretches back, as has been seen, into the Middle Ages, or even a sign of the swing of a stylistic pendulum in the recurrent cycles of literary fashion. Any explanation is made yet more tentative by the possibility of irony in the use of stylistic features belonging to the past. Such problems are less acute in the latter part of the period.

One notable feature of anti-feminist writing in the earlier part of this period is its conformity of style with that of traditional moralists such as Puget de la Serre and the author of the *Tableau des piperies des femmes mondaines*; these writers may in turn be associated with the 'style Nervèze' of the sentimental novel first described by Reynier, which is characterized by the presence of oxymoron, chiasmus, conceits, elaborate and unusual similes, and extraordinary metaphors drawn from a wide range of human activities: navigation, war, architecture, book-production, surgery, among others.[11] Initially this style was described as 'précieux', although more recent critical opinion has designated it as baroque; certainly the former epithet could hardly be applied to Trousset's *Alphabet* or de Vaux's *La Magdeleine au desert*. In both anti-feminist and moralistic works the attack on beauty as a worldly value, the preoccupation with death, and the contrast drawn between appearance and reality in the obsessive use of cosmetic imagery all recall baroque themes.

In spite of his avowed distaste for this manner of writing,[12] Trousset is particularly rich in examples of it, as passages already quoted indicate;[13] in his dedication to 'la plus mauuaise [femme] du monde' he declares his alphabet to be

Pedagogue pour redresser ton ignorance, maistre pour enseigner ta

---

[11] On the 'style Nervèze', see Reynier, *Le roman sentimental*, pp. 318–40; Magendie, *La politesse mondaine*, i. 277–92; R. Bray, *La préciosité et les précieux de Thibaut de Champagne à Jean Giraudoux*, Paris, 1948, pp. 101–7; Adam, 'Baroque et préciosité'; Lathuillère, *La préciosité*, i. 209.

[12] See *Alphabet, Au Lecteur*, p. 19: 'si [mes] discours ne sont pas assez bien affriandez d'vn langage Pindarique et affecté comme desireroient les mistodins de nostre temps: ie croy que tu m'excuseras, et ne me sçauras malgré de n'estre partisan des nouueautez, et trop curieux indigateur des dictions inuentees, par gens bigarrez et farcis d'impressions estrangeres, m'arrestant plustost aux discours Laconiques, et aux sentences succulentes et moelleuses, qu'aux fripperies des termes ambageux, fantatiques et amphibologiques.' [13] See above, pp. 39, 42–3, 133.

propre cognoissance: miroir pour voir tes impertinences: phare pour
venir à bon port d'vn sainct amendement, guide pour te conduire en
la voye du salut seurement, quadran pour reigler les heures de tes
passions, lumiere pour esclairer ton entendement, heraut pour crier
contre tes vices à tout moment, ambassade pour t'annoncer les bri-
gantins de ton honneur et de ton contentement, mords et camords,
pour refrener tes folles affections: marteau pour briser et fracasser tes
pernicieux desseins, et tonnerre en fin, pour esbranler, effrayer et
escraser la pierre de ton endurcissement.[14]

Here may be noted the abuse of enumeration which characterizes
much of this writing, and the pursuit of bizarre metaphors which
we find also in anti-feminist definitions of woman: Chrysostom's
designations of the *mala mulier* are repeated by Trousset,[15] who
also describes woman as 'vn puits si estroit que ceux qui s'iettent
dedans, ne sçauroit s'en retirer sans la corde d'vne grace speciale
et particuliere',[16] and Ferville, perhaps remembering Semonides'
comparisons of women with animals, produces the following
definition:

La femme

> *C'est vn Cameleon qui se poussant de vent*
> *N'aime point vn suiet qu'alors qu'il est present*

C'est vn Pirauste, qui haissant la temperature, ne veut point de plus
heureuse fin que de se consommer parmi les flammes de sa concupiscence.

C'est vne Cygalle, qui ne veut dépendre ses iours qu'en vains
plaisirs.

C'est vne Locuste, qui ne veut que sautiller parmi les fresles fleurettes
d'vn terrestre aueuglement.

Vn Colac qui apres auoir erré nonchalamment parmi les goulfes
marins, reuient en fin honteusement mourir dans sa riue fangeuse. . . .[17]

Another eight definitions follow, three of which are connected
with the sea (comparisons to Scylla, a newt ('triton Geneuois'),
and a torpedo fish), which may bring to mind the widespread
popularity of such images, with their baroque connotations of
inconstancy and movement.[18] The unusual nature of both vocabulary and metaphor may also be noted; Trousset shows in a

[14] *Alphabet*, pp. 14–15.   [15] Ibid., pp. 3–4: *PG* lix. 485–90.
[16] *Alphabet*, p. 176.
[17] *La méchanceté des femmes*, pp. 62–4. The passage so impressed Trousset that he
quotes it in his *Alphabet* (pp. 209–10).
[18] See also Trousset, *Alphabet*, pp. 175, 337; Caillet, *Tableau du mariage*, p. 90,
quoted above, p. 112.

similar way a predilection for archaic or obscure epithets, often placed before the noun to give added effect: 'cuitable contagion', 'la beauté nompareille . . . des odiferantes fleurs de mon petit labeur', 'ses charmes Plutoniques', 'leur coüarde infamie' are some examples.[19]

In moralistic literature, apostrophe is often associated with such features of style: de Vaux's address to the would-be womanizer has already been quoted (above, p. 66); in the *Tableau des piperies des femmes mondaines*, similar passages are to be found:

Vous Dames barboüillées farcies de mille vices roturiers, montées dans vn cloaque d'ordure, plongées dans des sangs corrompus, enfondrées dans vn bourbier de sensualité, aussi bien que vos Amans desesperez qui exhalent tant de cuisans souspirs . . .

O monde maintenant tout gaucher, fait au rebours, et à contrefil, qui fait prendre l'escorce aux Dames pour l'arbre, l'ombre pour le corps, le masque pour le visage, et le tableau pour la chose exprimee![20]

Enumeration and extended metaphors and similes are also in evidence.[21] In general moralistic writers are more discreet in their deployment of such devices than anti-feminists; it is even rarer to find passages of this sort in texts favourable to women, although Lescale's *blason* of female beauty is reminiscent of the same techniques:

Ses cheueux longs, delies, et blonds, doucement ondoyants par dessus les espaules, nous monstrent que de son temperament elle est gratieuse. Son front est le tableau, où la paix se voit despeinte, et ses yeux n'estincelent qu'amour et concorde. Ses ioües meslees du teint de roses et de laict, nous enseignent qu'elle surpasse esgalement les douceurs du goust de l'vn et de l'odeur des autres. Sa bouche vermeille comme l'Aurore, nous promet que le soleil du repos humain se leue chez elle . . .[22]

Such conceits contrast sharply with the expressions of physical horror at the uncleanliness of woman found in moralistic and anti-feminist texts.

The similarity of style in passages from moralistic and anti-

---

[19] *Alphabet*, pp. 145, 337, 370, 374.
[20] *Tableau des piperies des femmes mondaines*, ff. 159ᵛ, 116ᵛ.
[21] See Valladier's comparison of woman with the devil (*La saincte philosophie de l'ame*, pp. 813-14), and Puget de la Serre, *Entretien des bons esprits*, pp. 491-2, quoted above, p. 70 n.
[22] *Champion des femmes*, f. 41ʳ⁻ᵛ.

feminist texts is most apparent in references to cosmetics. Invectives against 'pecheresses fardées de plastres auec des visages peints et desguisez'[23] are reminiscent of such patristic texts as Tertullian's *De cultu mulierum*, both in style and content; one is faced again with the problems of disguised quotation and plagiarism referred to above. Pulpit oratory may also be a common influence: Trousset was a Franciscan, Valladier the *prédicateur ordinaire du Roi* in 1612–13, and it seems likely that the authors of the *Tableau des piperies des femmes mondaines* and the *Courtisane dechifree* of 1642 (which plagiarizes both Trousset and the *Tableau des piperies*) are both clerics. Desportes's 'Stances du mariage', imitated by Courval-Sonnet, Deplanches, Motin, and Du Lorens, and quoted at length by Trousset and others at this time,[24] may also be linked with both style and content of moralistic and anti-feminist works; all would seem to be manifestations of the 'anteros baroque' of which Madeleine Maurel speaks. Writings hostile to the female sex do, therefore, provide evidence which supports this critic's claim for the privileged position of women in baroque art.

Next to be considered is the question of vocabulary in this period. This has already been investigated in one major critical work with a view to elucidating the ethical patterns of Corneille's plays.[25] It is of primary concern here to show how vocabulary is used, in Marino's phrase, to 'far stupir';[26] to do this it will be necessary to indicate what common assumptions it betrays and how these are contradicted and yet at the same time upheld.

Part of the lexical area of terms denoting women should first be mentioned.[27] Where Latin has four words which are frequently

---

[23] *Tableau des piperies des femmes mondaines*, f. 29ʳ; see also ibid., ff. 26–30; Ferville, *La méchanceté des femmes*, pp. 95–6; Trousset, *Alphabet*, pp. 256–78; *La courtisane dechifree*, p. 132.

[24] See above, pp. 30 n., 97; Trousset, *Alphabet*, pp. 50–1; *Brief discours pour la reformation des mariages, passim*.

[25] O. Nadal, *Le sentiment de l'amour dans l'œuvre de Pierre Corneille, Étude conjointe*: 'De quelques mots de la langue cornélienne et d'une éthique de la gloire.'

[26] 'La Murtoleide', in *Opera*, ed. A. Asor Rosa, Milan, 1967, pp. 852–3:
È del poeta il fin la meraviglia
(Parlo de l'eccellente, non del goffo):
Chi non sa far stupir, vada a la striglia.

[27] See A. Grisay, G. Lavis, and M. Dubois-Stasse, *Les dénominations de la femme dans les anciens textes littéraires français* (publication de l'Institut de Lexicologie française de l'Université de Liège), Gembloux, 1969, for a treatment of the Latin and medieval background to this paragraph.

used (*mulier, femina, domina, uxor*), French in this period has only
two which are used with the same frequency, *femme* and *dame*.
Femme is the generic, biological term ('vn nom commun aux
Filles comme aux Mariées'[28]), differentiated from *dame* in what
appears to be a sociological way by Picou in his liminary poem to
Gerzan's *Triomphe des dames*:

> Ce n'est pas seulement le Triomphe des Dames
> De qui les deux attraits captiuent les Amans
> Ce sçauant Escriuain par ses raisonnemens
> Fait triompher de nous tout le sexe des femmes.[29]

In anti-feminist pamphlet literature, *femme* refers almost exclusively to married women of indeterminate social status, and the
connotation of marriage is retained in some uses of the description 'femme forte'. Religious moralists classify women as *vierge,
femme, veuve* (translating the Latin words *virgo, uxor, vidua*), in
which classification *femme* has again connotations of marriage.
Dame is used on the one hand as a means of address to members
of the leisured bourgeoisie and above, and on the other in a way
reminiscent of the medieval use of the word, embodied in such
texts as the Marian *Esclavage des devots de la B. V. Marie, emperière
du monde*, which appeared in 1629:

[Pratique de l'esclavage, item 4] : Vous vous frapperés de quelque coup
de discipline, ou ferés autre chose semblable en considération des
mancquements commis au service de vostre Dame et Maistresse.

   [Motif pour s'exciter à servir fermement la Vierge en esclave, item 6] :
N'est-ce pas la pratique des courtisans du monde de s'appeler et de se
porter en esclave des créatures qu'ils affectionnent et desquelles ils
dépendent? Que ce soit aussi l'usage des Courtisans du Ciel et de
Marie.[30]

It is perhaps because of these connotations of service and deference that *dame* is more popular in titles of feminist treatises in
the early part of the period, in which great respect for women is
a cornerstone of the argument, than in the works of the regency
of Anne of Austria, in which the word *femme* is predominant in
titles, laying stress on the biological difference which writers

---

28 Grenaille, *L'Honneste fille*, i. 157.
29 Gerzan, *Le triomphe des dames*, 12ᵛ.
30 *Esclavage des devots*, ed. P. Delattre, *Revue d'ascétique et de mystique*, xxx (1954),
352–5.

such as Du Bosc and Le Moyne claim to be the sole distinguishing factor between the sexes.

The importance of names as definitions, stressed in the Renaissance by such works as Pontus de Tyard's *De recta nominum impositione*, is of interest here, as it survives in the practice of giving what are often false etymologies to account for properties of the name's possessor. This is more common in anti-feminist literature in this period (the derivation of *putain* from *puteo*, and *mulier* from *mula* or *mollior* are examples), which is perhaps to be expected, as it has been shown that this current of writing has close links with the preceding century.[31] Another Renaissance (and for that matter, scholastic) method of describing the properties of a being was by epithets, and collections of these in alphabetical form under subject were published in the sixteenth century, drawing both on Latin verse (Ravisius Textor's *Epithetorum opus*, published in 1524 and frequently reprinted) and on the Pléiade poets (Maurice de La Porte's *Epithetes*, which appeared in 1571, and was reprinted in 1580, 1581, 1593, 1602, and 1612). These compendia provide an insight into attitudes prevalent in literature, which are applicable in this period also, as the conclusions of the study of moralistic writers indicate.[32] Under *femme*, La Porte lists the following epithets:

Muable, tromperesse, cheueluë, malitieuse, compagne de l'homme,

[31] A feminist example is found in Couvay's *Honneste maistresse* (Ch. 1: 'Du nom de maistresse, de son antiquité et de son pouuoir', pp. 1–15). The predilection of the Renaissance for anagrams (also seen as mystical keys to the meaning and definition of names) survives also in some feminist writing of the period (e.g. Suzanne de Nervèze's anagram of Anne-Marie-Maurice d'Austriche ['Diane Armee Mars Cherit Ta Vertu'] in *Les genereux mouuemens d'une dame heroïque et pieuse*, Paris, 1644, p. 43). See also Ronsard, *Sonnets pour Helene*, ed. Smith, Paris and Geneva, 1970, pp. 109–10.

[32] See above, pp. 65–71; the community of outlook of moralists and anti-feminists is indicated also in the epithet lists found in their works: Trousset describes woman as 'orgueilleuse, superbe, mondaine, sotte, curieuse, voluptueuse, cruelle, colere, babillarde, infidelle, enuieuse, quereleuse, iniurieuse, dangereuse et ennuyeuse, menteuse, ialouse' (*Alphabet*, p. 15); Ferville's list emphasizes three female failings, arrogance, inconstancy, and lubricity: '[la femme] est inconstante, volage, mobile, desloyalle, infidelle, instable, legere, variable . . . glorieuse, outrecuidee, presomptueuse, superbe, arrogante, iniurieuse, importune, eshontee, lasciue, cupide, effrenee, lubrique, auare, mesdisante, intemperee, incontinente, cruelle, barbare et endiablée' (*La méchanceté des femmes*, pp. 64–5); Maillard describes woman as 'souuent legere, inconstante, vaine, superbe, impatiente, desireuse de liberté, subiecte à ses passions, moins capable de raison' (*Le bon mariage*, p. 290), but also balances his picture of woman with an equally unflattering account of man, attributing the vices of both sexes to the fall.

belle, pusillanime, gente, babillarde, fine vengeresse, sotte, volage, indiscrette, furieuse, superbe, reuesche, mammeluë, enuieuse, passion-nee, barguignarde, chiche, desdaigneuse, charmeresse, imbecille, double, fiere, delicate, legere, inutile, venimeuse, lasciue, fardee, ialouse, fascheuse, impatiente, mensongere, propre, desloyale, mesna-gere, auare, fragile, mauuaise, obstinee, soupçonneuse, incorrigible, paoureuse, aspre, mariee, quereleuse, vile, dissoluë, perruquee, variable, impudique, fraudulente ou frauduleuse, criarde, assotee, pleureuse ou pleurarde, cauteleuse, passion de l'homme, miserable.[33]

These epithets fall into quite easily identifiable groups, reflecting the prevalence of a set of commonplaces about the female sex which are often expressed in terms of biblical, classical, and patristic *loci*. The figure of the *femme forte* is, as has already been pointed out, in many ways the antithesis of the depiction of womankind embodied in these commonplaces, of which the following are the most important to this study:

Fragilior sexus (*le sexe fragile, infirme, faible, imparfait*; La Porte has *imbecille, pusillanime, assotee, sotte, fragile*). The fragility referred to can apply to either the body (reflecting no doubt the medical beliefs about woman's imperfect generation drawn from Aristotle) or the mind. In the latter case, it indicates weakness and sus-ceptibility to passion (La Porte: *passionnee, furieuse*), and more precisely to certain vices and mental states often associated with women: lubricity (La Porte: *impudique, lasciue, dissoluë*), jealousy described in Du Ryer's *Lucrece* as a 'cruelle et lasche passion'[34] (La Porte: *jalouse, enuieuse, soupçonneuse*), fear (La Porte: *pusillanime, paoureuse*), which Corneille makes the dominant epithet for the female sex ('le sexe craintif'), but which is excusable when the fear applies to the conservation of honour or the survival of a lover. The epithets *incorrigible, malitieuse, mauuaise, impatiente* in

---

[33] *Les epithetes,* Lyons, 1593, ff. 173ᵛ–4ʳ; cf. *Le grand dictionnaire françois-latin,* ed. Nicod and P. de Brosses, Lyons, 1625, p. 613, s.v. *femmes*: 'belles, muables, vierges pudiques, humaines, mortelles, rusées en amour, tromperesse, passion de l'homme, miserable, fier animal, courtoise, honneste, de doux entretien, sçauante, gentille, indocte, mal'habille, delicieuses, qui sous robes trop precieuses du rang des nobles abusoyent, atteincte de la mort *Rons[ard]*'; p. 625, s.v. *fille*: 'badine, ieune, sotte, de renom, souueraine, venerable de Lemnos, cruelle et sotte beste, dure, fiere, rebelle, rude en amour, inexorable, inhumaine, douce, amiable, honneste, belle, *Rons[ard]*'. It is clear from this epithet dictionary how such lists as that of La Porte were compiled.

[34] *Lucrece,* I. ii, p. 13.

La Porte's list might also be grouped under the heading *fragilior sexus*.

When referring to the fragility of the body, the commonplace is naturally less hostile to women, as it pays tribute to their physical beauty (which, as has been seen, is often described as compensation from nature for their lack of valour and physical force) (La Porte: *belle, gente, propre, delicate*). It is interesting that La Porte lists the moral qualities associated with physical fragility under the diminutives *femmette* and *femmelette*, and perhaps more strikingly under *mere*:

[*Femmette* et *Femmelette*]: Simple, douce, peu-caute, ioyeuse, docile, prudente, iolie, belle, bellotte, debonnaire, amoureuse, brune, nice, gaye, amiable, ieune, mignonne ou mignarde, diligente, honneste, soulas de l'homme, fidelle, gente ou gentille, ouuriere, ingenieuse, actiue.[35]

[*Mere*]: Douce, nourrissante, ou nourriciere, feconde, benigne, chere, pitoyable, debonnaire, soigneuse, venue, miable, soucieuse, charitable, amoureuse, secourable.[36]

By virtue of their *delicatesse, mollesse*, women are seen as the comfort and civilizing force of men (La Porte: *compagne, soulas de l'homme, secourable, benigne, charitable, nourrissante ou nourriciere*); the attribution of such qualities as pity, compassion, clemency, liberality, gentleness, love is also connected with physical weakness. The susceptibility of women to love (La Porte: *amoureuse*; cf. Isabelle in *Don Sanche d'Aragon*: 'je puis aimer, puisque enfin je suis femme'[37]) is perhaps the most important literary commonplace about them; by virtue of their fragility, they are opposed to the harsh strictures and inhuman codes of men (described by them as 'brutalité'[38]) and it is due to their influence that clemency triumphs over vengeance; this is implied in Cinna,[39] and explicitly stated in Mairet's *Marc-Antoine*.[40]

[35] *Les epithetes*, f. 174ʳ. [36] Ibid., f. 263ᵛ.
[37] *Don Sanche d'Aragon*, II. ii.
[38] Corneille, *Horace*, IV. iv; cf. Tasso's use of the word 'ferità' in his *Discorso della virtù eroica e della carità* (*Prose diverse*, ed. Guasti, ii. 190), and *Nicomachean Ethics*, VII. i. I.
[39] *Cinna*, IV. iii.
[40] *Le Marc-Antoine*, V. iv, p. 77:

> (Caesar) Antoine a desrobé sa vie à ma douceur,
> Qui l'auoit accordée aux larmes de ma sœur;

see also Pauline in *Polyeucte*, III. iii.

Tears and sighs are also associated with woman's physical weakness, which has a debilitating as well as a humanizing effect. *Volupté, oisiveté, luxe* are all described as effeminate, and said to result from *mollesse*.[41]. The *grâce du langage* which is another manifestation of feminine *délicatesse* may also be seen as affectedness or *mignardise*. There is a hidden side to the endearing qualities of gentleness, for in the *femme offensée*, hate, cruelty, and a desire for vengeance are all the more extreme ('non est ira super iram mulieris'[42]). Such violent emotions represent, however, power and strength of purpose, and are therefore germane to feminism. The *femme vengeresse* is a common figure in drama (e.g. Emilia, Medea, Cleopatra), and is sometimes identical with the *femme charmeresse*, the female magician, another powerful female figure, one of whom is made by Rousset a symbol of baroque.

The physical fragility of women is sometimes paradoxically associated with brute strength, thus forming a composite androgynous warrior beauty. The musings of the warrior Clarofilant in Du Verdier's *Roman des dames* shows how writers exploit the paradox and extravagance embodied in this combination.[43] More often, female characteristics and physical attributes ('teint delicat', 'beauté', 'ton de voix') are given to male characters, indicating the predilection of the age for the mixing of opposites and again producing the strange combination of beauty and bellicosity. Such figures abound in the pastoral, but may also be found in tragi-comedy and even tragedy.[44] They fall outside the iconographical tradition of depicting men with coarser and more deeply coloured skins than women, and conflict with the beliefs about masculine sturdiness and robustness, referred to, for example, in Hardy's *Didon*.[45]

[41] Although not in La Porte's *Epithetes*, *molle* is a frequent epithet for women in this period (see Ravisius Textor, *Epithorum opus*, Basle, 1592, p. 333, s.v. *Foemina*, and *Le grand dictionnaire françois-latin*, pp. 472 and 904; also Du Bosc, *L'honneste femme*, iii. 188, quoted above, p. 69).

[42] Ecclus. 25 : 23. Verses 17–36 of this chapter are the source of many commonplaces about the female sex.

[43] *Le roman des dames*, i. 163–4, quoted above, p. 207.

[44] e.g. the Prince in Gilbert's *Marguerite de France*, Aristobule in Tristan's *Mariane*, Massinisse in Mairet's *Sophonisbe*.

[45] To the argument that a change in climate will endanger his health, Aeneas replies :

> Aux corps effeminez appartient ce scrupule,
> Des climats, pour le mien, la difference est nulle.

> (*Didon*, iv. ii, in *Théâtre*, ed. Stengel, i. 45.)

Varium et mutabile semper femina (*Aeneid*, iv. 569)[46] (*inconstante, infidèle, bizarre, capricieuse, instable*; La Porte: *muable, volage, legere, variable, desloiale*). The theme of inconstancy is often associated with the baroque, and women, being of the inconstant sex, are thereby allied to its spirit. This commonplace is most frequently associated with love: it is of course unusual to claim that women are more constant than men (a theme of the popular *Heroides* of Ovid); the chapter entitled 'De la belle et stable amitié des femmes' in *Le triomphe des dames* of 1599 and the title of Bronzini's feminist tract of 1622 (*L'advocat des femmes, ou de leur fidelité et constance*) are examples of the paradoxical use of the epithets *stable, fidèle, constant*. Gilbert, in 1650, was to go as far as to suggest that women love more rationally, and that this accounts for their greater constancy.[47] The description of the male sex as the 'sexe maudit, ingrat, leger' in Scudéry's *Didon*[48] and elsewhere is an example of a similar reversal of epithet.

Du Bosc and Le Moyne go further, and exploit the ambiguity of the word *constance* (meaning either constancy, or stoic apathy), making this reversal an occasion to underline the heroic qualities of the female sex: impassivity, loyalty, prudence, resoluteness, *fermeté de cœur*.

An extension of this commonplace is found in the words which interpret the fickleness of women as calculated and malicious (*fourbe, rusée, dissimulée*; La Porte: *tromperesse, fine, double, desloiale, cauteleuse, fraudulente ou frauduleuse*). This distrust of feminine motivation is also associated with a feminist reaction to male inconstancy in love, by which women such as Guarini's Corisca take many lovers as a defence against male promiscuity, and thus ensure their equality to men: 'jouer les hommes pour n'en être pas victime', as Rousset puts it.[49] This disguising of thought and intention, itself reminiscent of many baroque themes, is found also in more physical terms in imagery drawn from cosmetics (La Porte: *fardee, perruquee*) which has already been noted. Moralistic

[46] 'Mutabile semper' in one of Flamen's *Devises et emblesmes d'amour* (pp. 20–1).
[47] 'Les femmes . . . ayment plus parfaitement que nous: comme leur amour est l'ouurage de leur raison, cette mesme raison, qui les rend froides pour ceux qui leur doiuent estre indiferens, les rend constantes pour ceux qu'elles doiuent tousiours aymer' (*Panegyrique des dames*, p. 26).
[48] *Didon*, IV. ii, p. 73.
[49] *La littérature de l'âge baroque en France*, pp. 42–3; cf. Ninon de Lanclos, quoted by Émile Magne as saying 'les hommes jouissent de mille libertés que les femmes ne goûtent pas . . . je me fais donc homme' (*Ninon de Lanclos*, Paris, 1925, p. 62).

literature condemning the use of cosmetics deploys these epithets with both a literal and a figurative meaning; the baroque themes of mask and metamorphosis are of course prominent in such contexts.

Finesse, *vivacité*, and *subtilité*, used to describe the feminine mind (the last has medical overtones, as women are said to have a 'sang plus subtil'), are used sometimes to describe a positive quality ('pénétration d'esprit') and more often with pejorative force to describe the female facility for *tromperie*. In the *femme forte*, these vices are countered by *franchise héroïque*: 'conseiller, menasser, offrir, refuser, tout à descouuert, sans dissimulation, mais pourtant fort sagement'.[50] The association of women with political intrigue (explicit in *Nicomède*) is contrasted with the fearless honesty of such figures as Pulchérie in *Héraclius* and Semiramis, as she is described in *La femme genereuse*.[51] Political action is set against this 'prudence généreuse, qui marche à visage découvert, qui prévoit le péril sans s'émouvoir, et ne veut point d'autre appui que celui de sa vertu', in the words of Corneille in the preface to *Nicomède*.[52]

Meretrix (*la femme mondaine*). The biblical commonplace 'omne quod est in mundo concupiscentia carnis est, et concupiscentia oculorum, et superbia vitae'[53] has already been quoted in connection with the trio of vices *volupté*, *avarice*, *ambition* which are often associated at this time. The *femme mondaine*, being *in mundo* and *de mundo*, embodies these faults. *Voluptas* is of course traditionally opposed to *virtus*, and as the latter is often associated with masculinity, so is the former with the female sex: 'la concupiscence', writes Baudoin, translating Tasso, 'pour estre vne passion molle, et tres delicate en l'ame, est vn symbole de la femme'.[54] For the *femme forte*, heroic chastity is clearly the corresponding virtue and it is perhaps because of this association of women with *voluptas* that so much stress is laid on chastity as a heroic virtue.[55] Avarice is a frequent accusation against women (La

---

[50] Du Bosc, *La femme heroïque*, i. 257; cf. Montaigne, *Essais*, ed. Thibaudet and Rat, ii. 17, p. 630: 'Aristote estime office de magnanimité hayr et aimer a descouvert, juger, parler avec toute franchise, et, au prix de la verité, ne faire cas de l'approbation ou reprobation d'autruy'; cf. also *Nicomachean Ethics*, iv. 8.
[51] *La femme genereuse*, p. 45, quoted above, p. 231 n.; see also *Pertharite*, i. ii.
[52] *Théâtre*, ed. Lièvre and Caillois, ii. 389.	[53] 1 John 2 : 16.
[54] *Les morales du Tasso*, Paris, 1632, p. 263.	[55] See above, pp. 83–5.

Porte: *auare*), but it is sometimes transmuted into a positive quality to become 'œconomie' or 'vertu mesnagere'. It is of course inconceivable in heroic figures, for it is directly opposed to liberality.[56] Ambition presents a difficult problem for moralistic writers about heroic women, for it is considered to be a not particularly blameworthy property of high birth, together with 'noble fierté' (distinct from *superbia*, since it is justified). The superiority of ambition over love as a passion is asserted on more than one occasion by Corneille who expressly disregards the morality of such a preference.[57] Du Bosc and Le Moyne remain tactfully silent about worldly ambition in their feminist works, although the former condemns it in passing in the third part of his *Honneste femme*.[58]

Other vices associated with the *femme mondaine*—pretentiousness, vanity, affectation, arrogance—have been discussed in detail elsewhere. They are countered in the *femme forte* by references to humility, simplicity, modesty.

Reversals similar to those noted in connection with these commonplaces may be pursued further into the realm of the vocabulary of behaviour, but with less conviction. In the field of the vocabulary of love, androcentric terms are allied to the idea of possession (*prendre, ravir, posséder*), whereas gynaecocentric terms imply self-abandonment (*se donner, s'abandonner, se sacrifier, mourir en soy pour revivre en autruy*). It is not uncommon to find a reversal of this usage in the early years of the century, as, for example, in the following extract from the *Apologie de la constance*:

Si vne Dame te possede desia, c'est accuser sa beauté d'impuissance de dire qu'vne autre te puisse rauir, et rompre en vn instant les chaisnes qui te retiennent son captif. Si elle a eu le pouuoir de te prendre, pourquoy ne l'a-elle pas aussi de te retenir . . .[59]

---

[56] See *Les morales du Tasso*, pp. 122-3, where liberality is described not only as a heroic, but also as a masculine virtue; and *Eudemian Ethics*, iii. 4.

[57] '[La] dignité [de la tragédie] demande quelque grand intérêt d'Etat, ou quelque passion plus noble et plus mâle que l'amour, telles que sont l'ambition ou la vengeance . . .' (*Discours de l'utilité et des parties du poème dramatique*, in *Trois discours sur le poème dramatique*, ed. L. Forestier, Paris, 1963, p. 46); see also Cléopâtre's speech in *Pompée*, 11. i, quoted above, p. 191.

[58] *L'honneste femme*, iii. 407.

[59] *Apologie de la constance*, ff. 37-8; see also *La femme genereuse*, p. 48, and Sorel, *Francion*, ed. Roy, iii. 79: 'je ne demande pas encore a vous posseder, repartit Francion, mon souhait est seulement de vous daigniez auouer que vous me possedez.'

The reverse case (gynaecocentric terms applied to men) is not infrequent in *précieux* literature. An associated area of vocabulary is that of captivity (of which the above extract again offers an example), commonly used by men in drama and love poetry.[60] Gynaecocentric terms are conspicuously absent from Corneille's plays; this may be attributed to the tendency towards solipsism shown by his characters, who could not conceive of an *abandon de soi*. In any case, his slighting assertions about the status of love in tragedy are well known.[61] When describing their *tendresse* his characters resort to political terms which they apply to their affection (*régner, être souveraine, avoir des droits sur le cœur, vivre sous les lois d'une maîtresse*). This use of political vocabulary in the sphere of love is paralleled by the use of the vocabulary of love in the sphere of politics (*cruel, ingrat, inhumain, froideur, rigueur, dédain* of princes; *faveurs* and *service*). The use of such vocabulary and of the vocabulary of conquest and defeat in the sphere of love may be seen as a disguised compliment to a passion often associated with women; but such a suggestion can be no more than tentative, not only because the exchange of vocabulary between love and politics is a universal commonplace, but also in face of the low assessment of love in many of the plays of the period, proclaimed even by women themselves:

> On se lasse bientôt de l'amour d'une femme;
> Mais la soif de régner règne toujours sur l'âme.[62]

As for the political behaviour of women, the association of intrigue and double-dealing with them has already been mentioned.[63] *Audace, superbe, menacer, braver* form a group of words also relevant in this context, indicating their reaction to their political and physical impotence, and implying that their behaviour is more arrogant than their position justifies.[64] Such words are often applied to men, but it is doubtful whether this is done with the intention of casting doubt on the masculinity of their actions.

[60] e.g. Hardy, *Didon*, III. ii, where Didon uses such vocabulary with the clear intention of inverting the normal relationship of man to woman in love.

[61] Cf. his letter to Saint-Évremond dated 1666, in which he says: 'j'ai cru jusques ici que l'amour était une passion trop chargée de faiblesse pour être la dominante dans une pièce héroïque' (*Œuvres complètes*, ed. A. Stegmann, Paris, 1963, p. 862)

[62] Rodelinde in *Pertharite*, III. iii.

[63] See *Nicomède*, IV. ii, quoted above, p. 193.

[64] On the identification of woman with misrule and rebellion, see N. Z. Davis, *Society and culture in early modern France*, Ch. 5: 'Women on top', pp. 124–51.

The vocabulary connected with the manifestation of physical weakness offers a clearer case of reversal. *Larmes, pleurs, soupirs, plaintes, trembler, évanouir* are all used of male characters in the pastoral; *tendres sentiments, dignes faiblesses, crainte, frayeur, peur, impuissance, lâche, mou,* all words reflecting the moral susceptibilities of women, are applied to male characters in drama (Antiochus and Seleucus in *Rodogune* are notable examples). The heroic woman, often in direct contrast to the weak man, is free from such frailty, and faces life with impassive firmness.

A final note may be added on some words which express concepts having in close proximity either pejorative or eulogistic connotations. That such words are exploited by writers of the period is indicated by the following passage from the dialogue in *La femme genereuse*:

[Le courtisan]: Ie ne veux pas contester sur toutes ces pointilles, ie cede aux femmes l'opiniastreté.
[La femme genereuse]: Dites constance, Monsieur, vous abusez des termes, et en faites vn mauuais employ.[65]

Contiguous pairs of words similar to this which have been touched upon above are *grâce du langage* — *mignardise, finesse d'esprit* — *tromperie, économie* — *avarice*. An interesting pair, *éloquence* — *babil* (La Porte: *babillarde, criarde*), is much discussed in literature about the value of conversation with women, in which feminists such as Scudéry praise their 'éloquence naturelle', apparently without irony.[66] The use of such contiguous terms is indicative of a playful attitude to words, and an exploitation of their ambiguities, which is sometimes seen as a feature of baroque writing.

It is clear from the above examples that the heroic woman is not only free of all the unworthy attributes of womankind, nor simply possessed of masculine virtues; she also retains the qualities associated with the frailty of women (beauty, gentleness, clemency, compassion), thus forming an antithesis of woman in moral attributes, and a fusion of man and woman in her entirety,

---

[65] *La femme genereuse*, p. 205; cf. La Porte: *quereleuse, revesche, obstinee*. Trousset also remarks on such contiguous pairs of concepts (*Alphabet*, pp. 150–1).
[66] See also *La responce des dames et bourgeoises de Paris au Caquet de l'accouchée*, in *Recueil général des caquets de l'accouchée*, ed. E. Fournier, Paris, 1855, p. 207, where the association of *éloquence* and *caquet* is clearly ironic, at the expense of Marie de Gournay.

superior to one and the other sex. The two levels of favourable
comparison (*femme forte* v. *femme faible*; *femme forte* v.
homme) place her in an enviably dominant position. She is, however,
often meant to be an exemplar of the virtues, dormant or active,
in all women, and thus an inconsistency arises, for her superiority
may only be maintained if her privileged position as an exception
to her sex is also upheld.

A more important inconsistency is exposed when the assumptions which underlie these comparisons are examined. It would
seem that at the basis of all the reversals pointed to above is an
attitude to ethics which divides passions and moral attributes
into predominantly male and predominantly female categories.
Corneille, when describing *vengeance* and *ambition* as 'passions
nobles et mâles', is betraying such an attitude, and it would
probably be possible, as has been seen, to classify other passions
for their dominant sexual implications.[67] Such polarities as *force–
faiblesse, fermeté de cœur–mollesse, vertu–volupté*, even perhaps words
which are connected with either dominance or subservience
(*puissance–impuissance*) may be seen to be parallel with the polarity
homme–femme. By such a scheme, men who act in a feeble, con-
cupiscent fashion could be said to be effeminate, and women who
act courageously, with decision and force of will, could be said
to be masculine, producing a simple reversal of sexual attributes
in individuals. It is clear that these polarities are used in this way
by such writers as Hardy, Corneille, Du Bosc, Grenaille, and Le
Moyne.

It is, however, the stated intention of feminist writers to
persuade their readers that 'virtutes animo non sexu judicande',
that 'la vertu de l'homme et de la femme n'est qu'vne mesme
vertu'.[68] If virtues and vices are neither male nor female, but
categories relating exclusively to the soul, then the pairs of opposite qualities mentioned above no longer run parallel, as it were,
with the polarity *homme–femme*, but cross it, providing another
dimension of judgement. Thus *homme* no longer implies *force,
vertu, constance*, nor does *femme* imply *faiblesse, volupté, inconstance*;
but rather *homme* and *constance* are two unconnected dimensions,
implying the existence of an infinity of possible dimensions

[67] See *Les morales du Tasso*, pp. 122–3, and *La femme genereuse*, pp. 95–6, for
classifications of virtues according to sex.
[68] Motto on the frontispiece of Du Bosc's *La femme heroïque*.

defined by opposites, such as *grandeur–bassesse* or *vieillesse–jeunesse*. Now it is clear that if moral attributes are to be considered to be no longer linked to sex, feminist writers are guilty of a fundamental inconsistency, for they rely on reversal to cause surprise and press their case, at the same time as denying that this reversal exists, or should cause surprise; Le Moyne and Du Bosc are clearly both aware of this inconsistency, although they make no attempt to resolve it,[69] and it may be sensed in such passages as the following from Puget de la Serre's *Portrait de la Reyne*:

Ie ne m'étonne pas si le Sage met au nombre des choses les plus difficiles à treuuer vne Femme forte, puisque de siecle en siecle, il semble que l'vn laisse le defi à l'autre de nous la faire voir. En effet ce sexe a eu en partage les douceurs et les graces, céte sorte de presens affectez au corps en rendit la nature si delicate, que l'ame a de la peine d'agir puissamment, si la force de ses actions dépend de la force des organes. De maniere que ce sexe, qui ne peut s'eleuer au dessus de son temperament, tire sa force de sa vertu plûtôt que de sa nature, et c'est ce qui oblige le Sage sans doute à mettre vne femme forte *au rang des merueilles du monde. Mais que son étonnement cesse* aujourd'huy, et qu'il ne doute plus de la rencontre de cette femme, puis qu'elle paroît aux yeux de toutes la terre sous le visage de nôtre Auguste Reyne, *comme la plus Genereuse, et la plus Magnanime qui fut iamais.*[70]

In this passage one is urged to be surprised not to be surprised: or perhaps not to be surprised to be surprised. This combination of *nil admirari* and *admirari* will be encountered again below.

A further development in this manipulation of language and ethics is suggested by the following passages from Grenaille's *Honneste mariage*:

A voir ce beau dessein [Arria killing herself to encourage her husband Paetus to do the same], suiuy de l'execution, qui ne prendroit Arria pour son mary, et son mary pour Arria? Ne faut-il pas confesser que la force est icy foible, et que la foiblesse est icy forte?

Si tost que [les femmes] ont changé l'ordre de la Prouidence, et qu'au lieu que les desirs de la femme doiuent estre subordonnez à la

---

[69] See Le Moyne, *Gallerie*, pp. 10–11, quoted above, p. 49; Du Bosc, *La femme heroïque*, i. 41–2, where he claims that the virtues of the sexes are equal but different, which contradicts both the motto on his frontispiece and the argument developed in the introduction to his book (ibid. i. 23–34).

[70] *Portrait de la Reyne*, pp. 112–13. The italicizing is my own.

puissance du mary, ceux du mary le sont à ceux de la femme, on void vn homme qui deuient femme, et vne femme qui deuient homme.[71]

Here may be detected, beyond the reversal of moral attributes in individuals, the transformation or metamorphosis of values by which a new schema (*force/femme*, *faiblesse/homme*) is produced; in iconology such a metamorphosis is (perhaps playfully) upheld, as has been seen. Thus one finds united in a single artistic production self-exclusive or contradictory uses of language, which adds tension and unresolvedness to the style of these texts; such features are often linked with baroque.[72]

Of all ethical terms applied to women, *vertu* and *honneur* are most frequently subjected to the complex usage described above. Such phrases as 'courage viril', 'fermeté de cœur masle', 'vertu plus que masle' are often encountered in these texts; where a traditional schema of *vertu* is respected, such phrases may simply be elucidations of usage, distinguishing *vertu masle* from *vertu feminine* (that is, moral strength from the preservation of chastity). 'Vertu plus que masle', on the other hand, suggests the creation of a new schema, by which women are capable of greater moral strength than men; this may be perceived in the account of the death of the heroine in *Sainte Catherine*:

[Maximin]: Dis moy comme elle est morte?
[Valere]: En personne constante,
En courage heroïque, en Reyne trop constante,
Ces exemples fameux de generosité,
Que la memoire garde à la posterité,
Qui brauerent pour Rome, et les fers, et les flâmes,
En sa comparaison, sont morts comme des femmes . . .[73]

Here the scale of values is not only overturned, and the schema reversed, but women are also seen to achieve a level of virtue never reached by men. Mention has already been made of Aquinas's commentary on the *Nicomachean Ethics* referred to at length by Du Bosc, according to which heroic virtue is said to cause the apotheosis of its possessor;[74] the death of heroines such as

[71] *Honneste mariage*, pp. 279, 189.
[72] See Eugenio d'Ors, *Lo barocco*, p. 36; Madeleine Maurel, *XVIIe siècle*, lxxxiv-lxxxv. 19.
[73] Anon., *Sainte Catherine*, v. vi, p. 90.
[74] See above, pp. 82, 231.

St. Catherine exemplifies this, as they are possessed of *vertu divine* by the action of grace. Other writers are explicit on the subject:

L'experience nous a bien fait connoistre depuis, que plusieurs hommes estoient tous de chair, par leur mollesse et lascheté, et qu'vn nombre incroyable de femmes estoient toutes composées d'os, comme si elles n'auoient point de chair, si esloignées elles ont esté des plaisirs sensuels, et si puissantes à esclorre de hauts desseins, que les hommes n'osoient tant seulement entreprendre ny conceuoir d'y atteindre.[75]

La diuersité de sexe ne cause pas de difference essentielle dans les ames, veu qu'elle ne consiste que dans le corps: en ce sens les filles peuuent auoir vn grand courage dans vne chair extremement fresle, et parmy toutes les infirmitez de la nature conceuoir de fort genereux desseins. La vertu se perfectionne dans la foiblesse. La volonté ne depend point des organes en ses plus hautes operations, et la grace de Dieu se plaist à faire des efforts extraordinaires, où la nature ne peut monstrer que son impuissance.[76]

Women's frailty, therefore, adds lustre to their virtue, and enables them to outshine even men.

When applied to women outside the context of the comparison of the sexes, *vertu* means, in most cases, chastity or virtuousness, and may be synonymous with *honneur*. Yet this last notion is not only conceived of in terms of chastity by writers at this time: in many of Corneille's plays a woman's honour is associated with more masculine considerations, especially rank-consciousness, family pride, and status. Heroines set out, almost as if they were men, to avenge family honour, and become intimately associated with the glorification and preservation of the family unit against state, and even husband. In the context of devotional writing, virgin martyrs are ascribed an honour which is decidedly militant, and where they are said to defend 'l'honneur de la Chrestienté', even perhaps military.[77] *Honneur* prevents figures like Zenobia and Cleopatra from being subjected to a Roman triumph; suicide is the preferable alternative. In all this, the word takes on implications of courage and pride of status when applied to women, and

[75] Dinet, *Theatre françois*, ii. 4.
[76] Grenaille, *Honneste fille*, ii. 139–40; see also L'Archevesque, *Les grandeurs de la mere de Dieu*, p. 569, quoted above, p. 67.
[77] See Guerry, *Traicté de l'excellence du sexe fœminin*, p. 23, who talks of the 'faits heroïques de tant de dames d'honneur et hault courage', where the phrase 'dames d'honneur', which is usually synonymous with 'femmes vertueuses' or 'femmes chastes', is given masculine associations by juxtaposition with 'hault courage'.

yet still retains its associations with chastity, thus placing the heroic woman again in a superior position to both sexes, free from the weaknesses and vices of both men and women.

The association of heroic vocabulary and imagery with women may also be considered here. This is drawn from the masculine-dominated fields of war and politics, and from the sphere of martyrdom and miracle (*sublime, divin, prodige, merveille, miracle, inspiration*). The deployment of such vocabulary is clearly intended to evoke *admiratio*, not only by surprise but also by magnificence. *Illustre, généreuse, heroïque, forte, vaillante, magnanime* are common epithets for the heroines of Du Bosc and Le Moyne, and their implications are strengthened by images of armies, battles, victories, triumphs, trophies, empires, conquest, glory.[78] The brilliant reputation attributed to these *femmes fortes* runs counter to the traditional view that a woman's reputation should not pass beyond the doors of her own house. Similar imagery and vocabulary are applied to the Virgin Mary and to virgin martyrs, who are praised for their 'masculine' qualities (*constance, résolution, fermeté de cœur, élévation*) as well as those associated with devout women (piety, charity, humility, compassion).

There is also considerable use of terms of leadership and royalty: *reine, majesté, princesse, haute naissance, élévation* (which can have this sense). Le Moyne is even forced to postulate noble birth for one of his more obscure heroines.[79] The presence of this group of words is perhaps to be explained by the equation of high moral virtue with the social fact of high birth.

Finally, the vocabulary of moral and aesthetic approbation should be mentioned. *Haut* and *beau* are very often used as epithets indicating moral approval ('belle conception', 'belle observation' are phrases often found in the margins of printed sermons), as one would expect from an age in which *plaire* and *instruire* are rarely separated.[80] More striking is the use of such epithets as *agréable, qui plaît, qui charme*. Like Marino's 'crudeltà che piace', these are often used to indicate the paradoxical beauty of what is considered to be ugly, or disagreeable, or horrific in

[78] See below, p. 259.

[79] *Gallerie*, pp. 265–6 (in the section entitled 'la Judith françoise'): 'ne m'interrogez point de sa naissance: cette colere bien-seante, et cette fierté modeste et composée, vous asseureront mieux que moy qu'elle doit estre de bon lieu.'

[80] Cf. Grenaille's use of 'beau dessein' to describe suicide (*Honneste mariage*, p. 279, quoted above, p. 251).

some way, such as war, death, marriage (described in Baudoin's translation of Tasso's discourse on the subject as a 'joug agreable'[81]). Important in such combinations of words is the rôle of art, which is the force which transforms the unattractive subject into what is pleasing. The paradoxical beauty of the rose ('etiam armata placet') is used as an emblem for female chastity by Le Moyne,[82] but it may equally well apply to the beauty of female warriors—Mareschal's *Sœur valeureuse* is described as a 'guerriere agreable',[83] and Madame de Saint-Balmon possesses, according to Le Moyne, 'tout ce qui force, tout ce qui plaist';[84] in both cases, the paradox may be sensed. More extreme cases are not infrequently met in the drama of our period:

> La fille de Caton nasquit parmy les armes,
> Les horreurs des combats ont pour elle des charmes
> (Guérin de Bouscal, *La mort de Brute et de Porcie*,
> I. v, p. 20)

> J'adore ma foiblesse, et sa honte me plaist
> (The king in Boyer, *La sœur genereuse*, I. ii, p. 13)

> La mort la moins difforme, est vn monstre d'horreur ...
> [on hearing of the suicide of Cleopatra]
> Certes cette action courageuse qu'elle est,
> En me desobligeant me rauit et me plaist
> (Caesar in Mairet, *Le Marc-Antoine*, v. vii–viii, p. 92)

The *maraviglia* of such lines need hardly be stressed.

Thus vocabulary is used to shock, surprise, and disconcert; by reversal, by contradiction, by magnificence, by ambiguity. One does not find a balanced use of words in which categories are clearly distinguished and oppositions and polarities maintained; there is a constant play on the inadequacy of oppositions which exposes moral ambiguities and confusions, but upholds them at the same time by implicit reference to the generally accepted opinions under attack.

In the sphere of syntax, as has already been indicated, persuasive rhetoric and the rhetoric of eulogy are much in evidence, and this should not be surprising in view of the didactic purpose

[81] *Les morales du Tasso*, p. 294. [82] *Devises heroiques et morales*, p. 19.
[83] In Du Ryer's liminary poem for Mareschal's *La sœur valeureuse*.
[84] *Gallerie*, ëë3ᵛ.

underlying much of feminist writing, and of the constant pre-occupation with the evocation of *admiratio*. It is more than probable that the elements of formal rhetoric to be considered here were conscious devices of style to feminist writers, since there exist rhetorical treatises of this time which deal with the question of the composition of eulogies. These are intended for either secular or ecclesiastical use, and it is of interest here to consider briefly an example of each sort.

Frischlin's *Methodus declamandi in laudatione, thesi de laudibus mulierum demonstrata* of 1606 deals with both the rhetoric of eulogy, and how this may be applied to a feminist subject. The author sets out his method on the pattern of traditional rhetoric—*dispositio, inventio, elocutio*—of which only the last element need concern us here. Having collated his material by *loci*, Frischlin proceeds to demonstrate how to 'amplify' it. Here Cicero is taken as a model, and Frischlin's readers are advised to adapt periods from one or other of his speeches to their own subject. This leads not only to a predilection for sonorous expressions and periphrasis, but also to a heavy emphasis on the most useful techniques of *amplificatio*: superfluous negative clauses, repetitious enumeration, paralipsis, unnecessary comparisons, apostrophe, frequent appeals to the reader or listener. An example from Frischlin's declamation will illustrate this:

Viri verò cum intelligerent, è latere viri desumptam esse faeminam, non putarent esse viro inferiorem faeminam, aut ei subjectam; sed omnino scirent faeminam esse viro parem, et iisdem ornatam donis, quibus vir prae aliis cunctis animantibus praepelleret.[85]

Aut ei subjectam, et iisdem ornatam donis, quibus vir prae aliis . . . , the *non . . . sed* construction, and even the repetition of *faeminam* may all be seen as amplifying features.

Mazarini's *Art de bien prescher*, published in translation by Baudoin in 1618, may be taken as an example of an ecclesiastical rhetoric. This contains an exemplary panegyric of Saint Agatha, and is reminiscent in many ways of Frischlin, notably in its biographical approach and its reliance on *loci*. As one would expect, there is a greater number of *sententiae* in this work, centred on a moral theme (virginity), but the methods of eulogy remain essentially the same. The fact that sermons are written for public

---

[85] *Methodus declamandi in laudatione*, Strasbourg, 1606, p. 19. This passage is very reminiscent of glosses on Gen. 2 : 22 (e.g. that of Gennadius, *PL* lxxxv. 1635).

declamation is of course significant, and leads to a higher incidence of apostrophe, not only to the Almighty and the congrega-
tion, but also to the subject of the sermon.[86] This declamatory
element, which can also be conveyed in printing by the use of
typographical techniques, such as capitalization and the deployment of type faces of different sizes, is very conspicuous in the
works of clerics such as Du Bosc and Le Moyne.

Rhetorical devices commonly found in feminist prose writing
are in no way peculiar to it, but are characteristic of its style.
They are usually found in greatest abundance in those sections
which reflect on a narrative. Rhetorical questions are of course
common, and when grouped, as in the passage quoted from
Grenaille's *Honneste mariage* (above, p. 251), may be quite effective.
They often form an elementary structure to which other devices
are added; thus, in the quotation from Grenaille, there is a double
antithesis and an example of a Ciceronian construction which
invites the complicity of the reader ('ne faut-il pas confesser?').
This complicity presupposes a male readership, which feminist
writers sometimes acknowledge: Le Moyne asks his reader to
confess with him that '*nostre* Achab ne valoit gueres mieux que
leur Iesabel',[87] and Susanne de Nervèze also refers specifically to
her male audience.[88] The invitation to agree with the writer is
given more point if the act of agreement is made to seem reluc-
tant or grudging: 'reconnoissons donc', 'auoüons donc', 'il faut
auoüer sans passion'.[89] Le Moyne provides a good example of this
in his comment after recounting a heroic deed of Semiramis,
whom previously he had denounced as an unsuitable model of
behaviour for women ('ie ne voy pas pourquoy l'impudicité des
Dames, sera iustifiée par la valeur de Semiramis conquerante et
impudique'):

Auoüons qu'il y eut bien du magnanime et de l'Heroïque en ce transport. Auoüons que ceste teste demy-coëffée, estoit soûtenue d'vn grand
cœur: qu'elle estoit des plus fortes et des plus capables: et qu'il ne
pouuoit y auoir de Couronne trop grande ny trop haute pour elle.[90]

[86] This may also be found in Marian works: e.g. L'Archevesque, *Grandeurs de la
mere de Dieu*, pp. 479–80, quoted above, pp. 71–2.
[87] *Gallerie*, p. 12; the italics are my own.
[88] *Œuvres spirituelles et morales*, pp. 91–2.
[89] For examples of this see Machon, *Discours ou sermon apologetique*, p. 89; Grenaille,
Honneste fille, i. 32; Du Bosc, *Honneste femme*, ii. 297–8; Scudéry, *Femmes illustres*,
i. 18.   [90] *Gallerie*, pp. 174, 316–17.

Here may also be seen the use of repetition and enumeration (the latter often being no more than a disguised form of the former), both in construction and in epithets ('forte–capable', 'grande–haute', 'magnanime–heroïque'); these are universally encountered features of amplification. Du Bosc very frequently employs enumeration, and combines its use with that of interjections and exclamations in the declamatory manner, as is indicated in the following passage from his *Femme heroïque*, describing the predicament of the defeated Thomyris:

Que de malheurs l'attaquent en mesme temps; que d'euenemens funestes! elle voit vne armée ennemie au milieu de ses Estats, elle la voit victorieuse, la sienne défaite, son fils prisonnier qui se tue de regret; et apres toutes ces pertes, en état d'en faire encore de plus notables; se voyant sur le point de perdre, et son Royaume, et sa liberté, et sa vie mesme: Elle est attaquée de tous costez, et de la douleur, et de la crainte; l'auenir luy doit causer autant de frayeurs, que le passé de regret: et cependant parmy tant de malheurs et de pertes, elle ne s'abandonne pas aux pleurs, mais elle pense au remede, dit Iustin; ô grande ame, s'il en fut iamais! ô grand cœur et vrayement heroïque![91]

Antithesis is again conspicuous in this passage, both in the over-all construction and internally ('ne s'abandonne aux pleurs' —'pense au remede').

A technique popular with these writers is the refutation of imaginary opponents. Le Moyne, it is true, refutes Tasso and Guez de Balzac in sections of the *Gallerie*,[92] but he also invents imaginary anti-feminists whose arguments he exposes in passages quoted above (p. 48). Scudéry, Du Bosc, and Grenaille all employ the same technique of persuasion.[93] Paralipsis is also used in this way to prevent the reader from disagreement: 'on sçait que', 'toutes les Dames sçauent', 'n'est-ce pas', 'peu de gens ignorent' are not infrequent formulas.[94] There is a parallel in drama in the use made of enthymeme, which is examined below.

[91] *La femme heroïque*, i. 226–7; cf. Justinus, *Historiae Philippicae*, i. 9: 'amisso tanto exercitu, et quod gravius dolendum, unico filio, Tamyris orbitatis dolorem non in lacrimas effudit: sed in ultionis solatio intendit.'

[92] *Gallerie*, pp. 171–5, 250–5.

[93] *Femmes illustres*, i. 99–100; Du Bosc, *Honneste femme*, iii. 7–9; *Honneste fille*, i. 309–10.

[94] See, for examples, Le Moyne, *Gallerie*, p. 252; Grenaille, *Plaisirs des dames*, p. 34; Scudéry, *Femmes illustres*, i. 18; Du Bosc, *Honneste femme*, iii. 7.

The enumeration of negative clauses, reminiscent of Frischlin, is found in many writers, notably Le Moyne, whose succeeding clauses form a crescendo in the rhythm of the sentence:

Les Femmes doiuent apprendre de cét exemple [Porcia], qu'il ne tient pas à leur Sexe qu'elles ne soient fortes: que leurs foiblesses sont des vices de la Coustume; et non pas des defauts de la Nature: et qu'vn grand Cœur ne s'incommode non plus d'vn corps delicat . . .[95]

A similar crescendo in the structure of the sentence, this time achieved with the use of more complex constructions (*D'autant . . . que, si . . . que*) is found in *La femme genereuse*, in a passage in which the predilection for antithesis and parallel constructions is again in evidence:

Les combats par les armes arriuent rarement, et ceux de la continence se font et les iours et les nuicts, et quasi à tous les momens de la vie, ausquels les femmes estans assiduës, elles sont les veritables guerrieres, et font voir la plus heroïque vaillance qu'on puisse conceuoir. Et leur constance y paroist d'autant plus genereuse, et leur patience et longanimité d'autant plus ferme et immobile, qu'elle est attaquée par les hommes les plus agreables à leurs yeux, et par leur propre cœur, et la plus forte inclination de la nature, tout cela n'amollissant point leur courage.[96]

Most striking, however, is a combination of all these elements with apostrophe and hyperbolic language in a construction of even more marked crescendo (*non . . . non . . . mais!*), exemplified in the following extract from Poiré's *Triple couronne de la bienheureuse Vierge*:

Car vray Dieu! qui ne s'étonnera d'apprendre qu'vne femme conduise l'armée victorieuse du Dieu des armées, composée d'vn million de millions de bien-heureux Esprits, d'innombrables regiments de Patriarches, de Prophetes, d'Apotres, de Martyrs, de Confesseurs, et de saintes Vierges? Qui ne s'émerueillera d'entendre qu'elle commande non a treize cens mille gens de pié, cinq cens mille cheuaux, et cent mille chariots, comme Semiramis Reine des Assyriens; non à six vingts mille hommes comme Bunduique, que nous pourrions à bon droit nommer l'Amazone Angloise, ains aux troupes du grand Dieu, qui surpasse en nombre de combattans les étoiles du ciel, et le sablon de la mer . . .[97]

[95] *Gallerie*, pp. 208-9.   [96] *La femme genereuse*, pp. 138-9.
[97] *Triple couronne*, i. 156. Other examples of crescendos may be found in Grenaille, *Honneste fille*, i. 11ᵛ-2ʳ, quoted above, p. 231; L'Archevesque, *Grandeurs de la mere de Dieu*, pp. 479-80, quoted above, pp. 71-2; Du Bosc, *La femme heroïque*, i. 305.

Here may also be sensed the same interference with the perspectives of scale which has already been noted as a feature of book illustration.

All the devices briefly considered here are closely associated with the evocation of *admiratio*, either by surprise (antithesis, apostrophe) or by grandeur and magnificence (enumeration, correlatives, crescendo). At the same time, persuasive techniques are used to convince the reader of the necessity to emulate the heroines of feminist writing, who are almost without exception described as impassive and stoically indifferent to the external world. The reader is therefore urged simultaneously to *admirari* and to *nil admirari*. Again, tension and inconsistency (or rather contradictory elements) may be detected in the style of feminist writers.

In drama, the interrelationship of different planes of impassivity and *admiratio* is even more complex. In accounts of the deaths of heroines by execution or suicide, the narrator, himself obviously in a state of *maraviglia*, tells an audience from whom *maraviglia* is expected (for a figure with whom they are meant to identify?) of the reaction of those present at her death to her impassivity. Thus, from an impassive centre of interest, first a crowd is made to admire, then a narrator made to wonder at the combination of the crowd and the apathetic heroine (whose fear and pain seems to have been mystically transferred to those around her), and finally an audience is urged to admire the deep emotion of a narrator. Here a sort of crescendo of *admiratio* is created by a series of concentric circles around an impassive centre (crowd, narrator, audience) which is often further complicated by the fact that the audience has been witness to the struggles for self-mastery of the heroine, and knows of her inner *inconstance*.[98]

A further note about drama may be added at this point. The alexandrine is a very useful medium for chiasmus, parallel constructions, antithesis, enumeration, and emphatic vocabulary, and such devices are often used to stress the grandeur of heroines, although this is always at the expense of the rest of their sex; it is only by reference to the weakness of the mass of women that the strength of the exception may be established. Such praise of the heroic woman may therefore be seen in one light as the very antithesis of feminism, if it were not for the fact that such excep-

[98] See above, pp. 187.

tions are used as arguments for the existence of similar, but dormant, capacities in all women. A similar inconsistency to that discussed above in the context of vocabulary (p. 250) may be detected in the examples which follow:

> I'ay cru voir vne femme, et i'ay veu la vertu
> (Tarquin in Du Ryer, *Lucrece*, II. v. p. 33)

> [Cf. Si le sexe est blasmé pour vn peu de foiblesse,
> Tout le sexe est loüable à cause de Lucrece
> (id., ibid., p. 34).]

> . . . Qu'une femme enfin dans la calamité
> Me fasse des leçons de générosité
> (Sévère in *Polyeucte*, IV. vi)

> [Cf. Et faut-il qu'vne fille en cette extremité
> Vous fasse des leçons de générosité?
> (Porcia in Boyer, *La Porcie Romaine*, II. iv, p. 34)

> I'ay honte qu'vne femme, estant ce que ie suis,
> M'enseigne le moyen de borner mes ennuis
> (Antoine in Benserade, *La Cleopatre*, III. i, f. 19ʳ)]

Sometimes a form of enthymeme underlines the accepted opinions about capacities and faults in women:

> Mon père, je suis femme, et je sais ma faiblesse
> (Pauline in *Polyeucte*, I. iv)

> Je puis aimer, puisque enfin je suis femme
> (Isabelle in *Don Sanche d'Aragon* II. ii)

> Cesar . . .
> . . . porte vn cœur, Madame, et vous auez des yeux
> (Epaphrodite in Benserade, *La Cleopatre*, v. i, f. 41ᵛ)

> Tarquin porte vn Sceptre, et . . . Lucrece est femme
> (Brute in Du Ryer, *Lucrece*, I. ii, p. 16)

An even more compressed form of statement, embodying usually reversal, is also to be found in the drama of the period (e.g. 'Leur amour m'offensait, leur amitié m'accable' [Cléopâtre in *Rodogune*, IV: vii]); references to Christianity as the 'secte impie' in *Polyeucte* and other martyr plays also betray the delight in paradox and reversal, of which the opposition *femme forte–sexe faible* is but one example.

The elements of vocabulary and syntax examined here reflect, therefore, the prevalence in feminist writings of certain themes and stylistic features which are associated with the idea of baroque (inconstancy, reversal, mixing of opposites, contradictory elements tolerated in a single aesthetic production, appearance and illusion, metamorphosis). They also illustrate the purpose of many of the writers to 'far stupir' by upsetting accepted opinion and by producing ambiguities which distort ethical attitudes. The appeal to magnificence, seen in the exploration of the vocabulary of war and conquest, politics and kingship, is another indication of the overriding desire to impress the reader.

Admiratio has been discussed at some length already, but it is useful at this point to summarize the usual methods by which it is evoked. Paradox, or the close association of conventionally antithetical and incompatible elements or attitudes, is everywhere apparent, especially in the onslaught on accepted opinion and prejudice;[99] horror is present in the evocation of a reaction of shock to something which offends against *bienséance* (this has been seen to be common in book illustration);[100] magnificence may be detected in the introduction of imposing, superhuman elements which diminish the reader and violently alter the perspective between him and the heroine, magnifying and exaggerating the difference in stature (this is done visually in book illustrations, and by the use of literary and dramatic crescendos). All this is effected by the workings of art; the *crudeltà* of which Marino speaks in connection with the engraving of the 'Battaglia de' Lapiti' is only pleasing by virtue of Tempesta's skill as an

[99] Scudéry, for example, sets out to show in his *Femmes illustres* that contradictory attitudes and modes of behaviour can be justified; successive harangues have the sub-titles 'que l'amour est preferable à l'honneur'; 'que l'honneur est preferable à l'amour'; 'que l'amour ne doit point mourir auec l'amante'; 'que l'amour ne doit aller que iusqu'au tombeau'. One may sense here the predilection for comprehensive solutions to moral problems, as opposed to the clear definition of right and wrong.

[100] An example of the use of horror to evoke *admiratio* in literature is found in Grenaille's *Plaisirs des dames*, pp. 34–5: 'toutes les Dames sçauent l'histoire de Raymond Lulle, qui faillit à perdre l'esprit pour auoir veu la gorge d'vne Italienne. Quoy qu'il fist profession de Philosophie, il la prenoit pour Deesse, toute mortelle qu'elle estoit, et il mourut volontairement à soy-mesme, pour ne plus viure qu'à elle. Enfin son amour auoit banny sa raison. La Dame qu'il poursuiuoit, et qui auoit encore plus de vertu que de beauté, se resolut de le guerir par le mesme suiet qui l'auoit blessé. Elle luy monstra donc son sein parfaittement beau par le haut, mais rongé par le bas de deux ulceres incurables, et luy dit auec autant d'efficace que de douceur: Monsieur, vous voyez que vous aymez ce que vous deuriez haïr. Ce spectacle surprit tellement l'esprit de Lulle, qu'abandonnant l'affection de toutes les creatures, il s'adonna tout à fait à l'amour de Dieu.'

illustrator, the suicide of Cleopatra appeals to Caesar because it is an elegant gesture of moral dignity, Grenaille for the same reason describes Arria's self-immolation as a 'beau dessein'. When art is combined with a didactic purpose, complications inevitably occur. The claim that *admiratio* can have a morally regenerative effect, made by Corneille and Du Bosc,[101] not only appears doubtful in view of what the reader is urged to admire, but also, as has been pointed out before, because for at least one part of the time, he is urged not to admire.[102] Tension and unresolvedness are again encountered.

Fusion, reversal, and metamorphosis are also important aspects of the style which has been examined. Fusion (the combination of male and female attributes in one person), reversal (the inversion of male and female attributes for isolated cases), and metamorphosis (the changing of woman into what man is assumed to be) are closely related, and often difficult to disentangle. In some cases, feminist writers make a case for metamorphosis (as in *La femme genereuse*, where it is even claimed that men have become women), in other cases, for fusion (as in Du Bosc's *Femme heroïque*); in drama, reversal is most commonly encountered. Often, there is a deliberate play on ambiguity, as has been seen in the context of vocabulary, and as is also true of the depiction of such figures as Céladon in the pastoral. Once again, certainty is impugned, and illusion blended with truth.

Sacred oratory and the rhetoric of persuasion and of eulogy all contribute, then, to the style of feminist texts and passages reflecting feminist thought in this period. The evocation of *admiratio* through horror and surprise, and the deployment of paradox, metamorphosis, and the mixing of opposites in both vocabulary and syntax is strongly reminiscent of similar evocation by analogous methods in the visual arts, confirming the conclusions reached in the last chapter. This may be seen as particularly interesting, as the illustrations for the works of Du Bosc and Le

---

[101] See above, p. 229 n.; *Examen de Nicomède*, in *Théâtre*, ed. Lièvre and Caillois, ii. 392; *La femme heroïque*, ii. 524.

[102] The problem is acknowledged by Corneille; speaking of Cléopâtre in *Rodogune*, he writes: 'tous ses crimes sont accompagnés d'une grandeur d'âme qui a quelque chose de si haut, qu'en même temps qu'on déteste ses actions, on admire la source dont elles partent' (*Discours de l'utilité et des parties du poème dramatique*, ed. Forestier, p. 55; see also Bénichou, *Morales du Grand Siècle*, Paris, 1948, pp. 27–9).

Moyne are conceived of as an integral part of the whole; the common approach of illustrator and writer would seem to support the argument for a period style which embraces at least literature and the visual arts at this time. The fact that such comparisons break down later in the century should not cause surprise, for, as Raymond Picard has pointed out in his illuminating article on Racine and Chauveau, the generation gap between writers and engravers would account for their differing outlooks.[103]

An aesthetic which is characterized by a delight in metamorphosis, paradox, and the mixing of opposites is certain to exploit one of the fundamental distinctions in life as in literature, that between the sexes; but the contradictory nature of woman herself—both angelic and demonic, beautiful and ugly, pure and unclean, compassionate and vengeful, gentle and cruel—is in itself eminently attractive to such an artistic vision. Thus anti-feminism as well as feminism has its place in the baroque universe, in which woman is not only the Protean Circe, but also 'un symbole de délice et d'abomination',[104] enjoying the 'triunfo y derrota' of which Eugenio d'Ors speaks. This leads to the question whether feminism has closer links with baroque than anti-feminism, which, as has been seen, attracts similar features of style. In favour of the view that feminism is of greater importance, one may first adduce the fact that the new feminism of Du Bosc, Grenaille, and Le Moyne emerges at the same time as the development of what Rousset calls 'plein-baroque' out of 'pré-baroque' (1625–30).[105] It is interesting to note that before these 'années charnières', anti-feminist and moralistic texts reflect baroque features of style, and that subsequently one must turn to feminist texts to find them. Furthermore, there are strong indications that feminism has a greater influence on imaginative literature (especially drama) after 1630 than anti-feminism exerted before that date. Feminism and anti-feminism are allied to baroque in different ways: anti-feminism is often associated with the 'spectacle de la mort', with the evocation of horror, with the pursuit of the extravagant and the bizarre, but it does not exploit the reversal of commonplaces and the mixing of opposites as do feminist writers. It is here that the most persuasive evidence for the

---

[103] 'Racine and Chauveau', *Journal of the Warburg and Courtauld Institutes*.
[104] Maurel, 'Esquisse d'un anteros baroque'.
[105] *La littérature de l'âge baroque en France*, pp. 233–5.

greater importance of feminism may be found, for the tampering with ethical terms affects, as has been seen, not only feminist texts, but impregnates a great part of imaginative literature at this time. The heroine of this period, who combines beauty with strength, compassion with resoluteness, modesty with heroic virtue, is the incarnation of a fundamental dislocation in traditional moral attitudes; her depiction can only be understood in terms of the commonplaces she negates, upholds, and transcends simultaneously. In anti-feminist texts, on the other hand, one finds no more than reinforcement of widely held beliefs, albeit hyperbolically expressed. It is possible, therefore, to argue that feminism plays an important rôle in French literature, especially between 1630 and 1650, and that its popularity as a theme contributes to, and perhaps even influences, the development of baroque.

The alliance of feminism and baroque seems, however, to be above all a feature of the age of Louis XIII and Anne of Austria; before this, the rhetoric of feminist writing, although exploiting paradox, is too defensive and not energetic enough to reflect fully the baroque characteristics of the works of Du Bosc and Le Moyne, and subsequent defenders of woman, the *précieuses*, and *modernes* like Fontanelle and Perrault, also eschew such an approach. Perhaps the tension and unresolvedness which are characteristic of feminist texts at this time can only exist in historical circumstances in which opinions are evenly balanced, and may be swayed, if only fleetingly, by artistic means. During these queen regencies, the sense of the glorious present, the heroic deeds of female warriors, and literary activity by women seem to have opened up new horizons which are exploited by artists and writers in the ways analysed above; Louis XIV's majority and the depreciation of the 'morale héroïque' herald the return of the traditional moral order, and with it an attachment to firm divisions and the rule of common sense. The days of baroque feminism were over.

Postscript

THE heritage of the continental Renaissance in France may be clearly detected in the areas which have been scrutinized in this study. The tradition of didactic writing on topics such as marriage and social behaviour which stems from Erasmus and Vives, Castiglione and Agrippa, continues throughout the period considered here. It is reinforced in its liberal aspect by the writings of St. Francis of Sales, and is in evidence in courtesy books until the end of the century. This tradition is one of the forms through which society influences imaginative literature, as Magendie's exhaustive study *La politesse mondaine et les théories de l'honnêteté en France au XVIIe siècle* shows, and it becomes the medium for feminism after 1630.

Renaissance Aristotelianism is less well defined as an influence, but more pervasive; it impinges on this study above all in the view of woman as an inferior version of the male, with its physiological, political, and ethical implications. Both moralists and anti-feminists exploit the commonplaces which are associated with this view of woman, and even baroque feminists such as Du Bosc and Le Moyne rely on them, if only for artistic purposes. By 1660 it seems that these commonplaces are no longer authoritative, and Molière is able to place them in the mouth of Arnolphe in *L'Ecole des femmes* to show how out of date his views on women are:

> Tout le monde connaît leur imperfection:
> Ce n'est qu'extravagance et qu'indiscretion;
> Leur esprit est méchant, et leur âme fragile;
> Il n'est rien de plus faible et de plus imbécile,
> Rien de plus infidèle: et malgré tout cela,
> Dans le monde on fait tout pour ces animaux-là.
>
> (v. iv)

Such commonplaces do not, of course, die out altogether, but appear increasingly antiquarian as the century progresses.

In terms of literary history, it has been shown that there were two periods of intense feminist literary activity between 1610 and 1652. The first of these periods stretches from the publication of

Trousset's *Alphabet de l'imperfection et malice des femmes* to the end
of the debate centred on this work (1617–29); during this time,
some twenty refutations or counter-refutations were produced,
many of them the work of provincial writers, few possessing
individual merit. Only Trousset's *Alphabet* survives, and is
triumphantly republished throughout this period and indeed as
late as 1685, attesting a little-known aspect of the taste of the
book-buying public. The second period coincides with part of
the regency of Anne of Austria (1640–7), and is characterized by
a glorification of women and an enhancement of their prestige
which provoke little opposition. Again, an impressive body of
works is produced, and, in this case, writers are in the main
Parisian and better known: Le Moyne, Du Bosc, Grenaille,
Puget de la Serre. The second period coincides with a flourishing
of feminism both as a literary theme and as a feature of the
visual arts, and a marked intensification of social and political
activity by women.

These two periods are the high points in a more gradual development in social and political awareness: the attempt in the
early years of the century by St. Francis of Sales to bring Christian
teaching about marriage and social behaviour up to date; the
striking change in the literature advocating education for women
from the defensive tracts of Artus Thomas and Charlotte de
Brachart to the polemical writings of Scudéry, Du Bosc, and Le
Moyne; the investigation and formulation of codes of *honnêteté*
for women in the 1630s; the debate about the value of mixed
conversation and of literary and linguistic arbitration by women
in the 1640s, clearly related to the growing influence of the *salons*;
finally, the discussion of political problems concerning women
during the regency. Concurrent with this development is the
change in the medium chosen for feminist polemic: from the
traditional form described in the second chapter of this study,
it moves to moralistic writing, and from moralistic writing to
a unique combination of this with imaginative and artistic
elements as may be seen in Scudéry's *Les femmes illustres*, Du
Bosc's *La femme heroïque*, and Le Moyne's *Gallerie des femmes fortes*.

From the study of imaginative literature, there has emerged the
presence of social and matrimonial preoccupations concerning
women in novels and comedies; the survival of neo-Platonist
attitudes to woman in the pastoral tradition, in which a celebration

of femininity itself may also be detected; and, in tragedy and tragi-comedy, a depiction of the heroic woman which is in many ways similar to that of the *femme forte* in feminist writing. It is interesting to note that the traditional genre of feminist writing, marked by its preoccupation with the mystical prerogatives of women, appears in decades in which the pastoral also flourishes (1610–30); that the preoccupation with social and matrimonial questions in moralistic literature coincides with the production of comedies and novels in which these questions are also debated (1630–40); and that the emergence of the *femme forte* comes at a time when serious drama seems to be the dominant literary form. Such parallels are open to obvious criticism, as the chronology of literature is rarely so clear-cut and neat, but they suggest an inter-relationship between genre and prevailing social and artistic preoccupations which may repay further investigation.

The rise of feminism in the 1630s may also be seen in the context of certain social phenomena: the disrepute of erotic and hence also to some degree of anti-feminist literature after the trials of *libertins* in the previous decade; the growing importance of the leisured middle classes; the activities of the *salons*, and the related movement against pedantry; most important, the rôle played by female patrons such as Anne of Austria, Mlle de Montpensier, and Marie-Louise de Gonzague. It is also of interest that these figures attract far more prominent artists in the sphere of the visual arts than in that of literature: Rubens, Pietro da Cortona, Romanelli, Vouet, Mignard, Vignon, Bosse are of a different stature from Le Moyne, Desmarets, Puget de la Serre. One is tempted to conclude that painting and engraving stood in higher repute than literature at this time, in spite of the efforts of Richelieu.

In the context of all these developments may be seen the emergence of two literary and social types, described by Guez de Balzac in a famous letter to Mme Desloges as the 'femme cava-lier' and the 'femme docteur'. The 'femme cavalier', who loves hunting and masculine pursuits, appears in French society in such figures as the maréchale d'Ancre, the duchesse de Lon-gueville, and the duchesse de Chevreuse (all active in politics) as well as in the less prominent Mme de la Guette, Mme de Saint-Balmon, and Anne de Vaux (all female warriors). The involvement of Mlle de Montpensier in the Fronde both in a political and a military rôle marks the climax of this social phenomenon, which reflects the revival of feudal attitudes among the *grande noblesse* described by Bénichou in his illuminating study *Morales du Grand Siècle*. Like her social counterpart, the heroic woman of the novel and drama who fights, rides, and intrigues with men seems to disappear after the Fronde, although she may still be found in works of art conceived and planned during the regency of Anne of Austria, such as epics and epic novels.

The 'femme docteur', on the other hand, emerges into full prominence in the 1650s as the *précieuse*, endowed with a desire for learning and a determination to develop such feminine faculties as *finesse, pénétration, vivacité d'esprit*. The evidence presented in the fifth chapter of this investigation supports Lathuillère's thesis on *préciosité* which traces its origins to the beginning of the century. *Préciosité* is born of the feminist demands for education of the 1630s and 1640s, but, unlike these, it is a movement insti-gated and directed by women themselves. Du Bosc and Le Moyne write from a baroque stance when they argue in favour of educa-tion for women, since they adopt consciously a masculine point of view from which they are able to exploit paradox and mix opposites; the *précieuses*, while often extravagant in their language, arguments, and aims, are fundamentally in harmony with the position they are debating, as they are speaking on their own behalf. There is no dislocation or internal contradiction in the writings of Madeleine de Scudéry or the words of the *précieuses* recorded by Michel de Pure. The study of the 'femme docteur' and of writings in her favour supports therefore Antoine Adam's contention that *préciosité* is to be seen as a phenomenon of the mid 1650s, separate from the recurrent swing towards affectation, periphrasis, and euphemism in the pendulum of style. Whereas the 'femme cavalier', the heroic woman, is perhaps the finest achievement of this period from the artistic point of view, it is the 'femme docteur' (who embodies also, according to Jean Rousset, 'la bergère rebelle au dieu d'amour, jalouse de son autonomie' of the pastoral) who survives as a literary and social figure.

Common to both the earlier and the latter part of the period is the paradoxical nature of feminism, most clearly seen in the attack on *opinion commune* which marks the triumph of the extra-ordinary over the commonplace. This attack takes on a deeper meaning after 1630, when the social, political, and even military activities of women cause a reaction in literature, evoking on the one hand the hostility of writers such as Guez de Balzac, and on the other, the sense of the glorious present which may be perceived in literature, in book illustration, and in the visual arts. This 'weltliche Apotheose', to use Otto von Simson's term, contrasts strikingly with the 'mépris du siècle' of writers of the next generation, such as La Bruyère and Boileau. It impregnates the literary and artistic production of a decade (1640–50) which seems to be remarkable for the coherence and unified nature of its aesthetic outlook, imbued as it is with the evocation of wonderment, surprise, and horror by means of the skilful, even ingenious manipulation of paradox, the mixing of opposites, and the balancing of the commonplace with the extraordinary which allows both to retain meaning and force, as least momentarily. One of the keys to the interpretation of this literary production is the identification of the commonplaces in which it trades; it has been shown how *loci* about women drawn from intellectual debates and social and literary sources can aid such interpretation. These *loci* form part of the broad spectrum of ethical terms which are subject to the treatment described above, and which indicate the change from the baroque to the classical approach to art.

Bibliography

PRIMARY SOURCES

I. *Manuscripts*

COLLETET, Guillaume, *Vies des poètes* (BN N.A. Fr. 3073–4).

De la conversation des femmes ou il est traité sçavoir s'il est utile aux jeunes gens de les hanter, et de converser avec elles (BN N.A. Fr. 124, ff. 177–209, appendix in a different script, f. 210). *Terminus post quem* of appendix 1641 (mention of Gassendi's *De Nicolai Claudii Fabrici de Peiresc . . . vita*).

De l'excellence et noblesse du sexe fœminin (BN A.F. Fr. 24255, ff. 258–65). This is not, as Ascoli suggests, a translation of Lucrezia Marinella's *Nobiltà ed eccellenzia delle donne*.

JACOB, Louis, *Dictionnaire biographique des femmes écrivains, depuis l'antiquité jusqu'au XVIIᵉ siècle* (BN A.F. Fr. 22865). BN Cat. gives this title and no name of author. This is a copy of the *Bibliothèque des femmes illustres par leurs écrits* by Jacob, mentioned by Coste, *Eloges et vies des reynes . . .*, Paris, 1647, ii. 170; Jacob's work (although not this copy) was finished in 1646 (for attribution and date, see f. 198ᵛ). This work has been thought to be 'introuvable' (see A. Cioranescu, *Les romans de la princesse de Conti*, Paris, 1937, p. 16 n.).

MIRAMION, M. de, *Discours de la conversation des femmes scavoir si cest chose utille à la jeunesse* (BN N.A. Fr. 1554, ff. 1–10).

Mulieres virtutibus et scientia praeditae cum praefixis authoribus qui earum laudes scripserunt. Item traité de la perfection des femmes comparée à celle des hommes. Omnia ex MSS Domini Dubuisson-Aubenay (Maz 4398). The *Traité*, dated variously 1617 and 1618, is by 'le sieur D. B. B.'; probably Dubuisson-Baudot (François-Nicolas Baudot, sieur Dubuisson et d'Aubenay) himself.

RAMPALLE, sieur de, 'S'il se faut marier ou non. A Cleandre', in *Discours accademiques de Monsieur le Mareschal de Bassompierre en forme d'epistres a Monsieur de Balzac* (BN A.F. Fr. 645, ff. 45–51). Also printed in an expanded form in Rampalle's *Discours academiques*, Paris, 1647, pp. 233–79.

II. *Printed sources*

As well as giving locations for the rare works listed in this bibliography, I have included references to books which I have not been able to find, and have indicated the bibliography in which these are cited.

A Castro, Rodericus, see Rodrigues de Castro, Estevam.

Advis salutaire et tres-necessaire aux gens de bien, qui se laissent battre par leurs femmes, n.p., n.d., 8vo (BN Rés Y² 2753). Gay cites an edition dated 1615. This is a reprint of the *Advertissement salutaire aux confreres de la haute et basse, pauwre et riche, vieille et nouvelle, noble et roturiere confrairie des martyres persecutez par leurs deshonnestes, indiscretes et malavisees femmes*, n.p., 1610, 8vo; it appeared also, with a different title and in a slightly amended form, in 1651 (BM 12314 ee 35).

Agrippa, Henricus Cornelius, *De nobilitate et praecellentia foeminei sexus . . . declamatio*, Antwerp, Michaelis Hillenius, 1529, 8vo (BN Z 17290).

Allard, Marcellin, *La gazzette françoise*, Paris, Pierre Chevallier, 1605, 8vo (BN Rés Z 2814).

L'amazone françoise au secours des Parisiens. Ou l'aproche des troupes de Madame la Duchesse de Chevreuse, Paris, Jean Henault, 1649, 4to (Maz M 12441).

Amyraut, Moyse, *Considerations sur les droits par lesquels la nature a reiglé les mariages*, Saumur, Isaac Desbordes, 1648, 8vo (BM 5157 a 55).

Angenoust, Nicolas, *Le paranymphe des dames*, Troyes, Pierre Du Ruau, 1629, 8vo (Ars 8° S 3114).

Angot de l'Esperonnière, Robert, *La consolation des femmes en leurs accouchemens. Avec le bon traictement de leurs marys*, n.p., 1637, 8vo (BN Rés R 2179). This work, published without mention of author, first appeared in Angot de l'Esperonnière's *Exercices de ce temps* (1622) with the title 'Lucine ou la femme en couches'.

Les antitheses des dames de Cypre, contre le bachelier Erophile et le docteur Philarete. Par Madamoiselle I. D. C., Paris, Samuel Thiboust, 1621, 12mo (Ars 8° B 30649).

L'apologie de la constance, ou fleau des inconstans. Contre une harangue faicte en leur defense . . ., Paris, Jean Gesselin, 1598, 12mo (BM 12314 de 2). The dedicatory epistle is signed 'N. R.'.

Arrest de nosseigneurs de la Cour des Aydes donné en faveur des femmes. Portant permission aux vefves, et autres sans difference d'acquerir les offices de controoller au regallement des tailles, et de jouyr des droicts et privileges y attribuez suivant l'edict, Paris, François Saradin, 1633, 8vo (Maz 37297[53]).

Les articles des privileges accordés aux femmes pardessus leurs maris le jour de caresme-prenant, Paris, Anthoine Du Breuil le jeune, 1616, 8vo (BM c 39 a 15). The same *recueil factice* in the BM contains two other anti-feminist *facetiae*: *Les belles et diverses complexions amoureuses des femmes et des filles de ce temps*, Paris, Julien Le Dinde, 1621, 8vo; *Le vieillard jaloux tombé en reveries des cornes avec une expresse deffence aux femmes de ne plus battre leurs maris sur les peines y mentionnez*, Paris, jou[x]te la copie imprimée à Roüen, 1618, 8vo.

AUBERY, Jean, *L'antidote d'amour, avec un ample discours contenant la nature et les causes d'iceluy, ensemble les remedes les plus singuliers pour se preserver et guerir des passions amoureuses*, Paris, Claude Chappelet, 1599, 12mo (BN R 20795).

D'AUBIGNAC, François Hédélin, abbé, *Panegyrique funebre de tres-haute, tres-puissante et tres-excellente princesse Madame Charlotte Marguerite de Montmorancy, veufve de feu tres-haut, tres-puissant et tres-excellent prince Monseigneur Henry de Bourbon Prince de Condé . . .*, Paris, Charles de Sercy, 1651, 4to (Maz M 14882).

—— *La Pucelle d'Orleans, tragedie en prose*, Paris, François Targa, 1642, 12mo (BN Rés Yf 3955).

—— *Zenobie. Tragedie*, Paris, Augustin Courbé, 1647, 4to (BN Rés Yf 329).

D'AUBIGNÉ, Théodore-Agrippa, *Œuvres complètes*, ed. E. Réaume & F. de Caussade, 6 vols., Paris, 1873–7.

D'AUDIGUIER, Vital, *Epistres françoises et libres discours . . . seconde edition reveüe, et augmentee par l'auteur*, Paris, Pierre Billaine, 1618, 8vo (BN Z 14323). First edition in 1609.

D'AUDIGUIER DU MAZET, Henri, *Le censeur censuré. Dedié au sieur de Sandricourt*, n.p., 1652, 4to (Maz M 12626).

D'AUTEUIL, Charles Combault, baron, *Blanche, Infante de Castille*, Paris, Antoine de Sommaville & Augustin Courbé, 1644, 4to (Maz 17503).

BALESDENS, Jean, *Les vies des très-illustres et très-sainctes dames, vierges et martyrs de l'Eglise . . .*, Paris, 1633, 8vo. Cited by Cioranescu.

Le balet des fols aux dames. Dansé au Marest du Temple, n.p., 1627, 8vo (BN Yf 979).

BALINGHEM, Antoine de, *Scriptura sacra in locos communes digesta*, 2 vols., Cologne, Wilhelmus Friessem, 1659, 4to (Lyons). An earlier edition appeared in 1621 at Douai.

—— *La toute-puissante guerrière representée en la personne de la sacrée Vierge Marie*, Douai, 1625, 12mo. Cited by Cioranescu.

—— *Le triomphe de chasteté et totalle défaicte de fol amour . . .*, Lille, 1616, 8vo. Cited by Cioranescu and Gay, who gives Saint Omer as the place of publication.

BALZAC, Jean-Louis Guez de, *Lettres . . . seconde partie*, 2 vols., Paris, Pierre Rocolet, 1636, 8vo (BN Z 14361–2).

BARBARO, Francisco, *De re uxoria libri duo*, Amsterdam, Joannes Janssonius, 1639, 12mo (Ars 8º S 3326). First published in 1513.

BARBO, Giambattista, *L'oracolo overo invettiva contra le donne*, Venice, Giovanni Dominico Rizzardi, 1616, 12mo (All Souls).

BAUDOIN, Jean, *Les penitentes illustres. Avec des advis aux dames de toutes conditions*, Paris, Jean Rémy, 1647, 8vo (Maz 32233).

—— *Recueil d'emblemes divers*, 2 vols., Paris, Jacques Villery, 1638, 8vo (BN Z 17520–1).

BENSERADE, Isaac, *La Cleopatre*, Paris, Antoine de Sommaville, 1636, 4to (BN Rés Yf 213).

BERNIER, Abraham, *Apologie contre le livre intitulé Alphabeth de la meschanceté des femmes. Par laquelle l'on void l'excellence de leurs vertus et perfections*, Paris, Joseph Bouillerot, 1618, 12mo (Lincoln Cathedral Chapter House Library).

BÉROALDE DE VERVILLE, François, *La Pucelle d'Orleans restituee*, Tours, Sebastien Molin, 1599, 12mo (BN Rés Y² 1537).

BERTHAULT, François, *Le bouquet historial, recueilly des meilleurs autheurs grecs, latins et françois*, Paris, Jean Cochart, 1668, 12mo (Brotherton Library, Leeds). Cioranescu cites an edition in 1635.

BESLY, Jean, *Plaidoyer de Maistre Brusquet, advocat, sur les mondanités des femmes et pucelles*, Fontenay-le-Comte, 1617, 8vo. Cited by Cioranescu.

BOUFFLERS, Adrien de, *Le chois de plusieurs histoires et autres choses memorables, tant anciennes que modernes . . .* , Paris, P. Mettayer, 1608, 8vo (BN G 21411). Dedicatory epistle is signed 'A. D. B.'; Barbier gives the name of the compiler.

BOUVOT, Antoine Girard, *Judith, ou l'amour de la patrie, tragædie*, Langres, 1649, 4to (Ars 4º B 3631). Name of author and imprint are written in a seventeenth-century hand on the title-page.

BOYER, Claude, *La Porcie Romaine. Tragedie*, Paris, Augustin Courbé, 1646, 4to (BN Rés Yf 344).

—— *La sœur genereuse. Tragi-comedie*, Paris, Augustin Coubé, 1647, 4to (BN Rés Yf 333).

BRACHART, Charlotte de, *Harengue faicte par Damoiselle Charlotte de Brachart surnommee Aretuze qui s'adrese aux hommes qui veuillent deffendre la science aux femmes . . .* , Chalon-sur-Saône, Jean des Preyz, 1604, 8vo (BN R 54526).

BRÉGY, Charlotte Saumaise de Chazan, comtesse de, *La reflexion de la lune sur les hommes*, Paris, Antoine de Sommaville, 1654, 8vo (Ars 8º B 22218).

—— *La sphere de la lune, composée de la teste de la femme*, Paris, Antoine de Sommaville, 1652, 8vo (BM 717 e 17). Title-page gives author as 'Mlle de B***'; the attribution is that of Cioranescu.

Brief discours pour la reformation des mariages, Paris, Anthoine Du Breuil, 1614, 8vo. Reprinted in Fournier, *Variétés historiques et littéraires*, iv. 5–16.

BRINON, Pierre de, *Le triomphe des dames*, Rouen, Jean Osmont, 1599, 12mo (Ars 8° S 3078). Dedicatory epistle signed 'P. D. B.'; Cioranescu gives the name of the author.

BRONZINI, Cristoforo, *L'advocat des femmes ou de leur fidelité et constance. Dialogue contre les medisans de ce temps. Traduit d'italien en françois, par S. D. L.*, Paris, Toussainct Du Bray, 1622, 12mo (BM 8416 a 27). 'S. D. L.' is le chevalier de L'Escale, according to Dubuisson-Aubenay.

BURSATI, Lucrezio, *La vittoria delle donne: nelle quale in sei dialoghi si scuopre la grandezza donnesca e la bassezza virile*, Venice, Evangelista Deuch., 1621, 8vo (Maz 22545).

CAGNOLI, Belmonte, *Difesa di Semiramide*, Avignon, Giovan [Jean] Piot, 1638, 8vo (BN O²d 26).

CAILLET, Paul, *Le tableau du mariage representé au naturel. Enrichi de plusieurs rares curiosités, figures, emblemes, histoires, loyx, mœurs et coustumes de diverses nations. Et illustré de fleurs poëtiques et oratoires, des plus celebres auteurs anciens et modernes*, Orange, Estienne Voisin, 1635, 12mo (Ars 8° B 22235).

CALLOT, Jacques, *Vita beatae Mariae Virginis Matris Dei emblematibus delineata. Vie de la bien-heureuse Vierge Marie . . .* , Paris, François Langlois, 1646, 4to (BM 636 g 32[1]).

CAMUS, Jean-Pierre, *Les spectacles d'horreur, où se descouvrent plusieurs tragiques effets de nostre siecle*, Paris, André Soubron, 1630, 8vo (Maz 25148).

CANDELA, Joannes Dominica, *XIV discours de l'heur et bien de l'estat de virginité et continence composés par le R.P. Jean Dominique Candela de la Compagnie de Jesus. Et traduictz d'italien en françois par le P. Antoine Vivieu de la mesme Compagnie*, Toulouse, Vve I. Colomies & R. Colomies, 1608, 12mo (BN D 27737). Sommervogel cites the Italian original (*Del bene della S verginità, discorsi XIII*, Palermo, 1599).

CAUSSIN, Nicolas, *La cour sainte, dixiesme edition*, Paris, Sebastien Chappelet, 1640, 8vo (BN Rés Z 3254—but only an extract [ii. 219–484]). See Sommervogel for the bibliography of this work; the first edition of vol. 2 seems to date from 1629.

CERIZIERS, René de, *Les trois estats de l'innocence, contenant l'histoire de la Pucelle d'Orleans, ou l'innocence affligée, de Geneviefve, ou l'innocence reconnuë, d'Hirlande, ou l'innocence couronnée*, Paris, Estienne Loyson, 1659, 12mo (BN Y² 7653-4). Cioranescu cites an edition dating from 1640.

CHAPELAIN, Jean, 'Discours contre l'amour', reprinted in J.-E. Fidao Justiniani, *L'esprit classique et la préciosité au XVIIe siècle*, pp. 109-39.

—— *Opuscules critiques*, ed. A. C. Hunter, Paris, 1936.

—— *La Pucelle ou la France delivrée. Poëme heroïque*, Paris, Augustin Courbé, 1656, fol. (BN Rés Y 70).

CHARRON, Pierre, *De la sagesse, trois livres . . . derniere edition*, Paris, David Douceur, 1613, 8vo (BN R 31148). First edition in 1601.

CHASSENEUX, Barthélemy de, *Catalogus gloriae mundi*, Geneva, Philippus Albertus, 1617, fol. (BN F 1717). First edition in 1528; this work is reprinted as late as in 1649.

CHOLIÈRES, Jean Dagoneau, alias Nicolas, sieur de, *La forest nuptiale, où est representee une varieté bigarree, non moins esmerveillable que plaisante, de divers mariages selon qu'ils sont observez et pratiquez par plusieurs peuples et nations estranges: avec la maniere de policer, regir, gouverner et administrer leur famille*, Paris, Pierre Bertault, 1600, 12mo (BM 8415 aaa 31).

—— *La guerre des masles contre les femelles: representant en trois dialogues les prerogatives et dignitez tant de l'un que de l'autre sexe. Avec les meslanges poëtiques du sieur de Cholieres*, Paris, Pierre Chevillot, 1588, 16mo (Ars Rés 8° B 32908). Another edition in 1614.

Complainte des mal mariez, avec l'enfer des amoureux. Le tout mis par dialogue fort plaisant et recreatif pour resjouyr les melancholiques, Rouen, Abraham Constant, 1605, 8vo (Ars 8° B 30648).

Consolation aux dames, sur la deffence des passemens, poincts-coupez et dentelles, n.p., n.d., 8vo (BN Ye 18967). Cf. *Consolation aux dames sur la reformation des passemens et habits*, n.p., n.d., 8vo, reprinted in Fournier, *Variétés historiques et littéraires*, viii. 140-6, and *Consolation sur l'entretien des dames pour la réformation des habits*, cited by Magendie, *La politesse mondaine*, i, Bibliography.

La constance des femmes nouvellement descouverte, Paris, Jean Martin, 1627, 8vo (BN Rés Y² 2564).

Coppie de la responce pour les dames du Parlement de Paris, à la lettre des dames du Parlement de Bordeaux . . ., n.p., 1650, 4to (BHVP 126492).

CORBIN, Jacques, *La Royne Marguerite. Ou sont descrites la noblesse, la grandeur de ceste grande princesse, sa beauté, ses vertus. Avec un racourcy des dames illustres de l'antiquité . . .*, Paris, Jean Berion, 1605, 8vo (BM G 13940).

CORDIER, Jean, *La famille saincte; où il est traitté des devoirs de toutes les personnes qui composent une famille*, Paris, Claude Sonnius & Denis Bechet, 1643, 4to (BN D 7187).

CORNEILLE, Pierre, *Théâtre complet*, ed. P. Lièvre & R. Caillois, 2 vols., Paris, 1961.

—— *Trois discours sur le poème dramatique*, ed. L. Forestier, Paris, 1963.

COSNARD, Marthe, *Les chastes martirs*, Paris, Augustin Courbé, 1651, 8vo (BN Yf 4837).

COSTE, Hilarion de, *Les eloges et vies des reynes, princesses, dames et damoiselles illustres en pieté, courage et doctrine, qui ont fleury de nostre temps, et du temps de nos peres. Avec l'explication de leurs devises, emblemes, hyerogliphes, et symboles*, Paris, Sebastien Cramoisy, 1630, 4to (Maz 18643). A second and enlarged edition was published in two vols. in 1647 (Paris, Sebastien Cramoisy & Gabriel Cramoisy, 4to : BN G 6031–2).

La courtisane dechifree, dediee aux dames vertueuses de ce temps, Paris, Jacques Villery, 1642, 8vo (Ars 8° S 3138). Dedicatory epistle is signed 'I. F. C. D. S. S.'.

COURVAL, Thomas Sonnet de, *Satyre menippee sur les poingnantes traverses et incommoditez du mariage. Avec la Thimethelie ou censure des femmes . . . troisiesme edition, reveuë de nouveau par l'autheur, et augmentée d'une deffence apologetique contre les censures de sa satyre du mariage*, Paris, Jean Millot, 1610, 8vo (BM c 39 c 15). The *Satyre menippee* and the *Censure des femmes* first appeared in 1608; the *Deffence* in 1609, with the title *Responce à la contre-satyre*.

COUVAY, Louis, *L'honneste maitresse*, Paris, Guillaume de Luyne, 1654, 8vo (BN R 24102).

CRESPET, Pierre, *Le jardin de plaisir et recreation spirituelle*, 2 vols., Lyons, Heritiers de Benoist Rigaud, 1598, 16mo (BN D 13559).

CROUS, Marie, *Abbregé recherché de Marie Crous pour tirer la solution de toutes propositions d'Aritmetique*, Paris, Jacques Auvray, 1641, 8vo (Maz 30047[1]).

Cupido triumphans, vel ratio cur sexus muliebris omni amore, et honore sit dignissimus, Utrecht, Wilhelmus Strick, 1644, 12mo. 'Autore H. H. V. O. G.'.

CYRANO DE BERGERAC, Savinien, *Lettres*, ed. L. Erba, Milan, 1965.

DADRÉ, Jean, *Loci communes similium et dissimilium, ex omni propemodum antiquitate, tam sacra, quam prophana collectorum, quibus docendi ratio perfacilis, dicendi verò copia longè uberrima, theologiae caeterarumque artium studiosis omnibus accessura est*, Cologne, Arnoldus Mylius, 1603, 8vo (BN D 85556).

DECRET, Claude, *La vraye veuve, ou l'idee de la perfection en l'estat de viduité . . .*, Paris, Gaspard Meturas, 1650, 4to (BN D 7277).

DEPLANCHES, Jean, *Les œuvres poetiques*, Poitiers, Julian Thoreau, 1612, 12mo (BN Rés p Ye 388).

DES ARMOSINS, Dydimus, *Les trophees celestes, ou se peuvent voir les genereux et immortels faicts des femmes illustres* . . . , Lyons, Thomas Arnaud d'Armosin, 1620, 4to (BN Ye 34165).

DESFONTAINES, le sieur, *La veritable Semiramis. Tragedie*, Paris, Pierre Lamy, 1647, 4to (BN Yf 534).

DESMARETS DE SAINT-SORLIN, Jean, *L'Ariane*, Paris, Matthieu Guillemot, 1639, 4to (BN Rés Y² 720). This novel first appeared in 1632.

—— *Jeux historiques des rois de France, reines renommées, geographie et metamorphose*, Paris, Nicolas Le Clerc & Florent Le Comte, 1698, 12mo (BN Rés 8º L⁴² 3). An earlier edition appeared in 1644.

—— *Les visionnaires*, ed. H. Gaston Hall, Paris, 1963.

DESPORTES, Philippe, *Le mariage honni par Desportes, louangé par Blanchon, Le Gaynard, Rouspeau*, ed. H. Vaganay, Mâcon, 1908.

DIEZ, Filippo, *Summa praedicantium: ex omnibus locis communibus locupletiss[ima]*, Lyons, Pierre Landry, 1592, 4to (BN D 7349).

DINET, François, *Le theatre françois, des seigneurs et dames illustres. Divisé en deux parties. Avec le manuel de l'homme sage, et le tableau de la dame Chrestienne*, Paris, Nicolas & Jean de la Coste, 1642, 4to (BN 4º L²1 I).

Discours de l'ennemy d'amour et des femmes, see *Nouveau recueil des pieces les plus agreables de ce temps*.

Discours en la faveur des dames contre les mesdisans. Disputé entre deux dames, Cleophile et Clorinde, et un gentil-homme nommé le sieur Cloridan, Paris, Abel L'Angelier, 1600, 12mo (Ars 8º S 3125).

Discours merveilleux de la vie actions et deportemens de Catherine de Medicis Royne Mere; declarant tous les moyens qu'elle a tenus pour usurper le gouvernement du Royaume de France et ruiner l'estat d'iceluy, n.p., selon la copie imprimée à Paris, 1649, 8vo (Maz 52007). First edition dates from 1579.

Disputatio perjucunda qua anonymus probare nititur mulieres homines non esse: cui opposita est Simonis Gedicci . . . defensio sexus muliebris qua singula anonymi argumenta distinctis thesibus proposita viriliter enervantur, The Hague, I. Burchornius, 1641, 12mo (Ars 8º S 3038). First edition dates from 1595.

DU BOSC, Jacques, *La femme heroïque, ou les heroïnes comparées avec les heros en toute sorte de vertus*, 2 vols., Paris, Antoine de Sommaville & Augustin Courbé, 1645, 4to (BN R 5989–90).

—— *L'honneste femme, seconde edition, reveue corrigée et augmentée par l'autheur*, Paris, Jean Jost, 1633, 4to; *seconde partie*, Paris, André

Soubron, 1634, 4to; *troisiesme et derniere partie*, Paris, Augustin Courbé [1636], 4to (BN R 6227–9). First edition of the first part is Paris, Pierre Billaine, 1632, 8vo. All references are made to the 1633 edition of this part, the long preface of which was written by d'Ablancourt (see Tallemant des Réaux, *Historiettes*, ed. Adam, ii. 244).

—— *Nouveau recueil de lettres des dames de ce temps. Avec leurs responses*, Paris, Augustin Courbé, 1635, 8vo (BN Z 14308).

DU CHESNE, André, *Figures mystiques du riche et precieux cabinet des dames, où sont representées au vif, tant les beautez, parures, et pompes du corps feminin: que les perfections, ornemens et atours spirituels de l'ame*, Paris, Toussaintz Du Bray, 1605, 12mo (Ars 8° s 3115).

DU LAURENS, André, *Historia anatomica humani corporis et singularum eius partium multis controversiis et observationibus novis illustrata*, Frankfurt, Matthaeus Beckerus [1600], fol. (Queen's).

DU LISDAM, Henri, *L'ambition, la volupté et l'avarice*, Lyons, Claude Morillon, 1613, 8vo (BN R 34358).

DU LORENS, Jacques, *Les satyres*, Paris, Jacques Villery, 1624, 8vo (BN Ye 7690).

DU MOULIN, Pierre, *Premiere decade de sermons*, Geneva, Jaques Chouët, 1642, 8vo (BN D² 7276).

DUPLEIX, Scipion, *Liberté de la langue françoise dans sa pureté*, Paris, Denys Bechet, 1651, 4to (BM 12950 h 25).

DU PONT, Jean-Baptiste, *Le miroir des dames, où les effects d'une saincte amitié sont au vif representez*, Lyons, Thibaud Ancelin, 1605, 12mo (Ars 8° B 19391).

DU RUAU, Florentin, *Tableau historial des regences: ou se voit tout ce qui s'est passe pendant icelles depuis Clotilde jusques a Marie de Medicis a present regente ensemble leurs droicts et prerogatives*, Poitiers & se vendent à Paris chez Isaac Mesnier, 1615, 8vo (Maz 50021).

DU RYER, Pierre, *Esther, tragedie*, Paris, Antoine de Sommaville & Augustin Courbé, 1644, 4to (BN Yf 478).

—— *Lucrece, tragedie*, Paris, Antoine de Sommaville, 1638, 4to (BN Rés Yf 475).

—— *Les vendanges de Suresne, comedie*, Paris, Anthoine de Sommaville, 1636, 4to (BN Rés Yf 361).

DU SAULT, Nicolas, *La vie de Madamoiselle de Neuvillars, miroir de perfection pour les femmes mariees, et pour les ames devotes*, Paris, Sebastien & Gabriel Cramoisy, 1649, 8vo (Maz Rés 52355).

DU SOUHAIT, le sieur, *Les neuf muses françoises*, Paris, Jacques Rezé, 1599, 12mo (BN Rés p Ye 340[3]).

—— *Les pourtraicts des chastes dames*, Paris, Gilles Robinot, 1600, 12mo (Ars 8° S 3080).

DU TILLET, Dame, *La veritable response faite par les dames du Parlement de Paris, à la letre qui leur a esté escrite par les dames du Parlement de Bordeaux*, n.p., 1650, 4to (Maz M 12383).

DU VERDIER, Gilbert Saulnier, sieur, *Le roman des dames*, 2 vols., Paris, Jacques Villery, 1630-2, 8vo (Ars 8° B 22546-7). Probably the first edition, in spite of the assertions of Williams and Baldner, who date this novel 1624 and 1616 respectively.

EBERARTUS, Joachimus, *Bonus [sic] mulier, sive centuria iuridica practica quaestionum illustrium: de mulieribus, vel uxoribus*, Rhodiis [? Rostock], Daniel de Baretiis, 1616, 4to (Bodley Douce M 394).

ERASMUS, Desiderius, *Opera omnia*, Leyden, 1703-6.

Esclavage des devots de la B. V. Marie, emperière du monde. Praticque de se consacrer parfaictement à son service, Liège, Jean Ouwerx, 1629, 12mo (ed. P. Delattre, *Revue d'ascétique et de mystique*, xxx (1954), 348-60).

ESTIENNE, Antoine, *Remonstrance charitable aux dames et damoyselles de France, sur leurs ornemens dissolus, pour les induire à laisser l'habit du paganisme, et prendre celuy de la femme pudique et Chrestienne*, Paris, Sebastien Nivelle, 1585, 8vo (BM 851 b 10).

ESTIENNE, Henri, *Carmen de senatulo foeminarum, magnum senatui virorum levamentum atque adiumentum allaturo*, Strasbourg, Antonius Bertramus, 1596, 4to (Maz 1096).

Estranges propheties sur les mondanitez des femmes et des filles de ce temps, n.p., 1632, 8vo (BN Ye 21625).

L'excellence des femmes, avec leur response à l'autheur de l'Alphabet. Accompagnee d'un docte et subtil discours de la feu reyne Marguerite, envoyé sur le mesme suject à l'autheur des secrets moraux, Paris, Pierre Passy, 1618, 8vo (BN Rés R 2187).

Exhortation aux dames vertueuses, en laquelle est desmonstré le vray poinct d'honneur; avec l'Ecatomphile de Leo. Bapt. Albert, où est l'art d'aimer, Paris, 1597, 12mo (BM 8416 a 57). The *Catalogue Deneux* cites an edition in 1596. Other editions in 1598 and 1608.

Le fantastique repentir des mal mariez. Ensemble le reconfort des femmes qui se plaignent de l'absence et deffault de leur mary, Paris, se vend ruë Galande, aux Escolles de Picardie, n.d., 8vo (BN Rés Y² 3079). The *Catalogue Deneux* has an edition in 1623.

FARET, Nicolas, *L'honneste homme ou l'art de plaire à la court*, ed. M. Magendie, Paris, 1925. First edition dates from 1630.

La femme genereuse qui monstre que son sexe est plus noble, meilleur politique, plus vaillant, plus sçavant, plus vertueux, et plus œconome que celuy des hommes, Paris, François Piot, 1643, 8vo (Ars 8° S 3193). 'Par L. S. D. L. L.'.

FERRAND, Jacques, *De la maladie d'amour, ou melancholie erotique. Discours curieux qui enseigne à cognoistre l'essence, les causes, les signes, et les remedes de ce mal fantastique,* Paris, Denis Moreau, 1623, 8vo (Bod H 68 Art.). A later version of the banned *Traité de l'essence et guérison d'amour,* Toulouse, 1610.

FERVILLE, sieur de, *La méchanceté des femmes,* Paris, jouxte la coppie imprimé: à Caen, Pierre Rocolet, 1618, 12mo (Ars 8° S 3158). An edition of the *Cacogynie, ou méchanceté des femmes,* Caen, 1617, cited by Cioranescu.

FITELIEU, le sieur, *La contre-mode,* Paris, Louys de Heuqueville, 1642, 12mo (BN R 25963).

FLAMEN, Albert, *Devises et emblesmes d'amour moralisez,* Paris, Jean Rémy, 1648, 8vo (BM 12305 b 11). An earlier edition is cited by Weigert (*BN Cabinet des Estampes: inventaire du fonds français,* iv. 233–4: Paris, Olivier de Varennes, 1633, 8vo).

FRANCIS OF SALES, St., *Introduction à la vie dévote,* ed. F. Henrion, Tours, 1939.

FRISCHLIN, Nicodemus, *Methodus declamandi (posthuma) in laudatione, thesi de laudibus mulierum demonstrata,* Strasbourg, Johannes Carolus, 1606, 8vo (BM 011805 df 1).

GAILLAR, sieur de, *Le bouclier des femmes, contre les impostures et les calomnies des mesdisans de leur sexe,* Paris, Jacques Bessin, 1621, 8vo (Ars 8° S 3166).

GARDÉ (François), *La Judit de ce temps representee en la personne de tres-haute et tres-vertueuse princesse, Madame Louise de Lorraine . . . relligieuse . . . ,* Mons, François de Wandret, 1641, 4to (Ars 4° B 3888).

GAREL (Elie, sieur des Boisrichers), *Les oracles françois, ou explication allegorique du Balet de Madame, ensemble les paralleles de son Altesse avec la Minerve des anciens . . . ,* (Paris, Pierre Chevalier, 1615), 8vo (BN 8° Yth 13472). Title, publisher, and author all cited from the *Privilège.*

GERZAN, François Du Soucy, sieur de, *Le triomphe des dames,* Paris, chez l'autheur, 1646, 4to (BM 10661 g 2).

—— *La vraie philosophie des dames,* Paris, 1653, 4to. Cited by Cioranescu.

GILBERT, Gabriel, *Marguerite de France, tragi-comedie,* Paris, Augustin Courbé, 1641, 4to (BN Rés Yf 210).

—— *Panegyrique des dames,* Paris, Augustin Courbé, 1650, 4to (Maz A 11833).

—— *Semiramis. Tragedie,* Paris, Augustin Courbé, 1647, 4to (BN Rés Yf 345).

GILLET DE LA TESSONERIE, le sieur, *Sigismond duc de Varsav. Tragicomedie*, Paris, Toussainct Quinet, 1646, 4to (BN Rés Yf 252).

GLEN, Jean-Baptiste de, *Du debvoir des filles, traicté brief et fort utile*, Liège, Jean de Glen, 1597, oblong 8vo (Bod Douce G 234).

GOURNAY, Marie Le Jars de, *Egalité des hommes et des femmes*, n.p., 1622, 8vo (BN Z Payen 543). Reprinted in Mario Schiff, *La fille d'alliance de Montaigne, Marie de Gournay*, Paris, 1910, pp. 61–86, to which edition all references are made.

—— *L'ombre de la Damoiselle de Gournay*, Paris, Jean Libert, 1626, 8vo (BN Rés Z 2821).

GRENAILLE, François de, sieur de Chatounières, *Les amours historiques des princes. Contenant six narrations veritables, sous ces titres, l'amour jaloux, l'amour furieux, l'amour effeminé, l'amour desesperé, l'amour ambitieux, l'amour infidele*, Paris, Nicolas & Jean de la Coste, 1642, 8vo (Ars 8° B 18684).

—— *La bibliotheque des dames*, Paris, Anthoine de Sommaville, 1640, 4to (BN R 6237).

—— *La galerie des dames illustres*, Paris, 1643, 12mo. Cited by Gay.

—— *L'honneste fille, premiere partie*, Paris, Jean Paslé, 1639, 4to; *seconde partie*, Paris, Toussainct Quinet, 1640, 4to; *troisiesme partie*, Paris, Antoine de Sommaville & Toussainct Quinet, 1640, 4to (BN R 6233–5).

—— *L'honneste mariage*, Paris, Toussainct Quinet, 1640, 4to (BN 4° Y² 5692).

—— *L'honneste veuve*, Paris, Anthoine de Sommaville, 1640, 4to (Bod 4° M 56 Art.).

—— *La mode ou charactere de la religion. De la vie. De la conversation. De la solitude. Des compliments. Des habits. Et du style du temps*, Paris, Nicolas Gasse, 1642, 4to (BN Z 4022).

—— *Nouveau recueil de lettres des dames tant anciennes que modernes*, 2 vols., Paris, Toussainct Quinet, 1642, 8vo (BN Z 14310–1).

—— *Les plaisirs des dames*, Paris, Gervais Clousier, 1641, 4to (BN R 6221).

GRIGUETTE, Bernard, *Eloges des hommes illustres peints en la Gallerie du Palais Roial*, Dijon, Pierre Paillot, & Paris, Toussainct Quinet, 1646, 4to (BN Ye 1175).

GUARINI, Battista, *Il pastor fido. Le berger fidele*, Paris, Matthieu Guillemot, 1610, 12mo (BN Yd 3892).

GUERIN DE BOUSCAL, Guion, *La mort de Brute et de Porcie. Ou, la vengeance de la mort de Cesar, Tragedie*, Paris, Toussainct Quinet, 1637, 4to (BN Rés Yf 520).

GUERRY, le sieur, *Traicté de l'excellence du sexe fœminin, et des prerogatives de la Mere de Dieu*, Paris, Jean Petrinal, 1635, 8vo (BN R 24085). Dedicatory epistle is signed 'Guerry', which may be a pseudonym (? cured of misogyny).

Gynaeciorum sive de mulierum tum gravidarum parientum et puerperarum affectibus et morbis libri graecorum arabum latinorum veterum et recentium quotquot extant ..., ed. Israel Spachius, Strasbourg, Lazarus Zetznerus, 1597, fol. (Queen's). Earlier editions by different editors appeared in 1566, 1577, 1586–7.

Harangue faicte en la defense de l'inconstance, Paris, Abel L'Angelier, 1598, 12mo (Maz 27931).

HARDY, Alexandre, *Théâtre*, ed. E. Stengel, 5 vols., Marburg and Paris, 1884.

HEYWOOD, Thomas, *The exemplary lives and memorable acts of nine the most worthy women of the world: three Iewes. Three Gentiles. Three Christians*, London, Thomas Cotes and Richard Royston, 1640, 4to (Bodley 4° A 47 Art.).

Hippolytus redivivus id est remedium contemnendi sexum muliebrem, n.p., 1644, 12mo (Maz 77838). 'Autore S. I. E. D. V. M. W. A. S.'. G.-F. de Bure gives a different title (. . . *id est remedium amoris, sive ars contemnendi sexum muliebrem*), which makes more sense as the title of an anti-feminist work.

L'illustre conquerante ou la genereuse constance de Madame de Chevreuse, Paris, N. Charles, 1649, 4to (BN Lb37 483).

L'innocence et le veritable amour de Chymene, n.p., 1638, 8vo (BN Rés Z 3229). Attributed to Godeau by Jamet, in whose *recueil factice* on the subject of women this pamphlet is to be found.

JULIARD, Jean, *Les amours de l'amant converty* . . . , Lyons, Jean Didier, 1604, 16mo (Ars 8° B 20016).

JUVERNAY, Pierre, *Discours particulier contre la vanité des femmes de ce temps*, Paris, Jean Mestais, 1635, 8vo (BM 846 k 18[2]). The *Troisiesme edition*, Paris, Pierre Le Mur, 1637, 8vo (BN D 13684), to which all references are made, is illustrated.

LA BRUYÈRE, sieur de, *Replique à l'antimalice ou defense des femmes du sieur Vigoureux* . . . , Paris, Jean Petit-Pas, 1617, 12mo (Ars 8° S 3156).

LA COLOMBIÈRE, Marc de Vulson, sieur de, *Les portraits des hommes illustres françois qui sont peints dans la Gallerie du Palais Cardinal de Richelieu . . . ensemble les abregez historiques de leurs vies*, Paris, Henri Sara, Jean Paslé & Charles de Sercy, 1650, fol. (BN Ln1 2).

—— *Questions plaisantes et recreatives, avec leurs decisions, pour se divertir agreablement dans la compagnie des dames. Ensemble un discours problematique touchant le celibat et le mariage* . . . , Paris, Louis Chamhoudry, 1652, 8vo (Ars 8º B 30573).

LA FRANCHISE, sieur de, *La deffence des dames, ou bien responce au livre intitulé, Question Chrestienne touchant le jeu*, Paris, Philippe Lambert, 1634, 8vo (BN D 65750).

LA GUETTE, Catherine Meurdrac, dame de, *Memoires . . . escrits par elle-mesme*, The Hague, Adrian Moetjens, 1681, 12mo (BN 8º Lb³⁷ 4548 A).

LAHIER, François, *Le grand menologue des saintes, bien-heureuses, et venerables vierges* . . . , 2 vols., Lille, Nicolas de Rache, 1645, 4to (Madrid).

LAMBERT, Matthieu, *Discours du danger et peril qu'il y a de converser et hanter trop familiarement avec femmes, tant seculieres que religieuses*, Liège, Henri Hovius, 1596, 8vo (BN H 15671).

LA MOTHE LE VAYER, François de, *Considerations sur l'eloquence françoise de ce temps*, Paris, Sebastien Cramoisy, 1638, 8vo (Maz 20247).

—— *Quatre autres dialogues . . . faits comme les precedens à l'imitation des anciens*, Frankfurt, Jean Savius, 1716, 12mo (BN Z 16633). 'Par Oratius Tubero', i.e. La Mothe Le Vayer. First edition probably 1631 (see Tisserand, *La Mothe Le Vayer, Deux dialogues faits à l'imitation des anciens*, p. 19).

LA PORTE, Maurice de, *Les epithetes*, Lyons, Benoist Rigaud, 1593, 16mo (BM c 40 a 49). First edition dates from 1571.

L'ARCHEVESQUE, Nicolas, *Les grandeurs sur-eminentes de la tres-saincte Vierge Marie*, Paris, Guillaume Macé, 1638, 4to (BN D 8366).

LA VALLETTRYE, sieur de, *Œuvres poetiques*, Paris, Estienne Vallet, 1602, 12mo (BM 240 c 45).

LE BERMEN, Louis, sieur de la Martinière, *Le bouclier des dames, contenant toutes leurs belles perfections*, Rouen, Jacques Besongne, 1621, 12mo (BM 08416 e 64).

LE DELPHYEN, *Deffence en faveur des dames de Lyon, avec un bref discours de l'excellence et beauté de la femme*, Lyons, Pierre Michel, 1596, 8vo (Ars 8º B 11009).

LE FAULT, Guillaume, *Petit traicté contre l'abominable vice de paillardise et adultere qui est aujourd'huy en coustume* . . . , The Hague, Arnoult Meuris, 1629, 12mo (BN D 59018). Facsimile edition of 1868.

LE HEURT, Matthieu, *L'honneur des dames souveraines de la Chrestienté*, Poitiers, 1607. Cited by Cioranescu.

LE MAIRE, le sieur, *La Prazimene*, Paris, Antoine de Sommaville [& Augustin Courbé], 4 vols., 1638–43, 8vo (BN Y² 7328-31).

LEMAISTRE, Antoine, *Les plaidoyez et harangues* . . . , Paris, Pierre Le Petit, 1657, fol. (BN F 2496).

LE MOYNE, Pierre, *Devises heroiques et morales*, Paris, Augustin Courbé, 1649, 4to (BN Ye 1356).

—— *La gallerie des femmes fortes*, Paris, Antoine de Sommaville, 1647, fol. (Taylor).

—— *Les peintures morales, où les passions sont representees par tableaux, pacharacteres, et par questions nouvelles et curieuses*, Paris, Sebastien Cramoisy, 1640, 4to; *Les peintures morales, seconde partie de la doctrine des passions* . . . , Paris, Sebastien Cramoisy [1643], 4to (BN Rés R 1136–7).

LE PELETIER, Laurens, *De la chasteté, et combien l'incontinence est dommageable . . . Ensemble de la dignité et excellence du mariage. Et de la saincteté et vertu de plusieurs femmes et filles illustres*, Angers, Adam Mauger, 1635, 8vo (Queen's). 'Seconde edition'; there is no indication as to the date of the first.

L'ESCALE, le chevalier de, *Alphabet de l'eccellence et perfection des femmes. Contre l'infame alphabet de leur imperfection et malice*, Paris, Nicolas de la Vigne, 1631, 12mo (Ars 8° S 3151).

—— *Le champion des femmes, qui soustient qu'elles sont plus nobles, plus parfaites et en tout plus vertueuses que les hommes, contre un certain misogynes, anonyme auteur et inventeur de l'imperfection et malice des femmes*, Paris, Vve M. Guillemot, 1618, 12mo (BM 12331 a 35).

L'ESPINE, Timothée-René de, *La Macette, poëme satirique*, ed. E. Courbet, Paris, 1875. This appeared first in the *Nouveau recueil des plus beaux vers de ce temps*, Paris, Toussainct Du Bray, 1609, 12mo (pp. 414–36), with the title 'Discours du S. de l'Espine'.

—— *La parure des dames*, Liège, Ardt de Corswarem, 1606, 12mo (BN R 24113).

Lettre des dames du Parlement de Bordeaux aux dames du Parlement de Paris . . . , jouxte la coppie imprimée à Bordeaux, 1650, 4to (Maz M 11337).

Lettre d'un fameux courtisan à la plus illustre coquette du monde, Paris, 1649, 4to (BHVP 101209).

L'HERMITE DE SOULIERS, Jean-Baptiste, alias Tristan L'Hermite de Souliers, *La princesse heroïque ou la vie de la comtesse Mathilde, marquise de Mantoüe et de Ferrare*, Paris, Cardin Besongne, 1645, 4to (BN K 2949).

LIÉBAUT, Madame, *Les misères de la femme mariée, où se peuvent voir les peines et tourmens qu'elle reçoit durant sa vie*, Paris, Pierre Menier, n.d., c. 1597, 8vo, reprinted in Fournier, *Variétés historiques et littéraires*, iii. 321–31. This work also appeared in 1619 without name of author and with the title *Discours pitoyable, des lamentations de la femme*

L

mariée. Ensemble des miseres et tourmens qu'elle endure sous un mauvais mary [Lyons], Thomas Arnaud d'Armosin, 4to (BN Rés Y² 2768).

LORYOT, François, *Les fleurs des secrets moraux*, Paris, Claude Desmarquets, 1614, 4to (BN D 8596).

—— *Les secrets moraux*, Paris, Claude Chappelet, 1614, 4to (BN Rés R 1138).

LOTICHIUS, Johannes Petrus, see LOTZ, Johann Peter.

LOTZ, Johann Peter, *Gynaicologia: id est: de nobilitate et perfectione sexus foeminei*, Rintheln, Petrus Lucius, 1630, 8vo (BN R 18139).

LUIS DE GRANADA, *Sylva locorum communium omnibus divini verbi concionatoribus*, Lyons, Pierre Landry, 1586, 8vo (BN D 36689).

MACHON, Louis, *Discours ou sermon apologetique, en faveur des femmes*, Paris, T. Blaise, 1641, 8vo (BM 8415 b 18).

MAILLARD, Claude, *Le bon mariage, ou le moyen d'estre heureux, et faire son salut en estat de mariage. Avec un traité des vefves . . .* , Douai, Jean Serrurier, 1643, 4to (BN D 11452).

MAIRET, Jean de, *Les galanteries du duc d'Ossonne*, Paris, Pierre Rocolet, 1636, 4to (BN Yf 646).

—— *Le Marc-Antoine ou la Cleopatre. Tragedie*, Paris, Antoine de Sommaville, 1637, 4to (BN Rés Yf 357).

—— *La Sophonisbe, tragedie*, Paris, Pierre Rocolet, 1635, 4to (BN Rés Yf 591).

—— *Sylvie. Tragi-comedie pastorale*, ed. J. Marsan, Paris, 1932.

MALHERBE, François de, *Œuvres complètes*, ed. L. Lalanne, 5 vols., Paris, 1862–9.

La malice des femmes avec la farce de Martin Baston. Dediée à la plus mauvaise du monde, Troyes, Nicolas Oudot, 1659, 8vo (Ars 8° S 3165).

MAMBRUN, Pierre, *Dissertatio peripatetica de epico carmine*, Paris, Sebastien & Gabriel Cramoisy, 1652, 4to (BN Y 123).

MARCASSUS, Pierre de, *La reine des femmes, dediée à la Reyne*, Paris, 1643, 8vo. Cited in the *Catalogue Pichon*.

MARCONVILLE, Jean de, *De la bonté et mauvaistié des femmes*, Paris, Jean Dallier, 1564, 8vo (BN R 18275).

—— *De l'heur et malheur de mariage . . .* , Paris, Jean Dallier, 1564, 8vo (BN R 18276).

MARESCHAL, André, *La sœur valeureuse, ou l'aveugle amante. Tragi-comedie*, Paris, Anthoine de Sommaville, 1634, 8vo (BN Yf 6872).

MARGUERITE DE VALOIS, *Lettre*, in Loryot, *Fleurs des secrets moraux*, d1ʳ–d4ʳ.

—— *Mémoires*, ed. P. Bonnefon, Paris, 1920.

—— *La ruelle mal assortie*, see *Nouveau recueil des pieces les plus agreables de ce temps*.

MARINELLA, Lucrezia, *La nobiltà, et l'eccellenza delle donne, co' diffetti, e mancamenti de gli huomini* . . . , Venice, Gio. Battista Combi, 1621, 8vo (All Souls). First edition dated 1600.

MARINO, Giambattista, *La galeria*, Venice, il Ciotti, 1635, 12mo (BN Yd 6010–11).

—— *Opere*, ed. A. Asor Rosa, Milan, 1967.

MARTIN, Simon, *La vie de sainte Ulphe vierge*, Paris, Sebastien Huré, 1648, 12mo (BN Ln²⁷ 19921).

Le martire de ste Catherine, tragedie, Caen, Eleazar Mangeant, 1649, 8vo (BN Yf 4836).

MAZARINI, Giulio, *Practique pour bien prescher: où sont donnez les preceptes necessaires aux predicateurs, pour inventer, disposer, orner, apprendre par cœur et reciter un sermon. Traduitte* . . . *par J. Baudoin*, Paris, Jean Mejat, 1618, 12mo (Maz 24644).

MÉAT, le sieur, *La fille heroïque ou sainte Reine martyre*, Paris, Thomas Blaise, 1644, 8vo (BN Ln²⁷ 58012).

MÉNIER, Honorat de, *La perfection des femmes, Avec l'imperfection de ceux qui les mesprisent*, Paris, Julian Jacquin & Nicolas Alexandre, 1625, 8vo (BM 8416 aaa 35). An earlier edition in 1623 (Bibliothèque Inguimbertine, Carpentras).

La meschanceté des femmes avec leurs ruses et finesse . . . , Paris, Vve J. Promé, n.d., 12mo (Ars 8° S 3160).

Meslange de divers problemes, Paris, Augustin Courbé, 1647, 12mo (Ars 8° B 34805).

MEXIA, Pero, *Les diverses leçons de Pierre Messie* . . . *mises* . . . *en françois par C. Gruget* . . . *plus la suite de celles d'Antoine Du Verdier*, Tournon, Claude Michel, 1616, 8vo (BN Z 39341). First edition of Mexia's *Leçons* 1542; of Du Verdier's, 1577.

MIREMONT, Jacqueline de, *Apologie pour les dames, où est monstré la précellence de la femme en toutes actions vertueuses*, Paris, Jean Gesselin, 1602, 12mo (Ars 8° B 11012 Rés).

MONTAIGNE, Michel de, *Essais*, ed. A. Thibaudet and M. Rat, Paris, 1967 (Bibliothèque de la Pléiade).

MONTLUC, Adrien de, prince de Chabannais, comte de Cramail, *Les pensees du solitaire*, Paris, Anthoine de Sommaville, 2 vols., 1629–30, 8vo (BN Y² 9800–1). Contains *Les theses et conclusions du bachelier Erophile* (i. 253–81); see above, s.v. *Les antitheses des dames de Cypre*.

MONTPENSIER, Louise d'Orléans, duchesse de, *Mémoires*, in *Collection des mémoires relatifs à l'histoire de France*, ed. C.-B. Petitot and L.-J.-N. Monmerqué, 2ᵉ série, Paris, 1825, xl–xliv.

MOTTEVILLE, madame de, *Mémoires*, in *Collection des mémoires relatifs à l'histoire de France*, ed. Petitot and Monmerqué, 2ᵉ série, xxxvi–xl.

MOUSÉ, sieur de, *Les larmes de Floride essuyees par Minerve*, Paris, Louis Boulanger, 1627, 12mo (Ars 8° B 17333).

Les muses gaillardes. Recüeillies des plus beaux esprits de ce temps par A[nthoine] D[u] B[reuil], *seconde edition*, Paris, Anthoine Du Breuil, 1609, 12mo (BN Rés Ye 2744).

NERVÈZE, Antoine de, *La guide des courtisans*, Paris, Anthoine Du Breuil, 1606, 12mo (BN Rés Z 3250).

NERVÈZE, Suzanne de, *Les genereux mouvemens d'une dame heroïque et pieuse*, Paris, Jean Paslé, 1644, 8vo (Maz 28021).

—— *Œuvres spirituelles et morales*, Paris, 1642, 12mo (BN Rés Z 3208 [part of Jamet's *recueil factice* on the subject of women] contains an extract: 'Apologie en faveur des femmes', pp. 83–92).

NICLOT, Simon, *Le petit cabinet des vierges et ames chastes*, Reims, François Bernard, 1649, 12mo (Ars 8° T 8288).

Nouveau recueil des pieces les plus agreables de ce temps . . . , Paris, Nicolas de Sercy, 1644, 8vo (Maz 35569). This *recueil* contains (i) *La ruelle mal assortie*, attributed to Marguerite de Valois; (ii) *Les loix de la galanterie*, attributed to Charles Sorel; (iii) *Discours de l'ennemy d'amour et des femmes*; (iv) *Response à l'ennemy de l'amour et des femmes, faite par Erophile*.

OLIVIER, Jacques, see TROUSSET, Alexis.

Parænese aux filles et femmes, pour la modestie et honnesteté Chrestienne, n.p., n.d., 8vo (Ars 8° B 11009).

PASCAL, Jacqueline, sœur Sainte-Euphémie, *Règlement pour les enfants*, in *Lettres, opuscules et mémoires de Mme Périer et de Jacqueline, sœurs de Pascal, et de Marguerite Périer, sa nièce*, ed. P. Faugère, Paris, 1845, pp. 228–300.

PASSE, Crispin de, the Younger, *Les abus du mariage, ou sont clairement representez les subtilitez deshonnestes tant des femmes que des hommes dont ils usent pour se tromper l'un l'autre* . . . , n.p., 1641, oblong 4to (BM 554 a 33).

—— *Le miroir des plus belles courtisanes de ce temps*, n.p., 1635, oblong 4to (BM 685 d 27[2]).

—— *Les vrais portraits de quelques unes des plus grandes dames de la Chrestienté, desguisées en bergeres* . . . , Amsterdam, J. Broeesz, 1640, oblong 4to (BM 685 d 27[1]).

PHILIPPE D'ANGOUMOIS, *Discours sur la conversion d'une dame mondaine à la vie devote*, Lyons, Louis Muguet, 1617, 12mo (BN D 22913).

Plaidoyer d'un mari desesperé pour l'estrange et admirable caquet de sa femme. Apporté nouvellement de Grece en France, Paris, Claude Percheron, 1617, 8vo (Ars 8° B 30577). This tract, attributed by Gay to Libanius, first appeared in 1593 in the original Greek with a Latin translation by Fédéric Morel; in the same year, the first French version appeared, to be reprinted in 1594, 1595, and 1617.

POIRÉ, François, *La triple couronne de la bien-heureuse Vierge, Mere de Dieu* . . . , Paris, Sebastien Cramoisy, 1630, 4to (BN 5603).

POLMAN, Jean, *Le chancre ou couvre-sein feminin . . . ensemble le voile ou couvre-chef feminin*, Douai, Gerard Patté, 1635, 8vo (BM 1094 dd 8).

PONA, Francesco, *La galeria delle donne celebri*, Bologna, il Cavalieri, 1633, 8vo (BM 244 i 3). First edition, Rome, 1625.

PONTAYMÉRI, Alexandre de, *Paradoxe apologique, où il est fidellement demonstré que la femme est beaucoup plus parfaicte que l'homme en toute action de vertu*, Paris, Abel L'Angelier, 1594, 12mo (Ars 8° s 3201).

POTTIER, Nicolas, *La Vierge triomphante*, Mons, 1641, 4to. Cited by Cioranescu.

Pouvoir attribué aux femmes de cognoistre de causes legeres. Plus la deffence aux femmes de ne plus battre leurs maris sur peine d'encourir les peines cy apres mentionnees, Paris, Robert Tillon, 1615, 8vo (Bibliothèque Rothschild).

PUGET DE LA SERRE, Jean, *L'entretien des bons esprits sur les vanitez du monde*, Rouen, Louis Loudet, 1631, 8vo (BN R 40932).

—— *L'isthoire et les portraits des imperatrices, des reynes, et des illustres princesses de l'auguste maison d'Austriche, qui ont porté le nom d'Anne*, Paris, Pierre de Bresche pere et fils, 1648, fol. (Ste Geneviève Rés W fol 272 inv 348).

—— *Le martyre de sainte Catherine. Tragedie en prose* . . . , Paris, Antoine de Sommaville & Augustin Courbé, 1643, 4to (BN Yf 379).

—— *Le portrait de la Reyne*, Paris, Pierre Targa, 1644, 4to (Maz 17565).

—— *Le reveille-matin des dames*, Paris, Pierre Billaine, 1638, 12mo (BN Rés Z 3232[2]).

PURE, Michel de, *La prétieuse, ou le mystère des ruelles*, ed. E. Magne, 2 vols., Paris, 1938-9.

Le purgatoire des hommes mariez, avec les peines et les tourmentz qu'ils endurent incessamment au subject de la malice et mechanceté des femmes . . . , Paris, jouxte la coppie imprimée à Lyon par François Paget, 1619, 8vo (reprinted in Fournier, *Variétés historiques et littéraires*, iv. 81–5).

Question celebre. S'il est necessaire, ou non, que les filles soient scavantes. Agitée de part et d'autre par Mademoiselle Anne Marie de Schurman Holandoise,

et le Sr André Rivet Poitevin, le tout mis en françois par le Sr Colletet,
Paris, Rolet Le Duc, 1646, 8vo (BN R 24049). This work first appeared in Latin with the title *Amica dissertatio inter nobilissimam
virginem Annam Mariam a Schurman et Andream Rivetum de ingenii
muliebris ad scientias et meliores literas capacitate*, Paris, 1638, 8vo (Ste
Geneviève M 8° SUP 20 Rés).

RACAN (Honorat Du Bueil, marquis de), *Les bergeries et autres poésies
lyriques*, ed. P. Camo, Paris, 1929.

RAMPALLE, sieur de, *Discours academiques*, Paris, Augustin Courbé, 1647,
8vo (Ste Geneviève X 8° 832 inv 1844).

RANGOUZE, sieur de, *Lettres panegyriques aux plus grandes reynes du monde,
aux princesses du sang de France, autres princesses, et illustres dames de la
cour*, Paris, 1650, 8vo (BN Rés Z 2272). 'Imprimées aux dépens de
l'autheur'. In Jamet's *recueil factice* on the subject of women (BN
Rés Z 3210), there is a fragment of an earlier edition of 1649.

RAVISIUS TEXTOR, Joannes, alias Jean Tixier de Ravisy, *Epithetorum
opus absolutissimum*, Basle, Leonhardus Ostenius, 1592, 4to (BM 625
e 7). An earlier edition in 1524.

—— *De memorabilibus et claris mulieribus: aliquot diversorum scriptorum
opera*, Paris, Simon de Colines, 1521, fol. (BM 612 l 3).

RAYNAUD, Theophile, *Dissertatio de sobria alterius sexus frequentatione
per sacros et religiosos homines*, Lyons, Michael Duhau, 1653, 8vo
(BN D 12876).

*Recueil des exemples de la malice des femmes, et des mal-heurs venus à leur
occasion. Ensemble les execrables cruautez exercees par icelles*, n.p., n.d.,
8vo (BN Rés Y² 2731). BN has another edition, Paris, Pierre Hury,
1596, 8vo (Y² 61719).

Recueil des plus excellens ballets de ce temps, Paris, Toussainct Du Bray,
1612, 8vo (BN Rés Yf 4226).

Recueil général des caquets de l'accouchée, ed. E. Fournier, Paris, 1855. This
work first appeared in a collected edition in 1623.

Recueil general des questions traitees ez conferences du Bureau d'Adresse,
5 vols., Paris, Bureau d'Adresse, 1638–55, 4to (BN Z 4039, 4043–6).
Another edition in 1666 (Lyons, Antoine Valançol, 12mo: BM 1136
a 34).

REGNAULT, le sieur, *Marie Stuard Reyne d'Ecosse, tragedie*, Paris, Toussainct Quinet, 1639, 4to (BN Rés Yf 1445).

RÉGNIER, Mathurin, *Œuvres complètes*, ed. G. Raibaud, Paris, 1958.

La rejouissance des femmes sur la deffence des tavernes et cabarets, Paris,
Imprimerie de Chappelain, 1613, 8vo (reprinted in Fournier,
Variétés historiques et littéraires, x. 175–85).

Response à l'ennemy de l'amour et des femmes, faite par Erophile, see *Nouveau recueil des pieces les plus agreables de ce temps*.

Response de la plus fameuse coquette de l'univers, à la lettre du plus malheureux courtisan de la terre, Paris, 1649, 4to (Maz M 11848).

RHODIGINUS, Caelius, see RICCHIERI, Camillo.

RICCHIERI, Camillo, alias Caelius Rhodiginus, *Lectionum antiquarum libri xxx*, Basle, Hier. Froben & Nicol. Episcopius, 1542, fol. (BN Z 410).

RICHY, Jules de, *Le temple de pudicité*, Paris, Silvestre Moreau, 1616, 8vo (BN Ye 32187).

RIPA, Cesare, *Iconologia, overo descrittione di imagini delle virtu, vitii, affetti, passioni humane, corpi celesti, mondo e sue parte*, Padua, Pietro Paolo Tozzi, 1611, 4to (Taylor).

RIVET, André, see *Question celebre* . . . .

RODRIGUES DE CASTRO, Estevam, *De universa muliebrium morborum medicina*, Hamburg, Zacharias Hertelius, 1662, 4to (Queen's). This is the fourth edition; the first appeared in 1603. The 'pars prima theorica' is entitled *De natura mulierum*.

RODRIGUEZ DE LA CAMARA, Juan, *Le triumphe des dames*, Paris, Pierre Le Caron, n.d. (BN Rés R 934).

ROLBAG, Gregorius, *Certamen masculofoemineum super aequitate utilitate et necessitate differentiarum sexus in successionibus, quibus exstantibus masculis excluduntur foeminae in Italia, Gallia, Hispania et Germania*, Speyer, Joannes Philippus Spiessius, 1602, 4to (Bodley 4° R 4 Jur. Seld.).

ROMIEU, Marie de, *Discours admirable de l'excellence des femmes* . . . [Lyons], Thomas Arnaud d'Armosin, 1619, 4to (BN Ye 20358). This is a reprint (with minor modifications) of the *Brief discours que l'excellence de la femme surpasse celle de l'homme*, which appeared in the *Premieres œuvres* of 1581.

ROTROU, Jean, *Œuvres complètes*, ed. Viollet-Le-Duc, 5 vols., Paris, 1820.

SAINT-AMANT, Marc-Antoine de Girard, sieur de, *Œuvres*, ed. J. Bailbé, 4 vols., Paris, 1971.

SAINT-ÉVREMOND, Charles de Saint-Denis, sieur de, *La comédie des académistes*, ed. G. L. van Roosbroeck, New York, 1931.

SAINT-GABRIEL, sieur de, *Le merite des dames*, Paris, Jacques Le Gras, 1655, 8vo (Ars 8° S 3117). Expanded editions in 1657 and 1660.

SANDRICOURT, sieur de, *Le censeur du temps et du monde* . . . , 4 vols., Paris, 1652, 4to (BHVP 100478–81).

—— *La response de Sandricourt, sur la these couchée en la 2. partie du Censeur du temps et du monde* . . . *et l'examen de la piece intitulé, Le censeur censuré*, Paris, 1652, 4to (Maz M 11863).

SARASIN, Jean-François, *Œuvres*, ed. P. Festugière, 2 vols., Paris, 1926.

Satire des dames contre les chevalliers du carouzel, par M. A. D. R. Avec la response des chevaliers aux dames, par I. B. L. C., n.p., 1612, 8vo (BN Ye 7515).

SCHURMAN, Anna Maria van, see *Question celebre* . . . .

SCUDÉRY, Georges de, *Le cabinet* . . . *premiere partie*, Paris, Augustin Courbé, 1646, 4to (Maz 10918). This is, according to Mongrédien, 'la seule partie qui ait jamais paru' (*RHLF* xl. 415).

—— *Didon, tragedie*, Paris, Augustin Courbé, 1637, 4to (BN Yf 471).

—— *Les femmes illustres, ou les harangues heroïques, avec les veritables portraits de ces heroïnes, tirez des medailles antiques*, Paris, Antoine de Sommaville & Augustin Courbé, 1642, 4to; seconde partie, Paris, Toussainct Quinet & Nicolas de Sercy, 1644, 4to (BN X 3457, 3457bis). Parts of this work are almost certainly the work of Madeleine de Scudéry.

SCUDÉRY, Madeleine de, *Artamene ou le grand Cyrus, seconde edition*, 10 vols., Paris, Augustin Courbé, 1650–4, 8vo (Taylor). First edition 1649–53.

—— *Un tournoi de trois pucelles en l'honneur de Jeanne d'Arc. Lettres inédites de Conrart, de Mlle de Scudéry et de Mlle du Moulin*, ed. E. de Barthélemy and R. Kerviler, Paris, 1878. The letters date from 1646 and 1647.

SEBASTIEN DE SENLIS, *Epistres morales: où toutes les dames qui pretendent au paradis, treuvent les vertus d'une cour sainte et celles des cloistres reformés*, Paris [1645], 8vo (BN D 15812).

Les secrettes ruses d'amour. Où est monstré le vray moyen de faire les approches, et entrer aux plus fortes places de son empire, Paris, Thomas Estoc, 1610, 12mo (BN Enfer 766).

Les singeries des femmes de ce temps découvertes, et particulierement d'aucunes bourgeoises de Paris, n.p., 1623, 8vo (reprinted in Fournier, *Variétés historiques et littéraires*, i. 55–63).

SOREL, Charles, *L'anti-roman ou histoire du berger Lysis*, 4 vols., Paris, Toussainct Du Bray, 1633–4, 8vo (Ars 8° B 21267).

—— *De la connoissance des bons livres*, Paris, André Pralard, 1671, 8vo (Taylor).

—— *Histoire comique de Francion*, ed. E. Roy, 4 vols., Paris, 1924–31.

—— *Les loix de la galanterie*, ed. L. Lalanne, Paris, 1855. See also *Nouveau recueil des pieces les plus agreables de ce temps*.

Tableau des piperies des femmes mondaines, où par plusieurs histoires se voyent les ruses et artifices dont elles se servent, Paris, Jean Denis, 1632, 12mo (Ars 8° S 3163).

Tableau historique des ruses et subtilitez des femmes . . . , Paris, Rollet Boutonné, 1623, 8vo (Ars 8° S 3161). 'Par L. S. R.'; Quérard interprets this as 'le sieur Rolet'.

TASSO, Torquato, *Aminte fable boscagere . . . traduicte d'italien en françois par G. Belliard*, Rouen, Claude Le Villain, 1609, 12mo (BN Rés Yf 3786).

—— *Les morales . . . traduictes par J. Baudoin*, Paris, Toussainct Du Bray & Augustin Courbé, 1632, 8vo (BN R 52177).

—— *Le prose diverse* . . . , ed. C. Guasti, 2 vols., Florence, 1875.

TEMPESTA, Antonio, *Figurae biblicae*, n.p., n.d., oblong 8vo (BM 555 a 21).

—— *Imagini di molte SS vergini Romane nel martirio*, Rome, n.d., 8vo (Bodley Douce T 35).

Les tenebres de mariage . . . , Rouen, Loys Costé, 1602, 12mo (BN Rés Ye 2724–35). A collection of *facetiae*, including the *Discours joyeux de la patience des femmes obstinees contre leurs maris* and *Le plaisant quaquet et resjuyssance des femmes, pource que leurs maris n'yvrongnent plus en la taverne*. Techener's collection *Les joyeusetez faceties et folastres imaginacions de Caresme-Prenant, Gauthier-Garguille, Guillet-Gonin, Roger-Bontemps, Turlupin, Arlequin, Moulinet* . . . , Paris, 1830, contains 10 *facetiae* on the subject of women and marriage, some in common with Loys Costé's collection, all of which first appeared in the first sixty years of the sixteenth century.

THÉOTIME, *Question Chrestienne touchant le jeu, addressee aux dames de Paris, sçavoir si une personne addonnee au jeu se peut sauver, et principalement les femmes*, Paris, Jean Mestais, 1633, 8vo (BN D 13520).

THOMAS, Artus, sieur d'Embry, *Discours contre la mesdisance*, Paris, Lucas Breyel, 1600, 12mo (BN R 24408[1]).

—— *Qu'il est bien seant que les filles soyent sçavantes. Discours*, Paris, Lucas Breyel, 1600, 12mo (BN R 24408[3]).

TILLIER, François, *Le premier et second livre du Philogame ou amy des nopces*, Paris, Guillaume Bichon, 1586, 16mo (Ars 8° S 3338). Earlier edition in 1578.

Un tournoi des trois pucelles en l'honneur de Jeanne d'Arc . . . , see SCUDÉRY, Madeleine de.

Le triomphe des merites de Mademoiselle, Paris, Jacob Chevalier, 1652, 4to (Maz M 10351).

TRISTAN L'HERMITE, François, *La Mariane. Tragedie. Quatriesme edition reveue et corrigee*, Paris, Augustin Courbé, 1644, 4to (BN Rés Yf 507). First edition in 1637.

—— *Les plaintes d'Acante et autres œuvres*, ed. J. Madeleine, Paris, 1909.

TROUSSET, Alexis, *Alphabet de l'imperfection et malice des femmes . . . dedié à la plus mauvaise du monde*, Paris, Jean Petit-Pas, 1617, 12mo (BM 1070 f 12). 'Par Jacques Olivier'; for attribution and other details see above, p. 31. All references are made to the Rouen edition, David Ferrand, 1631, 12mo (Bodley 8° B 133 Th).

—— *Explication des armes de la Reine Mere*, Paris, Julian Jacquin, 1622, 8vo (BN Lb³⁶ 2128).

—— *Responce aux impertinences de l'aposté capitaine Vigoureux: sur la defense des femmes*, Paris, Jean Petit-Pas, 1617, 12mo (Ars 8° S 3154). 'Par Jacques Olivier'.

TURNÈBE, Adrien, the Younger, *Response à un curieux, demandant pourquoy les hommes s'assubjettissent aux femmes*, Rouen, Charles Gendron, 1598, 12mo (Maz 58200). 'Par A. T.'; attributed in the Catalogue of the Bibliothèque Mazarine to Turnèbe. Published together with the *Exhortation aux dames vertueuses* (Rouen, Charles Gendron, 1598, 12mo: for other editions see above, s.v. *Exhortation . . .*), of which Turnèbe's work is a refutation.

TYARD, Pontus de, *Solitaire premier*, ed. S. F. Baridon, Geneva and Lille, 1950.

D'URFÉ, Honoré, *L'Astrée*, ed. H. Vaganay, 5 vols., Lyons, 1925–8.

VALLADIER, André, *La saincte philosophie de l'ame, sermons . . .*, Paris, Pierre Chevallier, 1614, 8vo (BN Rés D 15505).

—— *Speculum sapientiae matronalis, ex vita Franciscae Romanae . . .*, Paris, Jean Richer, 1609, 4to (Ste Geneviève Rés H 4° 1654 inv 1753[3]). Cioranescu records a French translation in 1611.

VANDENBUSCHE, Alexandre, *Sommaire des dames illustres et vertueuses . . .*, Rouen, Claude Le Villain, 1603, 32mo (Ars 8° B 21972). An earlier edition appeared in 1574–5, with the title *Le recueil des dames illustres en vertu* (cited in the *Catalogue Lignerolles*).

VARIN, Jean-Philippe, *Les espines du mariage, pour retirer les jeunes gens et autres de folles et precipitées amours*, Paris, Fleury Bourriquant, n.d., 12mo (BN Rés R 2175). An edition dated 1604 is cited in the *Catalogue La Vallière*; Cioranescu records an edition in 1607.

VASLET, Raymond, *Question de médicine . . . sçavoir si l'esprit suit le sexe*, ed. M. Gille, *Revue pratique de biologie appliquée*, xxiv (1931), 39–45. This thesis dates from 1666.

VAUX, sieur de, *La Magdeleine au desert. Avec les meditations sur les attributs de la Vierge, sur le vendredi saint, sur la croix, sur le saint sepulchre, et sur les amours du monde*, Paris, Nicolas Gasse, 1629, 8vo (BN D 42582).

VERNON, Jean-Marie de, *L'amazone chrestienne, ou les avantures de Madame de S. Balmon*, Paris, Gaspar Méturas, 1678, 12mo (BN Rés Ln²⁷ 18234).

VIAU, Théophile de, *Œuvres complètes*, ed. M. Alleaume, 2 vols., Paris, 1855.

—— *Œuvres poétiques*, ed. J. Streicher, 2 vols., Geneva, Paris, and Lille, 1951–8.

VIGOUREUX, le sieur, *La defense des femmes, contre l'alphabet de leur pretendue malice et imperfection*, Paris, Pierre Chevalier, 1617, 12mo (BM 1070 f 12[2]).

VION DALIBRAY, Charles, *Les œuvres poetiques*, Paris, Antoine de Sommaville, 1653, 8vo (BN Ye 7759).

VIVES, Juan Luis, *De institutione foeminae Christianae*, Antwerp, Michaelis Hillenius, 1524, 4to (Bodley Arch B e 30).

VOITURE, Vincent, *Poésies*, ed. H. Lafay, 2 vols., Paris, 1971.

WOLFF, Johannes Ulricus, *Discursus: de foeminarum in jure civili et canonico privilegiis, immunitatibus et praeeminentia*, Rostock, Mauritius Saxo, 1615, 4to (Bodley 4° H 19 Art Seld).

SECONDARY SOURCES

I. *Bibliographical*

Only those reference works which were of assistance in establishing the bibliography of primary sources are listed here.

ASCOLI, G., 'Bibliographie pour servir à l'histoire des idées féministes depuis le milieu du xvıᵉ siècle jusqu'à la fin du xvıııᵉ siècle', *RHS* xiii (1906), 99–106.

BALDNER, R. W., *Bibliography of seventeenth-century French prose fiction*, New York, 1967. This is an amended and expanded version of Williams's bibliography (see below).

BARBIER, A.-A., *Dictionnaire des ouvrages anonymes*, 4 vols. and suppl., Paris, 1872–9.

BRIQUET, F.-B., *Dictionnaire historique, littéraire et bibliographique des françaises, et des étrangères naturalisées en France*, Paris, 1804.

BRUNET, J., *Manuel du libraire*, 6 vols. and suppl. (2 vols.), Paris, 1860–80.

BURE, G.-F. de, *Bibliographie instructive: ou traité de la connoissance des livres rares et singuliers*, 9 vols., Paris, 1765.

Catalogue d'une collection de facéties . . . par S. de S., Dresden, 1875.

CIORANESCU, Alexandre, *Bibliographie de la littérature française du XVIe siècle*, Paris, 1959.

—— *Bibliographie de la littérature française du XVIIe siècle*, 3 vols., Paris, 1966–7.

DEAKIN, T., *Catalogi librorum eroticorum*, London, 1964.

DENEUX, L.-C., *Catalogue d'une partie de la bibliothèque de M. L.-C. Deneux* ..., Paris, 1844.

DENIS, F., MARTONNE, A. de, and PINÇON, P., *Nouveau manuel de bibliographie universelle*, 3 vols., Paris, 1857.

GAY, J., *Bibliographie des ouvrages relatifs au mariage, aux femmes et à l'amour*, 6 vols., Paris, 1871–3 (revised edn., 4 vols., Paris, 1897).

GIRAUD, J., *Manuel de bibliographie littéraire pour les XVIe, XVIIe et XVIIIe siècles français, 1921–35*, Paris, 1939; *1936–45*, Paris, 1956.

GRAESSE, J. G. T., *Trésor des livres rares et précieux, ou nouveau dictionnaire bibliographique*, 8 vols., Dresden, 1859–69.

HEREDIA, R., *Catalogue de la bibliothèque de M. Ricardo Heredia* ..., 2 vols., Paris, 1892.

JACOB, L., *Bibliographica gallica universalis* ..., 4 vols., Paris, 1644–54.

JAMET, *Table du recueil de Jamet sur les femmes* (MS.: BN Rés Usuel).

LABADIE, E., *Nouveau supplément à la bibliographie des mazarinades*, Paris, 1904.

LACHÈVRE, F., *Bibliographie des recueils collectifs de poésies publiés de 1597 à 1700*, 3 vols. and suppl., Paris, 1901–6.

—— *Glanes bibliographiques*, 2 vols., Paris, 1929.

—— *Nouvelles glanes bibliographiques*, Paris, 1933.

—— *Les recueils collectifs de poésies libres et satiriques publiés depuis 1600 jusqu'à la mort de Théophile, 1626*, Paris, 1914.

LANÉRY D'ARC, P., *Bibliographie raisonnée et analytique des ouvrages relatifs à Jeanne d'Arc*, Paris, 1894.

LANSON, G., *Manuel bibliographique de la littérature française moderne*, Paris, 1921.

LA PORTE, J., and LA CROIX, marquis de, *Histoire littéraire des femmes françoises, ou lettres historiques et critiques*, vol. 1, Paris, 1769.

LAPORTE, M. A., *Bibliographie clérico-galante*, Paris, 1879.

LA VALLIÈRE, Louis-César de la Baume le Blanc, duc de, *Ballets, opéra, et autres ouvrages lyriques, par ordre chronologique depuis leur origine* ..., Paris, 1760.

—— *Catalogue des livres de la bibliothèque de feu M. le duc de la Vallière*, 3 vols., Paris, 1783; *2e partie*, 3 vols., Paris, 1784.

LIPENIUS, M., *Bibliotheca realis juridica*, Frankfurt, 1679.

MARRACCI, H., *Biblioteca mariana* . . . , 2 vols., Rome, 1648.

MARTIN, H.-J., *Livre, pouvoirs et société à Paris au XVIIᵉ siècle (1598–1701)*, 2 vols., Geneva, 1969.

MONGRÉDIEN, G., 'Bibliographie des œuvres de Georges et de Madeleine de Scudéry', *Revue d'histoire littéraire de la France*, xl (1933), 224–36, 412–25, 538–65; xlv (1935), 547–9.

MOREAU, C., *Bibliographie des mazarinades*, 3 vols., Paris, 1850.

MOUHY, le chevalier de, *Tablettes dramatiques, contenant l'abrégé de l'histoire du théâtre françois* . . . , Paris, 1752.

NIJHOFF, M., *La femme: qualités—travaux—histoire: catalogue des livres anciens et modernes et de gravures en vente chez Martinus Nijhoff* . . . , The Hague, 1898.

PEDDIE, R. A., *Subject index of books before 1880*, 4 vols., London, 1933–48.

PICOT, E., *Catalogue de la bibliothèque de M. le baron de Rothschild*, 5 vols., Paris, 1884–1920.

PRAZ, M., 'Bibliography of emblem-books', in *Studies in seventeenth-century imagery*, Rome, 1964, pp. 235–576.

QUÉRARD, J.-M., *Les supercheries littéraires dévoilées*, 3 vols., Paris, 1869–70.

RENOUARD, P., *Répertoire des imprimeurs parisiens*, Paris, 1965.

TOINET, R., 'Les écrivains moralistes au XVIIᵉ siècle: essai d'une table alphabétique des ouvrages publiés pendant le siècle de Louis XIV (1638–1715), qui traitent de la morale', *Revue d'histoire littéraire de la France*, xxiii (1916), 570–610; xxiv (1917), 296–306, 656–75; xxv (1918), 310–20, 655–71; xxxiii (1926), 395–407.

UNGHERINI, A., *Manuel de bibliographie biographique et d'iconographie des femmes célèbres* . . . , 3 vols., Turin and Paris, 1892–1905.

WATT, R., *Bibliotheca britannica; or a general index to British and foreign literature*, 4 vols., Edinburgh, 1824.

WILLIAMS, R. C., *Bibliography of the seventeenth-century novel in France*, Paris, 1931. See above s.v. BALDNER, R. W.

II. *General*

ABENSOUR, L., *La femme et le féminisme avant la Révolution*, Paris, 1923.

—— *Histoire générale du féminisme des origines à nos jours*, Paris, 1921.

ADAM, A., 'Baroque et préciosité', *Revue des sciences humaines*, July–Dec. 1949, 208–24.

—— *Histoire de la littérature française au XVIIᵉ siècle*, 5 vols., Paris, 1962.

298 *Bibliography*

D'ANGERS, J.-E., 'Sénèque et le stoïcisme dans l'œuvre du cordelier J. Du Bosc (1632, 1643, 1645)', *XVIIᵉ siècle*, xxix (1955), 353–77.

ARNAUD D'AGNEL, G., *Les femmes d'après S. François de Sales*, Paris, 1928.

ASCOLI, G., 'Essai sur l'histoire des idées féministes en France', *Revue de synthèse historique*, xiii (1906), 25–57, 161–84.

BABELON, J.-P., *Demeures parisiennes sous Henri IV et Louis XIII*, Paris, 1965.

—— 'L'Hôtel de l'Arsenal au xviiᵉ siècle', *L'œil*, cxliii (1966), 26–35, 55–8.

BABOU, H., 'De la vertu des femmes au xviiᵉ siècle', *Revue nouvelle*, ix (1846), 53–90, 279–93.

BADY, R., 'François de Sales maître d'honnêteté', *XVIIᵉ siècle*, lxxviii (1968), 3–20.

BAUDIN, M., 'The stateswoman in seventeenth-century French tragedy', *MLN* liii (1938), 319–27.

BAUMAL, F., *Le féminisme au temps de Molière*, Paris, 1923.

BEALL, C. B., *La fortune du Tasse en France*, Oregon, 1942.

BÉNICHOU, P., *Morales du Grand Siècle*, Paris, 1948.

BLUM, A., *Abraham Bosse et la société française au XVIIᵉ siècle*, Paris, 1924.

—— *L'œuvre gravé d'Abraham Bosse*, Paris, 1924.

BLUNT, A., *Art and architecture in France, 1500–1700*, London, 1953.

BOLLÈME, G., *La bibliothèque bleue: littérature populaire en France du XVIIᵉ au XIXᵉ siècle*, Paris, 1971.

BRAND, C. P., *Torquato Tasso*, Cambridge, 1965.

BRAY, R., *La formation de la doctrine classique en France*, Paris, 1931.

—— *La préciosité et les précieux de Thibaut de Champagne à Jean Giraudoux*, Paris, 1948.

BREMOND, H., *Histoire littéraire du sentiment religieux en France*, 12 vols., Paris, 1921–36.

BRUNETIÈRE, F., *Questions de critique*, Paris, 1889.

CASEVITZ, T., 'Mlle de Gournay et le féminisme', *Revue politique et littéraire*, lxiii (1925), 768–71.

CHARRON, J.-D., 'Le thème de la "métamorphose" dans l'Astrée', *XVIIᵉ siècle*, ci (1973), 3–14.

CHÉROT, H., *Étude sur la vie et les œuvres du P. Le Moyne*, Paris, 1887.

CIORANESCU, A., *Les romans de la princesse de Conti*, Paris, 1937.

CIRCOURT, A. de, 'La société française et les femmes illustres au xviiᵉ siècle', *Bibliothèque universelle*, vii (1860), 5–40; viii (1860), 34–71.

CLÉMENT, L., 'Le *Carmen de senatulo foeminarum* d'Henri Estienne', *Revue d'histoire littéraire de la France*, i (1894), 441–5.

COLIE, R. L., *Paradoxia epidemica: the Renaissance tradition of paradox*, Princeton, 1966.

COUSIN, V., 'Les femmes illustres du xviie siècle', *Revue des deux mondes*, i (1844), 193–203.

—— *La société française du XVIIe siècle, d'après Le grand Cyrus de Mlle de Scudéry*, 2 vols., Paris, 1858.

CRELLY, W. R., *The painting of Simon Vouet*, New Haven and London, 1962.

CROZET, R., *La vie artistique en France, 1598–1661*, Paris, 1954.

CURTIUS, E. R., *Europäische Literatur und lateinisches Mittelalter*, Berne, 1948.

DAVIS, N. Z., *Society and culture in early modern France*, London, 1975.

DELTOUR, F., 'De l'éducation littéraire des femmes au xviie siècle', *Revue des cours littéraires*, ii (1864–5), 249–61.

D'ORS, E., *Lo barocco*, Madrid, 1945.

DOUMIC, R., 'Le féminisme au temps de la Renaissance', *Revue des deux mondes*, cxlix (1898), 921–32.

DU BLED, V., *La société française du XVIe siècle au XXe siècle*, 3e série, *XVIIe siècle*, Paris, 1902; 4e série, *XVIIe siècle*, Paris, 1904.

DULONG, C., *L'amour au XVIIe siècle*, Paris, 1969.

DUPORTAL, J., *Contribution au catalogue des livres à figures du XVIIe siècle (1601–33)*, Paris, 1914.

—— *Étude sur les livres à figures en France de 1600 à 1660*, Paris, 1914.

EDELMAN, N., *Attitudes of seventeenth-century France towards the Middle Ages*, New York, 1946.

EHRMANN, J., *Un paradis désespéré: L'amour et l'illusion dans L'Astrée*, Paris and New Haven, 1963.

FAGNIEZ, G., *La femme et la société française dans la première moitié du XVIIe siècle*, Paris, 1929.

FAGUET, E, *Le féminisme*, Paris, 1910.

FEUGÈRE, L., *Les femmes poètes au XVIe siècle*, Paris, 1860.

FIDAO-JUSTINIANI, J.-E., *L'esprit classique et la préciosité au XVIIe siècle*, Paris, 1914.

FLACHAIRE, C., *La dévotion à la Vierge dans la littérature catholique au commencement du XVIIe siècle*, Paris, 1916.

FLUTRE, L.-F., 'Du rôle des femmes dans l'élaboration des *Remarques* de Vaugelas', *Neophilologus*, xxxviii (1954), 241–8.

FOURNIER, E. (ed.), *Variétés historiques et littéraires*, 10 vols., Paris, 1855–63.

FRANÇON, M., *Notes sur l'esthétique de la femme au XVIe siècle*, Cambridge, Mass., 1939.

FREUDMANN, F. R., *The Memoirs of Madame de la Guette, a study*, Geneva and Paris, 1957.

FUKUI, Y., *Raffinement précieux dans la poésie française du XVIIe siècle*, Paris, 1964.

GASTÉ, A., *La Querelle du Cid*, Paris, 1898.

GAUDEMET, J., 'Législation canonique et attitudes séculières à l'égard du lien matrimonial au XVIIe siècle', *XVIIe siècle*, cii–iii (1974), 15–30.

GEORGES-RENARD, L., 'La femme et l'éducation sous la minorité de Louis XIV', *Revue internationale de l'enseignement*, xlix (1905), 206–20.

—— 'Les femmes et la politique religieuse sous la Fronde', *Revue politique et parlementaire*, xlv (1905), 315–28.

GIBSON, W., 'Women and the notion of propriety in the French theatre (1628–43)', *FMLS* xi (1975), 1–14.

GOMBRICH, E. H., *Symbolic images: studies in the art of the Renaissance*, London, 1972.

GRANDMAISON, C. de (ed.), 'Description du Château de Richelieu par un anonyme du milieu du XVIIIe siècle', *Nouvelles archives de l'art français*, 2e série, Paris, 1882, 211–37.

GRISAY, A., LAVIS, G., and DUBOIS-STASSE, M., *Les dénominations de la femme dans les anciens textes littéraires français*, Gembloux, 1969.

GUEUDRE, M.-C., 'La femme et la vie spirituelle au XVIIe siècle', *XVIIe siècle*, lxii–lxiii (1964), 47–77.

HAINSWORTH, G., *Les Novelas exemplares de Cervantes en France au XVIIe siècle*, Paris, 1933.

HATZFELD, H., 'A clarification of the baroque problem in the Romance literatures', *Comparative literature*, i (1949), 113–39.

—— *Literature through art: a new approach to French literature*, New York, 1952.

HAUTECŒUR, L., *L'histoire des châteaux du Louvre et des Tuileries*, Paris and Brussels, 1927.

HENKEL, A., and SCHÖNE, A., *Emblemata: Handbuch zur Sinnbildkunst des XVI. und XVII. Jahrhunderts*, Stuttgart, 1967.

HOBERT, E., *Die französische Frauensatire unter Berücksichtigung der antiken Tradition*, Marburg, 1967.

HOFFER, P., *La dévotion à Marie au déclin du XVIIe siècle*, Paris, 1938.

HOFFMANN, P., 'Préciosité et féminisme dans le roman de Michel de Pure', *Travaux de linguistique et de littérature*, v, 2 (1967), 23–34.

HOLMÈS, C. E., *L'éloquence judiciaire de 1620 à 1660*, Paris, 1967.

HOURTICQ, L., *La Galerie Médicis de Rubens au Louvre*, Paris, 1920.

ILSLEY, M. H., *A daughter of the Renaissance: Marie Le Jars de Gournay; her life and works*, The Hague, 1963.

ISARLO, G., *La peinture en France au XVIIe siècle*, Paris, 1960.

IVANOFF, N., 'Le Roland furieux et la querelle des femmes au xvie siècle', *Revue du XVIe siècle*, xix (1932–3), 262–72.

JORAN, T., *Les féministes avant le féminisme*, Ière série, Paris, 1911; 2e série, Paris, 1935.

JUNG, M.-R., *Hercule dans la littérature française du XVIe siècle*, Geneva, 1966.

KELSO, R., *Doctrine for the lady of the Renaissance*, Illinois, 1956.

LA BROSSE, O. de, CAFFAREL, H., and GEORGES-THOMAS, M., *S. François de Sales: les femmes mariées*, Paris, 1967.

LAIGLE, M., *Christine de Pisan, Le livre des trois vertus: et son milieu historique et littéraire*, Paris, 1912.

LANCASTER, H. C., *A history of French dramatic literature in the seventeenth century*, 9 vols., Baltimore and Paris, 1929–42.

LANSON, G., 'Les stances du mariage dans *l'École des femmes*', *Revue politique et littéraire*, 4e série, xii (1899), 718–20.

LARNAC, J., *Histoire de la littérature féminine en France*, Paris, 1929.

LATHUILLÈRE, R., *La préciosité, étude historique et linguistique*, vol. 1, Geneva, 1966.

LEFRANC, A., *Œuvres de François Rabelais, Le tiers livre*, Paris, 1931.

LEGOUVÉ, E., 'Les femmes et le génie littéraire du xviie siècle', *Revue bleue*, ii (1890), 449–54, 481–5.

LE GUINER, J., *Les femmes dans les tragédies de Corneille*, Paris, 1920.

LEINER, W., *Der Widmungsbrief in der französischen Literatur, 1580–1715*, Heidelberg, 1965.

LEVI, A. H. T., *French moralists: the theory of the passions, 1585 to 1649*, Oxford, 1964.

—— 'The neoplatonist calculus', in *Humanism in France*, ed. A. H. T. Levi, Manchester, 1970, pp. 229–48.

LIVET, C.-L., 'Les femmes de la Fronde', *Revue européenne*, iii (1859), 529–51, 726–58.

McBRIDE, R., 'The sceptical view of marriage and the comic vision in Molière', *Modern language forum*, v, 1 (1969), 26–47.

Bibliography

McKendrick, M., 'The *bandolera* in Golden Age drama', *Bulletin of Hispanic Studies*, xlvi (1969), 1–20.

Magendie, M., *L'Astrée, analyse et extraits*, Paris, 1928.

—— *L'Astrée d'Honoré d'Urfé*, Paris, 1929.

—— *Du nouveau sur L'Astrée*, Paris, 1927.

—— *La politesse mondaine et les théories de l'honnêteté en France au XVIIe siècle, de 1600 à 1660*, 2 vols., Paris, 1925.

—— *Le roman français au XVIIe siècle de L'Astrée au Grand Cyrus*, Paris, 1932.

Magne, E., *Les femmes illustres, Ninon de Lanclos*, Paris, 1925.

—— *Voiture et l'Hôtel de Rambouillet. Les années de gloire, 1635–48*, Paris, 1930.

Mandrou, R., *Classes et luttes de classes en France au début du XVIIe siècle*, Florence, 1965.

Marsan, J., *La pastorale dramatique en France à la fin du XVIe et au commencement du XVIIe siècle*, Paris, 1905.

Matulka, B., 'The feminist theme in the drama of the Siglo del Oro', *Romanic review*, xxvi (1935), 191–237.

Maulde la Clavière, R. de, *Les femmes de la Renaissance*, Paris, 1898.

Maurel, M., 'Esquisse d'un anteros baroque', *XVIIe siècle*, lxxxiv–lxxxv (1969), 3–20.

Merlet, G., *Causeries sur les femmes et les livres*, Paris, 1865.

Mondadon, L. de, 'Les françaises du xviie siècle', *Études*, ccxiv (1933), 578–92, 703–20.

Mongrédien, G., *Madeleine de Scudéry et son salon*, Paris, 1946.

—— *Les précieux et les précieuses*, Paris, 1940.

—— *La vie littéraire au XVIIe siècle*, Paris, 1947.

Nadal, O., *Le sentiment de l'amour dans l'œuvre de Pierre Corneille*, Paris, 1948.

Nisard, C., *Histoire des livres populaires ou de la littérature de colportage*, 2 vols., Paris, 1864.

Payer, A. de, *Le féminisme au temps de la Fronde*, Paris, 1922.

Pellet, E., *A forgotten French dramatist, Gabriel Gilbert (1620?–1680?)*, Johns Hopkins, Paris, and Oxford, 1931.

Picard, R., 'Racine and Chauveau', *Journal of the Warburg and Courtauld Institutes*, xiv (1951), 259–74.

Picart, Y., *La vie et l'œuvre de Simon Vouet*, i: *Les jeunes années et le séjour en Italie*, Paris, 1958; ii: *Simon Vouet premier peintre de Louis XIII*, Paris, 1959.

Bibliography 303

PISTORIUS, G., 'Vlasta: le thème légendaire des amazones dans les littératures occidentales: première partie: France, Allemagne, Angleterre', *Comité d'études culturelles franco-tchécoslovaques*, ii (1957), 22–53.

PORTEMER, J., *La femme dans la législation royale des deux derniers siècles de l'Ancien Régime*, Paris, 1959.

REYNIER, G., *La femme au XVIIᵉ siècle: ses ennemis et ses défenseurs*, Paris, 1929.

—— *Le roman réaliste au XVIIᵉ siècle*, Paris, 1914.

—— *Le roman sentimental avant L'Astrée*, Paris, 1908.

RICHARDS, S. A., *Feminist writers of the seventeenth century, with special reference to François Poulain de la Barre*, London, 1914.

RICHARDSON, L. M., *The forerunners of feminism in the French literature of the Renaissance*, Baltimore, London, and Paris, 1929.

RIGAL, E., *Alexandre Hardy et le théâtre français à la fin du XVIᵉ et au commencement du XVIIᵉ siècle*, Paris, 1889.

ROGERS, K. M., *The troublesome helpmate: a history of misogyny in literature*, Seattle and London, 1966.

RONZEAUD, P., 'La femme au pouvoir ou le monde à l'envers', *XVIIᵉ siècle*, cviii (1975), 9–33.

ROUSSELOT, P., *Histoire de l'éducation des femmes en France*, 2 vols., Paris, 1883.

ROUSSET, J., *L'intérieur et l'extérieur*, Paris, 1968.

—— *La littérature de l'âge baroque en France: Circe et le paon*, Paris, 1954.

ROY, E., *La vie et les œuvres de Charles Sorel*, Paris, 1891.

SALOMON, H. P., *Tartuffe devant l'opinion française*, Paris, 1962.

SAYCE, R. A., *The French biblical epic in the seventeenth century*, Oxford, 1955.

SCHIFF, M., *La fille d'alliance de Montaigne, Marie de Gournay*, Paris, 1910.

SCHUELLER, T., 'S. François de Sales et les femmes', *Annales Salésiennes*, lv (1959), 129–43.

SCREECH, M. A., 'The illusion of Postel's feminism', *Journal of the Warburg and Courtauld Institutes*, xvi (1953), 162–70.

—— 'La querelle des amyes', *BHR* xxi (1959), 103–30.

—— 'Rabelais, de Billon and Erasmus', *BHR* xiii (1951), 241–65.

—— *The Rabelaisian marriage*, London, 1958.

SECOND DE TURIN, 'Une apologie littéraire et doctrinale de la dévotion séculière d'après le capucin Philippe d'Angoumois', *XVIIᵉ siècle*, lxxiv (1967), 3–25; lxxv (1967), 3–21.

SIMPSON, J. G., *Le Tasse et la littérature et l'art baroques en France*, Paris, 1962.

STEGMANN, A., *L'héroïsme cornélien, genèse et signification*, vol. 2, Paris, 1968.

SUTCLIFFE, F. E., *Guez de Balzac et son temps*, Paris, 1965.

—— *Le réalisme de Charles Sorel*, Paris, 1959.

TAPIÉ, V.-L., *La France de Louis XIII et de Richelieu*, Paris, 1967.

TELLE, E.-V., *L'œuvre de Marguerite de Navarre et la querelle des femmes*, Toulouse, 1937.

THOMAS, A.-L., *Essai sur le caractère, les mœurs et l'esprit des femmes dans les différens siècles*, Paris, 1772.

THOMAS, K. V., 'Women and the Civil War Sects', *Past and present*, xiii (1958), 42–62.

THUILLIER, J., and FOUCART, J., *Rubens' life of Marie de' Medici*, New York, 1967.

TISSERAND, E., *La Mothe Le Vayer, Deux dialogues faits à l'imitation des anciens*, Paris, 1922.

TRELOAR, B., 'Preciosity: a social and literary study', Oxford D.Phil. thesis, 1949.

—— 'Some feminist views in France in the seventeenth century', *AUMLA* x (1959), 152–9.

VÈZE, R., alias Jean Hervez, *Les femmes et la galanterie au XVIIᵉ siècle*, Paris, 1907.

Vies des dames qui ont été les plus célèbres dans le XVIIᵉ siècle par leur piété et leur dévouement pour les lettres, Paris, 1817.

VILLEY, P., *Sources d'idées du XVIᵉ siècle*, Paris, 1912.

WALTHER, H., *Proverbia sententiaeque latinitatis medii aevi. Lateinische Sprichwörter und Sentenzen des Mittelalters in alphabetischer Anordnung*, 5 vols., Göttingen, 1963–7.

WEIGERT, R.-A., 'Deux marchés passés par Simon Vouet pour les décorations de l'appartement d'Anne d'Autriche au Palais-Royal (1645)', *BSHAF* (1951), 101–5.

—— 'L'illustration française de la première moitié du xviiᵉ siècle', *Le portique*, v (1947), 111–28.

WHITFIELD, J. H., 'La belle Charite: the Italian pastoral and the French seventeenth century', *Italian studies*, xviii (1963), 33–53; xxiv (1969), 76–92.

WICKELGREN, F. L., *La Mothe Le Vayer, sa vie et son œuvre*, Paris, 1934.

WILSON, D. B., *Descriptive poetry in France from blason to baroque*, Manchester, 1967.

WIND, E., *Pagan mysteries in the Renaissance*, London, 1967.

WINEGARTEN, R., *French lyric poetry in the age of Malherbe*, Manchester, 1954.

YATES, F., *French academies in the sixteenth century*, London, 1947.

Index

In this index, references are given to authors, illustrators, anonymous works, historical figures, and major topics; there are no entries for famous women of antiquity or myth. Where a work has been referred to in the text, it has been indexed under the name of its author (e.g. references to *L'Astrée* are to be found under d'Urfé, Honoré). References are not given to the notes where a name occurs on the text of the same page.